The English Civil War

The English Civil War

Myth, Legend and Popular Memory

Charles J. Esdaile

Pen & Sword
MILITARY

AN IMPRINT OF PEN & SWORD BOOKS LTD.
YORKSHIRE - PHILADELPHIA

First published in Great Britain in 2024 by
Pen & Sword Military
An imprint of
Pen & Sword Books Ltd
Yorkshire - Philadelphia

Copyright © Charles J. Esdaile, 2024

ISBN 978 1 39903 748 8

Typeset in INDIA by IMPEC eSolutions
Printed and bound in England by CPI (UK) Ltd.

Pen & Sword Books Ltd. incorporates the Imprints of Pen & Sword Archaeology, Atlas, Aviation, Battleground, Discovery, Family History, History, Maritime, Military, Naval, Politics, Railways, Select, Transport, True Crime, Fiction, Frontline Books, Leo Cooper, Praetorian Press, Seaforth Publishing, Wharncliffe and White Owl.

For a complete list of Pen & Sword titles please contact

PEN & SWORD BOOKS LIMITED
47 Church Street, Barnsley, South Yorkshire, S70 2AS, England
E-mail: enquiries@pen-and-sword.co.uk
Website: www.pen-and-sword.co.uk

or

PEN AND SWORD BOOKS
1950 Lawrence Rd, Havertown, PA 19083, USA
E-mail: uspen-and-sword@casematepublishers.com
Website: www.penandswordbooks.com

MIX
Paper | Supporting
responsible forestry
FSC
www.fsc.org
FSC® C013604

In memory of Sealed-Knot comrades Sergeant Andrzej Ciupka and Corporal John Biller, both of Sir Gilbert Hoghton's Regiment of Foot, and Ensign Andrew Simmonds and Sergeant Steve Earnshaw, both of John Lilburne's Regiment of Foot, and also of all those who perished in the wars of 1642 to 1651, in the hope that, if any of them are yet still 'unquiet souls', they will one day rest in peace.

Table of Contents

Preface

First of all, a word of explanation. In brief, a study of the English Civil War may seem a very odd project for a Napoleonic specialist to become engaged in. Yet for anyone who knows me, the appearance of this book will come as no surprise. Ever since I was taken to see the film 'Cromwell' as a small boy in 1968, I have been fascinated by the Civil-War era, whilst forty years' service in the ranks of the Sealed Knot has done nothing to diminish my interest. In short, if Wellington and Napoleon have dominated my professional life, Prince Rupert and Oliver Cromwell have at the very least played a prominent role in my private one. As my long-suffering off-spring will attest, meanwhile, whenever they were dragged round mediaeval castles, the talk was never of what occurred in the days of Stephen, John, Edward I or Henry VI, but rather of what occurred in those of Charles I. Writing this book, however, has not just been a piece of self-indulgence. On the contrary, it seems to me that one issue which university historians need always to remain deeply aware of is the public understanding of history, for it is really only through grasping where our undergraduates are coming from that we can take them where we want them to go. This in turn means nurturing an awareness in our common-rooms not just of the vagaries of the way in which our subject is taught in schools and colleges, but also of all forms of popular history. Today, of course, the general public's understanding of the past, such as it is, is in large part the product of film and television, but in days gone by the chief source would rather have been song and story in the form of an oral tradition passed down from generation to generation until a range of antiquarians began to catalogue it in the late eighteenth century. Much of the material concerned, above all the folk-tale, has now, alas, largely fallen by the wayside, and it has therefore been omitted from the bounds of the current study, yet it is not to be despised and in other circumstances could well have been incorporated into its pages. To take an example that is very local to me, from the Isle of Man comes the legend of the Moddey Doo (pronounced 'Morva Do') or

Black Dog, this describing how the garrison of Peel Castle, an important fastness held by troops of the Royalist Earl of Derby, was terrorised into good behaviour by a mysterious hound of enormous size that appeared in their guardroom every night and frightened one of their number to death after he mocked his fellows for imagining that it had been sent to watch over their conduct, said hound never being seen again.[1]

Strange as this legend is, it is positively normal beside a story that comes to us from Hampshire. So bizarre is the tale concerned that it is worth recounting in full. In brief, one night in 1648 a poor villager from the tiny hamlet of South Baddesley was awakened from his slumbers by a heavily-cloaked stranger who offered him a purse of gold if he would carry a secret message to King Charles who was currently imprisoned on the Isle of Wight. At first the man demurred, saying that he had no way of getting across the Solent, but the stranger assured him that all would be well, whereupon he duly made his way to the nearby port of Lymington. On reaching the shore, to his astonishment, he was accosted by a gigantic cormorant who told him to mount upon his back. Screwing up his courage, the villager bestrode the bird's shoulders and very soon he found himself winging his way across the Solent. So far, so good, but clouds were rolling in from all sides and so the cormorant lost his way, eventually depositing him not at Carisbrooke Castle but rather in the very midst of Parliamentarian-held Southampton. Totally unaware of where he was, the unfortunate Hampshire hog asked where the king was and, not surprisingly, was soon brought before the governor who immediately decided he must be a Royalist secret agent. Sentenced to hang, the man was marched to the gallows and the noose placed around his neck, only for the whole structure at the very last moment to take off like a sky-rocket and soar high into the air before plunging back to earth and embedding itself in his little garden in South Baddesley. Next thing the unfortunate villager knew, he was waking up in his own bed and thinking he had dreamed the whole thing, only to discover, first, that the purse of gold he had been promised was lying hidden in the chimney and, second, that the gallows had been transformed into a beautiful elm tree.[2]

Impossible to believe? Ridiculous even? Certainly, but that is not the point, what such stories represent being a terrifying world in which the populace lived their lives in fear in the midst of events so extraordinary that every certainty was set upon its very heels, a world in which almost anything could happen and probably would. All this, however, is a matter for another author, what we will rather look at here being rather Stuart spectres and Roundhead revenants, these being figures that very much remain a foundation of the Wars of the Three Kingdoms' historic memory. That this is so is not surprising. Thus, for many generations prior to the advent of mass education, tales of hauntings and the supernatural were integral to the way in which the populace remembered the past, whilst, further back still, whether as unhappy souls condemned to serving time in Purgatory before attaining salvation or the direct agents of either God or the Devil, for both Catholics and Protestants ghosts were also an important part of religious belief. In just the same way as the giants, trolls, dwarves, pixies, leprechauns and fairies of folk tales were beyond doubt a folk memory of a time when *homo sapiens* shared the land with earlier species of humanity, so ghostly monks and Cavaliers were the means by which the turmoil of the Reformation and the mid-Stuart crisis were recalled, just as before them, or so one presumes, equally ghostly Roman centurions, Viking raiders and Norman knights served the same purpose in respect of earlier periods of trauma.

For a professional historian to take an interest in ghost stories, then, is not so very odd.[3] All the more is this the case, meanwhile, if consideration is given to the nature of the many anthologies of ghost stories that can be found on the shelves of any bookshop. These are replete with incident, certainly, but they are not replete with history. Thus, in turning their pages, it becomes clear that the authors of such works have rarely realised that, particularly with regard to stories that relate to battles and sieges, one way to explain their raw material is to explore the historical events on which they were actually based, or, if said events are unknown to them, to seek out events on which they might be based. It is this methodology that I hope lends a measure of originality to this book, for, rather than simply cataloguing hauntings, it seeks to place them in their cultural and historical context alike. For those who wish to engage in the practice, it can certainly help provide the wherewithal to go ghost-hunting, while, for those whose business is ghost-walks or ghost-weekends, it is sincerely hoped that its content will provide them with fresh material, but *The English Civil War: Myth, Legend and Popular Memory* is intended to do far more than either. Whether it is successful in attaining its objectives, it is not for me to judge, but in writing it I have found myself learning much more history than I would ever have imagined.

Of what, meanwhile, does the raw material for this work consist? Though a number of ghost stories have come down to us from the time of the Civil Wars, stories which are duly discussed in their proper place, it is not with them that we shall be primarily interested. Instead, what we will be looking at are rather the tales that have been recounted in the three centuries or more since Charles I and Oliver Cromwell went to their rest. Such tales are certainly numerous – at the last count, the number of places in England and Wales identified, some of them many times over, as being the haunt of well-known personalities of the period, lesser individuals who yet have names attached to them, or, most commonly, unknown officers and men of the two camps, stands at 233. It goes without saying, of course, that there is no verifying whether the apparitions really took place, are genuinely related to the Civil War rather than, say, the later Jacobite conflicts or could be augmented by others whose association with times Cromwellian has long since been lost, but the mere fact that there are so many is enough to suggest both that their investigation – something in which scholars of the era have thus far singularly failed to engage[4] – is warranted, and that their existence suggests the virulence of common memories of conflict. As for the organization of the project, it will be found that it has been divided into a series of regional case studies containing both a narrative of the military events concerned and a discussion of the ghost stories which pertain to them. If that is seen as giving too much attention to military history, then so be it, but it is difficult to see how else meat can be added, so to speak, to the bones of our spectres, while such an approach is also useful as a means of illustrating the conflict's extraordinarily wide reach in terms of personal experience as well as the source of an additional level of originality: narratives of the battles and campaigns of the Wars of the Three Kingdoms are numerous, but, without exception, they have all been top-down accounts retailing a single story that begins at Edgehill in 1642 and ends at Worcester nine years later, when the reality was rather one of a series of parallel struggles waged in different regions that only rarely intersected with one another, but yet ensured that fear and misery was spread wholesale, that the conflict, indeed, was a constant presence. It will be noted, however, that no attempt has been made to cover Ireland, Wales or Scotland: in part this is for reasons of space, but in part, too, it reflects a paucity of material that is distinctly odd given the Celtic cultures of all three countries, the total number of relevant hauntings that have so far been identified within their borders numbering a mere eleven.

One last question to examine in this preface, I suppose, is the issue of whether or not I myself believe in ghosts. Setting aside one rather disturbing incident in the course of a Sealed-Knot event at Bolsover Castle which neither I nor any of the friends who also experienced it have never been able to offer a satisfactory explanation, I have never had anything remotely supernatural happen to me, but, according to family legend, around 1891 my grandfather saw a figure he later identified as a Roman soldier while playing marbles in the street in which he was living in Southampton, while, a few nights after my father died in January 1987, my mother had a very powerful and, indeed, comforting vision of him standing over her bed. Exactly what they saw, I do not know, but I do know that the experiences were very real to them, and that I therefore cannot discount the possibility of ghosts altogether. In the same way I know many members of the Sealed Knot and the English-Civil-War Society who are prepared to swear blind to strange experiences of a sometimes chilling nature: the thunder of horses' hooves in empty lanes, Civil-War soldiers appearing or disappearing before their very eyes, even large bodies of troops marching along beside them.[5] Tricks of the eye? The fruit of imagination, exhaustion or even drink? Perhaps so, but the people concerned were in some instances very shaken by what they had seen, whilst in a number of cases the same things were seen or heard by a number of different witnesses. Sceptics, of course, will remain unconvinced, and, in the pages of this work, readers will find plenty of alternative explanations for the stories that have come down to us relating to Civil-War England, yet, in the end, the matter will never be susceptible of proof one way or the other. Whilst this may well be the only work on ghosts that I will ever publish, it is therefore impossible to believe that it will be the last word on the subject.

Finally, it may, perhaps, be necessary to appeal to the sympathy of my readers. As I would be the first to admit, this work could certainly be more complete than it is in its listing of the Stuart spectres, but it is the product of times that have, like those of 1642-51, as been sad as they have been distracted. Written, as it has been, in the context of the Covid-19 pandemic, it is necessarily devoid of at least a measure of the depth that access to serious research libraries would ordinarily have offered. However, faced by a choice of intellectual paralysis or proving that the pen is mightier than the virus, I felt that there was but one way to go. For good or ill, this work is the result, and I can but hope that it is accepted in the same spirit of good faith in which it is offered.

With explanation and apology out of the way, we come to the question of my many debts. In the first place, of course, I cannot but mention Pen and

Sword without whom, of course, this project would never have seen the light of day. In the second, there are those friends in the re-enactment world who have shared stories of hauntings with me, including, most notably, Elene Kkoulla. In the third, there is the host of specialists on the Wars of the Three Kingdoms, some of them academics and others independent scholars, whose work I have plundered with as much ruthlessness as any general of King or Parliament. To attempt to list them all is to risk causing offence by failing to recall one name or another, but, with all due apology, they include John Adair, John Barratt, Martyn Bennett, Jack Binns, Malcolm Braddick, Stephen Bull, Charles Carlton, David Casserly, David Cooke, Barbara Donagan, Wilfred Emberton, Glenn Ford, Peter Gaunt, Andrew Hopper, Trevor Hunt, Ronald Hutton, Stuart Jennings, John Kenyon, John Morrill, Peter Newman, Stuart Reid, Roger Richardson, Trevor Royle, Michael Seed, Roy Sherwood, Mark Stoyle, David Underdown, Malcom Wanklyn, John Wardman, Cecily Wedgwood, Austin Woolrych and Peter Young. And, finally, there is Sinéad, without whose love, patience and gentle encouragement this work would have no more substance than the spectres it seeks both to catalogue and to place in their historical context.

Charles J. Esdaile, Peel, 5 November 2023.

Chapter 1

The Blast of War

I t is a historical truism that times of great local, regional, national and international trauma are likely to be reflected in stories of the supernatural. All the more, meanwhile, is this the case when it comes to the experience of war: if any dead can be classed as being 'unquiet', it is surely those who have perished on the battlefield, and ended up, always assuming that there is anything left of them to bury, flung into mass graves without the slightest degree of ceremony. Of this connection between the horrors of war and the unworldly, examples are legion. Thus, in *A Supernatural War: Magic, Divination and Faith during the First World War*, Owen Davies has shown how the horrors unleashed in the years succeeding 1914 provoked a massive vogue for such practices as spiritualism as bereft parents, wives and children sought desperately to establish contact with the proverbial 'lost generation', not to mention a spate of visions and visitations, whether they were the famous 'Angels of Mons', the apparition of Our Lady repeatedly seen by a group of peasant children at the Portuguese village of Fatima in 1917, the vision of the same personage that thousands of Russian troops were reported to have seen in the sky above the battlefield of Augustovo in October 1914, or the ghost stories recounted by large numbers of front-line soldiers, some of them benign and some of them less so.[1] Not surprisingly, ghost stories also abound in respect of the battlefields of the American Civil War and many other sites associated with the conflict (famously, the White House has reputedly been visited many times by the spectre of Abraham Lincoln).[2] Just as gripped by supernatural visions of a bloodstained past was Germany, where widespread stories of a 'wild hunt' in the form of a host of terrible riders thundering across the skies may well have been a folk-memory of the hordes of Attila the Hun.[3] In present-day Vietnam, popular memories of the conflict of the 1960s and early 1970s are suffused with phantoms who ostensibly continue to make demands of the living and, whether real or not, stand proxy for the manner in which the war generation and its successors have interpreted the struggle.[4] In eighteenth-century Scotland the Seven Years' War saw five different witnesses in two different places claim to have seen a battle involving Highland soldiers being fought out in the sky at precisely the same time as 300 such men were falling in an action in North America.[5] As Spain erupted in chaos following the news that Napoleon Bonaparte had decided to overthrow the Bourbon dynasty in favour of his elder brother, Joseph, the city of Zaragoza was gripped by an episode of mass psychosis in which large numbers of people claimed to have seen a palm tree - a symbol of purity associated with Our Lady - in the sky above the basilica of the Virgin of the Pillar, an event that all and sundry interpreted as a call to arms.[6] And finally, it is worth noting that, as the Russians closed in on the Silesian city of Breslau in 1945, the city was awash with wild tales to the effect that the patron saint of Silesia, Saint Hedwig, had appeared in the skies above the city with her arms outstretched as if to shelter the inhabitants.[7]

That the English Civil War should very much fit into the pattern delineated above is hardly surprising. In brief, the years from 1642 to 1651 witnessed a national tragedy of a sort that had not been experienced since the Black Death of 1349. Of this there is abundant evidence. Take, for example, the oft-cited case of the Shropshire village of Myddle. Extraordinarily enough, thanks to the work of a local chronicler named Richard Gough, in this case we have a precise relation of the fate of the twenty-one men from the locality who marched off to war from 1642 onwards, no fewer than eight of whom lost their lives for certain, six more disappearing without trace and another coming home badly disabled thanks to a severe wound that left him with a crooked leg.[8] In all, according to the admittedly controversial figures advanced by Charles Carlton, in England alone total combat deaths came to some 86,000, to which of course must be added many scores of thousands of men who subsequently perished from the effects of wounds.[9] Nor was it just men who turned soldiers who suffered the ravages of war. If comparatively few civilians perished as a result of violence (the vast majority of those who lost their lives in this fashion probably fell prey to fire or bombardment rather than the edge of the sword), there was no protection against the epidemics of typhus and plague that spread in the wake of the military movements of the two sides. In so far as this phenomenon is concerned, we need look no further than the much-besieged town of Newark and its environs. One of the last places in mainland Britain to give up to the victorious Parliamentarians, by the time of its surrender almost one third of the original population had been consumed by three successive attacks of typhus, a further one of diarrhoea and, finally, one of plague so severe that it killed as many as all the other epidemics put together.[10] If possible, even worse off was the neighbouring village of East Stoke, where plague carried off 159 of its c.300 inhabitants in the six months from May to December 1646.[11] Yet, bad though much-beleaguered Newark and its surrounding district was, dotted around the country are many other examples: in Berkshire - an area much garrisoned, traversed and fought over by the contending armies - for instance, the number of burials in the period 1643-44 has been calculated as being 119 per cent above the average for the 150 years from 1558 to 1728, while in some particularly unfortunate places - Reading, Henley and Windsor, for example - the death toll could rise to three or even four times the norm; in Plymouth 2,845 people, or fully one quarter of the population, are recorded as dying of disease in the siege of 1644-45; between March and December 1645, Leeds lost some 1,300 men, women and children - perhaps one fifth of the population - to plague alone; and, finally, in Bristol an epidemic of typhus killed some 2,000 people in 1643-44.[12] In the graphic words of Parliamentarian cleric John Quick, then:

> This flaming sword of God is furbished ... to make a great slaughter, and, in execution of its commission, reads in circuit throughout the whole land, keeping its assizes in every corner ... of the kingdom, slaying and destroying sinners by hundreds and by thousands from one end of the nation unto [the other].[13]

To the ravages of the 'grim reaper', meanwhile, could be added the physical damage inflicted on the built environment: Chester, for example, saw many of the buildings along its main streets levelled to the ground by the sustained use of indiscriminate artillery bombardment aimed at terrorising the population into rising against the authority of the Royalist governor, Sir John Byron, other places that suffered badly from artillery fire including Lichfield, Newark, Scarborough, Exeter, York and Pembroke; the Hampshire town of Alresford and the Somerset one of Langport were both burned to the ground in an attempt to block the advance of the Parliamentarian armies who had just worsted the Royalists in nearby battles, a similar fate befalling Faringdon, Denbigh and Bridgenorth when their Royalist garrisons were driven in and forced to take refuge in the castles that dominated all three settlements; Chester, Exeter, Gloucester, Hereford,

Newcastle, Oswestry, Stafford and Worcester all lost most of their suburbs to attempts to ensure the defenders a clear field of fire; Bolton, Leicester, Farndon, Alton, Maidstone and Torrington suffered severe damage when fighting spilled over into their streets; Belvoir, North Scale, Castle Bolton, Shrawardine, Raglan, Donnington, Boarstall and Brampton Bryan were but a few of the many villages that were totally destroyed; numerous manor houses and stately homes were left in a state of complete ruin after bitter experiences of siege and assault, including, most notably, Basing House in Hampshire and the Lancashire examples of Hoghton Tower and Lathom, while dozens of others were put to the torch so as to deny their use to the opposition; and, finally, the list of castles that were slighted in the aftermath of the Civil Wars is so extensive as to render the choice of choosing examples completely invidious.[14] As for what life was like amid the ruins, here is Parliamentarian chronicler Joshua Sprigge on what he saw following the fall of Bristol in September 1645: 'The people [were] more like prisoners than citizens, being brought so low with taxation [and] so poor in habit and so dejected in countenance, [and] the streets so noisome and the houses so nasty as that they were unfit to receive friends or freemen till they were cleansed.'[15]

At first glance, all this might seem to be confined to those parts of the country that were theatres of actual conflict, and it is in fact the case that considerable parts of the country - Essex, Cambridgeshire, Norfolk and Suffolk; Hertfordshire, Middlesex, Bedfordshire and Buckinghamshire; Kent, Surrey and Sussex; Cumberland and Westmoreland other than the frontier city of Carlisle; and wide swathes of Wales - saw either no action at all or brief episodes of violence confined to one or two towns and castles. Equally, safe behind the imposing ring of earthen fortifications thrown up to keep it from harm, London saw the war out without a shot being fired. However, the absence of bloodshed in no way equated to the absence of war. On the contrary, total war though the conflicts of 1642-51 were not, their presence yet reached out far beyond the zones in which most of the fighting took place. Setting aside the fact that both sides had much resort to requisitioning, arbitrary measures of taxation and the impressment of manpower - it was, of course, this period that gave the English language the word 'dragooning' - we come here above all to the institution of the garrison. In brief, from the moment when neither side succeeded in obtaining a decisive victory at Edgehill, the Royalists and the Parliamentarians alike found themselves engaged in a contest in which everything revolved around the sinews of war, sinews that could only be guaranteed by the physical control of large expanses of territory. To secure their hold on this or that area, then, the two sides had to resort to stationing bodies of men in virtually every town and village, these troops being ensconced in convenient manor houses and castles hastily protected by earthern bastions and redoubts, such bases also serving to hamper the task of enemy generals seeking to advance on more important centres of power and providing jumping-off points for raids into enemy territory. In consequence, however far they lived from the latest seat of operations, the populace had to co-exist with armed men born, at least in the case of the majority of the rank and file, to the lowest, crudest and most ill-educated sections of society, whose sensibilities had been more-or-less blunted by their time in the military, and who were commanded by men who had been in at least some cases brutalised by long experience of the horrors of the 'Thirty Years' War' and were by no means necessarily disposed to treat civilians with respect. All the more was this the case as there was no regular means of supplying the soldiery, the result being that for month after month the countryside round about was stripped of all it contained for miles in every direction. As the war went on, so the ever more straitened Royalists earned a particularly evil reputation in this respect, but the Parliamentarians could be just as bad, an especially egregious example being the governor of the captured Royalist stronghold of Compton Wynyates, one George Purefoy, who not only engaged in the usual requisitioning but also compelled large numbers of local inhabitants to labour on the defence works he threw up for many days without pay and detained men returning to their homes after deserting from the Royalist forces so as to hold them for ransom.[16]

Still worse, in terms of day-to-day life, the soldiery were not confined to walled strongholds from which they could dominate the landscape. On the contrary, in the absence of proper barracks, many men were rather billeted in private houses, thereby jeopardising the peace of the household, not to mention the chastity of its female members.[17] As one contemporary commentator lamented of the soldiers who swarmed on all sides, seemingly officers and men alike, 'What whoredom is committed among them! What maid escape un-deflowered? What wife departeth unpolluted?'[18] And, or at least so went the general refrain, when the soldiery were not womanising, they were wreaking other forms of havoc, whether acts of mindless vandalism or engaging in duels and drunken brawls and other acts of violence. To quote Fiona McCall, for example, 'Soldiers "ripped open the beds and bolsters" at the Orpe family home, "shaking out the feathers … upon the ground".[19] Equally, in Oxford, from the autumn of 1642 the capital of the Royalist cause, Christchurch Meadows, became notorious for duelling, while there were several cases of senior officers being assaulted in the streets by disgruntled subordinates, at least one such incident ending in murder.[20] Finally, to add insult to injury, with both sides frequently short of ready money, communities found that their men stationed in their midst were billeted on them according to the practice of free quarters, reducing them, as one early-war petition put it, to the status of 'mere conquered slaves' preyed upon by 'so many Egyptian locusts'.[21] To quote Tennant, indeed, 'Quarter and theft were usually inseparable.'[22] As for the sums that were drained from communities across the country in this fashion, they were beyond doubt quite considerable: to take some examples from Parliamentarian-controlled Buckinghamshire, for example, the cost to Haddenham, Chesham and Beaconsfield of the years from 1642 to 1646 was a minimum of £796, £1,493 and £1,286 respectively, while in Royalist Worcestershire the cost incurred by the transit of troops through the county in 1643 alone amounted to £1,813.[23]

If things were bad when soldiers were in garrison, they were still worse when they were on campaign. All too often in dire straits for want of adequate food and clothing, the men ignored the standing orders issued by both sides prohibiting plunder on pain of death and fell upon the towns and villages through which they marched without mercy (well-paid and supplied thanks to steady improvements in the administrative infrastructure of the Parliamentarian camp, the New Model Army is far less deserving of such strictures, but it did not, alas, make its appearance till 1645). As an example, we have only to look to the marches of the army of the Earl of Essex in the campaign of Edgehill. However much they might have sought to persuade themselves that their behaviour was targeted at suspected Papists or closet Royalists, the reality was clearly one of indiscriminate pillage. 'In a confused tumult', complained one Royalist chronicler, 'they rush into the house and as eager hounds hunt from the parlour to the kitchen, from whence by the chambers to the garrets … They rob the servants of their clothes [and] with the butt-ends of muskets … break open the hanging presses, cupboards and chests.'[24] Lest it be thought that this was mere diatribe, here are the thoughts of one of Essex's own officers: 'We are perplexed with the insolence of the soldiers already committed and with the apprehension of greater. If this go on, the army will grow as odious to the country as the Cavaliers.'[25] Needless to say, meanwhile, the Royalists were just as bad: as one unruly recruit proclaimed, indeed, 'We will make any man a Roundhead that hath anything to lose.'[26] And, as for the Scots, whichever side they happened to be fighting on at any given moment, they invariably alienated the local populace on account of their depredations, depredations that were undoubtedly rendered all the worse by the fact that they were operating on what was, after all, foreign soil.[27]

The result of all this, of course, was widespread destitution. If hostilities had in part been precipitated by the influx of refugees from Ireland in the wake of the rising of 1641, the ranks of these poor folk were augmented by many others, whether gentry driven from their halls by the depredations of the other side; villagers and townsmen whose homes were either burned out in siege or battle or torn down to clear fields of fire for the defenders of one stronghold or another; folk frightened by the general insecurity of the times into seeking the protection, generally illusory, of some fortified town or city; or, worst of all, civilians expelled from their home towns by governors anxious that, because their men-folk were away fighting in the forces of the enemy, they constituted a potential 'fifth column'.[28] For all concerned, the result was misery. As members of the gentry, the family of Sir John Harrison, a Royalist Member of Parliament who fled London for Oxford in 1642, were better off than most, but, even so, their situation was uncomfortable enough. To quote his daughter, Ann:

> We, that had lived to that time in great plenty and order, found ourselves
> like fishes out of the water ... From as good a house as any gentleman
> of England had, we came to a baker's house in obscure street, and, from
> rooms well-furnished, to lie in a very bad bed in an attic, to one dish of
> meat, and that not so well ordered, no money (for we were as poor as Job),
> nor clothes more than a man or two brought in their cloak bags ... [and] at
> the windows the sad spectacle of war [and] sometimes plague, sometimes
> sicknesses of other kinds, by reason of so many people packed together.[29]

Uncomfortable or not, the gentry could generally hope to make some sort of shift for themselves. Not so the middling and lesser sorts, something that greatly increased their suffering being the fact that the suburbs that were so regularly torn down in the name of the defence of towns and cities were almost invariably the very humblest of districts. As Mark Stoyle writes of the numerous individuals who petitioned the authorities of Exeter with tales of woe in the years after peace returned to the city in 1646, 'For all these poor distressed people, the Civil War had proved an unmitigated disaster.'[30]

Amid all this, meanwhile, taxation bit deep. Nor was it just a question of raising money by means that were already in existence. In the Parliamentarian zone, for example, a property contribution – the so-called Weekly Pay – was soon in operation, this measure being supplemented in July 1643 with a new purchase tax – the excise – on items such as beer, twine, sugar, linen and leather, while by April 1644 the Oxford Parliament had followed suit in both cases.[31] The demands of the war being what they were, too, the charges involved were repeatedly raised, the £3,000 per month property assessment initially levied by the Royalists on Worcestershire, for example, being raised to £4,000 in February 1644.[32] On top of these national systems, meanwhile, many local garrison commanders proved intent on milking their domains by a variety of charges of their own making, a good example being the governor of the Royalist outpost of Lichfield, Richard Bagot, who used the threat of outright plunder to extort additional sums of money from the towns and villages round about.[33] Given that there were plenty of communities that for longer or shorter amounts of time found themselves having to subsist both sides at once – for a good example, one might cite the Staffordshire village of Maveswyn Ridware, the accounts of its constable showing, as they do, that between November 1643 and October 1644 it rendered up £109 in support of the garrison of Royalist Lichfield and £44 in support of Parliamentarian Stafford[34] – as even some soldiers were prepared to admit, the cost to the beleaguered populace was very heavy. As a petition submitted to the Parliamentarian governor of Newport Pagnell complained, 'We may have just cause to fear that the people may rise and cut our throats, if an enemy approaches from whom they may expect some relief from such oppression … Their general expressions are that we eat the meat out of their children's mouths.'[35]

What, meanwhile, was the economic cost of war? Before 1642, England had for the most part been a prosperous country, but, in the short term at least, the clash between king and Parliament put paid to that. Industry, true, profited from the demand for all the arms and armour, clothes and footwear, and wagons and tents. However, if production boomed (though even this judgement can be qualified: while firearms were at a premium, this was far from the case with such commodities as fine furniture), trade did not, and the results were often extremely stark. To take an obvious example, in a development that was particularly unfortunate in view of the effects of the so-called 'Little Ice Age' (see below), London was hit hard by the Royalist seizure of control in County Durham in that the supply of coal on which the capital had come to depend very heavily for its fuel was brought to a complete standstill. This is, however, but one example, for, as one struggling merchant put it, 'There is no part of the Kingdom suffers, but London suffers: London is plundered every day in all the Kingdom over.'[36] At least until the Parliamentarians succeeded in ousting the Royalist cause in the north, then, the situation ranged from the grim to the near desperate. To quote one of the many petitions associated with the capital's growing 'peace-party' - in its own self an indication of the havoc wrought by the war - 'The multitude of poor people in and about this city (who, by reason of the cessation of trade, want employment and, consequently bread) infinitely abound.'[37] And, as things were in London, so they were elsewhere, a good example being the woollen industry of Wiltshire, the local clothiers being able to maintain only the most intermittent contact with London - hitherto their chief market - and frequently finding themselves deprived both of vital consignments of raw material and skilled workmen.[38] Nor was Wiltshire alone: another bastion of the cloth industry that was affected very badly was Yorkshire's Pennine fringe, while the inability of the colliers of Northumberland and Durham to ship their produce from the Tyne to the Thames meant that thousands of men suddenly found themselves stripped of a major part of their income: hence, perhaps, the unwonted ease with which the Parliamentarians on the one hand and the Royalists on the other were able to raise troops from among their inhabitants.[39]

To death, destruction, disruption, disturbance and destitution, meanwhile, was added climatic disaster. As is now widely recognised, from around 1600 until perhaps 1850 the world fell into the grip of the so-called Little Ice Age, a sudden cold snap that reduced the average temperature by enough to effect drastic changes in the weather and appears to have been at its worst in the first half of the seventeenth century. Winters were longer, thereby massively reducing the length of the growing season and reducing the yield of the harvest, a problem that was much intensified by repeated instances of prolonged drought in the autumn and winter, while, such as they were, the crops were frequently ruined by hailstorms, incessant rain or unseasonable frosts (in England, in particular, while low in yield, the harvests of 1642–45 seem to have been enough to stave off disaster, but the second half of the 1640s was a different matter: between 1646 and 1651 so terrible was the weather that not a single harvest survived, the result being that much of the country was reduced to the brink of famine). So bitter were winter temperatures, meanwhile, that, along with many other waterways in Europe and beyond, the River Thames frequently froze over to such an extent that it was possible to stage 'frost fairs' upon it, the fact that many ports were cut off by ice for long periods of time also inflicting serious damage on seaborne trade. For the unfortunate men condemned to fight the Civil War, the consequences are only too easy to envisage: with armies all too often lacking even the shelter of tents and all too often inadequately clad, the suffering of all and sundry was terrible, even if, just occasionally, extreme cold could have its uses, it being noted of Edgehill, for example, that many of the wounded left lying on the field all night were saved by the fact that the blood was literally frozen in their veins.[40]

Every casualty of war, of course, is a human tragedy, but it is extremely rare that we get a glimpse of the impact that such stricken fields had in the humble households from which the bulk of the dead and wounded stemmed. Not so in the case of the educated, however. Of the death of Sir Edmund Verney, killed fighting for King Charles at Edgehill while defending the royal standard, for example, his Parliamentarian son, Sir Ralph, wrote that the news was 'the saddest and deepest affliction that ever befell any poor distressed man'.[41] Less well-known but even more affecting were the words penned by sometime royal official Edward Pitt on the death of his soldier-son, William, from typhus at Oxford in 1643. As he wrote to his wife, Rachel, in the middle of what he termed 'the ice that has chilled our sad hearts', with William, 'sweet soul' that he was, gone, they had lost 'the greatest comfort of our lives'.[42] To the anguish of personal loss, meanwhile, was often added the pain felt by families and old friends torn apart by war. Thus, the Verneys were far from being alone in their division: Parliamentarian chronicler Lucy Hutchinson was the sister of the Royalist governor of Barnstaple, Sir Allen Apsley, while her husband, John, one of Parliament's chief champions in the Midlands, found himself on the opposite side to his cousins, the Byrons of Newstead Abbey; the king's commander in the south-west, Sir Ralph Hopton, discovered that his chief opponent was to be Sir William Waller, a dear comrade from the German wars; Richard d'Ewes was a Royalist, whereas his brother,

Sir Symonds, was a Parliamentarian; the first soldier to fall for Parliament at Marston Moor was a younger son of the prominent Lancashire royalist Sir Gilbert Hoghton; William Fielding, the first Earl of Denbigh, was a Royalist, but his eldest son, Basil, who inherited the title after his father died of wounds received at the fall of Birmingham in 1643, was a Parliamentarian; and no less a figure than Prince Rupert had an elder brother - the exiled ruler of the Palatinate - who was firmly wedded to the struggle against King Charles. There was, then, much despair. To quote Sir Hugh Cholmley, commander of the Parliamentarian outpost of Scarborough, 'I am forced to draw my sword not only against my countrymen, but many near friends and allies, some of which I know to be well affected in religion and lovers of their liberties.'[43] Finally, if many men found themselves divided from friends and family, such was the complexity of the choices that had to be made in 1642 that plenty of gentlemen found themselves having to favour cherished principles at the expense of others that were no less dear to them. Thus, famously, Sir Edmund Verney was as much a Puritan as any of the men who rode into battle on the other side at Edgehill, while Sir Thomas Tyldesley, a die-hard Royalist who fell in the action that took place at Wigan in the Third Civil War, had before 1642 been a bitter opponent of the religious policies of Archbishop Laud, believing that they 'came too near idolatry'.[44]

All this, meanwhile, was accompanied by a sense of not just the established order, but the whole fabric of society coming apart at the seams: one might think here of the execution of the king, of the elevation, albeit infrequent, of men of humble origin to positions of influence and authority; of the rise of sectarian religion; of the abolition of the bishops and the House of Lords; of the expression of non-conformist opinion of every sort in press and pamphlet literature alike; of the destruction of age-old foci of the community such as market crosses; of the desecration of cathedrals such as Lichfield and Worcester; of the ejection of clergy from their cures in favour of new men more prone to speak the language of hard-line Puritanism, a process very often accompanied by various forms of humiliation; of the crowds of apprentices who mobbed Parliament in the winter of 1641-42; of the wholesale abrogation of the rights of property by the sequestration of the estates of opponents by one side or the other; of the bands of 'clubmen' who by 1645 were defying the soldiers of both sides in wide expanses of the country; of the angry crowds who sacked the properties of a variety of recusant families in the Stour Valley riots of 1642; of the East-Anglian rent strikes of 1643; of the ever more challenging and, ultimately, downright rebellious behaviour of the large number of humble Fenland folk who had been deprived of a large part of their livelihood by a decade or more of sustained attempt to drain such expanses as the so-called 'Great Level', and turn them over to agriculture; of the Puritan-inspired prohibition of the celebration of Christmas imposed in 1647; of the communities of leadminers in the High Peak who rallied to the support of the king out of hatred for the ever more greedy and exploitative attitude of the local gentry who were the sole beneficiaries of their labours; of the behaviour of the common soldiers who over and over again rose in mutiny against their officers; and, finally, of the radical demands made by the Diggers and Levellers (this is not, of course, to imply that all of these developments alienated all and sundry – on the contrary, many of them possessed much support – but to say that Oliver Cromwell wanted liberty of conscience and considerable limitations on the power of the monarchy is not enough to whitewash his innate social conservatism).[45]

As if all this was not bad enough, probably still more frightening was the manner in which the conflict seemingly threatened the bonds by which women were kept in their proper place; for some of the population, at least, the prospect of social and religious revolution was exciting, but, whether Royalist or Parliamentarian, there was doubtless scarcely a man in the country of any social rank whatsoever who was not alarmed at stories of women adopting male attire, fighting as soldiers, turning preacher, setting up all-female congregations, taking the lead in bread-riots and political demonstrations, and even petitioning Parliament.[46] As Barbara Donagan has written, then, 'For civilians, it often seemed that the pillars of order, morality and civility had crumbled', that, to quote a popular ballad of the period, the world had been 'turned upside-down'.[47]

And, finally, there was the impact of the fighting itself. First of all, we can speak of this in human terms. In families across the land whether great or humble, there was the anguish caused by the absence of beloved husbands, fathers and sons and, with this, the almost total impossibility of discovering their fate. As one Susan Rodway famously wrote, 'My most dear and loving husband … I pray you to send me word when you do think you shall return. You do not consider I am a lone woman. I thought you would never leave me this long together.'[48] In much the same vein, meanwhile, we have the complaints of another London goodwife named Susan Owen. Thus:

Most tender and dear heart: I am like never to see you more, I fear, and ...
the reason is this: either ... the Cavaliers will kill you, or death will deprive
you of me, being full of grief for you which I fear will cost me my life ...
I do much grieve that you are so hard-hearted to me. Why could you not
come home with Master Murphy on Saturday? Could not you venture
as well as he? But you did it on purpose to show your hatred to me ...
Everybody can come but you ... Pity me for God's sake and come home.[49]

To make matters worse, many of the men concerned had not even gone to
war of their own accord. On both sides of the lines, the supply of volunteers
driven to enlist by poverty, or more rarely, conviction, was far from infinite,
and the result was that both king and Parliament resorted to the press. This
last, alas, is not a subject that has attracted much attention from English Civil
War scholars, but, to quote John Donoghue, 'During the Wars of the Three
Kingdoms ... both Royalist and Parliamentary armies conscripted soldiers for
the infantry ... Both sides could claim that forcing men to serve fell within
the just tradition of raising armies to put down domestic insurrections. The
scale of conscription during these conflicts, however, dramatically outpaced all
previous initiatives.'[50] The brunt of the burden inevitably falling on the poorest
and most vulnerable sectors of society, the result was much disaffection. Already
Britain's military involvement in the Thirty Years' War - something that saw up
to 120,000 men, the vast majority not gentry bent on adventure and the defence
of the Protestant cause, but rather miserable levies destined to fight as pikemen
and musketeers, take ship for Holland, Germany, Denmark or Sweden - had
caused great anguish, a number of contemporary reports suggesting that many
unwilling warriors committed suicide or cut off hands or fingers rather than let
themselves be shipped abroad.[51] We have no evidence of this sort from Civil War
England, but it is clear enough that military service in general and impressment
in particular were much hated.[52] Particularly when they had been radicalised
by religious fervour, the populace were willing enough to rush to arms when
it was a matter of defending their own homes - good examples can be found
in the Royalist attacks on Bolton and Bradford in 1642 and 1643 - while the
London Trained Bands had relished standing to arms at Turnham Green in
response to Charles' advance on London after Edgehill, but being marched off to
fight elsewhere was quite another matter. Sir William Waller, then, had endless

problems with the London Trained Bands regiments dispatched to reinforce him in his campaigns in Sussex and Hampshire in 1643-44, while it is no coincidence that the Leveller movement included freedom from any sort of impressment as a central part of its programme.[53] To make any difference in this respect, very particular issues had to come to play: as Mark Stoyle has pointed out, if Cornwall not only produced disproportionate numbers of volunteers for the Royalist cause but also disproportionate numbers of volunteers who were prepared to serve beyond its borders and carry the war to the enemy, it was because large parts of the county felt a strong sense that Cornish culture was under threat from a 'little England' tendency that regarded their inhabitants as little more than barbarians, while Wedgwood argues that the reason so many fenlanders turned out to fight in the forces raised in the area by Oliver Cromwell was they associated the Royalist cause with the speculators who had been draining and enclosing the wetlands on which they were so dependent for their economic well-being.[54]

The trauma brought by war was not just a matter of personal anguish. Like all other conflicts, the English Civil War was replete with sights of horror, while it was also fought in the midst of the so-called 'military revolution', a period in which warfare that was intensified by a move to professional armies and new levels of intensity and destruction, a period, too, in which combat was far more likely to impact the lives of the inhabitants than it had in earlier times. In the words of a treatise on the art of war published in the 1620s:

> I will only make a poor demonstration of the differences of former times (yet not above twenty years gone) and these modern times wherein many things are practised by way of alteration, and you shall consider what you are to trust unto in the war in this instant ... You then did skirmish by files ... [but] now whole ranks shoot at once ... You had many battles in those days, but now ... you hear not of one in seven years ... You had then great use of open fields, but now you are enclosed in trenches and the besieging of towns. You had then certain field-pieces which played over your heads, but now you have dangerous batteries ... which sweep away whole ranks with ... great bullets ... You did then know, I confess, ambuscades, stratagems ... and such like, but now you must be acquainted with open terror and see the cannon fired before your face. Yea, many times, though you be quiet in your trenches, yet shall the shot come thundering ... and

put ... all your martial discipline to no purpose; again, being in a town
subject unto battery, you are swept away sitting at your meat [or] walking
in the street.[55]

The truth, of course, was that war had always been horrific, but the constant
increase in the use of firearms certainly ensured that mutilation and other forms
of visible damage were far more common than had been their wont (and, in
addition, that wounds were more likely to be deadly to be more deadly: by the
time of the Civil Wars, military surgeons were perfectly capable of sewing up
the gashes left by edged weapons, but the entry and, especially, exit wounds
inflicted by lead musket balls were difficult to repair and the chances of infection
much higher).[56] To take just one example of the effects of artillery, in a treatise
on surgery published in 1686 Richard Wiseman recalled how he was summoned
to attend a Royalist soldier who had taken a round of case-shot full in the face:

The colonel sent to me ... to dress the man. I went, but was somewhat
troubled where to begin. His face, with his eyes, nose, mouth and forepart
of the jaws, was shot away, and the remaining parts of them driven in. One
part of the jaw hung down by his throat ... I saw the brain working under
the lacerated scalp on both sides between his ears and brows.[57]

Inherent in the use of cannon and muskets was, of course the use of gunpowder,
this being a commodity that was all too prone to being blown up by accident,
usually by careless soldiers lighting their pipes in the vicinity of magazines or
powder wagons. Needless to say, the results were horrific. Terrible explosions
of this sort occurred at Hoghton Tower in 1643 and Torrington in 1646, but
better documented than either is the misfortune that almost cost the Royalist
western army the life of its commander, Sir Ralph Hopton, in the wake of the
Battle of Lansdown. Richard Atkyns, a Royalist officer, was among the stunned
eye-witnesses:

It made a very great noise and darkened the air for a time, and the hurt
men made lamentable screeches. As soon as the air was clear, I went to
see what the manner was, [and] there I found His Lordship miserably
burned, his horse singed like parched leather, and Thomas Sheldon ...

complaining that the fire was got within his breeches, which I tore off as soon as I could. And from as long a flaxen head of hair as ever I saw, in the twinkling of an eye, his [face] was like [that of] a blackamoor.[58]

More men survived the ravages of gunpowder, cannon-shot and musket ball than might have been expected, but they were often scarred for life and left as little more than cripples: his thigh having been shattered by a musket ball at Lancaster in 1643, William Blundell of Little Crosby spent the rest of his days not only with the leg concerned several inches shorter than its fellow - a feature that earned him the nickname 'Halt Will' - but also in constant pain; equally, according to the petition for relief he submitted in 1651 wounded at the first battle of Newbury, Canterbury, artisan George Robinson spent a full year as a patient of Saint Bartholomew's hospital in London, having 'above three-score splinters of the bone of his leg at several times taken out to his great pains' and had since then 'been not alone disabled to follow his vocation' but also 'almost continually in intolerable pain ... of which he cannot hope of remedy during this life'.[59]

If injuries were fiercesome, meanwhile, battlefields were places of horror whose sights were such as to leave a deep impact on popular memory. In Lincolnshire, for example, a corner of the battlefield of Winceby where fleeing Royalists were trapped in an angle of two hedges is still known as 'Slash Hollow'; in Northamptonshire, a piece of ground near the village of Marston Trussel bears the name 'Slaughter Field' on account of the massacre of a number of fleeing Royalists there in the wake of the Battle of Naseby; in Wiltshire, the steep drop over which much of the Roundhead cavalry fled to its destruction at the battle of Roundway Down in July 1643 is to this day known as 'Bloody Ditch'; in Cambridgeshire, the village of Harston boasts a stretch of ground whose name - 'Blood Field' - commemorates an otherwise long-forgotten skirmish; and, finally, in Oxfordshire, the name of Digbeth Street in Stow-on-the-Wold, the site of the defeat of the last Royalist army in the first Civil War, is supposed to be a corruption of 'Ducks' Bath Street', so much blood having collected in its many ruts that ducks were able to paddle in it.[60] As to the vistas that gave rise to such legends, we can do no better than quote the account of First Newbury written by Henry Foster, a sergeant in the Red Regiment of the London Trained Bands. Thus: 'The next day I viewed the dead bodies. There lay about 100 stripped naked in that field where our two regiments stood in battalia. This night the enemy carried away about thirty cart-loads of maimed and dead men ... Fourteen lay dead in one ditch.[61]

If such sights were all too common, it was not just soldiers who found themselves caught up in violence; civilians, too, frequently found that they had blood on their hands. In various parts of the country - for particularly good examples, we might cite the West Riding of Yorkshire, the clothing districts of north-east Somerset, and the Staffordshire moorlands[62] - common husbandmen and artisans rallied enthusiastically to the cause of Parliament and turned out to fight as a species of 'home guard' whenever their home territories were threatened by Royalist incursions, while in places of Parliamentarian sympathy that were besieged by the king's troops - one thinks here of Barnstaple, Plymouth and Lyme - large numbers of the inhabitants took an active part in defence of the walls.[63] Also worth mentioning here are the veritable popular insurrections that swept areas of both Devon and Somerset - both of them counties where popular support for Parliament was generally strong and in some places very strong indeed - in protest at Royalist taxation, requisitioning and wholesale plundering - in 1645-46, these being so ferocious that they could only be suppressed at the cost of veritable punitive expeditions.[64] As we shall see, at around this same time there were disturbances in other Royalist-controlled counties, including, most notably, Shropshire and Herefordshire, yet it was not just the Royalists who faced such problems: on the contrary, such was the misery of the populace that in September 1645 parts of Wiltshire, Sussex - a county even more strongly Parliamentarian in 1642 than Devon and Somerset - and Hampshire were gripped by serious disturbances sparked by the heavy recruitment and increases in taxation necessitated by the formation of the New Model Army.[65] In the resultant skirmishes, blood was shed on both sides - for example, at Sturminster Newton on 19 June, Bridport on 3 July, Hambledon Hill on 4 August and Walperton on 19 September - and on occasion, too, there were cases of simple murder when stragglers or men otherwise detached from their units from one side or the other were pounced upon by angry civilians and done to death. Thus, in December 1643, at Dunsford in Devon, the commander of a Parliamentarian patrol sent to search the place for arms was shot dead by one of its householders; at Nuthurst in Sussex two Parliamentarian soldiers who had enraged the inhabitants by their conduct were done to death by a mob; at the Leicestershire village of Ravenstone a fugitive from the battlefield of Naseby had his brains beaten out by a serving girl armed with nothing more than the paddle from her wash-tub; and, in the wake of the battle of Worcester, many Scottish soldiers were, in Clarendon's words, 'every day knocked in the head by the country people and used with their barbarity'.[66]

These episodes of popular violence are grimly reminiscent of some of the scenes portrayed in the famous series of engravings produced by Jacques Caillaux depicting the horrors of the Thirty Years' War. Mercifully for all concerned, the conflicts of 1642–51 never came close to matching what went on in Continental Europe in those of 1618–48. A number of scholars have tried to argue that this idea has been much overstated, and, if they pushed the argument much too far, it is certainly true that the Civil War still witnessed incidents, scenes and situations that were bad enough, and, what is more, scenes and situations that were even more jarring given the fact that England was a peaceful society from which armed conflict had been absent for the best part of a century. Of these, prominent examples include the sack of Birmingham, Bolton, Liverpool and Leicester by King Charles' forces; the slaughter in cold blood of a number of Parliamentarian prisoners at Barthomley, Hopton Castle and Woodhouse Hall in 1643 and 1644; the massacre of around 100 Royalist campfollowers in the wake of the battle of Naseby; and the New Model Army's murder of several Catholic civilians caught up in the storm of Basing House.[67] As for prisoners of war, if the terms of their surrender generally guaranteed them life and limb, neither the Royalists nor the Parliamentarians had the resources to give them much more than accommodation in conditions that were at best spartan and, at worst, utterly appalling. For a particularly grim example in this last respect, we have only to turn to the 5,000 Scottish prisoners captured at the battle of Dunbar on 3 September 1651. Marched south into England in the middle of incessant cold and rain, they were eventually housed in Durham Cathedral (then shut up, like every other cathedral in England, by reason of the abolition of episcopacy), but in the month that it took them to reach their destination 1,000 of them fell prey to starvation or exposure, while another 1,500 perished in the winter, as witness the grave pit that was recently uncovered during renovation work on one of the buildings on Palace Green.[68] Equally melancholic, meanwhile, was the fate of some 1,300 Scottish prisoners reputed to have been packed into the parish church of Chapel-en-le-Frith in the aftermath of the battle of Preston in July 1648 for sixteen days, a fact that, even if it is true, as the legend goes that many others were too weak to move and were therefore left to their fate, makes it something of a wonder that only forty-four of them died before they were marched to a fresh destination.[69] In general terms, it is true that conflict became ever less 'civil' as time advanced, with the Parliamentarian forces being ever more inclined to avenge both themselves, and, as they saw it, the whole of England, against the men they perceived as the authors of the 'sad distracted times' in which they lived, a process that culminated in the execution of Charles I in 1649. However, from the very beginning the ranting of such preachers as Hugh Peters ensured a propensity for violence that was both inherent and truly chilling, while plenty of evidence can be found, too, of Parliamentarian agitators and pamphleteers such as the future champion of the most radical faction of the Leveller movement, William Walwyn, who were prepared to challenge the view espoused by Pym, Hampden and, for that matter, Oliver Cromwell that the war was essentially a conservative affair whose great rallying cry was 'king and Parliament', and demanded that it should be directed at Charles himself rather than some supposed coterie of evil counsellors, and that with a view to giving England a whole new constitution rather than some patched-up version of the situation pre-1642.[70]

Before bringing this section to a close, the issue of access to the wider world and the manner in which its doings impacted on those who learned of them is also worth considering. Poor though communications may have been and literacy at best limited, seventeenth-century England was by no means ignorant of current affairs. Thus, prior to 1642 the participation of large numbers of gentry and commoners alike as volunteers in the service of Gustavus Adolphus and his fellow champions of Protestant Europe, not to mention the periodic clamour for, first, James I, and subsequently his son, Charles I, to send troops to fight for the cause of Frederick of the Palatinate and his beautiful English queen, Elizabeth (the daughter of the first of these two monarchs and the sister of the second) ensured that the appalling sufferings endured by 'High Germany' were common currency, one incident that struck particular horror into the minds of all and sundry being the storm of Magdeburg by forces of the Empire in 1631 with the loss of 30,000 lives.[71] Meanwhile, as England slid ever deeper into crisis after 1640, so the supporters of Parliament turned to news-sheets and pamphlets as a means of publicising their grievances and putting pressure on their stubborn monarch. When the catastrophic *deus ex machina* of the Irish revolt burst upon the scene in the autumn of 1641, it was easy to spread the highly convenient notions, first, that the dangerously papistical, if not downright papist, Charles, was behind the insurrection, and, second, that the rebels were savages bent on the torture and killing of every Protestant in Ireland, who, even as things were, were guilty of the murder of literally hundreds of thousands of good English and Scottish folk amid circumstances of the most revolting cruelty. This last claim was driven home by a veritable bombardment of crude wood-cuts showing atrocities of every sort, but, in a sense, such stridency was so much wasted effort: so far as Protestant Englishmen were concerned, the mere fact that the rebellion was a Catholic one was enough to damn it out of hand, and all the more so with the horrors that the Spanish Armada was universally supposed to have been poised to unleash upon Elizabeth I and her subjects a memory deliberately kept alive, meanwhile, by a long-running exhibition in the Tower of London of suitably devilish weapons and instruments of torture that had ostensibly been recovered from the wreckage of the many galleons that had come to grief before they could make their way home to Spain. Also very useful here were the stories that had been coming out of the Spanish empire in the Americas for the past century or more of the slaughter and enslavement of the indigenous peoples (the fact that England's policy in Ireland was equally colonialist and potentially just as brutal was, of course, always conveniently overlooked). As Michael Braddick has written, then, 'Over the winter of 1641-2 politics in England was conducted against the backdrop of terrible stories from Ireland.'[72]

Once civil war became an established fact, meanwhile, so Parliamentarian pamphleteers added fuel to the flames by painting the Cavaliers as not just ruthless ruffians but, still worse, papist ruffians - it is by no means insignificant that 'cavalier' was a term derived from the Spanish word for gentleman - and turning the lamentable but nonetheless comparatively minor episodes that occurred at Birmingham, Bolton and Leicester into veritable replays of what had happened at Magdeburg. In Scotland, meanwhile, the success of the Marquis of Montrose in raising so much of the Highlands against the Covenant was quite enough in itself to spread further waves of anguish through society, just as, ironically enough, the march of a Scottish army into England in 1643 terrified a goodly part of the population of such shires as Northumberland and Durham. With the population of the Marches on the one hand and Devon and Somerset on the other alarmed out of their wits by the sudden eruption of Celtic armies drawn from Cornwall and Wales across their borders, from end to end of the British Isles the populace lived in fear of being murdered in their very beds at any time, if not worse. Although the particular anecdote relates to the Irish rebellion, the emotions caught by one inhabitant of Bradford in respect of an incident when the church service he was attending was disrupted by the arrival of some most frightening news were beyond doubt typical of those felt by many other individuals in many other places at many other times. Thus:

> About three o'clock in the afternoon a certain man ... came and stood up in the chapel door and cried out in a lamentable voice, 'Friends ... we are all as good as dead men, for the Irish rebels are coming. They are come as far as Rochdale and Littleborough, and will be at Halifax and Bradford shortly' ... Upon [this] the congregation were all in confusion: some wept, others ran out, others fell to talking ... Oh, what a sad and sorrowful going home had we that evening, for ... we knew not but incarnate devils and death would be there before us.[73]

Just as terrified, meanwhile, was the staunchly Parliamentarian Lady Brilliana Hartley, who found herself trapped deep in Royalist territory in the family home at Brampton Bryan in Shropshire. As she wrote to her son, Edward, 'If God were not merciful to me, I should be in a very miserable condition. I am threatened every day to be beset by soldiers. My hope is [that] the Lord will not deliver me into their hands, for surely they would use all cruelty towards me.'[74] Finally, there are the repeated instances of panic that gripped London in general, and Westminster in particular, as the Long Parliament got to grips with the work of reform, as on 19 May 1641 when a minor mishap in which a rather clumsy member of the House of Commons lent on a piece of woodwork in the chamber that could not take his weight and snapped it, producing a crack like a pistol-shot that sparked a wholesale stampede for the exits on the presumption that the chamber was under attack.[75]

As time went on, meanwhile, it was not just marauding armies that gave rise to such fear. By the end of the war, many Royalist soldiers had perforce become accustomed to sustaining themselves through wholesale plunder and, with the coming of peace, all too many of the officers in particular found themselves with no means of securing an honest livelihood. There thus emerged the phenomenon of the highwayman or 'gentleman of the road', the first followers of this profession including such veterans as Phillip Stafford, Zachary Howard and James Hind, all of whom had been captains in the service of King Charles. According to the myth that quickly came to surround them, such men were heroic figures who never failed to behave as gentlemen and concentrated their ire on figures associated with the Parliamentarian cause, but from the beginning their ranks were swelled by common footpads whose mores were of a different nature, while in many instances a life of crime blunted their sensibilities and led to a slide in their standard of conduct, if that is, it had ever been high to start with. And, of course, whatever the reality, the roads were unsafe, while even the humble could not sleep quietly in their beds (although a product of the eighteenth century rather than the seventeenth, the most famous highwayman of all, Dick Turpin, had started out as a burglar who made a habit of not just breaking into houses but also torturing the people he encountered therein).[76] As to whether the volume of crime was increased by war, it is difficult to say – there had, of course, been plenty of felons in the towns and countryside of Tudor and Jacobean England – but what is true is that, perhaps because of the wholesale indiscipline that took hold of the armies of King Charles, the latter's rank and file were much associated with petty larceny in the Restoration era. Here, for example, is an indignant Samuel Pepys, 'Of all the old army [i.e. the New Model], now you cannot see a man begging about the street ... whereas the other [i.e. the Royalists] go with their belts and swords, swearing and cursing and stealing [and] running into people's houses, by force often times, to carry away something.'[77]

Interregnum Britain, then, was a society in shock (hence, perhaps, at least in part, the witch hunts that convulsed East Anglia in the period 1645-50).[78] For something of the sense of loss and desolation that prevailed, one need only turn to the Anglican theologian Jeremy Taylor. Thus, devoted Royalist though he was, by 1650 Taylor was nevertheless inclined to advocate a policy of peace at any price. To quote one of his many tracts:

If we could from one of the battlements of Heaven espy how many men and women lie fainting and dying at this time for want of bread, how many young men are hewn down by the sword of war, how many ... orphans are now weeping over the graves of [the] father by whose life they were enabled to eat ... in all reason we should be glad to be out of the noise and participation of so many evils. This is a place of sorrows and tears, of great evils and a constant calamity.[79]

Just as eloquent, meanwhile, was Laudian divine William Chillingworth, for whom, it seems, there increasingly came to be little to mark the two sides out in terms of morality:

> Seeing publicans and sinners on the one hand against scribes and Pharisees on the other; on the one side hypocrisy, on the other profaneness; no honesty nor justice on the one side, and very little piety on the other; on the one side horrible oaths, curses and blasphemies, on the other pestilent lies, calumnies and perjury ... I profess that I cannot without trembling consider what is likely to be the effect of these distractions.[80]

With this assessment, there were doubtless observers on both sides who were only too ready to agree. In addition, there was a growing sense of guilt, a sense of guilt redoubled after the Restoration that in many ways England was but little changed from how she had been in 1642 - that in the words of the poet John Dryden, 'Thy wars brought nothing about.'[81] To quote Blair Worden:

> Only men with an uncomplicated sense of allegiance to God or King could reflect without discomfort, at the time or afterwards, on their own part in a conflict which intensified the discord it was meant to resolve ... Neither courage nor heroism quite hid the guilt, or anyway the unease, of civil war. The visual record of the conflict, if we except printed matter and woodcuts, is minimal. Even royalism, the more aesthetically aware of the two sides, produced nothing to parallel in aspiration, let alone in achievement, a work such as Velasquéz's celebratory triumph of the Spaniards over the Dutch at Breda in 1625.[82]

Chapter 2

Of History, Horror and Hauntings

According to the greatest narrative historian of the Civil War era, C.V. Wedgwood, the sort of lamentations with which we closed the preceding chapter were exaggerated. There had been death, destruction and disruption aplenty, certainly, 'but there was no damage that an active people could not remedy' and all the more so given the positive mood she claimed to grip the country. Thus, 'The powerful cry now was not for a return to the old ways, but for strenuous change and new solutions. Here was no weary resignation, but new demands and bold ideas.'[1] To write in this fashion, however, is to confuse the mind of Oliver Cromwell, the cavalry of the New Model Army, the burgeoning sects of London or the followers of John Lilburne with the mood of the country as a whole, and one may be forgiven for suspecting that widening the focus of investigation would produce a very different picture. Yet it is evident that shame and despair were not mixed with a desire to forget all that had passed. On the contrary, if the great emphasis placed on the political and military events of the Civil War and Commonwealth eras by the innumerable almanacs that were a major feature of popular culture is anything to go by, there was also an appetite for keeping their memory alive, and, indeed, for probing into exactly what had happened (published by the dozen every year, these works habitually contained a list of events from the Creation onwards, and, hitherto but little concerned with the recent past, said lists now featured numerous entries for such events as Edgehill, Marston Moor, Naseby and the execution of the king).[2] In this atmosphere of cataclysm and calamity on the one hand and commemoration and commentary on the other, it was but natural that, for all England's Protestantism, a creed that abhorred the supernatural and, in particular, belief in ghosts, these last being a phenomenon that Catholic tradition explained by reference to unquiet spirits trapped in Purgatory, or even suffering eternal torment in the fires of Hell, who had come back to urge the need for repentance, there should have been a return to reactions that might be deemed to have belonged to a different age.[3] Nor was it just a matter of the unquiet dead. Also at work were more secular forces in that, frightened, confused and more-or-less cast adrift, the populace began to turn to ghost stories as a means of recording, commemorating or explaining the troubled times in which they lived: in sixteenth-century France, indeed, the endless turmoil of the Wars of Religion had already inspired a rash of tales that clearly had their origins in the events and debates of the day.[4] And, as in France, so in Germany where the Thirty Years' War generated tale after tale of spectral soldiers marching along country roads, ghostly armies doing battle in the skies and night-time apparitions stalking castles, manors and taverns. To quote Aidan O'Lynn, for example, 'Following the Battle of Nördlingen ... for many years late at night in that same area a field game of drilling, drumming and firing pieces was heard ... Likewise, the location of the battle of White Mountain ... outside Prague was haunted by fiery riders [while] the site of another Protestant defeat at Stadtlohn ... where over 6,000 were killed by the Catholic League, was haunted long after by spirits.'[5]

That similar developments were likely to take hold in England - a country, be it said, in which the realities of war were particularly shocking given the fact that there had been no pitched battle on her soil since the suppression of the rebellion of the northern earls in 1569 - was clear almost from the very beginning of the conflict. Thus, a few months after the battle of Edgehill (fought on 23 October 1642), claims began to circulate among the local inhabitants that the struggle was being regularly waged anew in the skies above the fields in which it had taken place to the sound of muskets and artillery, the clash of arms and the screams of dying men and horses. A priest who the men who first claimed to have seen the phenomenon having travelled to the site to investigate and promptly reported that he had had precisely the same experience, it was not long before the strange events reached the ear of King Charles in his wartime capital of Oxford. Much intrigued, he sent a group of his officers to see if there was any truth in the story, and they, too, testified to having seen the phantom fighting, even going so far as to claim that they had recognised the figure of Sir Edmund Verney, a gentleman of Charles' personal suite who had been killed while carrying the royal standard, together with those of a number of other officers. From Oxford, meanwhile, the story travelled to London, and there it was quickly immortalised in print as *A Great Wonder in Heaven: showing the Late Apparitions and Prodigious Noises of War and Battles, seen on Edge Hill near Kineton in Northamptonshire. Certified*

under the Hands of William Wood, Esquire and Justice for the Peace in the said
county, Samuel Marshall, preacher of God's word in Kineton, and other Persons
of Quality.[6]

So much for the story, but why was it so widely believed? At the simplest level,
the answer is easy enough: to quote Diane Purkiss, 'Ghosts signify the dead who
have been denied, ignored, slighted; a ghost is the advocate of the silent corpses,
buried without rites, not given their due. The [Edgehill] dead were disfigured,
unrecognizable and therefore buried hastily in unmarked graves without the rites
of communal mourning.'[7] However, it was not just this. While the spirits of those
buried in unconsecrated soil might stalk the land, and all the more so if they had
simply been tipped into mass graves without any attempt at the formal rites of
burial, thanks to Christian beliefs in the Resurrection of Christ and the dead
rising from the grave at the Last Judgment, it was a common belief that the dead
could literally come to life in protest at their fate, in pursuit of revenge or, finally,
in an attempt to effect some purpose on the part of God, such as, for example,
warning humanity of the horrors of war. And, finally, as if all this was not enough,
for those of Catholic persuasion there was the issue of Purgatory: with soldiers
seen as being in and of themselves evil men or, at least, men willing to turn their
hands to acts of great evil, it followed that it was very unlikely that they would be
admitted to Heaven straight away, their spirits therefore lingering in the places
they died, a fate that was all the more likely if they had died with the blood of
battle on their hands.[8]

It was not just Catholics who were influenced by these last beliefs: if
Protestants rejected the concept of Purgatory, they had no difficulty with the idea
that the souls of the damned were condemned to wander the land for all eternity.
However, let us set all this aside in favour of the concept of 'a great wonder in
Heaven' referred to by the pamphlet cited above. Herein lies another key. In the
words of Darren Oldridge, a historian who has strongly challenged the thesis
advanced in Keith Thomas' seminal *Religion and the Decline of Magic* to the
effect that the rise of Protestantism not just eroded, but ended up overthrowing
altogether medieval society's obsession with the supernatural as the only means of
explaining the workings of the natural world, 'Great political events encouraged
speculation about the divine messages they contained and the violent insecurity
of the mid-seventeenth century probably increased the need to find indications
of God's will.'[9] Fearing that the disordered nature of the times might combine

with the emergence of rational thought, some Protestant divines even mobilised the undead as proof of the existence of afterlife and redemption (or, in the latter case, lack thereof), 1691 seeing no less a figure than Oliver Cromwell's sometime chaplain, Richard Baxter, publish an earnest volume entitled *The Certainty of the Worlds of Spirits and, consequently, of the Immortality of Souls, of the Malice and Misery of the Devils and the Damned, and of the Blessedness of the Justified, fully evinced by the Unquestionable Histories of Apparitions, Operations, Witchcrafts, Voices, etc., written as an Addition to many other Treatises for the Conviction of Sadducees and Infidels.*[10] However, it was not just a matter of mere functionalism. As Oldridge further observed, the forty years preceding the outbreak of the Civil War witnessed a 'movement in English Protestantism towards an "experimental" style of piety in which the devout scrutinised their lives and consciences for signs of grace'.[11] Such searches, though, were not confined solely to the internal. To quote Oldridge once again, 'The search for heavenly warnings, judgements and approbations in the wider world was, perhaps, a natural extension of this tendency.'[12] And, if people searched for them, it was because they believed that they existed. Take, for example, Thomas Juxon, a prosperous London confectioner who saw military service in the London Trained Bands and left a detailed journal of the years from 1644 till 1647. Juxon was clearly a well-educated man with a good head for business, while his many remarks on the political situation are often most acute, and yet on 11 February 1644 we find him writing solemnly that 'a great black eagle with fired eyes' was credibly reported as having suddenly appeared in the Duke of Saxony's dining room while that worthy was at table, whereupon it proceeded to 'set upon one of the chairs of state for three days and three nights, vomiting streams of fire a little before [it] vanished away'.[13]

To the seventeenth-century mind, then, there was nothing strange about the idea of ghosts, to prove which point we have only to turn to the work of William Shakespeare and other dramatists of the period. Thus, the former made much use of apparitions - to take just four examples, they feature in *Macbeth*, *Julius Caesar*, *Hamlet* and *Richard III* - while they also crop up in the works of less well-known figures such as Thomas Kyd, Cyril Tourneur and John Webster.[14] More obscurely, in 1640 two unknown female playwrights writing under the pseudonyms of Mary Tattlewell and Joan Hit-Him-Home made use of a well-known London ghost story as the central plank in a pamphlet that set out to refute the claims of contemporary misogynists, in particular one John Taylor, a more immediately topical note in the same vein being struck by an anonymous pamphlet published at York two years later in which the shade of a late-Tudor pamphleteer named Thomas Nashe, who had waged a ferocious war on the then opponents of the bishops - the so-called Brownists - was called up to rehearse the same arguments he had put forward fifty years before.[15] And, finally, in 1644 we find an unknown Parliamentarian pamphleteer commandeering the spectre of the Earl of Strafford for the purpose of haranguing Charles I and his followers on the evils of continuing to wage war on their countrymen and warning them that they too would come to grief.[16]

If writers famous and otherwise made use of the spiritual world, it was because the subject was both popular and topical. At the level of the learned, numerous treatises such as Ludwig Lavater's *Of Ghosts and Spirits Walking by Night* were in circulation, while at all levels of society tales of phantoms and apparitions were recounted, dissected and generally lapped up, for, as one contemporary writer put it:

> Of all the common and familiar subjects of conversation that are entered
> upon in company ... there is none so ready to hand, none so usual, as
> that of spirits, and whether what is said of them is true. It is the topic that
> people most readily discuss, and on which they linger the longest, because
> of the abundance of examples, the subject being fine and pleasing and the
> discussion the least tedious that can be found.[17]

If ghosts walked the earth, moreover, there were few places where one was more likely to encounter them than battlefields and other places associated with acts of violence. According to Carlton, in our day it 'would be absurd to pretend that ghosts really exist, haunting sites where men slaughtered one another long ago'.[18] However, in the England of 1642 it would have been suggesting the opposite that would have merited this judgement. Meanwhile, all the themes that we will address in this work were already in widespread circulation. To take an obvious example, headless horsemen - a figure that seems to have emerged in connection both with devotion to the Catholic Church's legions of saints beheaded for their beliefs and earlier Celtic traditions of head-hunting - had been ranging the country for hundreds of years, generally as a species of grim reaper associated with imminent death.[19] Also well-known, meanwhile, was the figure of the ghostly lady haunting this or that castle or manor house, the tradition here, too, being that such apparitions signified the impending demise of a prominent member of the family concerned.[20] All that was missing, then, were the iconic figures of the Cavalier and the Roundhead, figures that were in a most literal sense invented in 1642.[21] Finally, also well established were the settings in which ghosts could be expected to appear: such places as ruinous castles and monasteries, for example, were commonly believed to be the haunt of spirits who went by the name of 'powries' or 'dunters'.[22]

In the words of Andrew Martin, life in medieval (a term that can here be extended well into the early-modern period) England was 'a veritable phantasmagoria'.[23] So much for the history, but to return to events in Warwickshire in the bleak midwinter of 1642, what did the events in question really amount to? At the time that the vision of the battle of Edgehill was first seen, the battlefield was still littered with corpses of the slain, and one explanation is therefore that, caught out, perhaps, in a violent thunderstorm, the shepherds who were the first witnesses to have reported the story may have panicked and convinced themselves that they were witnessing a haunting, whereupon those who successively investigated the phenomenon in the weeks that followed, seeing nothing but clear skies and empty countryside, could not bear to reveal their gullibility, and instead chose to claim that they had seen the same sights and heard the same sounds; what we have, then, is a similar situation to the one in Napoleonic Zaragoza that we have detailed above.[24] An alternative explanation that has been advanced is that the visions were the result of ergot poisoning, ergot being a fungus with hallucinogenic properties that affects wheat exposed to very wet weather while it is growing, but this seems less likely: while ergot certainly caused particular individuals to see a wide range of visions, it does not have the ability to cause multiple observers to see the same thing.[25] Needless to say, the truth is impossible to establish at this distance, but the fact that it reached the public domain means that it is difficult to be anything other than rather sceptical with regard to a similar story that emerged following the battle of Naseby in 1645: one suspects that this was a 'copy-cat' effort staged by some pamphleteer eager to turn a dishonest shilling, and yet, once again, crowds of people appear to have visited the field to see the haunting for themselves, many of them afterwards going on to testify to its veracity. Finally, if the cautious observer cannot but doubt the Naseby story, still more concern must attach to reports of the same genre that surfaced in the Commonwealth. Take, for example, two pamphlets that were written in support of the Cromwellian régime entitled *Strange News from the North* and *The Five Strange Wonders in the North and West of England*. Published in 1650 and 1659 respectively, the former recounted the apparition in the Malton area of ghostly companies of armed men marching to and fro in the dead of night, and the latter a supernatural re-enactment of the battle of Marston Moor. Given that all the strange sights and visions that had supposedly been seen since 1642 were explained in terms of 'portents' sent by God, it is not difficult to spot the message embedded in the two texts concerned: in brief, support the Commonwealth or risk God's displeasure and, with it, the horrors of war coming back to haunt England in person.[26]

What was sauce for the Parliamentarian goose was just as much sauce for the Royalist gander. Presumably with a view to achieving an effect that was the very mirror image of those aimed at by the pamphlets noted above, on 29 June 1662 two members of the clergy rode into notably Puritan Dorchester excitedly proclaiming to all and sundry that they had been riding along the road that led to the town from the village of Winterbourne Abbas when they had suddenly observed a ghostly body of a horse on the crown of a hill a little way off.[27] The message was clear enough: Dorchester had to turn away from the path of rebellion or face the consequences. Still more dramatic in this respect, meanwhile, were the stories that began to circulate concerning events that were supposed to have occurred at the Gloucestershire manor of Chavenage House in May 1660. Thus, situated at the village of Beverston, at the time of the Civil War the house was the home of Nathaniel Stephenson, one of the two Members of Parliament for the shire. A moderate Parliamentarian who had raised a regiment of horses to fight the King, Stephenson was supposedly coerced into supporting the execution of Charles I, only to have a curse put upon him by his daughter, Abigail, when she discovered what he had done, and promptly develop a painful illness of which he finally died in 1660. As the family and its guests were assembling for the funeral, so a fine black coach drawn by four black horses appeared at the gate and drove straight up to the house, whereupon the onlookers were terrified to observe that the driver not only had no head but also to judge from his dress, was none other than Charles I. As this point, things got still more dramatic: the fully clothed figure of Stephenson having emerged from the door and got into the coach, at a crack of the coachman's whip, the horses set off back down the drive at a furious pace, only for coach and horses alike to explode in a ball of fire as they reached the gate.[28]

The message of this story was, once again, discernible even to the most obtuse of Englishmen: a *de facto* regicide, Stephenson was paying for his crimes. So far as the propagandists of the Restoration were concerned, of course, he was far from the only Parliamentarian suffering the fires of Hell, but an equally popular theme was that such figures as Cromwell, his son-in-law, Henry Ireton, and the president of the trial of Charles I, John Bradshaw, were condemned to wander the earth for all eternity, a number of devices being employed to portray them as recounting their misdeeds, admitting the justice of their punishment and lamenting the evils they had brought upon the country.[29] Somebody else of whom this same claim was made, meanwhile, was Parliamentarian colonel Thomas Rainsborough, a regimental commander in the New Model Army who fought at the siege of Colchester in 1648 and was later in the same year slain by a Royalist raiding party during the siege of Pontefract Castle, some unknown supporter of Charles I publishing a pamphlet in which the colonel's ghost attributes Rainsborough's passing to the part he had played in the execution of Sir Charles Lucas and Sir George Lisle in the wake of Colchester's surrender. Thus:

> Sir Charles Lucas and Sir George Lisle, two worthy men whom I did hate,
> The glory of the British isle, whom I did make unfortunate,
> With resolution stout they died, and called me traitor to my face:
> It did no whit abate my pride, I saw them fall in little space.
> The death of them revenged hath been on me, by those that loved them well:
> Sweet Jesus Christ forgive my slee [*sic*], for by my means those worthies fell.[30]

If Parliamentarians could deploy the concept of Divine punishment to legitimise the cause, then so could Royalists. With the Stuart cause reduced to its last extremity, haunting could even be employed as a weapon. We come here to a hilarious story concerning the erstwhile royal palace at Woodstock. Not in use as a royal residence for more than a century, by the time of the Civil War Woodstock was little more than an empty shell in not very habitable condition, but in 1649 a commission was dispatched by Parliament to set about the task of stripping its fabric of anything valuable. Hardly had they set foot in the place, however, when their nights began to be disturbed by happenings that were ever more dramatic and, withal, ever more terrifying – strange noises, sudden torrents of water gushing from chimneys without warning, furniture that was mysteriously flung about or overturned. This continuing night after night without a break, after some two weeks the commissioners fled in disorder, loudly claiming that the place was in the grip of evil spirits, only for it to be revealed after the Restoration that the haunting had been the work of an erstwhile Woodstock servant named Joseph Collins who had enveigled his way into the employment of the commission and proceeded to use his intimate knowledge of the building as a means of bamboozling his new masters into abandoning their task.[31]

Thus far we have been in the realms of communal experiences of the supernatural, whether real, imaginary or invented. There is, however, a far more common form of apparition, this being the kind that is seen by one person alone, usually in the dead of night. Interpreted in Catholic tradition, as we have seen, in terms of both warnings to repent and reminders of the need to pray for the denizens of Purgatory, such visitors could also be interpreted as the spirits of men and women treated unjustly by their betters who had come back to avenge themselves through the application of terror, that such an idea was current in seventeenth-century England being explicitly suggested by the writings of Lucy Hutchinson: left a widow when her regicide husband, Colonel John Hutchinson, died in prison in 1664, she imagined herself haunting the place of his death for ever more.[32] Indeed, from the very next year we have the strange tale of Samuel Bligh. Thus, the youngest son of the family that owned Botathan House near the village of South Peverwin, while still little more than a child, in 1662 Bligh impregnated a local girl named Dorothy Dingley, only for the latter to die in childbirth. Utterly lacking in remorse, the young man carried on with his normal life, which in his case meant attending a school kept in nearby Launceston by Protestant divine John Ruddle. Yet his peace of mind was short-lived, for some three years later, every day he began to see a vision of his dead lover passing through a field known as Higher Brown Quartils. More and more terrified, he eventually confided in his parents, who in turn summoned Ruddle, who agreed to accompany Samuel on his journey to school he next day. Confronted, to his utter astonishment, with the sight of the apparition himself, he sought the permission of his bishop to exorcise the haunted field, and, following a series of confrontations with Bligh's nemesis in which it, among other things, predicted the onset of the Great Plague, ostensibly succeeded in driving it away for good.[33] And, if some ghosts were the product of guilt, others were just as clearly the product of fear: as O'Lynn has pointed out, in the 1650s and 1660s a variety of individuals confided to their diaries or told members of their families that they had seen ghostly companies of soldiers marching across the land, while, as England slid ever deeper into political crisis from the late 1630s onwards, there are a number of instances of individuals recording witnessing Edgehill-style battles in the sky: in short, just as war was dreaded before it came, so it was dreaded, and that still more, after the guns had fallen silent, and it is therefore no surprise to find uneasy minds falling prey to the concept of portents sent by God as harbingers of doom.[34] Nor was it just a matter of the general issue of uncertainty and upheaval: in the summer of 1650 a phantom drummer beating the alarm appeared to several sentinels stationed on the walls of Edinburgh Castle, and the fact that this event was followed by the arrival of Cromwell's army just a few days later meant that it was immediately assumed that the apparition was a warning of their advance.[35]

Reformation or no Reformation, then, the admonitory ghost remained an important part of popular culture, and it is therefore no surprise to find instances of the phenomenon cropping up in the context of the Civil War. For an example of someone who thought he had been visited by such a spectre, indeed, we can turn to no less a figure than Charles I. In 1641 he had been forced to betray his loyal ally, the Earl of Strafford, to Parliament in the vain hope that signing the death warrant of the high-priest of 'thorough' would buy off Pym and his cronies. This was a decision he regretted for the rest of his life, and it is therefore no surprise to find that legend has it that, shortly before the Battle of Naseby, the king was twice visited in his lodgings at Daventry by the ghost of his erstwhile advisor and warned that he would not prevail and should therefore stick to his original intention of heading for Scotland rather than turning south to do battle with the New Model.[36] Then, too, there is the case of the king's commander in the north, the Marquis of Newcastle. Thus, when his army launched what proved to be an initial attack on Bradford in December 1642, Newcastle had been deeply shocked when a Royalist officer captured by the defenders was murdered in cold blood despite being promised quarter. Driven to fury, when his forces appeared before the town again in the wake of their victory at Adwalton Moor, the marquis therefore allegedly gave orders that every man, woman and child in the place should be put to the sword when it fell, only to countermand the order at the last minute thanks to a visitation of his quarters at nearby Bolling Hall by a female figure who pulled the sheets from his bed and repeatedly said, 'Pity poor Bradford'.[37] And, finally, just as the Commonwealth had sought to exploit the phenomenon of battles in the sky for its own purposes, so Royalists were not averse to exploiting the spirit world to convey messages of their own. On the contrary, as Oldridge notes, in the years immediately following the Restoration several Anglican priests reported apparitions in which they were warned, or so they claimed, that failure to repent - a covert reference to indulgence in any form of political turbulence - would lead to famine, plague and other disasters, a prediction that was, of course, neatly borne out by the terrible events of 1665 and 1666.[38]

As these latter examples show, some of the stories of individual hauntings that we have are beyond doubt the work of invention - a knowing attempt, in fact, to exploit various features of popular culture for political ends.[39] Meanwhile, if it happened at all, King Charles' confrontation with the ghost of the Earl of Strafford was as likely to have been a dream as much as it was anything else. There remains, however, a third category of experience and one that must have been genuinely terrifying for those who it affected. As we have already mentioned, it is by no means improbable that the experience of battle left many soldiers at the very least deeply disturbed, the result very likely being a considerable incidence of post-traumatic stress disorder (there is some debate about this: horrific though the experience of war could be, seventeenth-century soldiers were part of a society in which suffering was seen as the fruit of divine intervention in human affairs, usually in the form of the chastisement of sin, and it can be argued that this bred a more philosophical approach to the issue). The number of cases was therefore probably far fewer than would be the case today, while, as we have seen, there was much reluctance to recount personal experience in any detail. Inevitably, then, any discussion of the issue has little to go on. That said, go on it can. While the evidence is limited, it is clear that many men returned from the wars deeply scarred by their experiences.[40] In this respect let us begin by citing an interesting case raised by Charles Carlton. Thus, as he points out in his study of war in England in the early-modern period, in his memoirs the Parliamentarian Edmund Ludlow reported that he could not eat for several days after the Battle of Edgehill, a phenomenon that he ascribed to his jaws having forgotten how to masticate on account of his having eaten so little for so many days before the battle. However, as Carlton says, otherwise healthy human beings do not forget how to eat, and so one must turn to other solutions, of which an obvious one in his view is the well-documented issue of post-combat lock-jaw.[41] All this can, of course, be dismissed as so much speculation, but it is nonetheless significant that, like the soldiers of the First World War, many veterans seem to have chosen never to speak of their experiences in such years as was left to them after the fighting finally concluded.[42] At the same time, as O'Lynn has pointed out, the phenomenon of men who had fought in battle seeing visions was written about at some length in a number of treatises of the period. To quote just one of the several examples that he gives, 'Ludwig Lavater mentioned how many people saw ghosts due to "melancholy, madness, weakness of the senses, fear or some other perturbation"' [and] described how men '"subject to fear through great dangers … imagine strange things which … are not so"'.[43] So distressed was one Royalist veteran, O'Lynn continues, that he even crossed the boundary from haunted to haunting, killing himself and then returning to terrorise the area around his home as a headless horseman.[44] Who this unfortunate man was we are not told, but the essence of his trauma is captured all too well by some lines penned by Parliamentarian veteran George Withers. Thus:

> What ghosts are they that haunt the chambers of my breast,
> And, when I sleep, or comfort want, will give my heart no rest?
> Methinks the sound of groans are ever in my ear:
> Deep graves, deaths-heads and charnel-bones before me still appear.
> And, when asleep I fall, in hope to find some ease,
> My dreams, to me, are worst of all, and fright me more than these.[45]

If Withers is to be taken at face value, then he experienced flashbacks and hallucinations typical of extreme forms of post-traumatic stress disorder, and in the process saw figures for whom he had no other word than 'ghosts'. How common the phenomenon was among ex-soldiers we have no idea, but in this respect it is worth quoting Mark Stoyle's survey of a large number of petitions presented by Royalist veterans seeking assistance from the authorities in the years after 1660. Among these, true, there is no overt reference to psychological disorders, but, even so, their contents are suggestive enough. To take just one example, a certain Griffin Morgan recalled that, in one episode of the siege of Taunton, he was 'thrust through with a halberd in his thigh and shot through the other thigh with a bullet, and yet was not himself taken, but took some of the enemy prisoner and brought them away'.[46] As ever, meanwhile, those men who survived the war came away scarred by the memories of narrow escapes. Of the siege of Newark in 1645–46, Lucy Hutchinson, for example, wrote:

> Besides daily and hourly providences by which they were preserved from the enemy's cannons and sallies, there were some remarkable ones by which God kept [my husband's] life in this leaguer. Once, as [Sydenham] Poyntz and he and another captain were riding to view some quarter of the town, a cannon bullet came whizzing by them ... and the captain, without any touch of it, said he was killed. Poyntz bid him get off, but he was then sliding down from his horse, slain by the wind of the bullet; they held him up till they got off from the place, but the man immediately turned black all over. Another time [my husband] was in his tent and was by chance called out ... a cannon bullet came and tore down the entire tent and killed the sentinel at the door.[47]

Nor were civilians immune from such experiences. If Alice Thornton, daughter of Strafford's replacement as Lord Deputy of Ireland, had nightmares for the rest of her life, it was scarcely surprising. Caught in Chester during Brereton's brief advance on the city in the summer of 1643, she was almost killed when 'as I looked out at a window towards Saint Mary's church, a cannon bullet flew so nigh the place where I stood that the window suddenly shut with such a force whole turret shook'. When the dust settled, Thornton was in one piece, but even so it was as terrifying a moment as that experienced by any soldier. As she continued, 'It pleased God that I escaped without more harm save that the waft took my breath from me for that present and caused a great fear and trembling, not knowing from whence it came.'[48] Some civilians, meanwhile, found themselves witnesses to grim scenes of armed combat, in which respect we can again turn to Lucy Hutchinson. As she wrote of the Royalist assault on Nottingham, 'The Cavaliers marched in with such terror to the garrison, and such gallantry that they startled not when one of their leading files fell before them all at once, but marched boldly over the dead bodies of their friends under their enemy's cannon and carried such valiant dreadfulness about them as made very courageous men recoil.[49]

Of such moments night terrors are made. Meanwhile, if war traumatises those engaged in it, it can also brutalise them. According to Richard Baxter, one man so affected, perhaps, was a certain Welsh gentleman named Bowen whose story is recorded thus in a letter written by Colonel William Rogers, the governor of Hereford, on 23 August 1656:

> In the beginning of the late war, a gentleman of that county ... took arms under the Earl of Essex, and by his valour obtained ... the command of Lieutenant-Colonel. But as soon as the heat of the war was abated, his ease and preferment led him to a careless and sensual life, insomuch that the godly commanders judged him unfit to continue in England, and thereupon sent him to Ireland, where he grew so vain and notional, that he was cashiered the army, and, being then at liberty to sin without any restraint ... became an absolute atheist, denying Heaven or Hell ... About December last, he being in Ireland, and his wife (a godly gentlewoman ... concluded by all the godly people that knew her, to be one of the most sincere and upright Christians in those parts, as being for many years under great afflictions, and always bearing them with Christian-like patience) living in his house in Glamorgan, was very much troubled one night with a great noise, much like the sound of a whirl-wind, and a violent beating of the doors or walls, as if the whole house were falling in pieces. And being in her chamber, with most of her family, after praying to the Lord, (accounting it sinful incredulity to yield to fear,) she went to bed; and suddenly after, there appeared unto her something like her husband, and asked her whether he should come to bed. She sitting up, and praying to the Lord, told him that he was not her husband, and that he should not. He urged more earnestly 'What! Not the husband of thy bosom?' Yet [he] had no power to hurt her, and she, together with some godly people, spent that night in prayer, being very often interrupted by this apparition.[50]

Sent news of the haunting with its implicit warning that he would be denied the pleasures of the marital bed unless he mended his ways, Bowen repented of his conduct and returned home the same godly Christian that he had once been, the fact being that Baxter was clearly making use of the supernatural as a means of restoring order not just in the national sphere but in the domestic one, while at the same time offering a counter to those who argued that belief in ghosts and spirits and, more particularly, demons was mere superstition.[51]

As with so much of the subject of this work, what we cannot know far outstrips what we can. That said, it is quite clear that, by the time of the Restoration, the Civil War and Interregnum had become firmly embedded in the long tradition of English ghost stories stretching back deep into the Middle Ages, not to mention persistent belief in the concept of the revenant corpse. As we have seen, meanwhile, there was clearly a link to minds troubled by guilt, remorse and horrific memories of battle and privation. As the years passed, however, so the dynamic began to change. Year by year more and more of the veterans of the war passed away until at some point around 1700 the turmoil of 1640-60 was finally lost to living memory. Yet clearly it was not lost to memory altogether: passed on down the generations, stories of the experience of the mid-Stuart crisis continued to circulate at family firesides and in village taverns, and it was not long before these began to be transformed into ghost stories. Unfortunately, however, the oral tradition does not exist in isolation. As the years passed, old stories were embellished and new ones invented, while the onset of romanticism and its fascination with the 'gothic' gave rise to fresh interest in ghosts and the supernatural and, by extension, yet more excursions into the realms of imagination. In short, fiction and reality became ever more intertwined, a prime example of this phenomenon being the manner in which artists came to visualise the combatants. Thus, until deep into the current author's lifetime, Royalists were envisaged in terms of archetypal Cavaliers with flowing locks, gaudy clothes and broad-brimmed hats bedecked with plumes, and Parliamentarians as grim-faced Roundheads clad in buff coats, breast and backs and lobster-pot helmets. There is much that is interesting about such images, including, not least, the fact that both sides were envisaged as cavalrymen, the very class of soldiers who would have been most in evidence to the bulk of the populace (being mounted, cavalrymen were invariably used extensively for such duties as scouting, carrying dispatches, escorting convoys and engaging in such activities as pressing new recruits, foraging and requisitioning). Pikemen and musketeers, then, are not in evidence, and that despite the fact that it was they who formed the bulk of both armies.[52]

Let us, however, set that aside and rather consider not the figures that we do not have, but the ones that we do. If that is done, what immediately becomes apparent is a set of assumptions of a highly questionable nature. Thus, the Royalist is clearly a gentleman and the Parliamentarian a representative of social classes unable to afford such finery, even, indeed, a member of the populace as a whole. That said, socially disadvantaged though the Parliamentarian might be, he scores far more in other respects, being clearly, first, much better equipped and, second, or so it cannot but seem, grimmer, more determined and more business-like. Contained in the image, then, is a simple explanation of both the nature of the conflict and the direction that it took: in brief, it was a clash between rival concepts of government or even rival social classes, and at the same time one determined by the fact that one side was much better equipped than the other. In this last belief, at least, there is a large degree of truth, but, beyond that, matters are more complex. On both sides, the colonel of a cavalry regiment would have aspired to equip each and every one of his men with high 'bucket-top' riding boots, a thick leather 'buff-coat' that came well down the thighs, iron breast and backplates, an iron sheath protecting the bridle arm and finally one version or another of the classic 'lobster-pot' helmet. What we have, then, is very much the Roundhead of legend and, with it, a figure whose appearance is dominated by black (the armour of the common soldiers was usually coated in blacklead to keep it from rust, only officers having access to the resources needed to keep such equipment regularly burnished) and various shades of brown or, at best, yellow ochre. For much of the time, possessed as they were not only of the country's chief arsenals (the Tower of London and, thanks to the Bishops' Wars with Scotland of 1639-40, Hull) but also of economic resources that were infinitely superior to those of their opponents, the Parliamentarian forces could for the most part aspire to this norm. Not so, however, the Royalists, their regiments often riding into battle with neither armour, nor buff-coats or helmets. If only *faut de mieux*, then, the broad-brimmed hats typical of the men of the period would have been the most numerous type of head-gear just as the troops would have appeared more colourful, the absence of armour and buff-coats ensuring that the colours of the doublets or soldiers' coats worn under all the protective layers - typically, a mixture of reds, blues and greens - would have been well to the fore. Hence the emergence, of course, of our stereotypical cavalier.[53]

Thus far, our analysis has been confined to the cavalry troopers, dragoons, pikemen and musketeers who made up the rank-and-file. However, the confusion also extends to the officers. To begin with the epithet 'Roundhead', even the most cursory search of the portraiture of the Civil War will reveal not even a single Parliamentarian commander with the close-cropped locks favoured by the apprentice-boys of London on which the term was originally based. On the country, for men of property and breeding the fashion was to wear hair long and flowing as one more sign of status. Equally, officers being invariably expected to provide their own clothes, on both sides they would have been arrayed in a more-or-less identical fashion, and that one again made for the celebration of their social and military elevation, the fact being that Parliamentarian officers and commanders were just as likely to be bedecked with gold and silver lace and wearing doublets with sleeves slashed to show brightly coloured silk linings as their Royalist opponents or, for that matter, to take to the field wearing the full armour of the cuirassier, a figure redolent with association with the 'knights-in-armour' of the past. To make matters worse, meanwhile, as witness the best-known portrait of Sir Ralph Hopton, supporters of the king of Puritan views might favour garb as sombre as that of any radical divine.[54]

To conclude, then, we have here a clear example of how tradition is at best an imperfect guide to the past. That said, we also have a clear example of how it cannot be wholly rejected: the cavalry of the rival armies very often did look very different from one another, while those of the Royalists were fighting at a disadvantage that beyond doubt contributed to the triumphs of Cromwell's 'ironsides' at Marston Moor and Naseby. In this work we shall endeavour to apply much the same sort of analysis to the hundreds of ghost stories that are in circulation about the Civil War and, indeed, to suggest that they offer a window on aspects of the conflict - above all, the human experience thereof - that would otherwise be lost to history.[55] In the words of Sarah Priestly, the sometime heritage officer at Watford Museum, 'I do quite a lot of ghost-story telling ... Quite often, even if ... we don't know the facts exactly, there's a lot of historical information. Some of the legends that we have tell you an awful lot about the age: they tell you a lot about the people.'[56] That any project involving the paranormal must necessarily be a question of peering through a glass darkly, and, what is worse, peering through a glass darkly at material whose nature is of its very nature uncertain, if not downright dubious, the author is the first to admit. To proceed in this direction is *faut de mieux* to draw upon anthologies of ghost stories, but such works do not have the best of reputations, and that for good reason. As Hilda Davidson has written:

Many books on ghosts have appeared ... One type lists apparitions, manifestations, haunted houses and the like ... The poorest examples, devoid of precise references, or, worse still, furnished with fictitious ones, rank with vampire films and horror fiction, bringing the subject into such disrepute that serious scholars retreat in disgust from such polluted territory and conclude that ghosts are not worthy of academic interest.[57]

For a Civil War instance of the sort of carelessness complained of by Davidson, we might cite the case of Wardour Castle, a Royalist stronghold in Wiltshire that was heroically defended for six days in the first week of May 1643 against overwhelming odds by Lady Blanche Arundell, the wife of its owner, Lord Arundell, a cavalry colonel who was to be mortally wounded at the Battle of Stratton just a week later. At this point enter the compiler of *Britain's Haunted Heritage,* J.A. Brooks. As Brooks says, legend holds that the redoubtable Lady Arundell - she was some 60 years old at the time of the events concerned - is supposed to haunt the castle, either stalking the battlements or gliding along a path that leads to an ornamental lake. What is not true, however, is that Arundell was slain in the sack of the castle after its surrender in defiance of the terms that she had been granted: while the story of the sack is true enough, she was rather removed as a prisoner, eventually dying in London in 1649.[58]

To make matters worse, ghost stories are just that, namely *stories.* Those who claim to have seen apparitions of one sort or another - indeed, those who recount any personal experience - are wont to alter the details each time they do so, while the process by which such tales are handed down from generation to generation is akin to an eternal game of 'Chinese whispers'.[59] At the same time further confusion can be added by the efforts of mediums to interpret traditions of haunting for their audiences, a probable example of this problem being offered by Brodick Castle. Situated on the Isle of Arran, in 1642 this classic baronial pile was the seat of the leader of the Royalist cause in Scotland, the Duke of Hamilton, and today has a resident in-dwell in the form of a Grey Lady who is seen on some back stairs leading to the servants' quarters. Who this future was no one knew until a new housekeeper claimed that grasp the so-called 'sixth sight' had enabled her to identify the woman as a maidservant who had committed suicide after falling pregnant to a soldier of the Cromwellian garrison. That there was such a garrison is undisputed - during the invasion of 1650, soldiers of the New

Model Army did indeed occupy the castle - but it had been in the hands of troops representing one or other of the warring parties at the heart of Scottish politics for the previous ten years, and so there is every chance that the Grey Lady's lover was a Scot, and not just that but a Protestant Scot. Far better, then, than to shift the blame to a Sassenach outsider, a choice that at the same time lent weight to the self-proclaimed medium's words by tying her story in with existing traditions of Cromwellian oppression (to take just one instance of this legacy, a tree near an old mill in the Fifeshire village of Fordell is supposed to be haunted by the spectre of a hanged man, according to legend an apprentice named Jock who was put to death by marauding Parliamentarian troops in 1651).[60]

In general, it has to be said that the activities of mediums and self-proclaimed psychic researchers do little to advance the cause of those interested in ghosts from the point of view of historical memory. To be blunt, indeed, they are wholly counter-productive. Sometimes armed with a variety of impressive-looking equipment and sometimes not, such people visit haunted sites and endeavour to discover signs of supernatural activity. In such ghost-hunts, they claim to encounter physical manifestations of such phenomena - strange smells, mysterious drafts, hot spots, cold spots, ectoplasm, strange mists, orbs of glowing light, knocking, banging, sibilant whispers - and sometimes even to be rewarded by contact with the spirit of this or that person. At best, however, their stories do but find more-or-less plausible explanations for hauntings and the like reported by others - a good example is noted medium Derek Acorah's 'discovery' that a ghostly presence associated with the so-called Swiss Garden in the Bedfordshire village of Old Warden was constituted by the spirits of deserters who had been hung from a tree that once stood on the site[61] - but the people concerned all too often fall prone to what is clearly embellishment and invention. For instance, asked to investigate a sixteenth-century cottage near the battlefield of Naseby whose owners were much plagued by 'things that go bump in the night', a local medium solemnly reported that the problem was caused by the spirit of a Parliamentarian soldier who had been mortally wounded in the building while trying to detain a Royalist courier. While the sceptic might point out that lonely Cavaliers of the sort described are a staple of many Civil War ghost stories, that such an incident might have occurred is not impossible, but said medium then proceeded to undermine his chances of being taken seriously by anyone other than devotees of the paranormal by asserting that the truth of the story had been confirmed to him by none other than the spirit of King Charles I![62] In still other instances, meanwhile, we do not get any detail at all: when a team of ghost hunters visited the Lion Hotel in Shrewsbury in search of the Cromwellian soldier who was said to haunt it, they could do no more than solemnly confirm that there was indeed some sort of presence, while a visit to the battlefield of Stratton on the part of a Cornish group entitled 'Paranormal Investigation' discovered little more than that the site was 'an area soaked in rich heritage which can sometimes be tapped', though one woman did claim that she had encountered the spirit of one of the fallen with the help of her trusty pendulum.[63]

From folk-memory, then, it is all too easy to be caught up in a world of fake-memory. All this, however, is surely no excuse for failing to peer at all. That said, scientific process requires at least a measure of self-denial. Thus, in the first place, random tales of a Cavalier and his lady walking here or an Ironside trotting down a lane there will not be given too much attention. Confronted by such stories, one's natural instinct is to ask how much the person concerned had had to drink or to assume that the incidents were simply invented. Meanwhile, even if they are taken at face value, they serve to do little but suggest the existence of dim memories linking certain places with the Civil War, not to mention the probable existence of oral testimony that has long-since gone forever, a further reason for caution in this respect being the fact that ghosts have become an important part of the tourist and television industries alike: television schedules are replete with programmes chronicling the activities of teams of investigators of the paranormal and most major towns and cities offer organised 'ghost-walks', while, to quote Kathleen Eyre, 'It is considered a poor castle, a disappointing old house, which cannot come up with a satisfying phantom.'[64] In the second place, discounted, too, will be most of the dozens, if not hundreds, of tales that might well have Civil War links, but are not specifically associated with the period: for all one knows, every single one of the 'monstrous regiment' of unidentified white, green, blue and scarlet ladies of unknown provenance or identity reported from every corner of the country may have been cast off by Cavaliers or ravished by Roundheads, but, for all that, they cannot be drawn upon for the purposes of this study. And, finally, the claims of modern-day ghost-hunters to have seen spectral figures and even captured images of them on film will be paid still less heed: of their very nature, ghost-hunters go to sites of memory that they believe to be haunted and promptly have experiences of the sort that they expect; to quote one veteran ghost-hunter, indeed, 'When too many people know about specific phenomena at a location, it can taint the results.'[65] Rather, what we will be concerned about are those stories that offer a narrative of particular incidents or can at least be linked with such incidents. From ghost stories, then, we will return to the original oral histories, thereby ensuring that the wheel is turned full circle.

Chapter 3

The North-West

If there was one part of the country that was always likely to be affected very heavily by the conflict that broke out in 1642, it was the north-west: valuable recruiting grounds studded with potential fortresses, Lancashire and Cheshire also sat athwart a number of key strategic routes, namely the main roads to North Wales and the west of Scotland and the sea crossings to Ireland, while the city of Chester was one of the most important in the country, being outstripped only by London, York, Bristol and Norwich. Finally, far to the north, along with its eastern counterpart, Berwick-upon-Tweed, Carlisle was one of the two border fortresses blocking access to England from Scotland. Sooner or later, then, whoever took control of the area, the war was certain to visit its green pastures. To make matters worse, meanwhile, at the start of the conflict, the region was deeply split between king and Parliament: in Lancashire, the former held everything but Bolton, Blackburn and Manchester, whereas in Cheshire, the situation was reversed, Chester being Royalist and almost all the rest of the county Parliamentarian. Within weeks of the king raising his standard in Nottingham, the first shots of the conflict were ringing out on the far side of the Pennines. Yet the nature of the war in the north-west was always to retain a certain difference. Largely pastoral, the region was too poor to support the operations of large armies, and much of the action that it saw was therefore pretty minor: there were many sieges, certainly, but only at Preston in 1648 do we see a battle involving more than a few thousand combatants on each side, while it is notable that few of the war's most important commanders made more than very brief appearances; on the Parliamentarian side, Fairfax fought there for a few days at the beginning of 1644 and Cromwell for a few more in the summer of 1648, while Prince Rupert managed something less than two months in the lead-up to the battle of Marston Moor. All this being the case, it is hardly surprising that many of the standard texts on the history of the war spend little time on anything but the siege of Chester and the battle of Preston: in Maurice Ashley's *The English Civil War,* for example, there is no mention of events in Lancashire and Cheshire at all until the author reaches the battle of Nantwich, and the whole of 1644 is then dealt with in two brief passages, each of only four or five lines.[1] More oddly still, we find H.C.B. Rogers' *Battles and Generals of the Civil Wars* behaving in equally summary fashion, all it can say of the events of 1643-44 being as follows: 'Over Lancashire, Cheshire and Staffordshire there was waged a minor struggle which only occasionally impinged on the major theatres of operations. On 28 January [1644] Parliament's commander in Cheshire, Sir William Brereton, beat the local Royalist forces at Nantwich.'[2] More recent works, true, have done much to redress the balance, but, even so, one cannot but feel that even those deeply interested in the military history of the Civil Wars would be able to name more than one or two of the actions that took place in the region.[3]

Before we address the battles and campaigns, however, it is important to look at the manner in which the region became divided in 1642 in more detail. There was a certain particularity about this situation. In Lancashire, we have what appears to be a classic pattern of the chief towns, and especially those with manufacturing or trading interests, supporting the cause of Parliament, and the bulk of the gentry, epitomised in this instance by such families as the Hoghtons, the Gerrards and the Blundells, supporting that of Charles I (worth noting here is also the fact that the western parts of the county were a stronghold of recusancy; equally, if the towns were largely Parliamentarian, it was in part because of the rapid spread of Puritanism among their inhabitants).[4] In Cheshire, however, the situation was more complex. On the surface, certainly, we see an exact mirror image of the situation in Lancashire, but at base the differences were less obvious. Having done very well out of Charles I's sale of monopolies to raise money to fund his rule during the eleven years he ruled without Parliament, many of the city's most powerful merchant dynasties such as that of the Gamulls were firmly Royalist, and the result was that the king's cause was easily able to win the day. Yet, just as there were Lancashire gentlemen - Sir Ralph Assheton, for example - who were fervent Parliamentarians, one cannot assume that Chester was wholly loyal: when the Puritan pamphleteer William Prynne passed through the city on his way to imprisonment in Caernavon Castle in 1637, for example, he was waited upon by a significant element of the town council and offered much hospitality. As for the rest of the county, if towns like Nantwich, Middlewich and Macclesfield all followed the lead of their counterparts in Lancashire, the gentry was split in that its leading families were mostly for the king and its lesser ones for Parliament. Theoretically, then, the division of the spoils should have been more equal, but in the way the gentry chose sides was to prove disastrous for Charles. Thus, no sooner had the Commission of Array been issued than several of the local magnates – the only figures with the economic power to do so – threw themselves into raising regiments for service in the king's army. Without the men concerned, the latter would undoubtedly have gone down to defeat at Edgehill, but back in Cheshire there were few troops left to uphold the Royalist cause, the result being that the Parliamentarians were in effect presented with an open door.[5]

With this preamble out of the way, we may turn to the necessary task of providing the narrative that is the context of the ghost stories which this work seeks to discuss. For the sake of convenience, an overall survey of the fighting in the north-west of England may be divided into six phases, namely the campaigns in Lancashire from September 1642 until June 1643; the campaigns in Cheshire and North Wales from January 1643 till January 1644; Prince Rupert's campaign in Lancashire in May-June 1644; the collapse of the Royalist cause between the autumn of 1644 and the early months of 1646; the Preston campaign of July 1648; and, finally, the very brief Lancastrian involvement in the Worcester campaign of the summer of 1651. To adopt such a view is not to suggest that the operations concerned did not sometimes overlap with one another, nor, still less, that the mere fact that the fighting was at any given moment at its most intense in Lancashire meant that Cheshire was wholly quiet or *vice versa*, but, as a general guide, such a plan works well enough.

Let us begin, then, with the outbreak of the war in Lancashire. As early as 15 July this last county was the scene of the very first recorded death in the conflict – that of a linen weaver from Kirkmanshulme named Richard Perceval, who died in a brief scrimmage in Manchester occasioned by an ill-advised visit to the town on the part of Lord Strange, a prominent Lancashire magnate loyal to King Charles who was soon to inherit the title of Earl of Derby – but it was not until 25 September that serious military operations began when Derby, as we shall now call him, appeared before the hastily improvised defences that had been thrown up over the summer to protect Manchester and embarked on a siege of the town. As he proved over and over again, however, the Royalist commander was a lacklustre leader, and his operations turned out to be so ill-conducted that within a week he had abandoned his positions and withdrawn to Warrington.[6] There followed something of a lull in operations while well-meaning representatives of both sides sought desperately to obtain a local truce that would see Lancashire declare its neutrality (a development that we will also see in Cheshire), but this came to nought, and in late November fighting flared up again when Sir Gilbert Hoghton led a force of improvised troops to attack Blackburn, only to be thrown out of it almost as soon as he had overrun the weakly defended town by a column of 8,000 troops that had been dispatched from Manchester. In this last place, meanwhile, boosted by the town's considerable resources, the process of raising and equipping troops had proceeded apace, and the New Year saw the Parliamentarians in a state to take the offensive. As was also the case in Cheshire, the Royalists had before the battle of Edgehill sent a large part of such men as they had been able to organise in Lancashire to join the king's field army, while they had suffered serious losses in a second attack on Blackburn that had this time been beaten off without difficulty, and they were therefore soon in bad trouble, Leigh falling to the Parliamentarians with little in the way of resistance and Preston being stormed on 8 February after a fierce fight that cost the Lancashire Royalists many of their best leaders. Also occupied were Lancaster and Hoghton Tower, though in the latter case not without an accidental explosion that saw the gatehouse utterly destroyed and, with it, around sixty Parliamentarian soldiers, including their commander Captain, Starkie.[7]

Disastrous though the loss of Preston was, the next few weeks saw something of a resurgence of the Royalist cause in Lancashire. Thus, on 16 February a surprise assault on Bolton by a force of around 1,000 men that had been dispatched from Wigan was only driven off after fierce fighting, while 18 March witnessed a major Royalist assault on Lancaster, whereupon, having sacked the town and put much of it to the torch, Derby followed up this success by reoccupying Preston, the latter having been left but weakly defended. There followed a second attack on Bolton, but 'the Geneva of the North', as the staunchly Puritan settlement was known, this time beat off the Royalists without too much difficulty, the latter being further discomforted by a stinging Parliamentarian riposte in the form of a successful move on Wigan, most of whose garrison ending up fleeing in disorder apart from a handful of musketeers who took refuge in the tower of the parish church and kept up a steady fire until they were threatened with being blown up if they did not surrender forthwith. That said, however, an attempt to storm Warrington was repelled with as much ease as the latest Royalist attack on Bolton.[8]

At this point the honours of war were roughly even, but on 17 April disaster struck Derby's forces. Having mustered the bulk of his forces at Preston, the Royalist commander once more struck against Bolton, only to be ambushed by a much smaller Parliamentarian force commanded by Sir Ralph Assheton just east of Whalley. In their march on Bolton, having passed through the latter village, Derby's men had to descend into the steep-sided valley of the Sabden Brook, file across a narrow bridge and then climb up to the moors again via a lane lined by stone walls. Taking advantage of the fact that, in mounting the slope, the lane swung sharply to the left, thereby flanking the direction of Derby's approach, Assheton lined the walls with musketeers, and, as soon as the head of the column came in range, had his men fire a single massive volley. Seemingly completely unaware of the presence of the enemy, the Royalists, many of whom were raw recruits armed with little more than scythes and pitchforks, were taken by surprise, and the result was one of the worst panics of the war. Unable to deploy, the front ranks recoiled onto the ones behind, and within a matter of minutes Derby's entire army was fleeing back the way it had come, leaving the countryside strewn with weapons of all sorts. A brief stand, true, was made around the church at Whalley, but the triumphant Parliamentarians were not to be denied and the few troops ready to stand firm quickly crumbled in their turn. To all intents and purposes, it was for the time being the end of the Royalist cause so far as Lancashire was concerned: utterly disheartened, Derby himself fled to join Queen Henrietta Maria in Yorkshire, the latter having, as we shall see, recently landed at Bridlington with a large quantity of arms and munitions; Warrington, Wigan, Preston, Liverpool and the castles at Thurland and Hornby were all taken, mostly without resistance; and the bulk of the rank and file dispersed to their own homes, the few troops who remained loyal eventually making their way across the Pennines in their turn. All that was left was Derby's own family seat, Lathom House, this being held for the Royalist cause by the Earl's French wife, Charlotte de la Trémoille, and Greenhalgh Castle near Garstang.[9]

Following the battle of Whalley, Lancashire remained quiet for the rest of the year: nothing was done about the surviving Royalist garrisons other than to try to keep them from plundering the local inhabitants, while the only fighting was a number of skirmishes on the northern and western borders occasioned by small forces of Royalist troops attempting to mount raids into Parliamentarian territory, the most notable of these taking place at Blackstone Edge, Colne, Clitheroe, Thornton and Lindale.[10] All these probes were turned back, however, the only success to which they led being the temporary reoccupation of Thurland Castle, this last having to be subjected to a seven-week siege before it was finally retaken.[11] With the situation reasonably under control, then, the Parliamentarian commanders were able to send a number of troops to take part in operations elsewhere, including the ones in Cheshire to which we must now turn. Unlike Lancashire, Cheshire had at first had a very quiet civil war. There had been a brief disturbance in the capital on 8 August 1642 when the area's leading Parliamentarian, Sir William Brereton, an enthusiastic Puritan who had served as one of Cheshire's two representatives in the parliaments of 1640 and 1641, had entered the city and attempted to take control, but otherwise all had been quiet, the only event of any note being a brief visit on the part of Charles I in the last days of September. On the whole, meanwhile, this was exactly how the local gentry hoped to keep the situation. Almost all of its members were inclined to one side of the conflict or the other, but they were also bound together by numerous ties of friendship and marriage as well as terrified by the prospect of being caught up in fighting that was widely feared to be likely to be as terrible as anything going on in war-torn Europe, and the result was that, having avoided any serious hostility for months, a large number of the men empowered by the Royalist Commission of Array on the one hand and the Parliamentarian Militia Ordnance on the other met together at the village of Bunbury and issued a declaration of neutrality. To quote Dore, 'All the fortifications in the county were to be dismantled, [and] local troops disbanded and no fresh ones sent in from outside [while] the signatories were to use their good offices to bring about a national reconciliation between King and Parliament.'[12]

As with all such attempts to escape the war, the Treaty of Bunbury, as it became known, came to naught. Splendid though the idea of neutrality was, it could only be maintained if Cheshire could assert its views in the face of outside pressures, but the general unwillingness of the local notables to engage with the business of recruiting and military organisation rendered such a prospect out of the question. Of course, the contending parties might also choose to leave Cheshire alone, but, given its strategic location, this was most unlikely. Very soon, indeed, troops from both sides were heading for Cheshire bent on securing its resources for their respective war efforts. On the one side was Sir Thomas Aston, a prominent local Royalist who had sat alongside Brereton in the 'Short Parliament' and raised a force of cavalry and dragoons at the head of which he marched on Nantwich in the middle of January 1643, and on the other the self-same Brereton, now commander-in-chief of the Parliamentarian forces in the county, and a small force of troops that had been raised in Staffordshire. With the city of Chester firmly in the hands of the Royalists, the obvious target for both sides was Nantwich, then not only Cheshire's largest settlement other than the capital but also an important manufacturing centre. The Parliamentarian commander being infinitely more dynamic than Aston, it was Brereton who won the race, the latter consolidating his success by beating off the enemy in a short skirmish to the east of the town. Nantwich having previously received rough treatment at the hands of another Royalist, Lord Grandison, when he had briefly descended on the town, it thereafter remained a fervent bastion of the Parliamentarian cause. Pushing north towards Chester, meanwhile, Brereton occupied the 'salt towns' of Middlewich and Northwich, and for good measure on 13 March inflicted a heavy defeat on Aston when the latter tried to interdict his communications with Nantwich by reoccupying the former settlement.[13]

More than somewhat in disgrace, Aston was now called back to Oxford by King Charles, his place at the head of Cheshire Royalism being taken by Lord Capel, the latter also having been placed in command of Shropshire, Flint, Denbigh and Caernarvon. Unfortunately for the king's cause, however, though brave enough, Capel was not much known in the region, while the constant depredations engaged in by the ever poorly paid and supplied Royalist troops rendered the task of raising men and money ever more difficult. As for his generalship, it seems at best to have been mediocre. Whatever the reason, Capel proved little more successful than Aston. Temporarily distracted though Brereton was by the need to march south-eastwards with many of his troops to participate in the fierce fighting then raging in the northern parts of Staffordshire (see Chapter 5), on 17 May an attempt to take Nantwich (now heavily fortified) was driven off with almost contemptuous ease, matters going from bad to worse when the Royalist commander was chased from his headquarters at Whitchurch by a Parliamentarian counter-attack ten days later. Back from his campaigning in Staffordshire, Brereton now joined the fray and advanced on Chester at the head of his main forces and for a brief moment threatened it with attack, only to decide after a short bombardment that its defences were too formidable for him to meddle with. Yet this did little to reduce his ardour, the situation rather being fairly encouraging: the Parliamentarian authorities having decided to dispatch the owner of Chirk Castle (since January 1643 a Royalist garrison), Sir Thomas Myddelton, to try to raise an army in North Wales, there was the hope of substantial reinforcements, while on 4 August another assault on Nantwich on the part of Lord Capel was defeated. With Capel temporarily out of the way, Brereton and Myddelton promptly occupied Wem and then turned south to deal with Shrewsbury, but in the interim the Royalists were reinforced by several fresh regiments that had just been raised in North Wales and marched on Nantwich for a third time. Once again, however, launched on 16 October, the attack proved a complete failure, the Royalists showing little enthusiasm for an attack on the ramparts and immediately drawing off when news arrived that Brereton and Myddelton were marching post-haste to relieve the town. Determined to salvage something from his operations, Capel then essayed an assault on Wem, but the Parliamentarian garrison that had been left there stood firm and inflicted so many losses on his men that their morale fell apart, large numbers of the survivors taking to their heels and making off into Wales in a bid to reach the shelter of their home villages.[14]

The eclipse of Capel, who proceeded to shut himself up in Shrewsbury, opened the way for further offensive operations on the part of the forces of Parliament. As yet, Myddelton had done little to achieve the objectives that he had been given back in London, and so he and Brereton now moved to secure them forthwith. Conquering the whole of North Wales being far beyond the reach of their limited resources, they rather resolved to confine themselves to occupying a strip of territory on the left bank of the Dee, thereby sealing Chester off from supplies and reinforcements and at the same time establishing a secure base for further operations. On 9 November, then, the two Parliamentarian commanders launched a surprise attack on the Royalist outpost guarding the bridge spanning the Dee at Farndon, some ten miles upstream from Chester. Quickly overwhelming their defenders, they then pushed south-west to occupy Wrexham, thereby securing their rear against any thrust from Shrewsbury. With the Royalists helpless to resist, it was thereafter short work to march northwards towards the coast and place garrisons in Flint and Hawarden Castles, the result being that, exactly as planned, Chester was cut off from North Wales while the Parliamentarian threat to the city was augmented by the arrival, as mentioned above, of a number of troops from Lancashire. This success proved short-lived, however. In accordance with instructions he had received from the king, the English commander in Ireland, the Earl of Ormonde, had negotiated a truce with the rebels who had done so much to spark the Civil War, and just now begun to dispatch substantial numbers of troops to aid the Royalist cause. Hardly had Myddelton and Brereton come to rest, then, when they suddenly found themselves faced by what they estimated as 5,000 veteran troops who had landed at Mostyn. Fearing that Liverpool was potentially under threat, the Lancashire Parliamentarians hastily retired via the various fords that offered passage across the Mersey in the Warrington area. This leaving Myddleton and Brereton unable to tackle the new threat, they retreated back to Farndon, leaving the advancing Royalists to recapture Hawarden Castle, the latter surrendering after a brief siege (Flint, by contrast, had been abandoned without a fight).[15]

The brief campaign in north-east Wales proved the curtain-raiser to a far more dramatic episode, indeed, perhaps the most dramatic episode in the entire history of the war in the north-west. Thus, joining up with 1,000 cavalry who had been sent north from Oxford under a particularly battle-hardened Royalist officer named Sir John Byron who had been given the task of replacing the ineffectual Lord Capel, the troops from Ireland, all of whom were infantry, marched south and besieged the garrison of Nantwich, having first inflicted a sharp reverse on Brereton at Middlewich. For good measure, albeit in a manner that was far less dramatic than is commonly suggested, Beeston Castle was taken by a daring raid led by a seasoned veteran of the wars in Ireland named Thomas Sandford (according to the usual version of events, Sandford scaled the sheer cliff on whose brink the castle stands at the head of a small party of men and took the governor by surprise, but both a contemporary Royalist news-sheet and the local Parliamentary diarist Thomas Malbon make no mention of any such exploit and rather suggest that the attackers were let in via a postern by a Royalist sympathiser).[16] Meanwhile, the village of Barthomley saw an unpleasant incident in which a dozen Parliamentarian prisoners were put to death in cold blood after they had essayed defiance in the face of a troop of Royalist soldiers who had surrounded them in the church and called on them to surrender.[17] Nantwich, however, was ensconced - a word that dates from the Civil War - amid formidable earthworks that had been thrown up to protect the town over the past year, while it also had the enthusiastic support of the local population, terrified as the latter were at the prospect of being assailed by troops whom they, like many others in the Parliamentarian camp, believed to be composed of murdering Papists.[18] Nothing daunted, Byron closed in on the town and drove the defenders from the outposts they had maintained outside the defences in the parish church of the suburban village of Acton and also neighbouring Dorfold Hall, the former, in particular, witnessing fierce fighting. Siege operations carried on for the next fortnight, and then on 18 January the Royalists launched a general assault on three points of the defences. In this endeavour, however, Byron was no more successful than Capel had been: here and there a few men managed to establish a temporary foothold on the ramparts, but that was all, and by the end of the day several hundred Royalists had been killed or wounded. Nor was this the end of Byron's travails. Having escaped from the defeat at Middlewich, Brereton had got away to the east, and responded to the emergency by sending for help to all and sundry. With the Royalist cause in Yorkshire badly distracted by the appearance of a large Scottish army on the frontier in accordance with the terms of the Solemn League and Covenant, and its counterpart in Lancashire in near-total eclipse, the results were dramatic. Gathering together as many troops as he could, the Parliamentarian commander in Yorkshire, Sir Thomas Fairfax, hastened to the relief of the defenders, and on 25 January, he appeared on high ground to the north-west of the town. Disadvantaged by the fact that only part of his army could reach the field in time, Byron nonetheless essayed defiance, but he had badly misjudged the temper of his soldiers in that the troops who had come from Ireland – the whole, in effect, of his infantry – were low in morale, and but little inclined to fight for the cause of Charles I. Exactly what occurred is open to debate, but, after a short struggle, much of the Royalist foot ended up retreating to the area round Acton parish church where they laid down their arms without further resistance, Byron being left no option but to flee to Chester at the head of such of his cavalry as he was able to rally.[19] Nor was the defeat at Nantwich the end of it. Thus, over the next month Brereton's forces spread out across southern and central Cheshire so as to mop up Royalist resistance, the garrisons that they reduced by siege or bombardment including Crewe Hall, Doddington Hall, Adlington Hall and Wythenshawe Hall, somewhere else that fell to them being the Staffordshire outpost of Biddulph.[20]

As the winter of 1643-44 came to an end, then, the Royalist cause was in as much trouble in Cheshire as it was in Lancashire, while, as we shall see, the situation in Yorkshire was no better. With Charles also in serious danger in the south, where the army of Sir Ralph Hopton was heavily defeated at the Hampshire village of Cheriton on 29 March, sending troops to remedy the situation was scarcely easy. News that the Royalist forces in Yorkshire had received still worse a drubbing at Selby and, further, that the Marquis of Newcastle had been besieged in York by the combined forces of the Scots, Sir Thomas Fairfax and the Earl of Manchester persuaded the king to sanction a plan put forward by his leading general, Prince Rupert, to remedy the situation. The prince having just relieved Newark by means of a similar manoeuvre, what was proposed was a surprise attack from an unexpected direction designed to force the three enemy armies to abandon the siege. From the beginning this was a desperate enterprise - even if he managed to link up with Newcastle, Rupert was unlikely to be able to muster enough troops to defeat the northern Parliamentarians and their Scottish allies, the result being that the question could not but arise as to how York could be safeguarded in the long term - but there was no better plan to be had at the current moment, while the scheme did at least afford an opportunity of restoring the situation in Cheshire and Lancashire, the situation in the region having deteriorated still further since Nantwich in that the Parliamentarians had now closed in on Lathom House.[21] Stoutly held by Lady Derby, this stronghold was proving extremely defiant, the 300-strong garrison launching numerous sorties and causing their assailants much loss, but it was under constant bombardment and could scarcely be expected to defend itself indefinitely.[22]

Having gathered such troops as he immediately could at Shrewsbury, then, on 18 May Prince Rupert set out on his great expedition, thereby immediately placing Cheshire and Lancashire centre-stage in the conflict in a manner that had never been the case hitherto. Marching first east and then north, within a week he had defeated a small Parliamentarian force that had been sent to block his progress at Stockport. Hearing of his arrival, the forces attacking Lathom retired towards what they supposed would be the safety of Bolton, but the hope the latter represented proved illusory: not only were the town's defences far less impressive than those of Nantwich, but Rupert's forces had been swelled by large numbers of clubmen pressed by the Earl of Derby (having initially responded to his defeat at Whalley by fleeing to Yorkshire to join Queen Henrietta Maria,

Derby had been ordered by the latter to return to the Isle of Man, of which he was feudal lord and sole ruler, on the grounds that his presence was needed there to restore order in the face of serious disturbances that had broken out among the populace in protest at various reforms that he had recently imposed, but the presence of Prince Rupert had led him to make a hurried reappearance in the hope of restoring his prestige, more than somewhat tattered as this last was). When the town was attacked on 28 May, then, although a first assault was beaten off, a second one succeeded, and, much enraged by a grisly gesture of defiance in which a captured Royalist officer was strung up on the ramparts in plain sight, the Royalist forces swept into the town carrying all before them. What followed went down in the pamphlet literature, and, indeed, much of the historiography, as a 'massacre', but, as with the incident at Barthomley, to use such language is to go too far. Certainly the town was sacked and many of the defenders killed in cold blood, and certainly, too, dozens of civilians were cut down as they tried to protect their property or flee the town, but there was nothing to distinguish innocent civilians from the Parliamentarian rank and file, few, if any, of the latter ever having been issued uniforms, just as at least some of the civilians who fell were almost certainly caught in the crossfire rather than deliberately made away with, and others men serving in the town's 500-strong militia. Given that it turned out that well over half the regular troops in the town became prisoners, and, still more so, that the parish records list just seventy-eight dead, all but two of them men, it is clear that most of the wilder stories should not be taken at face value. Yet what happened was still grim enough, while there is no reason to think that all the horrible incidents detailed in the various accounts of the sack that did the rounds in the months that followed were fictitious: Bolton had earned a name for itself as a hotbed of radical Puritanism, and, with many of the men who Derby had brought to join Rupert staunch Catholics from the heavily recusant west of the county, it is by no means impossible that the killing was increased by long-standing religious tensions, something else that did not help in the slightest being the hanging of the hapless Royalist prisoner in between the first assault and the second (who, if anybody, sanctioned this action is unclear, and it therefore seems probable that it was the work of a handful of fanatical clubmen). As to the question of whether the scenes that transpired were morally acceptable, it has to be pointed out not only that, according to the laws of war, a town which had unsuccessfully attempted to resist an attempt to take it by storm was held to have lost all right to any protection but also that, once troops ordered to storm such a place were within the walls, it was impossible to stop them killing, burning, raping and pillaging at whim.[23]

Lathom House having been relieved and the Parliamentarian field army in Lancashire all but totally destroyed, Rupert was now free to head for York, but, in an action that suggests how important it had become to the Royalists to control the coasts of the Irish Sea, the prince rather elected to turn his forces round and head for Liverpool, something in which he was undoubtedly encouraged by claims on the part of Lord Derby that the garrison consisted of no more than fifty men. Already a major port that was fast coming to supplant Chester on account of the manner in which the River Dee had been silting up the latter's harbour, the future cathedral-city was an important garrison and had in consequence been heavily fortified, while the troops holding it had been hastily reinforced by the dispatch of 400 men from Manchester and the recruitment of various parties of sailors from several ships that happened to be in the Mersey estuary. When Rupert appeared before the town on 6 June, then, he found it a much tougher objective than he expected, and therefore spent several days bombarding the defences from batteries that were established in the vicinity of Bank Hall - a house on the northern outskirts of the town that had been the home of the governor, John Moor - and the modern-day landmarks of Saint George's Hall and Lime Street station. Time, however, was anything but on the Royalist side, and so on 10 June the prince elected to assault the walls. Delivered though the attack was in two different places, the garrison held firm, it being claimed in the pamphlet literature that they inflicted the rather unlikely total of 1,500 casualties for the loss of but sixty men of their own. Yet Rupert was not the man to be unduly affected by such a setback and on the night of 12 June he tried again. Seemingly taken by surprise and by now much shaken, the defenders broke and ran, the result being a second episode of pillage and murder, the city council later claiming that the number of dead amounted to 360, though, as at Bolton, how many of those who lost their lives were genuine non-combatants is unclear.[24]

Thus ended the campaign of Prince Rupert. With Liverpool safe in Royalist hands, the latter struck eastwards once more and marched on York via the out-of-the-way northern route that led across the Pennines via Skipton and Clitheroe. However, as scarcely needs to be said, there followed the defeat of Marston Moore. Rupert having stripped the region of as many troops as he could, the cause of north-western Royalism was therefore soon in as much danger as ever. First to feel the pressure was Lancashire. On 20 August a mixed force of infantry and cavalry that had escaped across the Pennines under Sir John Byron was routed by local Parliamentarian forces on Aughton Moor just south of Ormskirk and forced to flee into Cheshire via the ford that crossed the River Mersey at Hale, and by the end of the month Liverpool was again under siege. This time, however, there was no bombardment, the new Parliamentarian commander who had been sent to the region, Sir John Meldrum, resolving rather to reduce the town by blockade. With the garrison's communications with Ireland sealed off by a naval blockade and the Cheshire Royalists in no state to come to its aid, the town was clearly doomed to surrender, though the governor, Byron's brother, Robert, refused to give way until, at the beginning of November, when his starving garrison mutinied and left him with no other option but to submit forthwith.[25]

With the fall of Liverpool, Royalist Lancashire was once again confined to Lathom House and Greenhalgh Castle. Of these, the tiny garrison of the latter was clearly regarded as little more than a nuisance, the result being that operations against them were confined to a loose blockade that took until June 1645 to finally bear fruit. Given its greater prominence, Lathom might have been expected to have been taken a little more seriously, but resources were surprisingly scarce, while the local levies on whom the local Parliamentary commanders were relying appear to have been increasingly war-weary. Not until July 1645, then, did operations begin in earnest, but even then, the only fighting that took place was centred on the task of driving the garrison from the few outposts it had managed to maintain outside the walls. After that, however, it seems to have been decided that further attacks were not worth the cost in terms of manpower, and that it was better to rely on the workings of starvation, a method that at length brought the capitulation of the garrison on 3 December. Distant Carlisle having fallen victim for the same reason to the Scots army that had fought at Marston Moor after a siege that lasted from February to June 1645, Lancashire, Cumberland and Westmoreland were all alike free of 'malignants'.[26]

Not so Cheshire, however. Yet here, too, the Parliamentarians had the advantage and that by an enormous distance. To tell the story we must return to the aftermath of the battle of Marston Moor. With the departure of so many troops to take part in 'York March', the men left behind had been hard pressed, as proof whereof just one day after Ormskirk a small Royalist force was soundly beaten at Tarvin.[27] The arrival of the survivors of Byron's command might at first have seemed to offer a little hope, but, already worsted at Ormskirk, they were in no condition to fight and on 25 August were routed for a second time at Hampton Heath near Malpas, the few troops that got away - most of them cavalry originally recruited in Northumberland by the Marquis of Newcastle - thereafter making post-haste to join the king in the Royalist haven of South Wales.[28] Hardly had they reached safety than a fresh disaster struck the Royalist cause in Cheshire, albeit not in Cheshire itself but across the border in Wales. Early in September the strategically important but poorly defended town of Montgomery and its attendant castle was occupied by a Parliamentarian force commanded by Sir Thomas Myddelton. Much alarmed, the commander of the Royalist forces in Shrewsbury, Sir Michael Ernley, promptly marched to its relief, and succeeded in driving off the bulk of Myddelton's men, saving a single regiment that managed to withdraw into the castle. Within a few days, however, the Parliamentarians were back in the form of a 3,000-strong relief force commanded by Sir John Meldrum, only to find that more Royalist troops had arrived from Chester headed by Byron. There followed a battle that, if substantial, is but little known. Approaching the town from the north, the relief force was set upon by the Royalists near the spot where the road to Wrexham crossed the River Camlad. What then took place is unclear and all the more so as Byron's troops initially gained the upper hand, but, for whatever reason, the Royalists' morale suddenly collapsed whereupon the entire force broke and ran, leaving behind them 500 dead and wounded and another 1,500 prisoners.[29]

Montgomery was a disaster for the Cheshire Cavaliers in that, with recruits for the Royalist army and weapons and equipment of all sorts in short supply, it cost Byron the loss of the last troops he could use to maintain an army in the field: from now on, indeed, the garrisons of Chester and Beeston Castle - the only other Royalist base in the county, Halton Castle, having been evacuated as being impossible to defend - could only hang on grimly in the hope that, if they got into difficulties, help would reach them from outside. As for the Parliamentarians, they were clearly ever more on the ascendant. Thus, already active in the northern part of the county - it was troops from his command that had gained the victory at Tarvin, a success that was repeated against a much larger contingent composed at Malpas three days later[30] - in the wake of the battle of Montgomery, Brereton closed in on both Chester and Beeston and,

much though Byron tried to impede him by a policy of vigorous raiding that led
to fierce skirmishes at such villages as Christleton, established a loose blockade
of both places. Desperate to keep Chester – the gateway to both Ireland and still
Royalist North Wales – safe, in February, and then again in March, the Royalist
high command organised successful relief attempts under, first, Prince Maurice,
and then Prince Rupert, though the price of these was the loss of Shrewsbury
to a Parliamentarian surprise attack facilitated by the withdrawal of much of the
garrison to help with the operations further north (see Chapter 7). Two months
later, meanwhile, more indirect assistance turned up in the form of the complex
manoeuvres that led to the battle of Naseby: marching as far north as Market
Drayton at one point as the king did, Brereton was panicked into abandoning his
positions and retiring on Manchester. With Naseby fought and won, however,
there was nothing to impede the Parliamentarians from returning and setting
about the city in earnest, and that despite the fact that, in the wake of the passage
of the Self-Denying Ordinance Brereton had been forced to travel to London
to plead for a renewal of his command (as an MP, the Cheshire leader was in
theory barred from exercising any authority over troops in the field, but, like
Cromwell, he was granted a series of temporary renewals that allowed him to
carry on as before).[31]

Very soon, then, Chester was not just blockaded but besieged, in respect of
which it did not help that the unfortunate Byron had been forced to surrender
a number of his already limited force of regular troops to reinforce the army
Charles took to Naseby. What, though, was the state of the defences? Early in
the war, the Chester authorities had ordered the construction of a line of earthen
fortifications that completely encompassed the bend in the River Dee in which
the city was situated, but the northern parts of the system had been progressively
abandoned, and, with them, the suburbs that they protected, on the grounds
that too many troops would be needed to defend them. On the eastern side of
the city, however, the outworks were still manned, not least because they denied
any force that might mount an attack the use of the high ground occupied by
the church of Saint John, this being an ideal position from which to bombard
the medieval walls (extremely tumbledown in 1642, these had been repaired
and in some sectors reinforced with earth, but the stretch opposite the church
happened to lack the latter refinement on account of the fact that it was backed
by a stretch of buildings that the town council had been unwilling to demolish).

Conscious, perhaps, of both the opportunities that the sector offered and the fact that Byron had just travelled to Mostyn to confer with his counterparts across the Welsh border, the Parliamentarian commanders – in the light of Brereton's continued absence, two middle-ranking officers named Michael Jones and James Lothian - resolved on a daring *coup de main*. Thus, during the night of 18-19 September, a force of 1,400 men was dispatched to launch a dawn attack on the eastern outworks. The defenders, it seems, were not keeping as good a watch as they should, and the result was that an advance party was able to scramble onto the summit of the bastion immediately overlooking the river, chase off the few Royalists in the area and, finally, throw open the gates so as to allow the entrance of the troops waiting outside. Taken completely by surprise, Byron's men had no chance to repair the damage and within a short time, the whole of the eastern suburbs was in the hands of the Parliamentarians, some of whom did not rest content with this success, but rather got through the East Gate and advanced as far as the cathedral close before they were finally overcome.[32]

No sooner had the Parliamentarians taken stock of their success, however, than news came in that no less a figure than King Charles himself was marching on Chester at the head of an army: having fled into south Wales in the wake of the battle of Naseby, the king had now resolved on making a desperate bid to join up with the forces of the Royalist commander in Scotland, the Marquis of Montrose, a gallant figure who for the past year had been winning battle after battle against the armies of the Covenant (that the king was chasing mirages is by-the-by, but so it was: not only had Montrose been badly beaten near Selkirk at the village of Philliphaugh on 13 September, but the only viable route across the frontier was blocked, for, having fallen to the Scots in June, Carlisle was now an enemy garrison). Hearing of the attack on the eastern suburbs of Chester when he reached the headquarters of the remnants of the Shropshire Royalists at Chirk Castle, Charles resolved on a two-pronged approach to the city whereby the king would enter it via the bridge across the Dee and get Byron to organise a sally while the bulk of his troops crossed the river further south and took Jones and Lothian in the rear. The best plan that could be devised in the circumstances, the scheme was rendered still more likely to succeed by the disheartening turn of events that had just afflicted the Parliamentarian forces. In brief, realising that time was short, the latter had hastily dragged up two cannon and put them in position in front of the church of Saint John, whereupon they immediately made use of them to bring down a twenty-foot section of the walls in the area to the south of the East Gate. This done, the way was open for an assault, and the night of 22 September therefore saw one party of Parliamentarians make straight for the breach while another equipped with scaling ladders rushed the wall on the other side of the East Gate. This time, however, the defenders were ready for them: putting up a fierce fight, indeed, they not only threw back both assaults but also managed to wound their respective commanders.[33]

Had the Royalists proved a little luckier, then, they might have pulled off a surprise victory, but from early in the day almost everything went wrong. On the morning of 24 September, true, King Charles rode across the bridge into the city, but on the other side of the Dee, the troops who had accompanied the king – the so-called 'Northern Horse' commanded by the redoubtable Sir Marmaduke Langdale – had got the upper hand in an initial clash with the enemy, only to be delayed in their march on account of being attacked from the south by a force of Parliamentarian cavalry led by Sydenham Poyntz. All might yet have been well, but the sortie that was supposed to be launched by the garrison of the city took a long time to get off the ground, with the result that many of the Parliamentary troops facing the eastern walls were able to march south to take on Langdale, the latter also having to face a renewed assault on the part of Poyntz. Badly outnumbered and further hampered by the fact that they had no infantry with which to oppose the enemy musketeers (part of the force sent up the river from Chester) who began to press in on their left flank, the Royalists fought well enough. However, they could not hope to prevail and, at length, turned and fled in all directions. Far too late, just at this moment the sortie finally materialised in the form of some 850 horse and foot commanded by the highly experienced Charles Gerrard, and a confused action ensued in the open ground to the east of the city, but the Royalists were flung into confusion by the many cavalrymen who had elected to try to break out of the trap by bursting through the troops hemming them in from the north and heading for Lancashire. In many cases literally ridden down and trampled underfoot, Gerrard's men were therefore quickly beaten in their turn. At more than 1,000 men in killed, wounded and prisoners, the Royalist losses were catastrophic, the plain fact of the matter being that King Charles, who had watched the action from the tower of the cathedral, no longer had either an army or a plan of campaign, in recognition of which the very next day he rode out of the city the way he had come with a small party of followers and headed west into the hitherto loyal bastion of North Wales in the hope that fresh troops might reach him from Ireland via the little port of Conway.[34]

Charles' attempt to break the siege having been defeated, there was now nothing to stop the Parliamentarians proceeding as they wished. In addition to the gun positions facing the east wall, fresh batteries were established in the ruins of the northern suburbs (these last had been torched following the decision to pull back to the city walls on that side of the city) and on the high ground across the Dee from the north-west corner of the defences, and a further period of bombardment soon brought down a section of the wall between the Goblin Tower and the Water Tower. Jones and Lothian being eager to end the siege before Brereton, an unpleasant character who was not much liked in the locality, could be restored to the command, as dusk fell on 9 October they launched a fresh assault with one column trying to get through each of the breaches and a third one seeking to escalade the wall between the Phoenix Tower and Sadler's Tower (now disappeared). Particularly in the vicinity of the new breach, the fighting was extremely fierce - the attackers, indeed, seem at one point to have got onto the walls - but at length such were their casualties that, at all three of the spots chosen for the attack, they were forced to retreat in disorder.[35]

Jones and Lothian, then, had failed in their gamble, and at the end of the month their worst fears were confirmed when Brereton reappeared with a fresh commission from Parliament and immediately took over the conduct of operations. Knowing that time was on his side - on 2 November one last attempt to relieve the city had been decisively defeated at the battle of Denbigh Green - and so the new arrival abandoned costly attempts to storm the walls in favour of starvation, not to mention terror tactics aimed at stirring up discontent among the populace. While the bombardment continued, then, its nature changed. Whereas his predecessors had spent the weeks since the assault of 9 October trying to hit strategic targets such as the tall water tower that stood beside the Bridge Gate and the various mills that kept the city supplied with flour, Brereton brought up a massive mortar and used it to lob heavy stone balls, explosive shells and primitive incendiary devices over the walls. How much damage resulted from these tactics has been subject to much debate, but it seems to have been quite substantial, many houses in Bridge Street and Eastgate Street being either burned down or damaged beyond repair. As for civilian casualties, the number is unknown, but one Royalist account mentions an old man, three women and three children being killed on the night of 10-11 December alone. All the while, Byron fought back as best he could, launching numerous sallies and dispatching his small force of cavalry to raid the Parliamentarian quarters in the villages round about via the bridge (protected by a detached fort on a hill overlooking the road to North Wales, this stayed open to the very end, while Brereton never had enough troops to seal off the area), but, as the weeks passed, so hunger and cold began to take their toll on the morale of his men, while the civilian population were still worse off. A hard man who had seen much service, Byron held out longer than might have been expected, but by the middle of January the city was in turmoil, the result being that he had no option but to enter into negotiations with Brereton, the remaining soldiers of the garrison finally marching out across the bridge on 2 February 1646.[36]

Byron's surrender, alas, did not put an end to Chester's sufferings. On the contrary, if there was no longer any fighting in Cheshire, Beeston Castle having been starved into giving up on 18 November, as spring moved into summer, so the city was hit by a devastating epidemic of plague that killed more than 2,000 people.[37] Nor was the war over: across the Dee the king still had many garrisons in North Wales, some of them - Denbigh, Holt and Hawarden - very close by. So determinedly were these held that it took until March 1647 finally to snuff the last of them - the remote fastness of Harlech Castle - out. For more than two years, however, Cheshire and Lancashire were at peace. Yet the respite proved short-lived. In the spring of 1648 fighting flared up once more thanks to a series of risings on the part of a mixture of erstwhile Parliamentarians discontented with the turn events had taken at Westminster and die-hard Royalists eager to strike one more blow for Charles I, while that monarch managed to add to the confusion still further by persuading the Scots to change sides in exchange for a promise to establish Presbyterianism in England. In the context of the north-west, it was this last that was most significant. As in the other major foci of the renewed conflict - Kent and South Wales - a number of disaffected local gentry took arms, but this would have been of little account but for the fact that on 8 July an army of some 15,000 Scots commanded by the Duke of Hamilton crossed the border near Carlisle and began to push southwards into England, in which process it was joined by a force of English Royalists headed by the indefatigable Sir Marmaduke Langdale. Hamilton, however, was possessed of only the most limited military talent and tarried in his advance despite winning minor skirmishes at Penrith and Appleby. The result was disaster, for, by the time that the Scottish invasion got moving, most of the outbreaks of rebellion in the rest of England had been suppressed. In consequence, it was not long before retribution descended on Hamilton's head. Far to the south-west, Oliver Cromwell had been besieging Pembroke Castle, and, having forced the latter's surrender on 11 July, he headed for Yorkshire where he linked up with the local Parliamentarian forces near Wetherby. Though outnumbered by odds of around two to one, the future Lord-Protector resolved to strike westwards across the Pennines to attack Hamilton, whose forces were now marching southwards through Lancashire.[38]

There followed what was easily the biggest battle that was fought in the north-west. Marching west by the very same route that Prince Rupert had followed in the opposite direction in 1644, on 17 August Cromwell caught Hamilton's army in the flank and rear as its main body was crossing the River Ribble at Preston (it is no credit at all to the Scottish commander that his cavalry was as far ahead as Wigan and his rearguard not yet past Lancaster). The only troops in a position immediately to oppose the oncoming Parliamentarians were Langdale's English Royalists, and, drawn up in a series of hedged enclosures to the east of the town, these put up a good fight, and that despite the fact that many of Cromwell's men were drawn from the fearsome New Model Army. Had Hamilton rushed up troops in support, Cromwell might even have been in serious difficulty, but in the event no more than a handful of cavalry were sent to Langdale's aid, the bulk of the Scottish army continuing to march across the narrow bridge that spanned the Ribble. Langdale's men being increasingly exhausted, the end was inevitable: after a four-hour battle, two regiments of Parliamentarian cavalry pierced their front while a force of Lancashire militia pushed down a narrow lane that took them down to the bridge and thereby cut them off, together with a number of Scottish infantry and cavalry, not to mention the Duke of Hamilton, the latter having stayed on the north bank of the river to supervise the defence (not that he did so in even the most remotely effective of fashions). In the event, Hamilton and his personal entourage managed to swim their horses across the swollen river, as did Langdale, while a few Scottish cavalry broke out to the north, but many hundreds of men were left to be taken prisoner. Finally, as if this was not bad enough, an enthusiastic assault on the bridge ensured that it ended the day in the hands of the Parliamentarians.[39]

Such was the scale of the disaster at Preston - the number of prisoners alone amounted to some 6,000 men - that there is little left to tell. Abandoning the field in the night, Hamilton fled southwards in the faint hope that he might secure fresh help from English Royalists, but the next day his surviving infantry were caught at the village of Winwick just to the north of Warrington, and were forced to surrender after a fierce fight that cost both sides many more killed and wounded. As for the cavalry, it succeeded in crossing the Mersey and plunging on into the Midlands, only to be caught in its turn at Uttoxeter, whereupon the hapless Hamilton laid down his arms, together with the 3,000 officers and men that were all that was left of his army. Far to the south, Colchester, a staunchly Parliamentarian town that had been seized by those Royalist forces which had succeeded in escaping the defeat of the Kentish uprising at Maidstone, continued to endure a siege even more terrible than that of Chester, while isolated groups were also holding out in the castles at Pontefract and Scarborough, but otherwise the Second Civil War, as the renewed conflict came to be called, was over.[40]

The battle of Winwick was not quite the end of the Civil Wars in so far as they affected the north-west. Thus, the Scottish invasion of England of 1651 that led to the battle of Worcester prompted the Earl of Derby to return from his Manx retreat yet again and make use of his substantial influence in the western parts of Lancashire to raise a fresh force of troops for the Royalist cause. In the brief campaign that followed, Derby showed greater energy and tactical skill than he had ever done before, but on 25 August he was trapped outside Wigan by a Parliamentarian force twice the size of the one he commanded and in the resultant action overwhelmed with the loss of most of his men, the sixty dead including Sir Thomas Tyldesley, a particularly ardent supporter of the king whose fall was commemorated in 1679 by a monument that still stands today.[41] Once more, though this time badly wounded, Derby got away, but, reach Charles II at Worcester though he did, he was accompanied by a mere thirty riders, most of them, one presumes, officers of one sort or another. Captured at the end of the battle that raged around that town on 3 September, the earl was put on trial for treason and sentenced to death, whereupon he was transported to Bolton – the scene, of course, of the 'massacre' of 1644 – and beheaded in front of the parish church, his journey from Worcester to his place of execution becoming commemorated, as we shall see, in a number of ghost stories, ghost stories, indeed, of the very sort to which we must now turn our attention.

The English Civil War, then, hit Lancashire and Cheshire very hard. If the two counties were the scene of no more than three major battles – four if one counts Whalley - they had yet seen much action with no fewer than eight major sieges and innumerable raids, skirmishes and attacks on fortified towns. Damage, meanwhile, had been extensive: much of Chester was in ruins, for example; Lancaster had been burned to the ground; and Lathom House erased from the landscape. In so far as Civil War ghost stories are concerned, then, it is hardly surprising that the region is very rich in the material that it offers. As was intimated in the second chapter, ghost stories come in many forms: thus, some are little more than bald claims that such and such a figure was seen in such-and-such a house or at such-and-such a spot, while others are far more detailed in that the figures concerned have a history and an identity attached to them that can be explored and in some cases even verified (something that does not apply to the apparitions themselves, of course: whether anything or anyone has ever actually been seen is not something that the current author is prepared to rule upon). As was also intimated in said chapter, the bulk of our attention will necessarily be on the second category, but it nevertheless seems appropriate to attempt a quick review of the many cases in which figures are said to have been seen without any attempt having, at least so far as is known, been made to make them the centre of a real story, or, for that matter, known historical facts have given rise to tales whose explanation is all too obvious. Such instances are, of course, of little use in analytical terms and yet their sheer number cannot but serve as evidence for the ubiquity of the English Civil War ghost.

Let us begin with the way known historical facts conjured up ghost stories. Of this tendency, the best example in the north-west concerns the Earl of Derby. As we have seen, the Royalist commander in Lancashire, having accompanied Charles II in his flight into exile in the wake of the battle of Bosworth as far as Boscabel, turned back and tried to make his way back to his fastness in the Isle of Man. In this, however, he was completely unsuccessful in that he had the misfortune to be recognised by a Parliamentarian patrol and taken prisoner. Ever unlucky as Derby was, just days before an Act of Parliament had been passed declaring anyone who was proved to have been in contact with the fugitive monarch guilty of high treason. This being the case, he was put on trial for his life at Chester and duly condemned to death by beheading. Unfortunately for the earl, however, he was not put to death on the spot, but rather condemned to being transported to Bolton for public execution there in revenge for the 'massacre' of 1644. An appeal for clemency (which to his credit was supported by Cromwell) having fallen by the wayside, Derby responded by trying to escape, only to be captured for a second time. There was, alas, no opportunity for another such bid: kept under close guard, the earl was transported to Bolton and executed in Church Gate in front of a still-extant tavern known as the Old Man and Scythe, a spot chosen on account of the fact that said tavern belonged to his estate.[42]

Hardly surprisingly, the severity of the earl's fate, and the steadfast courage and dignity that he maintained throughout - as he knelt at the block, his last words were 'Blessed be God's name for ever and ever. Let the whole earth be filled with His glory. Amen' - invested his memory with a dignity that his lacklustre generalship scarcely justified, and the result was that the story of his end was soon being commemorated by tales of supernatural happenings. Of these, the first concerns Stanley Palace, a Tudor mansion near Chester's Water Gate that had belonged to the Stanley family for generations. Out of respect for the earl, during his trial he was confined, not in some cell in the castle but rather the more comfortable quarters represented by said mansion, and his ghost, which is always seen in the form of a photographic negative, is in consequence said to roam the ground-floor rooms (for good measure, the upper floor of the building is supposed to be haunted by a woman in seventeenth-century apparel, though nothing is known in respect of who she was). This Chester haunting, however, is not the end of the earl's spectral proceedings. On the contrary, in Bolton his ghost has supposedly often been seen having what is generally assumed to be a last drink in the Old Man and Scythe, while it is said that, on rising from their seats, a number of patrons have discovered their posteriors to be soaked in blood.[43]

Derby being a prominent figure, he has conserved his identity, while such was the impact of the story of his passing that the executioner, one George Whewell, a Bolton man who according to tradition had lost his family in the 1643 assault and volunteered for the duty out of a desire for revenge, also has a place in the literature, a skull on show at the Pack Horse Inn in the Pennine village of Affetside being reputed not just to belong to him, but seemingly to object to being moved or otherwise interfered with (as to how the Pack Horse Inn became involved in the tale, it is claimed that Whewell was murdered in the vicinity by a vengeful Royalist).[44] Meanwhile, another known seventeenth-century figure remembered among Cheshire's ghosts is none other than Charles I, the latter having apparently been seen gazing from the tower of the cathedral at the ruin of his hopes on distant Rowton Heath, a further story having the king's spectre, this time headless, marking the anniversary of the king's execution by making an annual pilgrimage to the ancestral home of John Bradshaw (the judge who presided at his trial) at Marple.[45]

Tales of cathedrals, churches and old houses being visited by the shades of historical figures associated with them are probably only to be expected. However, both Chester and its surrounding county are stalked by a seemingly endless collection of nameless ghosts whose stories have been lost but who yet serve as a reminder of the Civil War. Beginning with the city itself, Morgan's Mount and Pemberton's Parlour, both of them towers on the north wall close to where the second breach was opened by the Parliamentarian guns, are reputedly the haunt - quite literally - of Cavaliers, some of them accompanied by richly dressed women, the presence of these figures generally being announced by a blast of icy air, while the Old King's Head in Lower Bridge Street is said to stalked by the ghost of a Cavalier killed in a duel who is seen only by unmarried women.[46] Meanwhile, turning to the wider county, a number of districts encompassed by the battlefield of Rowton Heath including Christleton, Waverton, Rowton Heath, Hoole Heath and Vicars Cross all lay claim to more-or-less frequent sightings of Civil War soldiers, one story of the men concerned that has survived stating that the apparitions seen from time to time in the vicinity of Brown Heath Road at Christleton are the ghosts of two Irish recruits taken prisoner in the fighting who paid the price for Parliament's hibernophobia.[47] At Nantwich the magnificent sixteenth-century building known as Churche's Mansion has been claimed by one medium in particular to be inhabited, not just by its most well-known spectre, namely the father of the man who had the building erected, but an unknown Royalist officer, while the patrons of the Black Lion Inn in Welsh Row - in January 1644 a suburb of the town that witnessed some of the worst fighting of the siege - have from time to time witnessed a Civil War soldier, seemingly in this instance a Roundhead, materialising from one of the walls in the public bar.[48] And, finally, Winnington Bridge - a crossing of the River Weaver near Northwich - is said to be haunted by two galloping horsemen, the latter having been identified, though on what evidence is far from clear, as a pair of Cavaliers fleeing Roundhead pursuers.[49]

Such narrative-devoid apparitions are also common in Lancashire. For example, at Speke Hall - in the Civil War the property of the staunchly Royalist Norris family - the ghost of a man dressed, or so it is claimed, like one of the

Three Musketeers, was encountered by a gang of workers in the 1950s and then again by a 13-year-old boy in the 1970s, incidents whose sting was considerably reduced by the fact that the apparition was described as being not just benign, but downright friendly and chatty.[50] Equally agreeable, meanwhile, is the handsome Cavalier who haunts the seventeenth-century Rake Inn in Littleborough, roaring with laughter all the while, though the same cannot be said of the spectre of Blackburn's Black Bull, this last supposedly being the ghost of a soldier named William Dutton who murdered the lover of some serving maid in the hope that he could enjoy her favours himself.[51] More spooky by far, then, is the case of the aptly named Skull Cottage near Appley Bridge, the building having got its name on account of a skull perched on a beam in a living room, the story being that said cranium belonged to a priest who was caught and killed in the building by Parliamentarian troops, and, further, that it visits misfortune on anyone who tries to move it.[52] From Foulridge, meanwhile, comes the legend of Tailor's Cross, a slab of stone originally marked by a crude carving of a pair of shears that has long since been lost, but is said to have marked the spot where a local tailor was shot by Cromwell's troops when he refused to help play his part in making up a fresh batch of uniforms, the unfortunate man concerned having for the next 200 years or more terrified passing night-time travellers by suddenly materialising and loudly bewailing his fate.[53] Rather less satisfying as a scene for a haunting is Dixon-Green Labour Club, Farnsworth, the building in which this institution is housed being frequented by a 'Blue Lady', a beautiful girl dressed in a blue silk dress with puffed sleeves thought, for reasons that have thus far gone unexplained, to be a victim of the Civil War.[54] In Middleton, School Lane is stalked by both a Roundhead and a Cavalier, both of whom are presumed to be victims of some forgotten fight (it is possible that this story is related in some way to the one involving the Middleton public house called the Ring o'Bells that is recounted below).[55] And, finally, herewith Terence Whitaker:

> On the edge of Turton Moors above Bolton a Cavalier has been seen to materialise out of a wall of some old cottages, and in broad daylight ...
> Saint Mary's churchyard at Rochdale has a sinister apparition which is seen quite often ... a man dressed in knee-breeches [who] has been seen gliding from the churchyard to the nearby river ... Bleak Rivington village near Horwich has a ghostly horseman who is said to ride [along] an old lane

within the precincts of the vicarage garden [though] only his head can be
seen, the ghostly body and horse hidden by the now sunken lane.[56]

Have the presences mentioned in these passages really been seen or otherwise
experienced? Perhaps, and, then again, perhaps not. What is clear enough is
they represent a verifiable reality in the form of a very strong folk-memory of
the seventeenth-century past. Confronted by sights of the utmost horror, the
people of Civil War England transmitted their experiences to the generations
that succeeded them and those generations in turn passed them on again, and, as
the detail of the tales altered from one teller to the next and their origins became
increasingly lost to sight, so, little by little, personal anecdote was converted into
ghost story. Nowhere is this more noticeable than in the case of the actual scenes
of armed conflict. As we have seen, stories that battlefields such as Edgehill,
Marston Moor and Naseby were haunted were in widespread circulation by
the time of the Restoration, while some of them can be traced back to within a
few months of the battles in question. Such tales remain commonplace, what is
notable being that they exist even in the case of actions of which there is almost
nothing in the way of historic memory. Thus, it is hardly surprising to discover
that the fields outside Nantwich which saw Sir Thomas Fairfax overcome Sir
John Byron should be held from time to time to reverberate with the crash
of musketry and artillery fire and the screams of the dead and dying – one of
them is even still called Dead Man's Field – nor that Chester anthologies retell
similar stories with respect to both the spot once graced by Sadler's Tower and
neighbouring Saint Werburgh's Street, a winding thoroughfare nestling in the
shadow of the cathedral, areas that alike witnessed fierce fighting in the first
Parliamentarian assault on the city.[57] Equally, with regard to Hoghton Tower, it
is all too predictable that one of its many ghosts is that of Captain Starkie, the
Roundhead commander who was blown up with many of his men in the great
explosion that destroyed much of the gatehouse in the complex's capture by the
Parliamentarians in 1643.[58] However, most telling of all are the stories that have
circulated in respect of the battles of Ormskirk and Winwick. Fought, as we have
seen, on 20 August 1644, the first of this duo of Royalist defeats is little known
even among Civil War *cognoscenti*, and yet we not only hear of the usual sounds
of battle – in this case galloping horses – but are also told of the precise spot
where they are most likely to be heard (usually at dusk), namely beside an old wall

bordering the Ormskirk-Liverpool road, what is strange about this being that it was precisely along the axis of this route that Byron's men fled as they made their way off the battlefield.[59] As for Winwick, the action in which the infantry of the Duke of Hamilton were overcome and forced to surrender by Cromwell, and, with it, one that is equally unknown, the A49 - the modern road whose line was followed by the Scots as they trudged south from Preston - is haunted a mile to the north at Newton-le Willows by the tramp of marching men, while a road called Hermitage Green Lane that marks the Scottish front line is marked by the lamentations of a number of captured soldiers who were allegedly hung from the trees that line its length.[60]

The battles of Ormskirk and Winwick are not the only instances in north-west England in which memory has become intertwined with stories of apparitions. Thus, from the Lune to the Mersey, Lancashire is spotted with stories of the ghosts of unhappy men, almost certainly fugitives from Hamilton's army, who either died of their wounds or were done to death by angry local clubmen or executed by the Parliamentarian forces. Thus, if no apparition has been recorded in these particular instances, the Fylde village of Staining is graced by a spot that forever smells of thyme and is supposed to mark the spot of the grave of some unfortunate Scottish soldier (thyme, it seems, was as much associated with Scotland in the early-modern period in northern England as the thistle, not least, perhaps, because a sprig of thyme was a field sign often employed by the much-feared 'border reivers'), while the atmosphere of evil that is said to mar one particular corner of Carr House, a seventeenth-century country residence near Tarleton, has been put down to the fact that it witnessed the death of another refugee from the *débâcle*.[61] Equally, the early sixteenth-century manor-house in Bolton known as 'The Hall in the Wood' is said to be haunted by a Cavalier killed in one of the upper bedrooms who is seen running up the main stairs in an effort to escape the men who had hunted him down, Foulridge's New Inn by a victim of the Battle of Preston and Thurnham Hall near Lancaster by yet another supporter of the king.[62] Not far away in Middleton, meanwhile, the Ring o'Bells is haunted by a Cavalier with a sad face dressed in a cloak and a lace collar carrying a sword, who somehow acquired the name Edward, and is believed to be a member of the family that owned nearby Stanycliffe Hall, a building, incidentally, that until its demolition in the late nineteenth century was reputed to be home to the ghost of another member of the same family who was murdered at some point in the Civil War period by a rebellious servant.[63] Further south, the Stork Hotel in Billinge - a village close to Winwick - has been the site of apparitions on the part of an angry figure who stamps around the public bar in high dudgeon, the story being that he was a prisoner who was murdered while being held in the cellar.[64] Then there is the rather happier tale of the Rock House Hotel, Barton upon Irwell, the 'in-dwell' here being a Royalist soldier who was being pursued by enemy troops but escaped by disguising himself as a yokel.[65] And, finally, a further clutch of unfortunate 1648 gallows fodder represented among the region's ghosts is constituted by the three Royalist soldiers imprisoned in Clitheroe Castle who were strung up for trying to escape and have according to legend haunted the place ever since.

Though the story appends to the campaign of Worcester rather than that of Preston, also worth mentioning here are events that are recorded as having taken place at Sandbach in Cheshire. Thus, in the days following the defeat of Charles II and the Scottish army he had led into England at Worcester on 3 September 1651, the senior Scottish general, David Leslie, led a group of survivors northwards in a desperate attempt to get back across the border. However, he and his followers did not get away unmolested. On the contrary, bivouacking for the night on a stretch of open ground outside the town, they were set upon by a large band of inhabitants out to avenge the ravages the Scots had inflicted on the area in their march south and a number killed or taken prisoner, the field concerned ever afterwards being known as Scotch Common. Nor was the popular memory of the events concerned restricted to a mere name: on the contrary, the bodies were dragged away and thrown in a nearby depression in the ground, which as time went on became associated with stories of a ghostly piper playing a lament for the dead and is therefore known as Piper's Hollow.[66]

If the battles of Ormskirk, Preston and Winwick and the campaign of Worcester are commemorated in this fashion, much the same is true of the siege of Chester. First up here come the severed heads that according to repute were in the past sometimes seen floating down the River Dee. To these there is attached a grotesque legend, namely that the Parliamentarian commander at the battle of Rowton Heath, Sydenham Poyntz, decided to undermine the morale of the defenders of the city by decapitating all the Royalist corpses found on the battlefield and throwing the resultant supply of heads into the river to drift downstream. This is assuredly so much nonsense - tough professional soldier though he was and anything but the most pleasant of men, Poyntz would no more have resorted to such a step than any other officer in England, for such was the general respect for the dead that to have done so would have been to sully his reputation beyond repair[67] - but it is entirely possible that the bodies of men drowned while trying to swim the Dee were clearly seen from the city walls in their journey towards the sea. What the story commemorates, then, is not a haunting at all, but rather a grim reality that those who witnessed it could never shake off, much the same being true of the sound of the terrible wailing that is supposed to emanate from the site of the plague pit known to have been dug on the bank of the river immediately in the rear of the Water Tower in the area now covered by Water Tower Gardens.[68]

Let us return, however, to the oddly situated 'Blue Lady' at Farnsworth. Whoever this last figure was, she may well fit in with a strong theme of traditional ghost stories, namely that of the young girl harshly treated by life. Whether they stemmed from the ranks of the humble or were the daughters of gentlefolk, the young women of the mid-seventeenth century were in an extremely vulnerable position in that those stemming from the ranks of the poor at best faced a life of drudgery while their more fortunate sisters were likely to be beset by one of endless boredom and frustration, not to mention the perils and pitfalls of an arranged marriage. And, of course, both groups were constantly vulnerable to philandering, sexual abuse and domestic violence, it being grimly symbolic in this respect that the upper floors of the Old Boot Inn in Chester's Eastgate Street, in the Civil War a notorious brothel, are said to resound to a cacophony of, on the one hand, male laughter, and, on the other, female moans.[69] With the coming of the Civil War, meanwhile, a bad situation could only get worse, for women frequently found themselves beset by traumas related to the struggle, this, too, being a theme that is highlighted by the stories of three ghosts whose identities are known, if only by repute, namely a girl named Mary Webb, a housekeeper named Grace Trygg and one Henrietta, a Chester innkeeper's daughter. Of these, the first was a servant at Wythenshawe Hall (a manor house in what is now the suburbs of Manchester) who was killed by Parliamentarian soldiers who had just stormed the building after she snatched up a musket and shot dead one of their officers to avenge the death of her lover, the latter being a member of the garrison who had been killed in the fight.[70] Next we come to Grace Trygg, a figure associated with Hockenhull Hall near the village of Duddon, the story being that she was decapitated by a group of Parliamentarian soldiers who she had angered by refusing to divulge the location of the valuables hidden on the premises by its absent Royalist owners, and is seen (minus her head) walking the lane that leads from the hall to the nearby A51 at a spot marked by a public house called 'The Headless Woman' (originally 'The Heedless Woman', but at some point renamed in commemoration of the unfortunate Trygg).[71] And, finally, there is the sad story of Henrietta. Thus, the daughter of the proprietor of the Blue Bell Inn, a hostelry a few yards from the North Gate, Henrietta had fallen in love with a soldier of the garrison and become pregnant with his child. Unfortunately for her, however, her lover was among the men who were killed in the belated sortie that was launched in the last stages of the battle of Rowton Heath, and the young woman was so distraught on hearing the news that she promptly ran down into the cellar and hung herself, the legacy, needless to say, being a forlorn figure that is seen at dusk either watching for the return of said soldier from the window in the side-wall of the building that looks out toward the gate or drifting down the stairs that lead to the cellar.[72] Once again, of course, one is forced to ask whether anyone really has seen these apparitions or whether they are purely the fruit of constantly repeated anecdote. This, however, is not the point, the important issue being, first, that they represent folk-memories of incidents that at the very least could have taken place and are highly suggestive of the way the populace remembered the conflict as a time of violence and arbitrary behaviour on the one hand and personal tragedy on the other. In terms of plausibility, meanwhile, still more probably needs to be accorded to a story that is attached to Tudor House, a half-timbered building in Chester's Bridge Street, the top floor of which is reputed to be haunted by the ghost of a Royalist officer billeted in the house whose head was struck from his shoulders by a stray cannonball while he was standing at a window taking the air.[73]

To conclude, then, the reports of Civil War paranormal activity that we have from north-west England are both widespread and in many instances closely linked either to historical events or to stories that have at least some degree of plausibility, the result being that they offer an insight into the popular experience and, indeed, memory, of the conflict. Particularly well-represented are the trauma of being caught up in a long siege; the vulnerability of women in seventeenth-century society, and all the more so in time of war; and the revenge wrought on both the Scottish soldiers defeated at Preston in 1648 and unhappy fugitives from the Royalist armies, this last being, perhaps, evidence of a certain retrospective feeling of collective guilt that emerged as memories of the plunder and pillage that was all too often the reality of the Cavaliers faded into the past (that said, the supporters of the king were anything but forgotten, the reality being that they retained a privileged possession in popular memory: of the fifty-six separate Civil War ghost stories that have come down to us from north-west England, only three feature Parliamentarians or their supporters, whereas the figure for their Royalist opponents is twenty-five). Interestingly, meanwhile, we also see a tendency to see the Parliamentarians as the villains of the piece: of the five stories from the north-west in which we hear of violence against civilians, in only one are the culprits Royalists. Finally, what is clear, too, is that ghost stories do not just crop up at random, but are concentrated in areas where there was much fighting: if fiercely contested Cheshire and south Lancashire positively swarm with Civil War ghosts, Cumbria, an area too poor and remote to see much action, has virtually none.[74] However, whether a similar picture can be obtained in respect to other parts of the country is another matter and one that we must now go on to establish.

Chapter 4

The North-East

D efined for the purposes of this work as the counties of Northumberland, Durham, Yorkshire and Lincolnshire, the north-east of England was to prove a scene of bitter conflict in the wars of 1642-46 and 1648 alike.[1] Positioned athwart the main route from Scotland into England and possessed of the country's second city, York, not to mention the vital port of Hull (and, with it, thanks to the 'Bishops' Wars' of 1639-40, the most important arsenal in the kingdom outside London), the fortress of Berwick (in 1642 the only place in the country furnished with modern fortifications), the coal of County Durham, the flourishing cloth industries of the West Riding and the lesser, though potentially still very useful harbours of Newcastle and Scarborough, like its counterpart across the Pennines, it was an area that neither side could afford to ignore. Just as it resounded to some of the very first shots of the First Civil War, it therefore resounded to some of the very last of the second, while it was no accident that the site of the biggest battle of all three fell within its borders. All this being the case, it is no surprise to find that it is just as peppered with ghost stories relating to the era, though, as before, it is first necessary to address the military narrative.

No sooner had the split between king and Parliament become overt than the north-east was pitchforked into the centre of events. Having fled London in the wake of the failed attempt to arrest the famous 'Six Members' and briefly taken refuge at Hampton Court, Charles and his suite made for York, not least because Yorkshire was known to be a centre of considerable loyalism. Before he arrived, meanwhile, there was a brief tussle at one of the gates when a newly raised troop of Parliamentarian dragoons tried to ride into the city, only to be set upon and driven off by a group of musketeers headed by one Captain Atkinson, albeit not without the latter being mortally wounded.[2] With the city thus secured, it was, then, at York that what became the chief army of the Royalist cause had its beginnings, just as it was York that was to be the first place in the country to experience the overcrowding, unruliness and general inconvenience consequent upon becoming a garrison. Meanwhile, it was also very soon the base for one of the very first military operations of the conflict, namely the unsuccessful Royalist attempt to seize control of Hull on 23 April 1642, pursued, though this was, by guile and persuasion rather than armed force (in brief, a small party of horse having gained access to the town the previous day on the pretext that Charles' second son, the future James II, to whom they were acting as escort wished to see the ships in the port – he was, after all, but 8 years old – to act as a 'fifth column', the king appeared before the walls at the head of such meagre forces as he had available and demanded to be let in in his turn, only for the governor, Sir John Hotham, to deny him entry and have the arrivals of the previous day, who had in the meantime done nothing whatsoever to help their royal master, expelled from the city).[3] An unscrupulous character who was friend of nothing but his own interests, Hotham was a most reluctant Parliamentarian – one suspects that his money, so to speak, was on the king – and he therefore let it be known to a variety of Royalist agents that he would gladly surrender the city if Charles would only march against it with a force sufficiently impressive for him to afford him sufficient pretext to open the gates. On 4 July, then, Charles set out from York with his entire army (now some 4,000 strong), but, by the time he arrived before the walls, it was too late: much suspected by the Parliamentarian leadership, the governor had been fenced about with more resolute figures, and the Royalist forces therefore found themselves met with defiance. Thus, thwarted, Charles embarked upon a siege, establishing batteries at such places as Hessle and Paull, but the defenders now had a new commander in the person of a Scottish soldier of fortune named Sir John Meldrum, this last's conduct of operations proving so vigorous that the Royalists quickly became discouraged. Dealt a particularly stinging blow by a successful sortie that destroyed a magazine that had been established at Anlaby, on 27 July the king raised the siege and fell back on York.[4]

With the failure of the attack on Hull, the epicentre of the war quickly moved away from the north-east, for, within a few days, Charles had left his temporary capital and embarked on the long series of manoeuvres that saw him raise his standard at Nottingham and fight the Battle of Edgehill. Behind him, however, he left a region deeply divided. Headed by the Marquis of Newcastle, the greatest magnate in the north of England, most of the local gentry sided with the king with the result that the Royalists were able to secure control of not just York, but also the town of Newcastle, while at the same time establishing a number of isolated garrisons such as Skipton, the seat of the Earl of Cumberland (see below).[5] Also very helpful was the Royalist seizure of Newark, a town that both commanded a major crossing of the River Trent and marked the point where the important communication links of Ermine Street and the Fosse Way crossed one another, and, in consequence, offered the hope of co-operation with Royalist forces in the Midlands and the south. Yet all was not well. Thus, the West Riding, a stronghold of Puritanism, had followed the lead of the staunch friend of that persuasion, Lord Fairfax, the situation being further complicated by the appearance of Parliamentarian garrisons at, among other places, Scarborough and Raby Castle. Very soon, then, the north-east was in the grip of a local struggle that was not really to intersect with the main course of the war till 1644.

In this petty campaign, the advantage was initially very much with the Parliamentarians, not the least of their opponents' problems being that the leadership of their cause was split between Newcastle, who had been given command of Northumberland and Durham, and the Earl of Cumberland, who fulfilled the same function in Yorkshire. Possessed of no military experience though he was, the former proved an able administrator, while, added to his enormous personal fortune, the fact that he faced little in the way of opposition meant that he was soon well on the way to building an impressive field force whose centrepiece was five regiments of infantry, the famous 'white coats' who were to cover themselves in glory at Marston Moor (there were also eight regiments of cavalry who will later figure in the text as the so-called 'Northern Horse').[6] That said, it would take some little time before he was ready to take the field, the result being that the initial Royalist advantage was soon under considerable threat. Unlike Newcastle, Cumberland turned out to be an ineffectual figure, and the result was that he was able to do little more than seek to hang on to such garrisons as the Royalists had been able to establish. By contrast, the Parliamentarians proved alarmingly aggressive, forces from Hull attacking Selby and Cawood Castle, home to the Royalist Archbishop of York, while the West Riding was overrun by forces raised by Lord Fairfax, who had quickly been appointed to the head of the Parliamentarian cause in the whole of Yorkshire and was ably supported by his son, Sir Thomas Fairfax, a man who was to go on to become, as we have seen, the victor of the Battle of Nantwich and one of the greatest commanders of the war, a Royalist attack on Bradford on 23 October being beaten off for good measure.[7] And, finally, not only did the Fairfaxes push eastwards to seize, first, Knaresborough Castle and then Wetherby, where on 21 November they defeated a force sent from York under Sir Thomas Glemham, but also, in the south of the county, Rotherham, Sheffield and Doncaster all fell into the hands of energetic Parliamentarian supporters.[8] Had the start of full-scale military operations not been delayed by abortive local peace negotiations, then the county might well have fallen into Parliamentarian hands in its entirety.[9]

Faced by this situation, Cumberland had no option but to appeal for help to Newcastle, and late November therefore saw the marquis march on York with 6,000 men. Mobilising a small force barely a tenth of the size of the one led by Newcastle, the son of the governor of Hull, another Sir John Hotham, rushed to block his way and managed to take up a strong defensive position at Piercebridge, a small village where the main road south crossed the River Tees. For all that they were badly outnumbered, much aided by the fact that the only way across the river was a single narrow bridge, Hotham and his men put up a brave fight when Newcastle attacked on 1 December, but the odds against the defenders were such that the day could only go one way, the Parliamentarians being driven from the field with heavy casualties.[10] Pushing south with all due haste, Newcastle reached York with no further difficulties, and on 6 December evicted the forces of the Fairfaxes from Tadcaster, which they had chosen to make their headquarters, following up this victory with a foray into the West Riding commanded by Sir William Savile.[11] Having first cleared the Parliamentarians from Leeds, Wakefield and Pontefract Castle, on 18 December Savile assaulted Bradford, only to be repulsed with some loss, the few regular troops in the town having been quickly joined by large numbers of civilians armed with staves, scythes and pitchforks.[12]

With their confidence thus restored, the Fairfaxes pushed east again and occupied Leeds and Selby, albeit in the case of the former only at the cost of a sharp contest that ended in bitter house-to-house fighting up and down Briggate.[13] Just as aggressive, meanwhile, was Sir Hugh Cholmley. Thus, hearing that a Royalist force was on its way to seize Whitby under Guildford Slingsby, on 14 January 1643, the latter sallied out with 500 men, and, having first seized Malton from the small Royalist garrison that had been established there, attacked Slingsby at Guisborough, not only routing the Royalists with ease but also capturing their commander. The victorious Parliamentarians then returned to Scarborough, only very shortly to hear that a large convoy of arms including sixteen cannon was on its way from Newcastle to York under the supervision of

Lord Eythin, Cholmley therefore rushing back north to try to intercept it, while in the meantime protecting his home base by augmenting the garrison that had been left at Malton with another one at Stamford Bridge. In this case, however, the Parliamentarian leader had over-reached himself, for Eythin had plenty of troops with him and had no difficulty in putting Cholmley's force to flight when it sought to block his passage of the River Tees at Yarm.[14]

At this point, matters might have gone very ill for Cholmley. Thus, now commander of Yorkshire as well as the counties further north, Newcastle left the Fairfaxes to their own devices and instead evicted the garrisons of Malton and Stamford Bridge. There might well have followed an attack on Scarborough, but on 22 February Queen Henrietta Maria, who had been across the sea seeking help in Holland, suddenly appeared at Bridlington with a large consignment of arms and ammunition and made her way to land in defiance of a squadron of Parliamentarian warships that had come up just too late to stop her.[15]

As can be imagined, the *deus ex machina* represented by the arrival of Henrietta Maria flung the Yorkshire Parliamentarians into confusion. Thus, much alarmed at the prospect of being struck what he feared would be a heavy blow, Lord Fairfax decided to retreat to the safety of the West Riding, a move that he decided to cover by detaching a rearguard of infantry and cavalry under his highly capable son. In order to achieve his objective, the latter made a surprise attack on Tadcaster, only himself to be taken by surprise when Newcastle's cavalry commander, Sir George Goring, marched to deal with him at the head of 2,000 horse. In the face of this sudden threat, the Parliamentarian commander beat a hasty retreat in the direction of Leeds (the nearest friendly garrison), and might well have got away had not his unruly troops, many of whom were ill-armed 'club-men', not persisted in wasting time by rifling every dwelling they passed along the way. The result was the Battle of Seacroft Moor, a running fight fought along several miles of the road from Tadcaster to Leeds on 30 March 1643. Repeatedly attacked by Goring, the Parliamentarians made it most of the way to their destination, but were eventually overcome when the Royalist horse succeeded in catching them from an unexpected direction on a stretch of open moorland just east of the town, almost all the surviving foot being forced to lay down their arms and marched off as prisoners to York.[16]

More than 1,000 of Fairfax's men having been lost in this affair, the Parliamentarian cause in Yorkshire was at a low ebb, and all the more so given the fact that, motivated by a mixture of concern for his own survival, dislike of Presbyterianism and, still more so, independency, disgruntlement at what had become apparent was the determination of Lord Fairfax to subordinate him to his command, fear for his family estates, and, last but not least, social conservatism, Cholmley did not just go to ground but actually changed sides.[17] Nor did it help that an attempt in late February to besiege the troublesome Royalist garrison in Newark had been an ignominious failure - led by the highly competent Sir John Henderson, the defenders had bid defiance to their assailants, whereupon the Parliamentarian commander, the utterly lacklustre Sir Thomas Ballard, had retired without pressing the issue - or that troops from Skipton took the Parliamentarian outpost at Kildwick Hall.[18] Yet the Fairfaxes did not give up, rather launching a spirited counterattack that saw them storm Wakefield on 21 May and take prisoner Lord Goring, along with sufficient junior officers and common soldiers to secure the exchange of the men taken at Seacroft Moor (indeed, according to Fairfax's own account, the action was launched with precisely this in mind, the common folk on whom he so much depended being much distressed by the loss of so many sons and husbands).[19] Blow, however, was soon followed by counter-blow, the next month seeing Newcastle strike at them yet again. Marching into the West Riding at the head of a powerful force, he bombarded a Parliamentarian outpost at Howley Hall into surrender and once more threatened Bradford, leaving the Fairfaxes with no option but to fight. On 30 June, then, battle was joined at Adwalton Moor. Though the numbers fielded by the two sides were about equal, it was the Parliamentarians who at first had the advantage in the fighting, the Royalists being steadily forced back, but every step the former advanced left them more tired and disordered. Sensing this perhaps, in a bold move that was completely to transform the situation, a Royalist infantry commander launched a timely counter-attack on what seems to have been his own initiative. Ably seconded by the Royalist cavalry, this move reduced the West Riding forces to chaos, and very soon they were either in full flight or laying down their arms, while, finding themselves in a position in which they had no chance of reaching their headquarters in Bradford, Fairfax *père et fils* were forced to flee the field with all haste and make for the safety of Hull.[20]

Adwalton Moor may have been a disaster for the Parliamentarian cause, but it should not be allowed to overshadow the extraordinary achievement of the Fairfaxes and their supporters: as has been pointed out, their defence of the

West Riding for eight months in the face of such heavy odds was a masterpiece of Fabian tactics.[21] With the Parliamentarian army in the West Riding in complete disarray, however, Bradford now faced a day of reckoning. The night after the battle, Newcastle took possession of nearby Bolling Hall, and, disturbed by an apparition though his slumbers may have been (see Chapter 2), the next day opened fire on the town with his artillery. All it took to reduce the few defenders to submission were a few shots, however, the marquis' troops penetrating the defences without the slightest difficulty virtually as soon as they were let loose upon them. Among the many prisoners was Sir Thomas Fairfax's wife, Anne, even if the ever-courteous Newcastle ensured that she was both well treated and safely conveyed to Hull. As for the populace, it was spared the massacre that was supposed to threaten on account of what had happened the previous December, though Newcastle's mercy did not extend to respect for their goods and chattels, the town being thoroughly pillaged of anything of value.[22]

Having thus disposed of Bradford and installed a garrison in the town, Newcastle now turned his attention to the situation in Lincolnshire. Striking east from Newark, in April 1643 a strong force of troops headed by Newcastle's cousin, Sir Charles Cavendish, had marched on Grantham. This place having quickly been taken by means of a surprise attack, Cavendish had then pressed on towards Boston, routing the local Parliamentarians under Lord Willoughby at Ancaster in the process. Much alarmed, the commander of forces of the Eastern Association, Lord Grey of Groby (confusingly enough, there was another Parliamentarian peer of the same title in the area, namely Lord Grey of Wark) responded by rushing reinforcements to his beaten subordinate and ordering him to force Cavendish and Henderson to retreat by threatening Newark.[23] As a first step Willoughby reoccupied Grantham, only to find that the gambit of marching on Newark had been rather more effective. Thus, hardly had he taken the town than on 13 May he was fallen on by the Royalists, these last managing to come up without notice and destroy a Parliamentarian outpost at Belton. Yet, in the event, fortune favoured Willoughby. Among the men who had arrived to reinforce him, then, was a regiment of horse commanded by the hitherto little-known Oliver Cromwell. A man for all his total lack of military experience possessed an instinctive grasp of the basic principles of warfare, Cromwell had, as is well known, formed a cavalry regiment – the famous 'Ironsides' – that was second to none in terms of recruitment, training and motivation. First serious action of his military life though the current clash was, the future Lord Protector charged the oncoming enemy, the force of his advance being such that his opponents turned tail and ran.[24]

Much lauded though it is by Cromwell's biographers, this very minor victory actually changed events very little.[25] Despite the fact that Cavendish was called away to Newark to help escort Henrietta Maria, who on 14 June had marched south from York accompanied by not just her precious convoy of arms and ammunition, but also a small army, on her way to Oxford, nothing further happened until July when Willoughby finally bestirred himself sufficiently to occupy the key town of Gainsborough. Now back again at Newark, Cavendish immediately made shift to remedy the situation by moving to besiege the town. Fearing that it would be retaken, Grey directed Cromwell to join forces with a contingent of troops from Nottinghamshire commanded by Sir John Meldrum, and on 28 July the two Parliamentarians hove into view from the south. Having been forewarned of their approach, Cavendish had pulled his men back to a steep hill on the further side of the town, and, in the clear hope that he would catch them disordered by the climb, charged his assailants as soon as they came within reach of his lines. The resultant fight at first surged to and fro with fortune going to first one side and then the other, but at length the Royalists over-reached themselves and thereby laid themselves open to a flank attack masterminded by Cromwell that soon had them reeling in disorder, Cavendish and many of his men being driven down the rear face of the hill into an area of waterlogged ground that lay at its foot. Among the many dead left sprawling in the latter's swampy pools was the Royalist commander – to this day the area is known as Candish Bog – but, for all that, the day did not end as well for the Parliamentarians as they expected. Pushing on northwards beyond the battlefield with his horsemen, Cromwell was suddenly confronted with the sight of a large Royalist army heading straight for him. The new arrivals being none other than Newcastle and the whole of his disposable force, the future Lord Protector could do nothing but turn tail and, along with Meldrum, beat a hasty retreat, leaving the marquis to mop up Willoughby and his garrison.[26]

The campaign of Gainsborough, then, ended with the Royalists in a strong position, but Newcastle did nothing to build upon his success, and that despite the fact that, pushed beyond endurance by the ever mounting financial demands imposed on it by Parliament, the town of King's Lynn had just risen in revolt under the leadership of a group of local Royalists. Instead, in a decision that has been much criticised ever since, he turned his troops around and headed for Hull, leave garrisons in Lincoln and Bolingbroke Castle though he did. With the benefit of hindsight, it can be seen that this move may have changed the war – had he pressed on, the marquis could possibly have shattered the forces of the Eastern Association and gone on to join the king at Oxford – but to march south leaving a strong enemy base in his rear was not an attractive prospect, and all the more so given that it was one that could easily be reinforced by sea, while, in the light of the secret negotiations of the previous year, Newcastle might also have thought that it would surrender without a fight. In reality, however, Hull was anything but an easy option. Having flirted with the idea of betraying the Parliamentarian cause once too often – they had earlier in the year gone so far as to sign a secret treaty with Newcastle whereby they promised that they would do nothing to impede the journey of Henrietta Maria to Oxford if he in turn would leave their domains in peace – the egregious Hothams had recently been overthrown in a coup headed by the deputy governor, Richard Overton, while both the garrison and the defences were much stronger than they had been in 1642, and the resolution of the defenders strengthened by the presence of the redoubtable Fairfax duo (Sir Thomas, indeed, had no sooner arrived in the city than he had been acclaimed as governor).[27] As a result of all this, besieging the place turned into a disaster for the Royalist cause. Impervious behind broad stretches of farmland that had been deliberately flooded to deny access to the walls, the defences could not be stormed, while Parliament's control of the sea meant that there was no chance of reducing the city by starvation either. With the weather, as ever in the Civil War, characterised by torrential rain and bitter cold, the Royalist forces suffered terribly and were soon falling prey to disease in very large numbers, while they were further discomforted by both Parliamentarian raids and an unusually high tide that flooded their siege works.[28]

As if all this was not bad enough, across the Humber the situation was getting darker once more. Lord Grey having proved less than successful as commander of the forces of the Eastern Association, he had been replaced by the Earl of Manchester, while Cromwell, now a lieutenant-general, had been given command of the whole of its cavalry. Very soon, meanwhile, the Parliamentarians had once more taken the offensive. Thus, Cromwell having first made a dash for the Humber to enable Fairfax and his cavalry – an arm of service of little use in a siege - to get across the river, Manchester sat down to besiege Bolingbroke Castle. Newark being the nearest Royalist garrison with the capacity to raise a field army, its governor, as before Sir John Henderson, rode forth to do battle at the head of a large force of horse and dragoons, duly winning a small action at Horncastle on 10 October, only to find himself ambushed by Cromwell and Fairfax deep in the wolds a day later. Known as the Battle of Winceby, the action that followed was a serious blow to the Royalist cause. With the front rank of the Parliamentarian forces composed entirely of the cavalry of the Eastern Association, a force that, thanks to Cromwell, was now well-drilled and highly motivated throughout, Henderson's men were swept away at the first charge and driven from the field with heavy losses, the result being that Newcastle had no option but to abandon the siege of Hull and also give up all hope of relieving Bolingbroke Castle, this last surrendering to Manchester on 14 November.[29]

Newcastle's travails were far from over, however. For much of 1643 the Parliamentarian leadership had been negotiating with the Scots to get them to enter the war in exchange for a promise to reform the Church of England. These negotiations having eventually brought success, the turn of the year saw a powerful Scottish army under the Earl of Leven march on Berwick. Crossing the border on 18 January, they pushed on very slowly towards the town of Newcastle, which at this point had but the thinnest of garrisons. Dropping everything, the marquis therefore rushed north with the bulk of his army and succeeded in getting there before the over-cautious Scots. Thus frustrated, Leven launched several attacks on the outer defences, but was beaten off and therefore decided to mask the town and cross the Tyne further inland. In this, he was further delayed by Newcastle, whose cavalry managed to deal him a sharp blow at Corbridge on 17 February under the command of Sir Marmaduke Langdale, a somewhat cadaverous figure who was to gain the nickname of 'the ghost'. However, such was the Scots' numerical superiority that they could not be checked forever, and on 28 February they crossed the Tyne at Ousebridge and headed east towards Sunderland, control of whose port would ensure that they could maintain their communications with Scotland, notwithstanding the Royalists' continued control of Newcastle. Far to the south, meanwhile, further danger was looming for the Royalist cause in that, commanded by Sir John Meldrum, in late February, the Parliamentarians had once more closed in on Newark and subjected it to a regular siege.[30]

Yet the Royalists were not yet finished. On the River Trent, their defences having been much reinforced over the previous year, the garrison of Newark put up a fierce fight and even managed to beat off a major assault that almost penetrated to the very heart of the town, thereby winning time for Prince Rupert to gather together a mixed force of cavalry and mounted musketeers, join up with the local Royalist field army under Lord Loughborough, and launch a surprise attack on Meldrum on 21 March that ended with the latter being trapped and forced to surrender, though he and his men were allowed to march away to join the nearest Parliamentarian forces, albeit at the cost of all their cannon, muskets and ammunition. Still worse, the prince did not attempt to follow up his victory, but rather headed back down the Fosse Way to pursue his designs on the north-west; the Eastern Association was panicked into abandoning Lincoln, the latter being swiftly occupied by the local Royalists.[31] And, as for the situation on the River Tyne, having slipped out of Newcastle before Leven had cut the Great North Road, the Royalist field army took up a position at Durham, thereby ensuring that the Scots, who had taken Sunderland on 4 March, could not threaten York.[32]

All well and good though this last development was, the Royalist commander knew that, with both Manchester and Fairfax loose on the southern borders of his domains, his one hope was to defeat Leven before the first two commanders could wreak havoc on the few troops he had left there. The Scottish commander, however, had no intention of giving him any such opportunity and, with both sides slowed down by heavy snow, there therefore followed several weeks of inconclusive manoeuvring. Eventually battle was joined at the village of East Bolden on 24 March, the action that followed seeing Newcastle launch a fierce attack on Leven, only to be driven back and forced to retreat to Durham.[33] So far as the Royalist cause was concerned, the results of Newcastle's failure were dire indeed. To protect his territory in Yorkshire from the Parliamentarians, he had left a large number of garrisons, of which, aside from York, the most important were Skipton, Pontefract, Bradford, Sheffield, Lincoln and Scarborough. In charge, meanwhile, was the governor of York, Sir John Belasyses, but, competent professional though he was, the latter had a major problem in that he could only put together a field army by drawing men out of his garrisons, this being something to which there were serious limits. The most that he would be able to concentrate being no more than 3,000 men, if that, he simply did not have the resources available to hold the Parliamentarians at bay for any length of time. Even as it was, the situation was bad enough for, still stiffened by that part of the army of Lord Fairfax that his son had not taken to fight at Nantwich (see Chapter 3), the garrison of Hull had been launching a series of raids that saw them go so far as occupying Whitby, while the forces of the Eastern Association were gathering strength in the southern reaches of Lincolnshire. Very soon, however, the outlook darkened still further in that, in the wake of his victory over the Cheshire Royalists, Sir Thomas Fairfax had ordered one of his subordinates, namely the extremely competent John Lambert, to advance on the West Riding with all of his infantry with the aim of re-establishing the area as the Parliamentarian stronghold that it had been prior to Adwalton Moor. Having marched across the Pennines via Sowerby and overcome a small Royalist outpost at Baildon, Lambert and his men appeared before Bradford on 3 March, and quickly crushed its small band of defenders, barricade themselves into the parish church though they had, following up this victory by occupying Leeds and Tadcaster and defeating a Royalist counter-attack at Hunslet on 5 March.[34]

With his situation deteriorating by the day, Belasyse realised that prompt action was needed to rectify the situation, and therefore gathered together such men as he could and marched for Selby where he rendezvoused with a force of cavalry that he had called forth from Newark under Sir George Porter. Turning west, he then headed for Bradford, and on 25 March launched a full-scale assault on the town. Almost succeed though this did, in the end the Royalists were repulsed, and the result was that Belasyse, weakened not just by the losses he had suffered in the fighting, but the desertion of his command by the Newark horse, Porter having greatly resented the manner in which he had been summoned to his rescue, was forced to retreat to Selby.[35] Here, however, he faced a disaster that was even worse in that Lord Fairfax had sallied forth from Hull and met up with both the men Lambert had commanded at Bradford and the 2,000 horse his son had retained with him at Nantwich, whereupon on 11 April he fell on Selby at the head of a force at least three times the size of the one commanded by Belasyse. Composed of veteran troops as they were, the defenders put up a fierce fight, but they could not possibly withstand such odds, the result being that, within a matter of hours, those men who had not been killed or wounded had almost all been captured, including, not least, their unfortunate commander.[36]

For Newcastle, of course, the news of the defeat at Selby could evoke only one response, and he duly left the Scots to their own devices and marched for York as fast as the roads would allow. Arriving just in time to stop the enemy from marching in all but unopposed, he quickly manned the walls and defied Fairfax and Leven to do their worst, while sending a desperate plea to King Charles for help, as well as trying to slow down the progress of his opponents by launching a series of raids on a number of strongpoints they had occupied on the outskirts of the city, such as, for example, the village of Acomb. At first, Fairfax and Leven could only mount a loose blockade, but in early June they were joined by Manchester and his army, the latter having first taken Lincoln in a three-day battle that ended on 6 May. The 8,000 extra troops that were now available making all the difference, siege operations now began in earnest. On 6 June, then, the Scots stormed two sconces that had been built in front of the western walls, while, having first blown a breach in the defences by means of a mine, ten days later Manchester's forces assaulted the precincts of what had been the abbey of Saint Mary's, only to be thrown back with heavy losses.[37]

Handling the defence with aplomb though he was, Newcastle could not hope to hold out forever, and the fear of losing York had therefore prompted the distant king to take action. Much beleaguered himself at this time, Charles could not come to the aid of the city himself, but, with Prince Rupert currently campaigning in Lancashire, there was a handy alternative that he was quick to seize. Very soon, Prince Rupert was marching across the Pennines at the head of every man that he could muster. By dint of taking the remote route via Skipton and Knaresborough, he took Fairfax, Leven and Manchester completely by surprise, thereby leaving them no option but to raise the siege. As Rupert knew, however, this was not enough, his only chance of preserving York on a permanent basis being to defeat the massive enemy forces facing him. Outnumbered three to two though he was, and that even with the addition of the garrison of York, on 2 July the prince therefore headed out of the city to attack the Parliamentarians and their Scottish allies. In the event, however, it was not him who did the attacking, but rather his opponents. Thus, the Royalists were much delayed in assembling their troops on the field and, the forces facing them having stayed quiet all day, they assumed that there would be no fighting until the morrow. No sooner had they started to make camp, however, than the enemy commanders launched a surprise attack that developed into a full-scale battle. Marston Moor being one of the most well-known battles of the English Civil War, there is no need to go into any detail here: suffice to say that by the time the last shots had been fired, the Royalist cause in the north-west had been damaged beyond repair amid scenes of terrible slaughter. With his own troops all but wiped out and his personal fortune reduced to nothing, Newcastle fled abroad, while such remnants of the forces brought across the Pennines by Rupert made their way back to Lancashire and thence to Chester or Newark. As for York, meanwhile, under the resolute Sir Thomas Glemham it held out for another two weeks before finally laying down its arms on 16 July.[38]

With the Royalist field army consigned to oblivion, the forces of Leven, Manchester and Fairfax now moved to eliminate the various Royalist garrisons that continued to dot the region. What followed was a series of sieges, some of them so prolonged and uneventful as to be mere blockades and others more short-lived but marked by bitter fighting, as was the case, for example, at Newcastle and Scarborough. Even before Marston Moor the Parliamentarians had taken Creyk and Cawood Castles, while by the end of the year these had been joined by their counterparts at Sheffield, Helmsley, Sandal, Bolton and Knaresborough, along with Newcastle, this last succumbing to starvation on 27 October.[39] Where they could, the Royalists hit back - the Skipton garrison, for example, launched a successful raid on some enemy horse quartered at Ripon - but, more often than not, their forays ended in defeat: caught by overwhelming numbers, a troop of dragoons were forced to surrender at Halton House, the same fate befalling 140 cavalry who were taken by surprise at Plumpton.[40] As 1644 moved into 1645, meanwhile, so other outposts joined the list: the town of Scarborough, for example, was stormed on 18 February, though Cholmley held out in the castle until 25 July.[41] Here and there there were brief moments of success, as on 1 March when the cavalry belonging to Newcastle's army that had escaped from Marston Moor relieved Pontefract Castle, besieged since Christmas Day of the previous year, other Royalist raids temporarily relieving Greenhalgh Castle and retaking Bolsover Castle and Welbeck.[42] Yet such operations became ever more risky - on 12 February, for example, 150 men of the Skipton garrison were pounced upon by a superior force of Parliamentarians in their return from a successful raid on Keighley and in the resultant skirmish lost one third of their strength - while the number of bases from which they could be launched continued to dwindle: if 25 July saw the surrender of Sir Hugh Chomley at

Scarborough, the garrison of Pontefract Castle had succumbed to blockade just four days before.[43]

The direction of events in Yorkshire, then, was all one way, but, before the guns fell silent, there was to be one last flurry of activity. The story begins with the arrival at Newark on 21 October of no less a figure than King Charles himself. Accompanying the monarch were some 500 cavalry under the command of Sir Marmaduke Langdale (the survivors of the disaster at Rowton Heath; see Chapter 3) and, in addition, the notorious Lord Digby, a figure as devious as he was incompetent who had become Charles' secretary of state. What followed was all too revealing of the dream-world that the Royalist high command was now inhabiting. Thus, for all that, low in morale and discipline alike, Langdale's men were quickly beaten in skirmishes at the local villages of East Bridgeford and Langar, Digby persuaded the king to let him and Langdale lead them to Scotland in a desperate bid to join up with the forces of the Marquis of Montrose.[44] Even had the secretary of state reached his goal, it would have made little difference, for Montrose had just been decisively defeated at Philliphaugh, but, in the event, initial successes at Doncaster and Cusworth were followed by a shattering defeat at Sherburn-in-Elmet on 15 October, an event that in turn doomed the very last Royalist stronghold in Yorkshire, namely Skipton Castle, not though the garrison laid down its arms till 21 December.[45]

In the Trent valley, too, all was in ruins. Following the departure of Digby and Langdale, Charles himself remained at Newark, but his presence in the town achieved nothing, and was marred by a violent scene between the monarch and Prince Rupert that led to the prince and many of his supporters leaving the former's service and riding out of the town in the hope of being allowed to go into exile.[46] Finally, with the Parliamentarians closing in, Charles abandoned Newark to its own devices and made for Oxford, the Royalists' situation being rendered still worse by the fact that many of the local commanders were bitterly at odds with one another. Very soon, then, they were in worse straits than ever: Shelford House was stormed with great slaughter on 3 November – in brief, it seems that the entire garrison of 160 men was put to the sword on the grounds that it had only sought quarter once the assault had actually been launched – this event in turn leading to the capitulation without resistance of other garrisons at Welbeck House and Wiverton.[47] Beyond the walls of Newark, all that was now left was Belvoir Castle, and even this was closely besieged, its garrison eventually being forced to give in on 3 February 1646.[48] With Belvoir gone, there remained Newark, which had been put under siege once again on 26 November. Headed by Sir John Belasyses, his captivity some time since brought to an end by a prisoner exchange, the garrison proved surprisingly aggressive and secured a number of minor successes, remaining so resolute that they were still holding out in the face of plague, starvation and bombardment when King Charles surrendered to the Scots at Southwell on 5 May 1646, only giving up even then at the direct orders of the king.[49]

The fall of Newark on 8 May 1646 did not quite mark the end of the Wars of the Three Kingdoms as far as the north-east was concerned. On the contrary, hardly had the Second Civil War broken out in 1648 than a group of Royalists seized Pontefract Castle while the garrison of Scarborough Castle mutinied and joined the rebellion. The result was two further sieges, of which the one at Pontefract lasted till 24 March 1649, but field operations were limited to a few clashes on the frontiers of Westmoreland between a small force at the orders of the same John Lambert who had played so important a role in the fighting in early 1644 and the Royalists who had risen on the far side of the Pennines under Sir Marmaduke Langdale. For the rest, however, Yorkshire and the rest were spared, and thus it was that, so far as the north-east was concerned, civil war passed into the realm of historic memory.[50]

As before, it now remains for us to examine how the ebb and flow of siege and battle and the impact that the trauma experienced by soldiers and civilians alike is reflected in the ghost stories that we have relating to the region. As usual, there are a variety of more-or-less vague reports of sightings of one sort or another: examples include the 'Cromwellian' soldier reported from Lindisfarne Castle; the mounted Cavaliers spotted on the moors at Buckstones near Marsden by a passing police patrolman in 1968; the squad of soldiers dressed in white – a description redolent of the Marquis of Newcastle's famous 'whitecoats' – glimpsed in a wood near Knaresborough in the nineteenth century; the Cavalier reputed to haunt Lincoln's County Assembly Rooms (a story that is somewhat undermined by the fact that the building dates only from 1745); the Cavalier, according to legend a Catholic who died of his wounds in the building, who is seemingly a regular at the Britannia Inn in Cleadon, a village close to the spot where Newcastle faced up to the Scots at Bolden Hill in March 1644, and the similar figure seen at the Black Horse Inn in nearby West Bolden; the Cavaliers linked to Watton Priory near Driffield, the Eyre Arms in the Derbyshire village of Hassop, whose lord of the manor was the strongly Royalist Sir Thomas Eyre, and the Old Queen's Head in the Pondhill district of Sheffield (reputedly the oldest building in the city); the group of seventeenth-century soldiers observed clustered beside a road just outside Wetherby; and, finally, the Cavalier seen walking to the ceiling through the air in spirals in the Sally-Port Tower in Newcastle as if he was ascending a long-lost staircase, and the spectre of a soldier killed while firing a cannon that is said to haunt the battlements of the same city's castle keep.[51] However, while not entirely to be scorned (see below), these are of little help except to remind us of the frequency of Civil War ghost stories, not to mention the familiarity of the public with the image of the Cavalier, and the capacity of places associated with the Civil War, as with those associated with murders and suicides, to turn shadows and moonbeams into visions of the past: in this respect it is no surprise to find Marston Moor - a battlefield that is particularly widely known - positively teeming with ghosts, including, not least, a headless Cavalier who is said to gallop across the battlefield and back again when the clock on Long Marston church strikes midnight.[52]

Moving on to cases that are rather more specific, we come first to the usual smattering of prominent personalities. Curiously enough, there are some incidents that might seem obvious candidates for ghost stories - most obviously, Queen Henrietta Maria's dramatic disembarkation at Bridlington under fire from Parliamentarian warships - which do not feature in the literature, while the Fairfaxes, Lord Leven and the Marquis of Newcastle are all absent from the scene. However, shades that do appear include those of, inevitably enough, Oliver Cromwell, who is supposed to haunt Long Marston Hall, the house where he spent the night before Marston Moor; King Charles I, who is associated with Newcastle's seventeenth-century 'Old George', which has a 'King Charles' room complete with a chair the monarch is supposed to have sat upon, and, in addition, the same city's Town Quay, where he stands looking out for a ship that would allow him to escape from the year or more he spent in the city in the custody of the Scots; Prince Rupert, who is held to haunt the house in which he lodged in Newark in the wake of the loss of Bristol; and, finally, Colonel John Bright, a young Parliamentarian from a prosperous Sheffield family of long standing, who led the recapture of that town in August 1644 and thereafter served for some while as its governor, Bright having been seen standing at the top of the stairs in the single wing that is all that remains of his family home, Carbrook Hall.[53] And, finally, there is County Durham's Raby Castle, which in the Stuart period was the home of the Vane family and is haunted by the decapitated head of Sir Henry Vane, a radical Parliamentarian who was executed as a regicide by beheading on Tower Green in 1662.[54]

Before moving on from this gallery of ghostly celebrities to other topics, there is one other story that is worth mentioning. We come here to the Ye Olde White Hart Inn. Situated in the heart of the oldest quarter of Hull, this is reputed to be the place where Sir John Hotham supposedly conducted discussions with a group of prominent citizens that led to his decision to declare for the cause of Parliament in 1642, and legend has it that it is haunted by the ghost of a 'Cavalier' – in this context, a figure to be understood simply as a member of the gentry – an image of whom was supposedly captured by a ghost-hunter in 2015; whether such a spectre has indeed been seen, meanwhile, the chamber where the meeting took place is known as the 'plotting room'.[55] Exactly what the story refers to is a little unclear – one suspects that its real subject was rather the brief presence in the city of the party accompanying the Duke of York – but, given that the Hothams were both executed for treason on Tower Green in January 1645, it would be faintly surprising that one or other them were not remembered in the city's legends. What is certainly the case is that they, or, to be more precise, Sir John Hotham the Elder, are remembered in nearby Beverley. Thus, discovering that his intrigues with Newcastle had been uncovered, the erstwhile governor slipped out of the city and made for York, only for him to be spotted and detained to the accompaniment of a sharp scuffle in which he was badly wounded by a blow from a musket-butt, an event that is said to be periodically re-enacted, albeit in sound alone – the clattering of hooves is followed by the noise of a struggle – in a narrow street just off the marketplace.[56]

As elsewhere, meanwhile, violence against women (and, in particular, violence against women by Parliamentarians) is a theme that is recurrent among the ghost stories of the north-east. To begin with a site that has already been mentioned, situated near Driffield, Watton Abbey (actually in origin not an abbey but rather a priory) is supposedly the home not just of the ghost of some unknown Cavalier, but also that of the then lady of the manor who, left alone in the house with just a handful of servants, was supposedly hacked to pieces after Marston Moor by a group of marauding Parliamentarians, and has repeatedly appeared to guests accommodated in the chamber in which she was murdered minus her head and dressed in bloody clothing with an infant in her arms.[57] Another story pertaining to brutal Roundhead troops, meanwhile, concerns the old vicarage in the West Yorkshire village of Kirkburton, the building being haunted by one Hester Whitaker, the wife of the then vicar, Gamaliel Whitaker, the unfortunate woman having been shot when a party of Parliamentarians came to arrest her husband on account of his well-known Royalist sympathies.[58] Finally, also in West Yorkshire is seventeenth-century East Riddlesden Hall near Keighley whose 'Grey Lady' is said to be the ghost of a woman murdered by her soldier husband when he returned from the wars and found her to be having an affair.[59]

If the example of Chester is anything to go by, it might be thought that York would offer up a similar wealth of ghost stories, but unfortunately this is not the case. Visual sightings of any relevance are, in fact, virtually non-existent, but, that said, there is some evidence of folk-memories of the siege of 1644. In so far as this is concerned, there are two sites where this is particularly the case, namely the cellars of Ye Old Starre Inn in Stonegate and the courtyard of the King's Manor, both of which are said to ring with the groans and screams of wounded soldiers on account of having been made use of as field hospitals, the Old Starre also being the spot where the city's only Civil War spectre - an important-looking officer dressed in fine clothes and a beaver hat - has made its appearance.[60] To return to the cries of the casualties heard in York, however, these pale into significance alongside a memory of the siege of Hull that is similarly preserved in legend, the story being that, before the construction of the suburbs that now cover the areas concerned, the fields around the town were haunted by the death-cries of wounded soldiers who were abandoned to the rising tide that flooded the Royalist siege works, not to mention skeletal hands seen reaching out of the ground in desperate appeals for help.[61]

It was not just the soldiers who suffered in the wars, of course. Mention has already been made of the terrible outbreak of plague that devastated the area centred on Newark following the surrender of the Royalist garrison in 1646. We come here to the story of Nan Scott, an inhabitant of the village of Holme who was so terrified by the ravages of the dreaded disease among her friends and neighbours that she fled to the village church and barricaded herself into a little chamber in the tower in the hope that she could thereby escape infection. Inevitably enough, after a few days her food and water ran out, and she was therefore compelled to venture out in search of fresh supplies, only to discover that the population had been all but entirely wiped out. Stricken with grief and remorse, she therefore returned to her refuge and shut herself up once more, this time for good, passing away, as she soon did, from thirst or despair. Whether Scott's shade has ever been seen is not recorded, but the story is well remembered while several ghost-hunters have from time to time reported strange noises and other supernatural effects.[62]

To conclude, then, for all the bitter fighting that it saw, the area stretching from Northumberland to Lincolnshire is not the most fruitful when it comes to the study of Civil War ghost stories. That said, the catalogue we have put together in their respect does echo several of the themes visible elsewhere in the country, whether the memory of leading personalities, the plundering of the rougher elements among the soldiery, the vulnerability of women in the face of military turmoil and, last but not least, the trauma inflicted on soldiers and civilians alike. Nor can it be denied that a number of the supposed sightings listed therein suggest very strongly that ghost stories constituted a major way memories of the historical past survived among the populace: for example, though a major action, the battle of East Bolden is all but entirely absent from the standard narratives, and yet not one but two village pubs in the vicinity boast phantom Cavaliers. What begs the question, however, is the manner in which places whose experience of the Civil War was just as traumatic as that of Chester – a good example might be much fought-over Bradford – have so much poorer a legacy when it comes to spectres, this being a query that might just as easily be posed of the region as a whole. Also very odd, meanwhile, is the absence of any Scottish soldiers among the Civil War ghosts of the north-east when their far less prolonged presence west of the Pennines is seemingly well remembered.[63] One argument might be that the industrialisation that gripped the West Riding and other areas was inimical to the survival of such tales, but this is somewhat undermined by the fact that, for all its shipyards and armament works, Newcastle has more Roundhead and Cavalier ghosts than York and that despite the fact that the latter is a city whose dependence on tourism gives considerable economic value to stories of the supernatural as well as one whose built environment might be thought to be conducive to the latter's survival. Nor is the deciding factor necessarily religious: if Lancashire was a stronghold of Catholicism - a faith that might be seen as promoting 'superstition' - in a way that could not be said of anywhere on the other side of the Pennines, the fact that Cheshire had comparatively few recusants did not get in the way of the survival of traditions of hauntings far stronger than those discernable in Yorkshire or Lincolnshire. What we have, then, is something of a mystery, albeit one that goes far beyond the scope of the current work.

Chapter 5

The Midlands

Stretching from Stafford and Derby in the north to the Chilterns in the
east and the Severn valley in the west to the fringes of East Anglia in
the east, the Midlands formed the veritable cockpit of the English Civil
Wars: indeed, it is probably the case that no other region had so continuous and
intense an experience of the conflicts of the era.[1] Thus, both the very first and
the very last serious military action in their long and complex narrative took
place at Worcester, while no fewer than four of their most important battles
- Worcester, Edgehill, Cropredy Bridge and Naseby - were fought within its
borders. Meanwhile, of the handful of towns in the country that experienced
the horrors of a sack, two of them - Birmingham and Leicester - were Midland
settlements. And, finally, when the king raised his standard, it was at Nottingham,
just as it was at Oxford, a city that was to experience a long and bitter siege, that
he established his wartime capital. In short, sadly for its inhabitants, the heart of
England became the heart of war, a fact that, as we shall see, is reflected in the
many ghost stories it was to generate.

As with other parts of the country, when war broke out the Midlands were
deeply divided. As might be expected, the manufacturing centres of Birmingham,
Coventry, Derby, Nottingham and Leicester were solidly Parliamentarian in
sympathy, while Oxford might have followed their lead had it not been for the
preponderant position enjoyed by its university. The gentry, however, were deeply
split with Lords Grey of Groby, Grey of Wark, Willoughby of Parham, Brooke
- the owner of Warwick Castle - and Saye and Sele and the powerful and well-
connected Hampden family of Buckinghamshire favouring the Parliamentarians
(something that in this last case was hardly surprising in view of the key role that
its most important member, John Hampden, had played in the opposition to King
Charles before 1642), and the equally important Hastings, Byron and Compton
coteries staying loyal to the throne. Very soon, then, the region was being drawn
upon by both sides for troops, while on 23 August, just one day after King

Charles raised his standard at Nottingham, not only did a Parliamentarian force sent from London to secure the region defeat a Royalist party at Southam, but a Royalist one made an unsuccessful attack on Warwick Castle. The troops who took part in these minor clashes being the advanced guards of many others - the Parliamentarians were quickly followed by the army of the Earl of Essex and the Royalists by those of King Charles - after a series of complicated peregrinations, there occurred first a clash at the village of Powicke just south of Worcester on 23 September in which Prince Rupert made an immediate name for himself by routing a Parliamentarian force that had tried to force its way across the River Teme, and then, following a further skirmish at King's Norton when a small force of Royalists collided with some 800 Parliamentarians under Lord Willoughby, exactly a month later, the battle of Edgehill. A classic of its type - both sides arrayed their troops with their cavalry and dragoons on each flank and their infantry and artillery in the centre - this last saw the 25,000 men on the field fight one another to a standstill, while, by the end of the bitter autumn day, losing perhaps one fifth of their strength in dead, wounded and missing.[2]

If neither side had destroyed the other at Edgehill, the battle was nonetheless a strategic success for the king: as the battle had been fought with the two armies reversed in respect to their lines of communication, Essex's failure to break the king meant that he was cut off from his base and London wide open to attack. Though it is far from certain what would have been the result - if the Parliamentarian field army was absent in the Midlands, the capital could still count on the six well-trained and well-equipped infantry regiments of its trained bands - at least in theory, a rapid march on London might have gained the king the decisive victory that had been denied him at Edgehill, but, to the dismay of Prince Rupert, Charles turned aside and instead marched on Oxford with a view to making it his headquarters. The immediate sequel to this choice - the storm of Brentford and the stand-off at Turnham Green will be dealt with elsewhere - but such details are by-the-by: what matters here is rather that the king faced the certainty of a long war and with it a very strong likelihood of defeat: even at the time that Edgehill was fought, it was clear that Parliament could count on the support of not just London, vital as it was, but also that of all of East Anglia and the south-east and much, too, of the south, and with them the richest agricultural areas of the country and the vital iron industry of the Weald. Nor was this the end of it, for the navy had come out against the king almost in its entirety, as had the key ports of Plymouth, Bristol and (as we have seen) Hull.[3]

To write in this fashion is, of course, to argue with the benefit of hindsight: in the winter of 1642 neither King Charles nor his opponents could be certain of what the future would bring, all that was open to them being to continue to wage the war. In the Midlands, this initially meant a bitter struggle for the contested areas in the north and the east of the region. In the wake of Edgehill, much aided by the manner in which the departure of many of the leading local Royalists to join the king's field army had weakened their hold on many localities, the Parliamentarians had been able to go on the offensive and seize Derby and Nottingham, but Charles' cause had also had its successes, friendly garrisons being set up in Worcester, Dudley Castle, Ashby de la Zouch Castle (the seat of the Hastings family and, in particular, its head, the Earl of Huntingdon), Belvoir Castle, Tutbury Castle, Stourton Castle, Hartlebury Castle, Bagworth House, Broughton Hall, Bretby Castle, Hillesden House, Burton-on-Trent, Bewdley, Lichfield and Stafford, the fact that many of these strong-points were to the west and north-west of Birmingham meaning that the king controlled the burgeoning workshops and foundries of the future 'Black Country').[4] In addition, of course, there was the king's new capital of Oxford and the circle of satellite garrisons that surrounded it, the latter including such places as Islip, Banbury and Woodstock. Though the armies of Essex and the king remained in winter quarters, the scene was set for a bitter local struggle in which the initiative initially rested with the Parliamentarians. Even before the first year of hostilities had come to an end, then, Bretby Castle and Burton-on-Trent had fallen to their forces, while the first two months of 1643 saw attacks on Ashby de la Zouch, Stafford and Lichfield. Of these last, the first two remained in the hands of their defenders, but Lichfield was a different story. Here, for want of any better citadel, the garrison had withdrawn into the moated cathedral close. Barricaded inside the medieval buildings of which this last was composed, the badly outnumbered defenders put up a good fight - the commander of the besieging forces, Lord Brooke, was even shot dead at extreme range by a deaf-mute named John Dyott armed with a fine rifled fowling piece - but in the end their assailants proved too strong for them and on 4 March the governor surrendered whereupon the cathedral was subjected to a veritable orgy of destruction. Fresh from his descent on Cirencester (see Chapter 7), Prince Rupert assembled a force to retake the town, the latter being an important link in the line of communications that linked Oxford with the Royalist fastnesses of York and Liverpool. The Parliamentarians being as keen to keep Lichfield as the Royalists were to regain it, the result was a fresh battle. Fought on 19 March, the action was known as Hopton Heath. In brief, the local Royalist commander, Henry Hastings, Lord Loughborough, the second son of the Earl of Huntingdon, was sufficiently heartened by the arrival of Spencer Compton, the Earl of Northampton, with the first of the troops got together by Rupert to launch an attack on the forces of Brooke's replacement, the 2,000 men commanded by Sir John Gell which was all that the Parliamentarians could put together in the first instance. Unknown to them, however, the very day that they chose to move, Gell was reinforced by a detachment of Cheshire troops that had marched to his assistance under Sir William Brereton, and the result was that Hastings and Northampton were held to a bloody draw, the price of which was much increased by the loss of the latter commander, the earl being cut down at the head of a desperate cavalry charge.[5] However, Gell had nonetheless suffered heavy casualties and he was therefore no longer strong enough to keep Lichfield secure and all the more so as Brereton had returned to Cheshire. Closing in on the garrison, which had once more ensconced itself in the cathedral close, on 8 April, Rupert subjected it to a regular siege and took it by assault two weeks later. En route to Lichfield, meanwhile, on 4 April the prince had fallen on the town of Birmingham after a detachment of Gell's men had tried to block his progress at an improvised barricade that had been hastily erected to block the southern approaches to the town at Kemp's Hill. As noted in Chapter 1, this was an episode that at the time gave rise to much controversy and has gone down in the modern historiography as an example of an English Civil War massacre: bursting into the streets, the Royalists are claimed to have cut down men, women and children by the score.[6] Ferocious though the protests of the Parliamentarians were, however, to describe the affair thus is to exaggerate a great deal: the town was ruthlessly plundered, certainly, and some eighty houses burned, while it would be naïve to think that some women were not raped or otherwise sexually assaulted, but few civilians appear to have lost their lives (the most detailed account we have puts the grand total at a mere seventeen, all but two of them men). At the same time, the context of the killing - namely, the active participation of some 300 of the populace armed with cudgels, hammers and pitchforks in the defence of the town, and the determined efforts of the Parliamentarian commander, one Captain Richard Greaves, to continue the struggle even after the Royalists had entered the streets - also have to be taken into account: no more than Bolton, then, was Birmingham Magdeburg.[7] Yet, whatever the truth of the matter, the affair had been a publicity disaster for Prince Rupert, while Brereton inflicted further embarrassment on him by capturing Stafford, Wolverhampton and Tamworth, thereby putting Oxford's communications with Chester and North Wales under serious threat and cutting Lichfield off from Ashby de la Zouch.[8] At length Brereton was checked by Eccleshall Castle, which endured a long siege that was only terminated on 30 August, but by this time fresh trouble had emerged in Cambridgeshire where the spring had seen Oliver Cromwell make his military debut by seizing Peterborough - a place whose authorities were strongly Royalist, but had been left without any sort of garrison - and overcome the defenders of Crowland Abbey near Spalding, an isolated Royalist stronghold whose garrison had been terrorising the area and beaten off several attacks by the local militia.[9]

If Brereton and Cromwell were successful in Staffordshire and Cambridgeshire, the Parliamentarian commander in Gloucestershire, Somerset and Wiltshire, Sir William Waller, was not so fortunate in his endeavours. Thus, fresh from a series of successes that had won him the appellation of 'William the Conqueror', on 29 May he sallied forth from Gloucester, and on the last day of the month appeared before Worcester, which he proceeded to attack, only to be driven off with some loss, his efforts having no other effect than to cause the troops inside to reinforce their defences.[10] At the same time, with Lichfield back in their hands, the Royalists re-established it as one of their chief garrisons in the area. Meanwhile, the importance of such places was emphasised by the march of Henrietta Maria from York to Oxford at the head of her great convoy of munitions. Accompanied by some 3,000 men drawn from Newcastle's army, most of them Lancashiremen who had escaped the disaster at Whalley, the queen first moved south to Newark, where she was joined by a further contingent of horse and foot under Sir Charles Cavendish. Striking west along the north bank of the Trent to confuse the Parliamentarians, the 'she-generalissima' as she laughingly now referred to herself seized Nottingham, whose garrison gave up the place without a fight in favour of retiring into the castle, and then on 2 July took Burton by storm, in which action Sir Thomas Tyldesley distinguished himself by leading a cavalry charge across the long bridge that provided the only direct access to the town.[11] With the Trent behind her and Burton secured for the Royalist cause by the establishment of a garrison, next stop for the queen was Stratford-upon-Avon where she was at length reunited with her husband, the latter having marched north to meet her from Oxford.[12]

For much of the rest of 1643, the heart of the Midlands remained quiet. However, in the summer there was a sudden flare-up on the frontiers of East Anglia. Departing from Newark, a force of 1,000 Royalists headed by the most prominent Royalist among the Cambridgeshire gentry, Lord Camden, made to attack Peterborough, only to be driven off by the local Parliamentarian commander in a skirmish that took place at the village of Millfield on 19 July. Left with no option but to beat a hasty retreat, Camden sought refuge at Burghley House, but Cromwell was hot on his heels and forced him to surrender on 26 July after the briefest of sieges.[13] Hardly had this matter been settled than the Eastern Association faced fresh problems. In brief, from one side of Parliament's territory to the other, taxation to meet the cost of the war effort was proving ever more burdensome, and, as we saw in Chapter 4, in August, whipped up by a clique of secret Royalists headed by Sir Hamon L'Estrange, the Norfolk town of King's Lynn rose in revolt in protest. An important port as it was, the place could in theory have been an important gain for the Royalist cause, but, with the Marquis of Newcastle currently preoccupied with his attempt to take Hull and the Newark garrison humbled by the defeat of Lord Camden, there were no troops available to succour it, the result being that the Earl of Manchester was left free to besiege L'Estrange, who put up a brave defence for a month before laying down his arms on 16 September.[14]

Needless to say, the lull in the Midlands-proper did not last. On the contrary, late in the year there was a flurry of minor activity that saw the Royalists take Leek and, albeit very briefly, Newport Pagnell (for reasons that are not quite clear, this last was evacuated after just a week), and their opponents Bagworth House in Leicestershire, Grafton Hall in Northamptonshire, Coughton Court in Warwickshire and Tong Castle in Staffordshire.[15] Further east, too, the Earl of Newcastle marched south into Derbyshire and Nottinghamshire and cleared most of both counties of Parliamentarian strongholds other than their respective capitals.[16] Confronted by the Scottish threat to Northumberland and Durham (see below), Newcastle soon headed north again, but the Parliamentarians in the area were not yet out of danger. The marquis had left behind garrisons at Wingfield Manor, Welbeck House and Staveley Castle, while the Newark garrison was also as aggressive as ever. On 10 January, then, a Parliamentarian convoy was almost taken in a fierce fight near the family home of the Royalist Byrons at Newstead Abbey while a week later the Royalists mounted an attack on Nottingham. Arriving before the town on 16 January, they drove in the troops that had been sent out to contest their passage by the governor, Colonel John Hutchinson, but the latter rallied the survivors in the castle, in which he endured a brief siege before driving the Royalists away by means of a surprise attack that caused them to flee in disorder.[17] It soon became clear, meanwhile, that Puritan Birmingham had not been remotely cowed by its sack at the hands of Prince Rupert, its inhabitants rather being bent on revenge. In the early autumn, then, a prosperous local iron-founder called John Fox, who had earlier in the war served as a captain under Lord Brooke, seized Edgebaston House, then the home of a prominent local recusant, and set up a garrison for which he quickly obtained many recruits from the surrounding district. By the turn of the year, the Parliamentarian commander, who was clearly an enterprising individual, went on the offensive, first of all taking nearby Aston Hall, whose owner, Sir Thomas Holte, had just requested the protection of a company of Royalist troops, and then launching a series of raids on such Royalist bases as Bewdley and Bromsgrove and even storming Stourton Castle, the latter promptly being turned into a fresh Parliamentarian garrison.[18]

Thoroughly outraged, the Royalists responded by claiming, quite unfairly, that the low-born Fox was a mere tinker, an accusation that has hung around his neck in much of the historiography ever since, and, not just that, but a glorified bandit bent on enriching himself from the plunder of the countryside, but, in reality, the Parliamentarian commander was little more than a nuisance; indeed, such were his depredations - very real, if motivated not by greed, but rather the fact that until the summer of 1644 he had no authority to engage in formal requisitioning - that he may even have alienated many inhabitants of the region who were otherwise favourable to the cause of Parliament. Nor was he able to make good his gains: in late March, Stourton Castle was retaken after a short siege, an attempt on the part of Fox to retake it being routed with much loss at Stourbridge Heath.[19] There were, true, more lasting successes elsewhere such as the capture of Biddulph House in Staffordshire after a month's siege on 16 February and the taking by storm of Hillesden House in northern Buckinghamshire a month later, but far more dangerous to the king were rather the main Parliamentarian field armies.[20] Having been firmly beaten at Market Drayton by Prince Rupert, who had been sent from Oxford to remedy the damage done by the defeat at Nantwich, on 4 March, the forces in Shropshire and Staffordshire under Sir Thomas Mytton and the Earl of Denbigh were no threat.[21] However, with the Royalist threat to southern England firmly smashed by the Parliamentarian triumph at Cheriton on 29 March, the victor of that battle, Sir William Waller, was ordered to join up with the army of the Earl of Essex and threaten Oxford. Had the two Parliamentarian commanders co-operated with one another in the manner that was intended, this might have caused Charles serious difficulties, for Prince Rupert, of course, was by now far away in Lancashire with considerable numbers of men who might otherwise have been available for service further south. Indeed, even as it was, the king was almost trapped in Oxford, an outcome that could easily have led to an immediate end to the war, there being no Royalist army either close or large enough to relieve the city, the magazines of which were in addition in no condition to sustain a siege. In the event, Charles slipped out of the trap with his cavalry and an improvised force of mounted musketeers, with hours to spare, but Oxford, and, with it, the bulk of the king's infantry, was still ripe for the picking. Alternatively, it would have been possible to mask Oxford and march in pursuit of the king, and all the more so as the latter's escape was barred by the troops of the Earl of Denbigh, who, having previously taken Rushall Hall, was currently engaged in the siege of Dudley Castle. Yet victory remained as elusive as ever, the fact that this was so being entirely the work of the Parliamentarian leadership in London. As we shall see, on 20 April the Royalist forces in the west had besieged the tiny Dorset fishing port of Lyme. In and of itself, the place was of little military value, but the defenders put up a gallant fight and therefore quickly became the darlings of the London news-sheets. Faced by strident demands that something should be done to rescue them, the Committee of Both Kingdoms therefore sent orders to Essex and Waller, directing the latter to march to the relief of Lyme, while the former pressed on with the campaign against the king. Detesting one another as they did (since the beginning of the year, they had been engaged in a series of bitter personal disputes whose roots lay, above all, in mutual jealousy), the two generals were all too happy to comply, and very soon they had parted company, the only change that they made to the instructions that they were given being to switch roles, so that it was 'Old Robin', as he was known, who ended up heading for Lyme).[22]

As Civil War strategic blunders go, the decision to send troops to relieve Lyme at this point was one of the greatest magnitude, for, with Prince Rupert absent in the north, the way was open for a victory of such magnitude that the war could have been ended at a stroke, and one can only profess astonishment at the manner in which so great a prize was flung away.[23] That there was no reason to expect that anything untoward might result is true enough: at the time that it issued the fatal order, the Committee of Both Kingdoms had no idea that Charles had escaped from Oxford and appears to have believed that he could be contained in the city by Essex's forces alone. This was not unreasonable as an expectation – had the king indeed been bottled up in his capital, all might yet have been well – but, as well as displaying a lamentable want of strategic insight, the Committee was at the very least risking an embarrassing reverse. Thus, with Charles on the loose at the head of a highly mobile 'flying army' and Parliamentarian numbers in the area reduced by half, it was impossible to maintain control of the situation in the manner that the Committee hoped, the infantry left behind at Oxford therefore having no difficulty in slipping out to join their royal master. Thus reinforced, the king could once more take the initiative, and there followed a cat-and-mouse game in which the rival armies marched relentlessly to and fro in the area between Oxford, Worcester and Stratford-upon-Avon. In this situation, the slightest slip could have led to disaster for either side, but, in the event, it was Waller who came to grief. Thus, much encouraged by the arrival of Denbigh, who had abandoned his operations at Dudley in favour of marching to the sound of the guns, and the capture of the Earl of Northampton's family seat, Compton Wynyates House, after a two-day siege, 'William the Conqueror' was spurred into a foolhardy attempt to break the deadlock. In brief, 28 June found the two armies marching parallel to one another up the valley of the Cherwell near Banbury with the river in between. Seeing that the Royalists had become badly strung out, Waller sought to take advantage of the situation by defeating his opponents in detail. Thus, while part of his army struck across the river via a narrow bridge at the village of Cropredy to split the Royalist army in two, he himself used a ford further south to attack Charles' rear. Good plan though this was, it was not good enough, Waller meeting such fierce resistance that he was brought up short and Charles enabled to concentrate superior numbers against the troops at Cropredy and put them to flight, capturing all their artillery. To put it mildly, it was not a good day for Parliament.[24]

In the wake of Cropredy Bridge, the focus of the Civil War once again shifted away from the Midlands: while Waller fell back on London in utter disorder, Charles marched into the west to settle accounts with Essex. That said, the Midlands were far from quiet, for in August Lord Saye and Sele had advanced from Leicester to besiege Banbury Castle. Held in check though the Parliamentarian commander was by the governor, Sir William Compton, such a threat to Oxford could not be tolerated by the Royalist high command, while further pressure was put on Charles by the fact that Compton put up a particularly sterling fight, beating back not one but two assaults on the breaches that were blown in his stronghold's medieval walls. Increasingly under threat from a new concentration of enemy forces to the south though he was, the king therefore dispatched 1,500 cavalry to relieve Compton under one of the latter's numerous brothers. This was to take a great risk, but, in the end, not only was Banbury saved but also Charles' troops emerged unscathed from the battle that followed at Newbury in October.[25]

Known as the Second Battle of Newbury, this action will be discussed elsewhere, all that needs to be said here being that, other than the fact that Compton Wynyates House remained in the hands of Parliament, the winter of 1644 saw the situation in the Midlands remain very similar to the state that it had been in the autumn of 1643. That all this changed was, of course, the result of the campaign of Naseby. In so far as this was concerned, operations began in April 1645 when Cromwell, now commander of the horse of the newly formed New Model Army, was ordered to strike westwards into the Cotswolds so as to cut off Oxford from Wales and the West Country, the first fruits of this move being the defeat of a Royalist cavalry brigade at Islip. Faced by this advance, the governor of Bletchingdon House, Sir Francis Windebank, surrendered without a fight (a move for which he very shortly paid for with his life: allowed to march for Oxford with all his men, he had no sooner entered the city than, accused of cowardice and dereliction of duty, he was arrested, court-martialled and shot). Moving on, Cromwell then routed a small force of Royalists commanded by Sir Edward Vaughan at Bampton and went on to attack Faringdon, only to be beaten off with some loss by its garrison. Still worse, however, on 3 May he was beaten a mile or two to the north at Radcot Bridge by Sir George Goring, who had come north from his current assignment – as we shall see, the siege of Taunton – at the head of 4,000 cavalry and mounted musketeers.[26] At this point, however, Cromwell's orders changed: much impressed by the fierce defence being put up by the governor of Taunton, Robert Blake, the Committee of Both Kingdoms – effectively the Parliamentarian high command – had in consequence directed the whole of the New Model to march to the town's relief. Turning south, Cromwell therefore joined a Sir Thomas Fairfax rewarded for his successes in the north with the command of the new force at Newbury. Taking the field in his turn in response, King Charles left Oxford and, after much argument with Goring, who had ridden up from Taunton for discussions as to what the Royalists should do next, resolved to take his forces north to preserve Chester from the growing threat represented by the troops of Sir William Brereton, while the western army resumed its attack on Taunton.[27]

Discovering that the king had left Oxford, the Committee of Both Kingdoms sent Fairfax fresh instructions, the Parliamentarian commander now being directed to besiege the Royalist capital, this last having, or so it was thought, been left ripe for the taking (that the garrisons left behind in the wake of Charles' departure were indeed too weak to hold their own is suggested all too clearly by the experience of the town of Evesham, this last falling to a surprise attack mounted by a force of troops from Gloucester on 26 May). In however disgruntled a mood from so much marching and countermarching, the New Model was therefore soon arrayed before Oxford, only for operations against the city to be abandoned almost before they started, though not before it had stormed the Royalist outposts of Boarstall House and Gaunt House. Thus, having marched as far as Market Drayton, Charles discovered that Brereton had retired from the environs of Chester and, at the urging of Prince Rupert, headed eastwards to threaten the Parliamentarian bastion of the East Midlands and East Anglia on the assumption that this would necessarily draw Fairfax and Cromwell away from Oxford. Initial target for the advance, it was decided, would be Leicester, a town that was known to be both ill-fortified and weakly held. Summoned to surrender, however, the governor refused to yield and on 30 May, then, he found himself facing a furious attack that, despite gallant resistance, carried the town in a single night.[28]

The cost of Leicester's resistance was the usual one associated with the capture of a town by storm in that the victorious Royalists subjected the inhabitants to a brutal sack – 'In the ruins of Leicester', remarked Nehemiah Wallington, 'you may behold a large map of misery, the townsmen, from the richest to the poorest, being all of them despoiled of their goods.'[29] – but the bad publicity that this brought was countered by the fact that Oxford was temporarily saved from any predicament it might have been in, first Cromwell and then Fairfax being ordered to head east so as to defend the approaches to London. At this point was taken one of the most crucial decisions of the war. With the New Model Army still many miles to the south, Charles could easily have marched northwards to join the Marquis of Montrose, who, as we have seen, was currently captaining a highly successful rebellion against the regime of the Covenanters, or retired to the Severn valley with a view to linking up with either Goring or the substantial Royalist forces in South Wales. Alternatively, there was always the refuge of Oxford and with it the chance of subjecting the New Model to the attrition and demoralisation consequent upon a major siege. Yet, persuaded by his secretary of state, the foolish and irresponsible George Digby, who was convinced, like many other Royalists, that the new army was at best a slender reed, the king instead elected to take on the New Model at once. To put it mildly, as Prince Rupert, at least, realised, if only because the Royalist army was outnumbered three to two, this was a very risky course of action and one which in the event proved to be disastrous. On 14 June, then, the over-confident Royalists attacked Fairfax near the village of Naseby, only to discover that the 'New Noddle', as they had labelled it, was too strong to over-match. On the right, true, the cavalry under Rupert routed most of their opponents, while the centre saw the veteran Royalist infantry throw the first line of their Parliamentarian counterparts into disorder, but Rupert's men threw away their success by galloping deep into Fairfax's rear with a view to pillaging the latter's baggage train. Still worse, on the right Cromwell routed the horse opposing him and, keeping his 'Ironsides' firmly under control, wheeled left and struck the Royalist infantry in the flank, most of the men concerned promptly laying down their arms. Covered by a sacrificial rearguard, Charles got away, as did most of the Royalist cavalry, but it was nevertheless a crushing defeat and one from which the Royalist cause never recovered.[30]

In exactly the same way as had been the case in the north in the wake of Marston Moor, Naseby led to the collapse of the Royalist position in the Midlands. Strongly held and defended by not only impressive earthern ramparts but also a ring of satellite garrisons, including, most notably, Woodstock, Boarstall House, Faringdon and Wallingford, Oxford was secure, while the king could also still count on plenty of strongholds in the area west of Birmingham, of which the most important by far was Worcester. Lichfield, too, was also still in Royalist hands as were Berkeley Castle, Tutbury Castle, Ashby de la Zouch and Belvoir Castle. Swelled by troops from places further north who had surrendered to the Parliamentarians but been given leave to march to the nearest Royalist stronghold, the garrison of Newark was also making a considerable nuisance of itself by beating up many Parliamentarian quarters and launching raids on such enemy positions as Torksey House, this last being burned to the ground. Yet what Charles no longer had was a field army capable of sustaining his hold on the areas concerned, all that had been salvaged from Naseby being a few thousand increasingly unruly horsemen. With matters in this state, a reckoning could not be long delayed. For a little while, with some exceptions – one such was Berkeley Castle, which was taken on 26 September – the king's garrisons were left undisturbed, for the New Model Army was kept fully employed in its reduction of Goring and the other western Cavaliers, not to mention such other isolated bastions as Basing House. However, beyond hanging on, the king's commanders could achieve little other than raiding the country round about – something that did nothing to endear them to the unfortunate local populace and in November 1645 led to an eruption of revolt in the Evesham area that was not just neutralist but actively pro-Parliamentarian, the insurgents fighting a number of skirmishes with parties of Royalist cavalry and taking part in several of the sieges that charted the eventual end of hostilities in the region.[31] With Goring long since out of the fight (see Chapter 8), the only hope was help from Wales, where the last Royalist general in the field, Sir Jacob Astley, had managed to get together a small field army at the head of which force he duly set out for Oxford. Yet, hardly had the news that the city's deliverance was at hand spread, than it was cruelly dashed, 21 March seeing the troops concerned forced to surrender at Stow-on-the-Wold by the forces of Brereton and Poyntz, these last having been released for operations elsewhere by the fall of Chester (see Chapter 3). With Astley gone, the Midland garrisons had come to the end of their stay of execution. Already one or two had succumbed – February, for example, had seen a Lord Loughborough disgusted with the Royalist cause surrender Ashby de la Zouch without a fight and go into exile[32] – and the others now found themselves facing extinction.

One by one, then, they were summoned to open their gates. Here and there demoralisation or want of resources caused the governors concerned to give up straight away, as was the case with the castles at Tutbury, Dudley and Hartlebury, but others were made of sterner stuff. Besieged as early as January, Banbury was not taken until 6 May, while at Bridgenorth, if the Parliamentarians broke into the town on 31 March, the garrison managed to pull back into the castle where it held out for another three weeks. Among the last places to fall were Lichfield, Oxford and Worcester, of which the first was besieged in late March, the second at the end of April and the third on 21 May, though in no case was any attempt made to storm the defences, the Parliamentarians instead preferring to rely on starvation and, at Lichfield and Worcester, bombardment (where there was fierce fighting, by contrast, was at several of Oxford's satellite garrisons: at Woodstock, for example, the garrison beat off an initial Parliamentarian attempt to storm the walls before being forced to surrender on 26 April). Particularly stoutly defended, Worcester held out till 23 July, and even then only gave up because it was almost completely out of powder. With Oxford and Lichfield already gone, so far as the Midlands were concerned, it was the end of the war, the only crumb of comfort for the Royalists being the fact that Charles himself escaped capture by slipping out of Oxford in disguise and turning himself in to the Scottish army that, as we have seen, was still besieging Newark, his hope being that he would be able to exploit the Covenanters' growing anger and frustration with Parliament and negotiate an alliance.[33]

After so torrid an experience of the years from 1642 to 1646, Midlanders probably felt that they had earned some respite. That being the case, it was but justice that the latter stages of the conflict between king and Parliament had only the most limited impact on their territory. Thus, in 1648 the region witnessed little more than mopping-up operations with the cavalry of the Scottish army that had been so comprehensively worsted at Preston and Winwick being rounded up at Uttoxeter; the Earl of Holland being detained after a short fight at Saint Neots in the wake of his short-lived rising in Surrey (see Chapter 7); and an isolated rising in Cambridgeshire that saw its leader, Michael Hudson, an erstwhile royal chaplain who had accompanied King Charles in his flight from Oxford in 1646, mount a desperate last stand at the fortified manor house of Woodcroft Castle.[34] Things were a little worse in 1651, true, but even then the impact on the Midlands was restricted to one small area alone. Thus, proclaimed by the Scots as their king following the execution of his father on 30 January 1649, the following year the Prince of Wales - now Charles II - had duly repaired to Edinburgh from his refuge in the devotedly loyal Channel Islands. Undeterred by the crushing defeat of the main Covenanter army at Dunbar on 3 September 1650 at the hands of Cromwell, as we have already seen, Charles struck south into England in the hope that this would spark off a Royalist uprising along the lines of the ones that had occurred in 1648. Outsmarting the New Model and its commander, both of them still in Scotland, Charles got as far as Worcester, but there was no sign of the hoped-for English support and on the anniversary of Dunbar Cromwell attacked him from the south and east. Although the battle that followed was fiercely contested, there was no stopping the Parliamentarians, and by dusk they had won the day, leaving Charles no option but to flee into exile via, not least, the famous oak tree at Boscobel. In and around the city, meanwhile, lay some 3,000 Scottish killed or wounded, the 10,000 prisoners subsequently being transported to Barbados as *de facto* slaves. Among the places caught up in the battle, meanwhile, was the self-same Powicke that had seen action in September 1642.[35]

The Civil Wars, then, may justly be said to have started and finished in the Midlands. It had, to put it mildly, been a traumatic nine years, the horrors of Edgehill, Hopton Heath and Naseby having been accompanied by numerous sieges and skirmishes that had been accompanied by much destruction: much of Bridgnorth had been burned to the ground, for example, while the repeated outbreaks of fighting at Lichfield had reduced the cathedral to ruins. And, finally, if Birmingham and Leicester had not been subjected to the wholesale massacres trumpeted in the Parliamentarian news-sheets, this was immaterial, the sack of the two places becoming twin icons of terror notwithstanding. As elsewhere in the country, then, it is no surprise to find that the Midlands afford much material to the collector of ghost stories. Indeed, no fewer than fifty of the region's cities, towns, villages, castles, stately homes and battlefields have been identified as the site of Civil War hauntings. Let us begin here with the usual crop of celebrities and other known individuals. In Oxford, then, the ghost of Charles I is supposed to have been seen both in the Bodleian Library and Christchurch College (his headquarters), in the latter case sometimes with his head and sometimes without, while Saint John's College and the spot in the gardens of Merton College known as Deadman's Walk boast those of, in the first instance, Archbishop Laud, and, in the second, the executed governor of

Bletchingdon House, Sir Francis Windebank (according to a woman who claims to have seen Windebank one evening while walking her dog, the unfortunate man appears standing erect against the college wall with his doublet flung back to bare his chest while staring fixedly at an invisible firing squad); in Worcester the Commandery - the Royalists' headquarters during the battle of 1651 - is haunted by Charles' field commander, the Duke of Hamilton, who, mortally wounded, perished in the building in the wake of the Parliamentarian victory; Elizabeth Washburne, the wife of prominent Worcestershire Royalist John Washburne, is supposed to appear on the pool that is all that is left of the moat at the family's home of Wichenford Court playing a golden harp in a silver boat drawn by four swans; at Bromham, Sir Lewis Dyve, a distinctly swashbuckling Royalist officer sentenced to death for his part in the Second Civil War, who, the very night before he was due to die, escaped his quarters in the Tower of London by dropping down a latrine shaft that overhung the Thames and swimming to safety, mounts guard over his impressive tomb in the village church; at Claydon House in Buckinghamshire, the heroic defender of the royal standard at Edgehill, Sir Edmund Verney, wanders the building searching for the hand that was slashed from his arm still clutching his precious charge; at Dudley Castle, the ruins play host to the Royalist governor, Sir Michael Leveson, a man who made himself so hated among the local inhabitants that his Parliamentarian captors had to protect him from a would-be lynch mob; and, finally, the keep of Bolsover Castle, one of the many homes of the Marquis of Newcastle, is associated with, if not the ghost of that worthy, than at least the scent of his pipe tobacco.[36] Then, too, there are the numerous anonymous ghosts reported from around the region, such as the woman in seventeenth-century clothing who has supposedly been seen at Aston Hall; the Cavaliers seen, in more or-less dramatic circumstances, at Eccleshall Castle, Codnor Castle, Hagley, Halton and East Retford; the groups of Civil War soldiers spotted in the grounds of Bradgate Park (the stately home at Loughborough associated with the childhood of Lady Jane Grey) and on the battlefields of Edgehill and Naseby; the courier claimed to gallop up to the main door of Middleton Hall in Northamptonshire; the spectres who stalk Upton-on-Severn's museum, Lichfield's King's Head public house - in this case, an ever jovial character notwithstanding the fact that he is by tradition the shade of a Royalist soldier mortally wounded in one of the sieges of the cathedral close - Leicester's Guildhall, Northampton's Hind Hotel, Mamble's

Sun and Slipper Inn, Sedgeley's White Lion Inn, Daventry's Wheatsheaf Hotel and Wordsley's Old Cat Inn; the galloping horsemen arrayed in plumed hats and flourishing swords charging an invisible enemy in fields near Worsham; the troop of supposed Parliamentarians seen readying themselves to ford the River Trent at Attenborough, and, last but not least, the duel between a Cavalier and Roundhead fought out in spectral fashion at Youlgreave in Derbyshire.[37] Finally, also belonging in this category are the re-enactments of one action or another in which terrified local residents have suddenly found themselves caught up, the most notable instances of this phenomenon having occurred at Hopton Heath and Grafton Regis, the village adjacent to the Royalist stronghold of Grafton Hall, captured, as we have seen, after a brief siege in December 1643 (this last instance is a rare example of a collective haunting in that the night of the three-hundredth anniversary of the defeat of the garrison was marked by thunderous sounds of battle that were heard across the entire village).[38]

As ever, such tales must be taken with a pinch of salt - we cannot know for certain either that anything really was seen, or, still less, supposing that such was the case, exactly what confronted the observers concerned (a spectre reported as a Cavalier, then, might just as easily be a Roudhead, or, for that matter, a highwayman) while, given the fact that took place in the middle of the Second World War, there is an obvious explanation for the disturbance to which the inhabitants of Grafton Regis were subjected in the form of some unheralded military exercise. What is far more interesting are the stories that either confirm the existence of folk-memories of particular events or hint at the lived experience of the period. Of the former category, although there are other instances - the sound of galloping horses heard in the cathedral close at Lichfield and at the bridge over the River Trent at Swarkstone near Derby that witnessed a minor skirmish in 1643; the noise of a troop of cavalry clattering through New College Lane in Oxford; the tortured screams that emanate from Leicester's Guildhall in testimony, or so it is said, to the sack of the town in 1645; the drum-beats heard at Marston Moretaine in Bedfordshire, seemingly the site of a minor skirmish; the sound of fighting heard at sixteenth-century Sinai Park House on the outskirts of Burton-on-Trent; or the musketry that crashes out at Elvaston Castle near Derby, where a line of bullet holes in the wall of the next-door parish church is maintained to mark the spot where prisoners were executed after the Parliamentarians overcame its Royalist garrison - the majority of these by far relate to Edgehill.[39] Associated with spectral activity almost from the very time of the battle, the area crops up again and again in anthologies of ghost stories. In the middle of the nineteenth century, then, an army was seen one night drawn up on the summit of the great ridge that had formed the Royalists' initial position, while in 1947 and 1950 there were reports of a ghostly white horse being seen at night by soldiers stationed at the military depot at Kineton, the charger in question supposedly being engaged in an endless search for its dead master, an officer named Henry Kingsmill who was buried in the church at Radway, where his tomb and effigy may still be seen, other men having claimed to have heard the sounds of a great battle while on sentry duty after dark. Clearly linked to the battle, too, are the stories from the nearby village of Lighthorne of phantom women lamenting the deaths of their menfolk and of a barn that is perpetually stained with the blood of wounded soldiers. And, finally, there is the case of the Anchor Inn at Warwick, this last being haunted by the ghost of its 1642 landlord, a man put on trial for looting the dead of Edgehill who was promptly swept off to Hell in the most dramatic of fashions by the Devil when he brazenly denied the charges that had been made against him.[40]

With this last tale, we come to the most interesting category of ghost story, namely those that reflect episodes touching upon the human experience of war (if the story of the landlord of the Anchor being taken down to the infernal regions by Satan himself is something that may well be doubted, it is perfectly plausible that he did go out to the battlefield to strip it of whatever he could and even that he experienced a sudden demise that was put down to punishment for his sins). As ever, the most important sub-group in the category concerned are those that relate to the sufferings and misuse of women. From Oxford, then, we hear of Prudence Bostock, a young girl deserted by her Royalist lover who haunts Magpie Lane, and from Kings Norton of the ghost of a maid-servant of Queen Henrietta-Maria's who died of illness contracted in her duties during the queen's stay in the village while en route to join her husband at Oxford in the summer of 1643 that has traditionally been identified as the 'in-dwell' of the Saracen's Head public house (originally a substantial private dwelling dating from the late fifteenth century).[41] Then, too, we have Hanborough's 'Old Mother Scalpepper' (actually one Mistress Jane Culpepper), an unfortunate woman who according to legend was murdered by some soldiers in the vicinity of the village and thrown in a convenient pond, the most recent report that we have of her speaking of a dripping-wet figure whose face is disfigured by terrible wounds.[42] Also guaranteed to inspire pathos are stories hinting at youthful heroism, of which good examples are those concerning Broughton Hall, the home of Parliamentarian elder statesman Lord Saye and Sele, which is haunted by the ghost of a young boy who is said to have been shot by a Roundhead soldier for shouting, 'God save the king!' after the place was retaken from the Royalist troops who had seized it some time previously, and the Three Tuns Hotel at Sutton Coldfield (reputedly the oldest building in the town) whose cellar is reputedly haunted either by - accounts differ! - a Royalist drummer murdered by Roundhead troops in cold blood, or a young Royalist soldier who was put in the pillory by the Parliamentarians and died in the course of his punishment, possibly because he was struck on the head by a stone (there is no reason to believe, as some versions have it, that he was literally stoned to death).[43] In this category, too, belong the region's two Second Civil War ghosts, namely, the Earl of Holland, who haunts Saint Neot's New Inn, the building in which he made his last stand before being taken prisoner and conveyed to London for execution, and Michael Hudson, who, according to legend, was killed in particularly brutal fashion by the Parliamentarian troops who broke into his refuge of Woodcroft Castle (fleeing to the battlements with his triumphant enemies in hot pursuit, he tried to save himself by climbing through a crenellation and clinging to the stonework outside, only to have both his arms severed by sword thrusts - hence the fact that his ghost has no hands - and fall to the ground where he was finished off by a blow from a musket butt).[44]

Like the haunting of the Reindeer Inn in Banbury by an unknown soldier who was hung in front of the building in 1644, all these stories speak of folk-memory while at the same time mirroring themes that we have already seen emerging from other parts of the country.[45] One such is, of course, the image of the Cavalier. In so far as this is concerned, one side of the coin is revealed by the apparition from Lichfield we have already encountered: though mortally wounded, the man concerned is unfailingly friendly and convivial, the very picture, indeed, of the gallant, not to say devil-may-care, attitude associated with the followers of King Charles.[46] Another such figure is the ghost of the village of Kempsey, a small place beside the River Severn on the old Bath road. A Royalist cavalryman named Fitzwilliam, it seems that the individual concerned was a dashing blade who in the war had enjoyed the favours of many women including one of the maidens of said parish. Finding himself back at Worcester in consequence of the campaign of 1651, he decided to seek the girl out once more and again succeeded in getting her into bed. Unfortunately, however, she had since wed no other than the village blacksmith, a choleric giant of a man who proceeded to catch the couple *in flagrante delicto*. Snatching his clothes, Fitzwilliam dropped out of the window onto the saddle of his horse, which was waiting below, but ruptured himself in the process. Screaming in agony, he galloped from the village in the direction of the Royalist camp, only to fall dead within a few minutes, the area having ever since been haunted by the hoof-beats of his terrified steed, while there are those who claim to have actually seen the spectre of horse and rider.[47]

If the tale of another womanising Cavalier is required, we can return to Royalist Oxford. As already noted, the more the fighting went on, the more the city became crammed with displaced supporters of King Charles, including, not least, the families of many officers fighting in his armies. Among the women and children concerned was one Mary Bayning, who was the wife of Sir William Villiers, Viscount Grandison. No more than a girl - she was but 14 when she wedded said nobleman in 1639 - Bayning found herself trapped in crowded lodgings in Jesus College, and, as is normal enough among bored and lonely women forsaken by their husbands in time of war, at some point acquired a lover. Who this gallant was is not recorded, but, returning to Oxford after being badly wounded at the storm of Bristol, Grandison discovered what had been going on, and promptly challenged the man to a duel. In doing so, however, the viscount had overestimated his strength, and, in the sword fight that followed in the garden of the college in which his wife was lodged, either collapsed from the effect of the wounds he had suffered at Bristol or was run through by his opponent. Duelling (though widespread) being prohibited by the ordinances of the Royalist army, the body was then secretly buried beneath the lawn, an act of impiety that, or so it is said, condemned the spectre of Grandison's killer to return again and again to search for the corpse in the hope of securing it Christian burial (the ghost is always seen digging holes in the garden, holes that, of course, have always disappeared by the next morning).[48]

If such was the obverse of how the 'King's shilling' was remembered, what was the reverse? In brief, tragedy and pathos. Over and over again, then, Cavaliers are lonely figures viewed in a fashion that is distinctly wistful, if not downright mournful (one of the few exceptions is the brutal Sir Michael Leveson). In Sutton

Coldfield, then, the gallopping hoof-beats heard in Yew Tree Walk are claimed to mark the passage of a lone Royalist desperately trying to outdistance his Parliamentarian pursuers; at Prior's Court, a half-timbered farm-house dating from around 1500 situated a mile or more south-east of the much fought-over village of Powicke, we hear of a fugitive Royalist who died in the building and was given a secret burial in a chimney; in various houses in a modern development on the outskirts of Droitwich, a Cavalier has seemingly appeared in people's living-rooms looking bewildered and lost; the 'in-dwell' of Bromsgrove's Ye Olde Black Cross is supposed to be a soldier left behind by his regiment who is forever engaged in a forlorn search for his erstwhile comrades; the Northamptonshire village of Marston Trussel is supposedly haunted by the ghosts of a group of Royalists cut down while trying to escape the disaster at Naseby, the place where they died being commemorated, as we have seen, by the name 'Slaughter Field'; and, finally, at Pavenham, a lane near the village is frequented by the ghost of a Royalist fugitive who was killed attempting to escape the Parliamentarian pursuers who were hounding him.[49]

The Cavalier, then, emerges from the ghost stories as an attractive figure, someone who was either a likeable rogue or an object of respect and pity as men who had sacrificed themselves for a lost cause. Not surprisingly, this is not true of their opponents. In this respect, we have already heard of a trooper shooting dead an innocent boy, of a Royalist drummer being put to death in cold blood, of a Royalist soldier who was supposedly stoned to death by his captors, and finally of the merciless treatment meted out to Michael Hudson at Woodcroft Castle.[50] However, pride of place in this litany of infamy should probably be occupied by the infamous Captain Thomas Bound, a truly dark figure who is seen roaming the village of Upton-on-Severn on his horse. A native of the place, Bound served as an officer in the Parliamentarian forces, and, whether unhinged by the horrors of war, an extreme misogynist or simply an out-and-out psychopath, he is subsequently said to have murdered two wives in succession, eventually committing suicide by drowning himself in the Severn. The only problem, of course, is that we do not know if Bound really was a Parliamentarian: as we shall see, it cannot but be suspected that there is a strong tradition of demonising the Roundheads by turning damaging stories that were actually told about their opponents against them.[51]

To conclude, then, much fought over as they were, the Midlands have more than their fair share of Civil War ghosts, while the stories that we have reviewed reflect much the same themes as we have seen in other places and, above all, suggest a society that was deeply traumatised. Furthermore, in almost every case, the places supposed to be marked by hauntings really were the site of Civil War activity, much of it little known or even completely forgotten. To quote one of the leading works on the subject, 'Yes, people invent sensational stories to attract attention. Yes witnesses often do not understand what they have seen, do not recall it properly, or filter their recall through aspects of their personalities. Even so, there are witnesses aplenty, and [one] must decide for [oneself] if every one of them is fraudulent or mistaken.'[52]

Chapter 6

The Severn Valley

However England is divided up for discussion in studies of this nature, there will always be judgements that are open to debate. Thus, in the case of *The English Civil War: Myth, Legend and Popular Memory* in particular, we have already seen Cheshire included in the chapter on the north-west and Yorkshire and, not just that, but parts of Derbyshire, Nottinghamshire and Lincolnshire in that on the north-east. The reasons for these changes are invariably rooted in the military narrative, but, as each decision is taken, others that make less sense are forced upon the author. This is particularly the case when it comes to the broad strip of territory stretching from the mouth of the River Severn to that of the River Dee. Definable as the Marches and composed of the counties of Gloucestershire, Herefordshire, Shropshire, Worcestershire and Cheshire, the area concerned can easily be justified as justifying a chapter in its own right, and yet Cheshire fits in far more closely with Lancashire than it does with Shropshire, while much of Worcestershire is difficult to exclude from a discussion on the Midlands. What one is left with is therefore a somewhat truncated affair consisting only of the first three counties on the list and parts of the fourth (essentially, the capital and the districts west of the Severn). What is left, however, is still a substantial slice of territory that enjoys a certain geographical unity, as well as one that was of great strategic importance on account of the major north-south artery of communication represented by the Severn and the various east-west routes that crossed the region and linked Wales with the rest of the country. Meanwhile, the area was thickly populated, garnished with the cathedral cities of Gloucester and Worcester and possessed of both the important woollen industry of southern Gloucestershire and the vital mineral deposits of the Forest of Dean, by 1642 a centre of the iron industry that was rivalled only by that of the Sussex Weald. And, finally, as if all this was not enough, just a few miles away lay Wales, for most of the war a bastion of the Royalist cause except in distant Pembrokeshire and, not just this, but King Charles' safest and most dependable source of manpower. If the area saw much fighting, then, it can scarcely have come as a surprise.[1]

As in many other parts of England, the population, and, more especially, the gentry, of the Severn Valley were anything but avid for war. That said, they could not remain apart from it, and the result was that by the autumn of 1642 both sides had been able to gather improvised forces of troops and establish *de facto* zones of control. In the north, due in part to the fact that there were particularly large numbers of recusants among the leading families, Shropshire was solidly Royalist, the Parliamentarians being confined to the eastern and north-eastern fringes of the county and the isolated stronghold of Hopton Castle in the extreme south (so unconcerned was the local leadership that it did not even raise a garrison for the county town).[2] At the other end of the Severn Corridor, by contrast, the situation was very different, the city of Gloucester, the Forest of Dean, and the whole of the southern part of the county around Stroud, Tewkesbury and Cirencester all being strongly Parliamentarian. As to why this should have been so, Puritanism having made great strides among the people and the propertied classes alike, part of the answer was religious, but there was also a degree of social conflict (in the Forest of Dean in particular, support for Parliament was fuelled by the pronounced royalism of Sir James Winter, a notorious recusant who had spent the last ten years or more trying to enforce a royal monopoly that gave him the sole rights to the area's timber and mineral wealth).[3] In between, the town of Hereford had been seized by the Parliamentarians, but much of the countryside bar a few strongholds such as Brampton Bryan, the country seat of radical Puritan Sir Robert Harley, was Royalist, as was the whole of Worcestershire west of the Severn, together with the county town.[4] That said, like much of the rest of the country, the fact that one side or the other was militarily dominant in a particular area did not mean that the population were wholly loyal to the cause concerned: If Shrewsbury and Worcester were both secured for the king in the Edgehill campaign, then, their inhabitants were in many cases staunchly Puritan and therefore extremely unhappy at the course events had taken. Only in a few instances, indeed, can we be certain that élite support for the Crown coincided with popular feeling, one such being Ludlow, a place that had been hard hit by the Long Parliament's recent abolition of the Council of the Marches of Wales, an important regional agency of the royal prerogative that had had its seat in the town and thereby brought much trade to its shops and hostelries.[5]

In so far as military operations were concerned, all was quiet. Not a shot was fired in either Shropshire or Gloucestershire for the rest of 1642; in Worcestershire there was a single skirmish at Ludeley; and in Herefordshire the only significant event was the evacuation of the county town by the Parliamentarians in December, the Parliamentarian commander in the west, the Earl of Stamford, having decided that he could not defend so isolated an outpost (plagued by Royalist raids such as the one that ended in a minor skirmish at Pontrylas on 13 November, Stamford was also dispirited by the utter failure of his efforts to augment the small force of troops he had brought with him with local recruits).[6] Nor did the situation get any better: while Stamford, as we shall see, took himself off into Devon to fight the Cornish Royalists, the forces he had been facing had chased their Parliamentarian enemies out of Tewkesbury and the son of the Earl of Worcester, a powerful magnate loyal to the king who was able to exert much control in south-east Wales, Lord Herbert, left free to gather a fresh army west of the Severn. To make matters worse, hardly had 1643 dawned than serious trouble erupted in Wiltshire. Thus, on 2 February, no less a figure than Prince Rupert launched a surprise attack on Cirencester. In fairness to the garrison, the town put up a fierce fight, but within the space of a few hours all resistance was at an end and a column of around 1,000 prisoners setting off on the road to Oxford, the town that they left behind being littered with the bodies of as many as 300 of their comrades and in large part in flames.[7] Faced with an urgent need to defend a Gloucester that was now extremely vulnerable, many of its outlying garrisons having had to be evacuated for want of men to sustain them, the Parliamentarian authorities in London responded by commissioning Sir William Waller to take charge of a relief effort at the head of a new force raised from the resources of the Western Association.[8]

A devout Puritan and highly experienced veteran of the Thirty Years' War, Waller had, as we shall, made a name for himself by suppressing Royalist support in Sussex in the autumn of 1642. With typical dynamism, he now headed into the west at the head of two regiments of cavalry, a handful of dragoons and a few small cannon, and marched by means of circuitous route that took him via Winchester, Salisbury, Shaftesbury, Bath as far as Bristol. Having first eliminated a particularly threatening Royalist base that had been established at Malmesbury (see Chapter 8), Waller now headed for Gloucester, Lord Herbert and his levies having emerged from their Welsh fastnesses, defeated a small Parliamentarian force at Coleford and stationed a detachment of 2,000 men commanded by Colonel Jerome Brett just two miles west of the city at Highnam House. Nothing daunted, Waller ordered the garrison to mount a sally against Brett as a feint, while he himself crossed the Severn at Framilode by means of a flotilla of barges and headed west with the aid of taking the Royalists in flank and rear. Fought on 27 March, the subsequent action saw Herbert's troops, the majority of them new levies who appear to have had little enthusiasm for soldiering, taken completely by surprise, and within minutes the whole assembly was throwing down its arms, Waller ending up with a haul of 1,400 prisoners and five field pieces.[9]

Eager to follow up this success, Waller next sent a small force to occupy Tewkesbury, which he believed to have been evacuated by the enemy, while he himself raided Monmouthshire, taking first the county town, then Usk and finally Chepstow. However, these sallies proved less than profitable, Tewkesbury turning out to be held by a strong garrison that quickly saw off Waller's men and Monmouthshire too poor to be able to offer him much in the way of resources, the various places taken by the Parliamentarians therefore soon being evacuated. In Waller's absence in Wales, meanwhile, Rupert's brother, Prince Maurice, had reoccupied Malmesbury, which had been left unoccupied for want of men and crossed the Severn with a view to cutting him off from Gloucester. However, by dint of a mixture of hard marching and good luck, the Parliamentarian commander managed to escape the trap at no other cost than a minor skirmish at Little Dean and even managed to slip a force into Tewkesbury, the troops that had beaten off his first attempt having been drawn out of the town to take part in the operations designed to catch him. Seizing Tewkesbury was an ingenious move, for it threatened to trap Maurice in his turn, but the prince saw the danger and marched hastily upstream to the next crossing, namely the bridge at Upton-on-Severn. Waller being just as well aware of the vital nature of this spot as his Royalist counterpart, at the head of the much diminished force left him by the time he had provided for the defence of Gloucester and Tewkesbury, he hastened to secure it, only to find Maurice's troops filing across the river and taking post in the fields south of the village. It was the early morning of 13 April. In the resultant battle - known as that of Ripple Field - being outnumbered by as many as two-to-one, Waller was badly beaten, but hardly had it been fought than Maurice received orders to rejoin King Charles to march to the relief of Reading, which, as we shall see, had just been besieged by the Earl of Essex. For the time being, then, the lower Severn Valley was secure, Waller even being able to march on the weakly held town of Hereford and intimidate its distinctly unimpressive governor into surrender.[10]

As we have seen, Waller was to go on to push his luck still further by means of an unsuccessful assault on Worcester, albeit at the cost of abandoning Hereford for want of troops to form a garrison.[11] However, for the time being, our attention must shift to the northern part of the region. Thus, boosted by their successes in Staffordshire and Cheshire, the forces of Sir William Brereton had taken the offensive in Shropshire and on 30 May stormed Whitchurch whose defenders, commanded by Sir Michael Woodhouse, were worsted after a fierce struggle.[12] At the other end of the county, meanwhile, the more than somewhat lacklustre local Royalists got together a field force under the governor of Hereford, Sir William Vavasour, and moved against isolated Brampton Bryan, only for the defenders to defy them under the leadership of Sir Robert Harley's wife, Lady Brilliana Harley, and hold out against a somewhat desultory siege that lasted from the end of July until the middle of September when it was at length abandoned (not that Lady Harley lived for very long to enjoy her triumph, very soon falling sick and dying of what may have been pleurisy).[13]

What saved Brampton Bryan were the momentous events taking place around Gloucester. Following the fall of Bristol in July (see Chapter 8), the Royalist armies of King Charles and Sir Ralph Hopton had marched on Gloucester, this last being rightly seen as a key target, commanding, as it did, both the lower Severn Valley and the main road into the southern parts of Wales. Anxious to spare the lives of their troops – losses at Bristol had been extremely heavy – the Royalist commanders elected to besiege the city, only to find that their operations were stymied by continuous rain that flooded their batteries and trenches. Meanwhile, assailed though they were by enemy mortars that hurled shells and incendiary devices over the walls every night, the populace rallied to the support of the young governor, Sir Edward Massey, and even under heavy fire laboured to make good the damage to the walls caused by the incessant Royalist bombardment. Left to itself, Gloucester would doubtless have fallen, but this proved anything but the case. On the contrary, in distant London, energised by the constant press reports lauding the courage of the defenders and only too well aware of Gloucester's strategic importance, the Parliamentarian leadership ordered the Earl of Essex to march to relieve Massey. Strengthened by a part of the London

Trained Bands, 'Old Robin', as he was known, duly set out to march west through the continuous rain, and on 8 September he arrived before the walls, the Royalists having in the meantime abandoned their works and withdrawn for some miles to the north; the siege, then, had lasted just one month. Meanwhile, by saving Gloucester, the Parliamentarians had also saved Brampton Bryan, news of the approach of the relief force having persuaded King Charles to send a messenger to Vavasour ordering him to bring all the troops he could spare to his support.[14]

In the wake of the relief of Gloucester, the Marches reverted to the petty warfare of the preceding months, and that but slowly. In Shropshire, as we saw in Chapter 3, the autumn of 1643 saw minor actions at Loppington and Wem, and in Gloucestershire Vavasour occupied Tewkesbury, while Massey launched a series of raids such as one that culminated in a small group of Royalist troops being besieged in the parish church of Taynton, but otherwise all was quiet. Not until the first weeks of 1644 did matters become more serious. Thus, in the interval since their salvation at the hands of the Earl of Essex, the defenders of Brampton Bryan had repaired their defences and established a satellite garrison at nearby Hopton Castle, a near derelict Norman stronghold. Thus provoked – the new Parliamentarian post was but five miles away – the Royalist governor of Ludlow, a newly arrived veteran of the war in Ireland named Sir Michael Woodhouse, decided to eliminate the challenge it represented, however vestigial (the defenders numbered just thirty-one men). As soon as the weather permitted, then, Woodhouse marched on the castle. Summoned to surrender, the governor, one Samuel More, returned a defiant answer and beat off an initial assault, only for Woodhouse to return a few days later with a much larger force. Two more summonses having been rejected, the Parliamentarian commander set about digging a mine beneath the walls, and this threat at last persuaded his opponent to sue for peace. As was perfectly within his rights according to the common practice of the period, the most that Woodhouse was prepared to offer was quarter for More himself and what amounted to a promise to spare the lives of the garrison in the first instance pending a decision on their fate. Hoping, perhaps, that there was a chance that his men would be shown mercy, on 13 March More duly surrendered, but in the event the result was far grimmer than he seems to have anticipated, Woodhouse in effect letting loose his soldiers on the Royalist rank and file to use them as they would. The men concerned being hardened veterans of the Irish conflict who were well aware of both how they were viewed in England as Irishmen (real or not) and their likely fate were they to be taken prisoner themselves, what followed was all too predictable. Thus, the twenty-nine men who had survived the siege were stripped of everything they possessed and then driven into a cellar beneath their quarters, the building then being fired over their heads. There were no survivors, but the incident can scarcely be regarded as an atrocity: More had held out in the face of no fewer than three offers of peace-terms, and Woodhouse probably acted as he did to discourage further acts of such defiance elsewhere.[15]

Cited over and over again in works wishing to portray the fighting of 1642–51 as an 'uncivil war' though it is, the fate of the garrison of Hopton Castle was very much an exception. Certainly, for all that he had shown himself to be a hard man, Woodhouse did not engage in the same behaviour when he moved on to Brampton Bryan shortly afterwards. Now led by one Nathaniel Wright, the defenders showed much spirit when the Ludlow troops appeared before their walls in early April, launching a successful sally that killed a number of the men engaged in digging siege-works, and refusing to be cowed by the heavy bombardment unleashed on them by Woodhouse, but, when they surrendered on terms after two weeks, the Royalist commander honoured his word to the letter. Meanwhile, their courage had not gone unrequited, for so many troops had been drawn in to deal with Brampton Bryan that Massey had been enabled to take the offensive at the head of the garrison of Gloucester, temporarily occupying Ledbury and Ross-on-Wye, storming Wilton Castle and threatening Hereford with a third occupation. This last place having been provided with a new governor in the person of the commander of a regiment newly arrived from Ireland, namely Nicholas Mynne, the Royalists succeeded in stabilising the situation, but, unfortunately for them, Mynne revealed himself to be distinctly over-ambitious, if not vain-glorious Thus, not content with sending troops to occupy Tewkesbury, a place that had always proved impossible to defend and was in fact promptly stormed by Massey, in July he launched a raid that almost reached as far as Gloucester, the only result of which was a Parliamentarian counter-stroke that routed his forces near the village of Redmarley and left him dead on the field along with 130 of his men.[16]

Meanwhile, a certain amount of fighting had also been taking place in Shropshire. On 28 December, Sir Thomas Mytton took Tong Castle, but March saw the Royalists strike back under no less a figure than Prince Rupert, Mytton being defeated at Market Drayton and Lillehall, ejected from Longford, Apley and Tong Castle, and forced to evacuate various small garrisons. Yet, being desperately needed for service elsewhere and, more especially the relief of York, Rupert could not remain in the area for long, and in his absence the pendulum swung back towards the Parliamentarians. Thus, on 23 June a force headed by the Earl of Denbigh captured Oswestry. Determined to retake the town, the nearest Royalist commander, Sir Fulke Huncke, immediately besieged it at the head of 2,000 men, but on 2 July he was beaten by a relief force led by Mytton. Encouraged by their success, Denbigh and Mytton then marched on Shrewsbury and on 4 July attempted to assault the town. Posted in the enclosures that spread in all directions beyond the walls, however, the garrison fought hard, progress being so limited that the end of the day saw the Parliamentarian commanders withdraw.[17]

The Parliamentarian offensive in Herefordshire having exhausted its momentum after the action at Redmarley, Mynne's forces were rallied at Hereford and the situation stabilised by the new governor, Barnabas Scudamore. However, the Royalists' travails in the region were anything but at an end. On the frontiers of Wales there were garrisons loyal to the king at Monmouth, Pembridge Castle, Newport and Chepstow, but in early September the first of these places was taken by Massey with the aid of a turncoat officer of the forces holding the town, a development that quickly prompted the surrender of the governor of Pembridge. Once again, however, want of men undermined initial success. Eager to make the most of their good fortune, the Parliamentarians resolved on the siege of Chepstow, but to do this they had to leave Monmouth in the hands of the weakest of garrisons, the result being that the Royalists were able to launch a counter-attack that had by the end of November given them back control of not just Monmouth but also Pembridge.[18]

Broadly speaking, then, so far as the Marches were concerned, 1644 can be seen to have ended in stalemate, the fact being that neither side were strong enough to prevail against the other. That said, the successes of Sir Thomas Mytton in northern Shropshire, and still more so the Royalist defeat at Montgomery in August (see Chapter 3) were hardly encouraging for the supporters of King Charles, while across the region there were clear signs that the populace were increasingly hostile to taxation, impressment and requisitioning: indeed, the winter of 1644-45 saw the emergence of 'club-men' movements in

Herefordshire, western Worcestershire and Shropshire alike. Of these, by far the most radical was the one that gripped the first of the three counties concerned. Thus, following the appearance of a number of manifestos demanding an end to requisitioning and the imposition of extra-legal authorities, foraging parties were chased away from various villages by angry crowds, while there were a number of tumultuous assemblies that were put down by force, something that only increased the general resentment.[19] In February 1645, meanwhile, there came a massive hammer-blow. In July 1644, as we have seen, the garrison of Shrewsbury had put up a good fight when it was attacked by the combined forces of Denbigh and Mytton, but the winter seems to have sapped its watchfulness, matters being compounded still further when Prince Rupert arrived in the town and drew out considerable numbers of men for service with the Royalist field army that he was putting together in the Midlands. Well aware of the situation in the town, on 22 February Mytton therefore launched a surprise attack and quickly gained entry in the face of little more than token resistance, the defenders promptly laying down their arms in exchange for terms that allowed them to retire to Ledbury (all, that is, other than thirteen men who were hanged on the grounds that they were Irish).[20]

Between them, the battle of Montgomery and the loss of Shrewsbury spelled the beginning of the end for the Royalist cause in the Marches. With the area denuded of large numbers of troops for field operations, there was little that the local leaders could do other than hang on to such garrisons as they still retained and effect the occasional relief operation. In Shropshire, then, the spring and summer of 1645 saw a serious defeat at Winstantow and the surrender of Royalist garrisons, many of them without much in the way of resistance, at Leigh Hall, Longner, Atcham, Madeley, Caus Castle, Stokesay Castle, Broncroft Castle, Tong Castle and Rowton Castle, the only bright spot in the situation being the fact that at High Ercall a Parliamentarian force that had embarked on a siege was defeated with heavy losses.[21] Further south, 22 April saw Prince Rupert drive a force of Parliamentarians led by Massey that had occupied Ledbury from the town in confusion, only for Royalist control of Herefordshire to be threatened by a far more dangerous foe in the shape of the Earl of Leven's Scottish army, this last having traversed Worcestershire and invaded the county from the east. Pushing westwards, the Scots, who were 10,000 strong, stormed a Royalist outpost at Canon Frome and then closed in on the capital, siege operations opening against this last on 30 July. Overwhelmingly outnumbered though he was, the governor, still Barnabas Scudamore, remained defiant, and the result was a five-week siege in which serious damage was inflicted on the city by bombardment. Food, however, was adequate, while the Scots, by contrast, experienced serious want and rapidly declined in spirit and discipline alike. What would have happened in the end is therefore open to question, but in the event, matters were settled by the appearance across the Severn of a large force of Royalist cavalry. The Scottish horse having been left behind when Leven marched on Herefordshire, Leven therefore abandoned the siege post-haste, thereby opening the way for the new arrivals to enter the town.[22] To the delight of many of the more loyal inhabitants, the column that rode in through the gates was headed by none other than a Charles I currently on the march for the final disaster that awaited him at Rowton Heath. That he was in the area at all was, of course, the work of the battle of Naseby, but this was the limit of the favour that said battle conveyed on Marcher Royalism. Elsewhere, by contrast, the triumph of the New Model Army had merely given rise to fresh misfortunes. Thus, in the summer further Parliamentarian attacks deprived the Royalists of the Shropshire garrisons at Dawley Castle and Lillehall Abbey, while on the borders of Wales October saw first Chepstow and then Monmouth fall to the Parliamentarians. In November a second siege of High Ercall eliminated a positon that had caused the king's enemies much trouble, and, finally, on 18 December Hereford fell to a carefully planned surprise attack headed by Colonel John Birch, a young officer eager for glory who had been charged with the task of doing what he could to distress the garrison. By the turn of the year, then, all that was left was Ludlow, Goodrich Castle and one or two fortified country houses such as Madresfield Court near Malvern. That being the case, it looked as if the struggle was all but over, but in fact there yet remained one last campaign to be endured. Thus, having laboriously put together a force of 3,000 men at Worcester, Sir Jacob Astley, the highly experienced professional soldier who had commanded the infantry of Charles' main field army, went on the offensive in the hope of drawing sufficient manpower from the Midland garrisons to put together a force big enough to confront the New Model Army. However, brave and competent though he was, Astley could not work miracles, 21 March seeing the Parliamentarian forces catch up with his troops at Stow-on-the Wold and force them to lay down their arms after a sharp fight on the rolling slopes north of the town, a philosophical Astley wearily telling his captors that they had done their work and could now go play unless it chanced that they fell out among themselves.[23]

There followed the usual mopping-up operations: Ludlow was taken after a month-long siege on 31 May; besieged as early as January 1646, Madresfield was temporarily saved when the Parliamentarian forces surrounding it drew off to join the operations against Astley, only finally surrendering when the garrison received news of the fall of Worcester; and, admittedly not assailed till June, Goodrich Castle held out until 31 July, by which time the walls were so battered that there was no hope of further resistance.[24]

Such, then, was the Marches' experience of the Wars of the Three Kingdoms (mercifully enough, the region was spared any involvement in the further outbreaks of fighting in 1648 and 1651). With the exception of the Gloucester campaign, the operations to which it played host had been relatively small in scale, while there had been relatively few battles or even skirmishes. That said, for the inhabitants, life was little easier than it was for their counterparts anywhere else. As Atkin writes of Worcestershire, for example, by 1646, it was 'a county worn out by the exactions of a war that few had sought or wished to participate in'.[25] And, in the same vein we have Bracher and Emmett's comments in respect of Shropshire. Thus: 'The war had a massive impact on civilians and touched the majority of people's lives in one way or another.'[26] In consequence, it is scarcely to be expected that the region should be free of Civil War ghost stories, true though it is that there seem to be rather fewer of them than is the case elsewhere. Let us begin with the trauma inspired by exposure to violence. Relatively limited though this last phenomenon may have been, in a number of places its memory was carried over to the supernatural, one such case being in Littledean Hall, Gloucestershire, the spot where two Royalist colonels named Wigmore and Congreve were killed when the house was stormed by the Parliamentarians reputedly being marked by bloodstains that could not be eradicated no matter how often they were scrubbed away. Also remembered in this fashion are the men slaughtered in cold blood at Hopton Castle; the spirits of Woodhouse's victims supposedly returning to the site of their deaths on each anniversary of their demise, and the casualties of Stow-on-the-Wold, where the King's Arms still resounds to the cries of the Royalist wounded who were carried there for assistance; and a group of Parliamentarian soldiers who died near the village of Aust in the vicinity of the present-day Severn Bridges when the boatman ferrying them across the river mistakenly put them ashore on a sand-bank that was promptly overwhelmed by the rising tide, their screams for help ringing out across the water to this day.[27] And, finally, along with a number of other ghosts, the Gloucestershire village of Prestbury boasts a headless horseman reputed to have been a Royalist courier killed by a Parliamentarian patrol who gallops down Mill Street before vanishing into thin air (in other versions of the story, the scene of the haunting is Shaw Green Lane and the manifestation no spectre as such, but rather just the clattering of hooves), and Shrewsbury's Dun Cow Inn a figure identified as a Dutch mercenary executed for murdering a fellow soldier.[28]

Next, perhaps, come those spectres that suggest no more than the memory of a time when the Marches swarmed with armed men. In Shrewsbury for example, a Civil War soldier was spotted in the Lion Hotel in the early morning one day in the 1990s, a team of ghost-hunters who later checked out the place reporting cold spots and strange lights; at the Shropshire village of Chatwall the lanes are roamed by a mounted Cavalier, while in Gloucestershire we have the cases of an area of high ground named Freezing Hill near the village of Wick that has on occasion played host to groups of Civil War soldiers; the old court-house in the village of Painswick, Charles I's headquarters during the siege of Gloucester, which is said to be haunted by both the ghost of the monarch himself and large bodies of men seen arming for battle; the headless horseman in seventeenth-century costume that haunts Woodchester Park near Nympsfield; the Civil War soldier who startles drivers at Broadwell by stepping out in front of them and then vanishing; and, finally, the spectral Cavaliers associated with Cirencester's King's Head and Fleece Inn, Stow-on-the-Wolds' aptly named Royalist Hotel and the district of Gloucester known as the Dukeries.[29]

Last but not least, we have the most interesting category of ghost story of all, namely that which commemorates particular individuals, the examples that we have from the Marches all being suitably dramatic. First of all, then, there is the case of Wilderhope Manor: situated near Church Stretton, this sixteenth-century building is haunted by the ghost of its Royalist owner, a major named Thomas Smallman, who, pursued by a troop of Parliamentarians, made his escape by riding his horse over the precipitous scarp slope of Wenlock Edge at a place known ever since as Major's Leap.[30] Smallman, it seems, made good his escape, but the protagonists of another Shropshire tale were infinitely less fortunate. According to tradition, then, the battlements of Goodrich Castle are haunted by the ghosts of a Royalist officer named Charles Clifford and his lover, Alice Birch, supposedly the daughter of the local Parliamentarian commander, John Birch: caught in the castle when it was besieged in 1646, the pair made a daring escape on horseback one stormy night, only to be drowned while attempting to swim the River Wye.[31] Just as unfortunate, meanwhile, were two Gloucestershire lovers named Roger and Beatrice, of whom the first was a veteran of the Royalist army and the second a member of a distinctly Parliamentarian household: in true Romeo-and-Juliet style, the two fell in love, only for Beatrice's two brothers, both of whom had fought for Parliament, to take great offence at the situation and lure her lover into an ambush on Dover Hill so as to murder him; utterly bereft, Beatrice promptly lost her wits, and died of grief, her ghost thereafter haunting the site of the murder, this last duly becoming known as 'White Lady's Gate'.[32] And, last but not least, we have Sherborne House, the country residence of John Dutton, a Gloucestershire gentleman elected to Parliament for the county in 1625 and 1640 who had been noted for his opposition to King Charles during the eleven years of the latter's personal rule, and yet nonetheless declared for the king, at least in some eyes a piece of treachery and one which, or legend has it, resulted in a curse condemning Dutton to haunt his ancestral home for all eternity.[33]

As we have seen, the Cavalier emerges from the ghost stories as an attractive figure, someone who was either a likeable rogue or an object of respect and pity as men who had sacrificed themselves for a lost cause. Not surprisingly, this is not true of their opponents. In this respect we have already met the infamous Captain Thomas Bound on his horse. A native of the place, Bound served as an officer in the Parliamentarian forces, and, whether a man unhinged by the horrors of war, an extreme misogynist or simply an out-and-out psychopath, he is subsequently said to have murdered two wives in succession, eventually committing suicide by drowning himself in the Severn.[34] To this epitome of the brutal Roundhead, meanwhile, can be added the ghost of Shropshire's Moreton Corbett Castle, a Puritan preacher who, notwithstanding its support for Parliament, was expelled by the family that possessed it on account of the extremity of his ranting, and avenged himself by cursing the site to eternal devastation.[35]

To return to the tale of Thomas Bound, the two women reputed to have been murdered at his hands have a significance all of their own in that they may be said to stand proxy for the strong theme we have seen elsewhere represented by the mistreatment of women that was commonplace in seventeenth-century society. As it happens, the Marches are bereft of stories of this sort that are explicitly linked to the Civil Wars, but Chalford in Gloucestershire does have a tale that has been dated by descriptions of the apparition concerned as relating to the Stuart period. In brief, then, a young milk-maid was seduced by one of her master's sons, only for the latter to get her pregnant and then abandon her to her fate, whereupon the unfortunate girl hung herself: last known to have been seen by some RAF aircrew in the Second World War, her spectre stands forlornly waiting for the faithless lover to appear at a particular stile outside the village.[36]

Relatively few in numbers though they are, then, the Civil War ghost stories of Gloucestershire, Herefordshire and Shropshire are redolent of many of the same themes that we have encountered elsewhere, as well as one or two others that are also relevant to the Civil War, including, most notably, the religious divisions underlying the conflict (one thinks here of the tale of the curse pronounced on Moreton Corbett Castle). That this is so is not to be wondered at, for the struggle was a constant presence, and one that bore hard upon the unfortunate inhabitants. Perhaps because many people in the Marches saw relatively few soldiers, there are relatively few reports of the latter's ghosts, but, for all that, memories of the days of Cavaliers and Roundheads must have been uniformly grim. Not for nothing, then, did John Wroughton call the book in which he discussed the experiences of Gloucester *An Unhappy Civil War.*

Chapter 7

The South-East

With the exception of East Anglia, no part of the country escaped the direct effects of war more lightly than the south-east of England (here defined as London and the Home Counties, i.e. Kent, Surrey, Sussex, Hampshire, Berkshire, Middlesex, Hertfordshire and Essex). Nevertheless, fighting did flare up from to time even in areas that otherwise saw little action – in Middlesex in 1642; in Sussex in 1642 and 1643; and in Surrey, Kent and Essex in 1648 – while Berkshire and Hampshire alike witnessed episodes of conflict that were far more sustained. Meanwhile, none of the inhabitants escaped the ravages of conscription, taxation and billeting, the result being that the wars of 1642-51 had much the same psychological impact as they did elsewhere. The economy, too, was hard hit. 'Such are the deadness of the times ... that much land lies waste, and none will use any but at very low rents', complained one report from Sussex.[1] As witness the petitions for assistance submitted to the courts in the years after the guns fell silent, the region therefore played host to much human misery: to name but three cases of misfortune that have come down to us from Hampshire, there was the father of three who had lost the use of his left hand in the service of the Parliamentarians and was left with no means of supporting his family; the sometime apprentice weaver who had been pressed into the Royalist forces, deserted to their opponents and served out the wars in the latter's service, only to find when he finally returned home that his master no longer had a place for him; and the goodwife of Andover who had lost her husband in battle and then been plundered of all her goods 'and was now like to perish for want of food and to be turned out of door naked'.[2] Nor was cultural disruption any less than it was anywhere else. 'All my ledger register books were taken away', lamented the clerk to the Chapter of Winchester cathedral, '[and] the records, charters, deeds ... and muniments lost... Divers of the writings ... were burned, divers thrown into the river; [and] divers large parchments ... made kites withal to fly into the air.'[3] When the Second Civil War was submerged by what appears to have been one of the worst summers in living memory, Hampshire Royalist Sir John Oglander was therefore probably far from alone in attributing the deluge to Divine displeasure. Thus:

> I conceive the Heavens were offended with us for our offence committed to one another, for, from Mayday to the fifteenth of September, we had scarce three dry days together ... As for the earth, it is turned almost to water. The rivers in the main have overflowed all the neighbouring fields, the rich vales stand knee-deep in water, and, with the current, much corn is carried away and haycocks [left] swimming up and down ... God mend all: first let us repent our bloody sins, [and] then we shall find His mercy.[4]

Across the region there had certainly been as much blood shed as there now fell rain. Indeed, even before Edgehill had been fought, the south-east was witnessing regular military operations. Broadly speaking, with Puritanism strongly entrenched in their ranks, both the gentry and the common people favoured the cause of Parliament. In so far as the former were concerned, we might cite the case of Hampshire's twenty-six Members of Parliament, of whom nineteen were Parliamentarian as opposed to just seven Royalist, while, if harder to quantify, the attitude of the latter is suggested by the enormous difficulty the party of the Sussex gentry who declared for the king in 1642 found in obtaining recruits (one of the abiding myths of the Civil War is that the yeoman class invariably followed the lead of the gentlemen whose land they farmed, the fact being that in reality there are dozens of examples where this was not the case).[5] In Kent, meanwhile, the petition presented to Parliament in March 1642 by a number of local gentry accusing Pym and his fellows of exercising arbitrary power and demanding that they reach a settlement with the king not only woke little in the way of a military echo in the months thereafter but also was quickly answered by a counter-petition that boasted some 6,000 signatures.[6]

From all this it follows that, across the region, it was infinitely easier for the everywhere more numerous supporters of Parliament to raise troops, the result being that there was never any chance that the Royalist cause would prevail. Had substantial help arrived from outside, it is possible that matters might have played out differently, but nothing of the sort occurred. In the wake of the battle of Edgehill, true, King Charles marched on London with his field army and on

12 November Prince Rupert destroyed two infantry regiments that were holding the town of Brentford in a struggle that left much of the place in ruins.[7] However, nothing came of this success. Reaching the then country village of Turnham Green, the Royalist army found its way blocked by the forces of the Earl of Essex, which had fallen back on the capital by a circuitous route; the 15,000-strong London Trained Bands, the strongest and best equipped example of its type in the entire country; and an enthusiastic mass of ordinary citizens armed with whatever weapons they could lay their hands on (much energised by the political confrontations that had preceded the war, London was overwhelmingly Parliamentarian in its sympathy, the Royalist 'fifth column' that it continued to harbour within its walls never being able to achieve anything of any note). After a day-long stand-off, the king therefore fell back on Kingston and its important bridge. From here, of course, he could have marched into Surrey and onwards into Sussex or Hampshire at will, but such a march would have exposed his base at Oxford to the risk of capture, and so after six days of indecision, he fell back the way he had come, thereby leaving his supporters south of the Thames exposed to retribution.[8]

Even as it was, Parliament had already been on the offensive in the south. Perhaps inevitably given its importance as a fortress, naval base and magazine, the first flashpoint was Portsmouth. In the summer of July 1642, the governor was Sir George Goring, a professional soldier of some ability who was also a prominent member of the local gentry and one of Hampshire's Members of Parliament. Over the past two years he had initially sided with the opposition to the king, but, like many others, had decided to change sides, albeit for no other reason than sheer opportunism, and on 2 August he duly declared for the Royalists. This move, however, soon proved to be a serious error of judgement, for no help proved forthcoming from the surrounding area whereas the Parliamentarians were quickly able to mobilise a scratch force of infantry and cavalry under the command of Sir William Waller and put Portsmouth under siege. To arrest the progress of his assailants, Goring launched a series of night-time raids, but the resultant skirmishes made little difference, while the morale of his motley garrison declined by the day, many of its members seeking refuge in desertion. Still worse, a Royalist attempt to secure the nearby Isle of Wight in which Goring had placed much hope collapsed after a few skirmishes and a brief siege of Carisbrooke Castle. In this situation, the end could not be long postponed, and, when the Tudor artillery fort of Southsea Castle was taken by a surprise attack on the night of 3 September, the Royalist commander sued for peace, the town being handed over to Waller four days later.[9]

With Portsmouth back in the hands of the Parliamentarians and Southampton already held by them, the focus of attention switched to Winchester. Held by local Royalist Member of Parliament, Sir William Ogle, the county town had at first evaded punishment, but in early to mid-December the peace its garrison were enjoying was shattered by the arrival in the area of a Royalist cavalry brigade commanded by Lord Grandison that had been raised in northern Hampshire and just participated in the sack of Marlborough (see Chapter 8), and was now retreating on its home territory. In hot pursuit was Waller, who had heard of Grandison's approach while engaged in the task of suppressing a small Royalist garrison that had been established at Farnham Castle and marched west to deal with him. Apparently believing that Waller was in lesser strength than was actually the case, Ogle sent the bulk of his garrison to aid Grandison, but the only result was a serious defeat at Wherwell on 12 December, the Parliamentarian commander following this up that same day with an assault on the town that was delivered with such vigour that the remaining defenders were overcome and forced to surrender (among the few to escape the disaster was Grandison himself, the peer, as we have seen, dying in Oxford a year later as a result of the wounds he sustained at the siege of Gloucester).[10]

Having crushed the Hampshire Parliamentarians, Waller moved on Sussex. Here the county town, Chichester, had initially fallen into the hands of the Parliamentarians, but the local Royalists had not remained inactive, and on 15 November a large party of gentry and their retainers headed by the High Sheriff, Sir Edward Ford, rode through the gates and chased out the enemy leaders. This done, Ford then sought to march on Lewes with the small band of cavalry and pressed country-folk that was the limit of his command, only to encounter a Parliamentarian force at Haywards Heath and be driven from the field in rout. Though most of the Royalists escaped to Chichester, Ford was in serious trouble, for Waller was literally at the gates. Having first seized Arundel Castle, where a small force of Royalists had established a garrison, the Parliamentarian commander closed in on the capital with 6,000 men. Operations to take the place began on 21 December, and within a few days, albeit not without a fierce fight, the 800 defenders had been driven from the suburbs and penned up inside the medieval walls. Threatened with an imminent storm, Ford realised that further resistance was futile, and on 28 December he duly laid down his arms, whereupon Waller and his men took control of the town, the cathedral being subjected to a violent episode of iconoclasm in the process.[11]

With London, Middlesex, Hertfordshire, Essex, Kent, Surrey and Sussex all unequivocally Parliamentarian, across the whole of the south-east of England only in Hampshire was there anywhere that still held out for the king outside the southern-most outposts of the Royalist capital at Oxford. We come here to the great palace of Old Basing, a Norman castle just outside the town of Basingstoke on to which had been grafted a splendid Tudor residence. Though deeply Catholic, its owner, the Marquis of Winchester, would from choice probably have stayed neutral, but his religion rendered him instantly suspect to the leaders of the Hampshire Parliamentarians, and so bullying and aggressive was their behaviour that in December he declared for the king. For the moment, he was left alone, Waller having been called away for the purpose of the operations in the Severn Valley we have discussed in Chapter 6, but the honest truth was that the existence of a Royalist garrison in Old Basing mattered not a whit in terms of the strategic situation. With the exception of Brentford and Turnham Green, the initial fighting in the south-east has not much figured in accounts of the Civil Wars, and yet it was absolutely crucial to their outcome, there being good reason to argue that, without the agricultural wealth of what was, after all, the most productive region of the country, the iron industry of the Weald and, *a fortiori*, the incalculable financial and commercial resources of the city of London, the Royalist war effort was doomed.

As 1643 dawned, however, this was anything but obvious, and so the Parliamentarian leadership was far from complacent. Quartered for the winter in a variety of garrisons in Berkshire and southern Oxfordshire, the formidable fighting force represented by the main Royalist army was still within striking distance of London, and it is therefore no surprise to find that the chief focus of the fighting in the south-east now shifted to the Thames Valley. The army of the Earl of Essex had spent the winter in the area centred on Windsor, and, after an initial probe of the Royalist positions that led to a minor skirmish at Brill, in April it duly sallied forth to strike a blow at the most accessible part of Charles' array, namely the four regiments of infantry and one of cavalry that had been posted to hold the town of Reading. Why this position had been assigned a garrison other than, perhaps, for reasons of prestige, is unclear, for it was not only very close to Essex's army but also cut off from the rest of the Royalist forces by the River Thames, positioned, as it was, on the southern bank of that waterway. Defences, of course, had been flung up over the winter in the form of the usual earthen rampart, but the governor, Sir Arthur Aston, was overly contemptuous of his opponents and does not appear to have made as good a job of the fortifications as might have been the case. Nor, meanwhile, was he a commander capable of getting the best out of his men, all accounts speaking of him as a deeply unpleasant character whose notorious Catholicism only made things worse. At all events, with food short too, when Essex closed in on the defences on 16 April, Royalist resistance was at best flaccid. Much alarmed, Charles and a Prince Rupert freshly returned from reducing Lichfield mounted a relief effort, but they were unable to pass the narrow bridge that carried the road from Oxford across the Thames at Caversham, while the garrison, now led by Aston's deputy, Sir Richard Fielding, Aston himself having been badly injured when a Parliamentarian cannonball struck his headquarters, had already entered into surrender negotiations by the time the relief force arrived, and therefore refrained from making any move to assist their would-be rescuers. On 27 April, then, Reading surrendered on terms that in the circumstances were extremely generous – Fielding and his men had merely to evacuate the town – not that this saved the unfortunate Royalist commander from facing a court-martial when he got back to Oxford on the (distinctly unfair) grounds of cowardice.[12]

Essex's army having been struck during the siege by a serious epidemic of typhus, the fall of Reading was followed by a lull in operations that allowed the Royalists to seize the initiative by mounting several large-scale cavalry raids, one of which led to the only substantial action of the summer, namely the clash at Chalgrove that led to the death of John Hampden, the close connection of Oliver Cromwell, who, next to John Pym, had been the leading figure in the opposition to Charles I before the outbreak of war.[13] Beyond that, however, all was quiet until September when, his army much reinforced, not least by five regiments of the London Trained Bands, Essex set out to relieve Gloucester, which, as we have seen, had been put under siege by King Charles and Prince Rupert. The resultant campaign soon taking 'Old Robin' out of the area, its results have already been recounted, but matters did not end with the rescue of Massey and his garrison. On the contrary, the attempted return of the Parliamentarian army to London produced the region's first major battle. Determined to avenge themselves on Essex, Charles and Rupert set off in hot pursuit, and, having slowed the Parliamentarian army by a spoiling attack at Aldbourne Chase, got across its path by occupying a ridge of high ground just south of the important strategic town of Newbury from which it was separated by the River Kennet. What followed was a bloody struggle that saw Essex's troops make desperate efforts to cut a way through the Royalist forces in the face of repeated enemy counter-attacks. By the end of the fighting – 19 September – the combined casualty-toll had reached around 3,000 men, but the king had clearly had the better of the day, for his army was still not only intact but also firmly ensconced in the same positions that it had occupied at the start of the day. Unfortunately for the Royalists, however, they had too little powder left to continue the fight, and that same night they in consequence slipped across the Kennet and thereby opened the way for Essex to resume his march on London. Charles and his men had not gone far, however, and the Parliamentarians had not made much progress before they were attacked by a substantial force of Royalist cavalry and commanded musketeers on Crookham Common near Aldermarston, the result being a sharp action in which Essex's rearguard was completely routed and his army only saved from complete defeat by a desperate stand on the part of two regiments of the London Trained Bands.[14]

As we shall see, situated, as it was, at the point where the main road from London to the west crossed the equally important highway from, ultimately, Manchester to Southampton via Birmingham and Oxford, Newbury had yet to have its fill of action in the Civil Wars, not the least reason for this being that, in the wake of the departure of Essex's army, the king established a garrison of some 200 men in Donnington Castle, a compact fourteenth-century stronghold on a ridge a little way to the north-west of the town. For the moment, however, the attention of the combatants once again switched to the counties further to the south and east. In brief, in line with what seems to have been a decision to abjure further operations in the Thames Valley in favour of a strategy based on clearing the whole of the south and west of Parliamentarians so as to open up the counties concerned to Royalist recruitment and taxation, while Prince Maurice was detached at the head of one force to deal with the defiant Parliamentarian strongholds of Lyme, Exeter and Plymouth (see Chapter 8), Sir Ralph Hopton (now ennobled as Lord Hopton) was given another and charged with an offensive into Hampshire and Sussex. At best, however, Hopton had no more than 3,500 men, while his attempt to recruit more troops was short-circuited by the arrival of news that a party of local Royalists led by the same Sir William Ogle who had headed the cause of King Charles in the area the previous year had taken the garrison of Winchester by surprise and bluffed it into surrendering the town. To explain this event, we have to take the situation in Hampshire back to the beginning of the year. In brief, although the Parliamentarians had established themselves in firm control of the eastern half of the county, its northern and western fringes had continued to be troubled by Royalist raiding – in mid-February, for example, Prince Rupert had swooped down on Alton in an attempt to seize a convoy of artillery pieces and ammunition wagons moving westwards from Farnham, only to be frustrated in a sharp action in the streets of the town by the 200-strong advance-guard of the convoy's escort – while the county was rendered still more vulnerable by Waller's departure, the only troops available for service within its borders other than the Trained Bands being a single regiment of cavalry and two small regiments of infantry. Nor was this paltry garrison well-led, the local Parliamentarian commander, Sir Richard Norton, proving singularly ineffectual, as witness the repulse of an ill-starred attempt on his part to seize a still very weakly held Basing House at the end of July. So far was the Marquis of Winchester from being overawed by Norton that, end though the episode did with a skirmish at Hursley in which the men concerned were routed, on 12 August a party of his soldiers raided the town from which he took his title. With Royalist cavalry commanded by the Earl of Crawford active in the New Forest, it is scarcely surprising that Ogle should have plucked up the courage to launch his *coup de main*.[15]

Enterprising though Ogle's action may have been, it sparked a chain of events that was ultimately to prove disastrous to the Royalist cause south of the Thames in that Hopton was left with no option but to send troops to support him and thus embark on offensive operations well before he was in a state to do so. To make matters worse, instead of keeping his army concentrated at Winchester, he rather allowed it to become spread out across a wide spread a wide spread of territory to the north and west, embracing not just Winchester but Alton, Andover and Salisbury. However, for the time being he was spared misfortune. Despite the fact, as we shall see, that his western endeavours had ended in defeat and humiliation, Waller had returned to the scene as commander of a new army whose role was to defend the southern approaches of London from a Royalist cause that was clearly in the ascendant, but, instead of heading west to deal with Hopton, 'William the Conqueror' chose instead to commence operations by reducing Old Basing. Unfortunately for him, this was now much more of an obstacle than it had been when Norton had attacked it in the summer. Thus, provided with a garrison of regular troops that had been sent from Oxford, it had also been fortified with a ring of imposing ramparts complete with ditches and bastions. On top of that, when Waller marched on Basing from his base at Farnham at the beginning of November, the weather was utterly dismal. Assailed by bitter winds and driving rain, the Parliamentarians launched a major assault on the northern sector of the perimeter on 7 November, only to be driven off with heavy losses after a full day of fierce fighting. A second attempt was made on 12 November, but once again the garrison stood firm, and, with his army much depleted by desertion and increasingly mutinous - in this respect the situation was not helped by the fact that several of the regiments under his command were drawn from the London Trained Bands - Waller was left with no option but to return to Farnham.[16]

While these abortive operations were in train, Hopton had gathered his wits and his army alike, and now, undoubtedly emboldened by the state of disorder so clearly gripping Waller's forces, a belief in which he was reinforced when an attempt to tempt his opponent into giving battle at Odiham on 28 November failed to elicit any response, resolved to obey the somewhat vague orders he had received to push as far eastwards as he could. Starting from Andover, he therefore first marched on Alton, which he garrisoned with the infantry regiment of Sir Richard Bolles and the cavalry brigade of the Earl of Crawford. With his army much diminished, for still other troops had been dispatched to Winchester, Alresford and Petersfield, the Royalist commander pushed eastwards into Sussex and on 8 December seized weakly held Arundel Castle whose eighty-strong garrison surrendered without a fight, the arrival of his forces in the county in the meantime encouraging the local Royalists to take control of Chichester.[17]

As strategic moves went, this advance was little short of suicidal, for Hopton had spread his army out across more than fifty miles of wintry countryside in the presence of an army that, if somewhat battered, was still intact, while being headed by a general who was notorious for his liking for rapid manoeuvre and surprise attacks. Perhaps the king's champion in the south hoped that the winter weather would immobilise Waller, but, if so, he was to be sadly disappointed. Thus, his forces having received substantial reinforcements from Essex's army, on the night of 12 December the latter marched on Alton by a circuitous route and took the defenders completely by surprise. Much to his discredit, Crawford mounted up his cavalry brigade and galloped to safety, but Bolles showed more spirit and put up a fierce fight in defence of the redoubt he had constructed around the parish church, only for him to be killed in the building's very pulpit and most of his men - some 850 - taken prisoner, 500 of whom immediately proceeded to 'turn their coats' and enlist with their erstwhile enemies. Meanwhile, insult was added to injury at the other end of the Royalist line when Norton rode out from Southampton that same day and drove out the troops who were in occupation of Romsey and Twyford.[18]

All this was but the beginning. A few days after surprising Alton, Waller marched on Arundel, drove the garrison from the town and placed the castle under siege. Gathering together all the men he could including a timely reinforcement of cavalry he had just received from Oxford, Hopton rushed to the rescue only to receive a message from the governor, a somewhat vain-glorious individual who appears to have been harbouring hopes of repulsing Waller on his own, that there was no immediate danger. Suspecting that he was probably outnumbered, Hopton paused in the hope that he could bring up some more troops, only to learn to his horror that, ill-provided for and low in morale, the castle had surrendered on 5 January. It was a crushing blow, for the prisoners amounted to another 800 men, many of whom proved just as willing as their counterparts in Alton to take service under Waller.[19]

The weather closing in at this point, both sides went into winter quarters, the guns now falling quiet for a while other than some lively skirmishing around Romsey, this last changing hands several times in the period when the main forces of the two sides remained at rest. Not until mid-March did operations resume. However, with both Hopton and Waller eager to fight a battle that could restore their somewhat battered reputations and reinforced by strong contingents from the king's Oxford army on the one hand and the forces of the Earl of Essex on the other, after that action became fast and furious. Thus, pushing into Hampshire in the direction of Winchester, Waller was challenged by his Royalist counterpart near the small town of Alresford, and there immediately followed the clash that became known as the Battle of Cheriton. Fought on 29 March 1644, this was a hard fight, but at the end of the day it was Hopton who found himself outmatched, and so, at length, he withdrew from the field and retired on Oxford.

Fortunately for him, however, Waller made no further efforts to seek battle and instead concentrated on clearing Hampshire of any remaining Royalists, the latter being driven from Romsey and Christchurch and also deprived of the outpost they had established at the Bishop of Winchester's residence at Bishop Waltham by dint of a three-day siege.[20]

By the end of April, all that remained to the Royalists was Winchester and Basing House, but major operations in the county now came to a halt on account of Waller's embarkation on the campaign that led to the Battle of Cropredy Bridge.[21] However, this did not mean that all was quiet. On the contrary, the garrisons of Donnington Castle and Basing House continued to make a serious nuisance of themselves, launching a series of raids that on occasion took them far afield. Thus provoked, the Parliamentarian Southern Association therefore assembled such forces as it could under the Sussex colonel, Herbert Morley, and in mid-June placed the Marquis of Winchester under siege once more. For some time, however, not least because of want of numbers, the peer's assailants limited their activities to a loose blockade, the result being that the garrison was able to persist with its raids. Only in mid-July did operations begin in earnest, and even then the defenders stood firm, launching repeated sorties, maintaining a heavy fire from the ramparts and even hurling stinking lumps of rotten meat at the Parliamentarians, while remaining defiant in the teeth of an increasingly heavy bombardment from cannon and mortars alike. To make matters worse, meanwhile, left all but unwatched, the garrison of Winchester became ever more emboldened, sending out raiding parties of its own far and wide. Gradually, however, exhaustion, disease and want of food combined to wear down the defenders, and, with desertions mounting by the day, it appeared that they might yet be overcome. In the event, however, a 1,000-strong relief force was scraped together from the various garrisons around Oxford around the nucleus of 300 men who had been released for service in the field by the surrender after a determined defence of a Royalist outpost at Greenland House near Henley. Commanded by a particularly energetic officer named Henry Gage, the relief column travelled by night and reached the vicinity of Basing House early in the morning of 11 September at the cost of a brief skirmish at Aldermaston. Appraised by fugitives of the Royalist approach, Morley drew up his men on Chineham Down to stave them off, and there followed a fierce little action fought out amid thick fog that eventually saw Gage drive Morley from the field and break through to the defenders, the latter having in the meantime sallied out and attacked the Parliamentarians in the rear. Basing House, then, was relieved, while Gage proceeded to add further laurels to his triumph by slipping back to Oxford without incident under cover of a further fog.[22]

With the local Parliamentarians in complete disarray, the fighting in Hampshire once more receded into the low-key business of raiding and requisitioning, the next area to experience full-scale military campaigning being rather Berkshire. Thus, in August Donnington Castle had been subjected to an unsuccessful attempt at escalade, while in the middle of September it was put under siege by forces dispatched from southern Oxfordshire, only, with its walls comprehensively breached, to be reprieved certain capture by the arrival of King Charles and his main field army in the wake of their triumphs in the Lostwithiel campaign (see Chapter 8).[23] In response, the forces of Waller and Manchester, which had been concentrated in the area west and north-west of London, together with such men who had been retrieved from the debris of Essex's beaten troops, made a concerted effort to bring the king to bay, the latter having not only lingered at Newbury but also weakened his forces by deciding to detach the Earl of Northumberland to the relief of hard-pressed Banbury. Hearing of this move, the three Parliamentarian commanders spotted a chance to catch Charles at a disadvantage, and within a short time 19,000 men were therefore bearing down on the mere 10,000 that was all that could be mustered to face them. Fought on 27 October, the resultant battle should by every right have been a disaster for the Royalist cause, for Charles was not only outnumbered by a factor of nearly two-to-one but also cut off from his base at Oxford, while he had also opted to take up a position on the north bank of the River Kennet rather than retiring to the infinitely preferable ground that he could have occupied on the further side. Yet the day did not go well for the Parliamentarians, the latter not only dissipating their fighting power by adopting a plan of attack that was unnecessarily complex, but also failing to set aside the rivalries that best their high command, of which the most important was the mutual loathing that separated the Earl of Manchester from his deputy, Oliver Cromwell (in some recent accounts, it is this last that is given the chief responsibility for the failure of the subsequent battle, it being argued that Cromwell deliberately held his forces back from fully participating in the action so as to discredit Manchester and thereby weaken the position of the Presbyterian party in the Commons). Nor did it help that, for all the lack of wisdom in fighting on the north bank of the Kennet, the Royalists had the benefit of good defensive positions, while their left flank was protected by the guns of Donnington Castle. After a day of fierce fighting, then, Charles' army was still intact, while the king proceeded to drive home the failure of his opponents by escaping with his forces to Oxford during the night.[24]

For all the disappointment of its results, the bungled fight at Newbury had consequences for the Parliamentarian cause that were massively positive in that it provided the impulse necessary to secure the passage of the Self-Denying Ordinance and the creation of the New Model Army. As we have seen, dramatic developments happened elsewhere in the wake of these developments, but, so far as the south-east was concerned, all was quiet other than the continual raiding of the garrisons of Basing House and Winchester. Thus, never more than a loose blockade after Gage's relief effort, the siege of the former was abandoned, while the Parliamentarians withdrew into winter quarters. In December, true, some excitement was elicited by the sudden appearance of Goring from the West Country at the head of a substantial force of cavalry, but, while he skirmished with Parliamentarian outposts at Crondall and Odiham, and demonstrated against both Farnham and Portsmouth, without infantry or guns he could achieve nothing concrete and soon rode away to head the Royalist army in the West. In the wake of his departure Waller pushed into the east of the county and occupied Alton and Petersfield, while Norton and Ogle engaged in some petty skirmishing in the Romsey area, but serious fighting there was none.[25]

What changed this situation, of course, was the Battle of Naseby. With the main Royalist army out of the picture, the Committee of Both Kingdoms was free to turn its attention to the more minor but nevertheless persistent nuisances represented by such places as Basing House. On 10 August, then, a force of local troops appeared before the defenders' positions and commenced siege operations. Progress, however, was very slow, and in late September it was resolved to reinforce the troops concerned with a detachment of the New Model Army under Cromwell. For reasons that are not quite clear, however, the future Lord Protector initially resolved to march not on Basing, but on Winchester. Arriving before the walls on 28 September, the next day he stormed the town. Fleeing into the castle, the defenders essayed defiance, only to be quickly placed under heavy bombardment. A particularly stubborn officer, Ogle hit back with a sortie into the streets, but this was repelled after fierce fighting, while a wide breach was effected

The Bluebell Inn, Chester; now no longer a tavern but a tapas bar, it is associated with the story of Henrietta, a young girl who hung herself in the cellar after her soldier-lover died in battle (author's collection).

The battlefield of Nantwich; fought on 26 January, 1644, the battle and the siege it brought to a close are remembered by a number of hauntings in and around the town (author's collection).

Hermitage Green Lane, Winwick; the site of bitter fighting in the last stand of the Duke of Hamilton's infantry following the Battle of Preston, the lane is rather remembered for the Scottish soldiers who were reputedly hung from the trees which overhang it after the battle was over. (author's collection).

Cromwell's Plump, an isolated clump of trees on the skyline of the Parliamentarian position at Marston Moor that is generally held to mark the spot from which Fairfax, Leven and Cromwell launched their attack on the forces of Prince Rupert (author's collection).

The blast of war: damage from the sieges of 1644 and 1645-46 is still visible in the surviving walls of Newark Castle (author's collection).

The church of Saint Giles, Holme: the tower is said to be haunted by the ghost of Nan Scott, a woman of the village who barricaded herself into the tower in a desperate attempt to flee the outbreak of plague that swept through the area in the wake of the fall of Newark in 1646 (Wikimedia Commons).

The King's Manor, York; caught up in fierce fighting during the unsuccessful assault of 16 June 1644, its courtyards are said to be filled with the screams and moans of the wounded (Wikimedia Commons).

The Commandery, Worcester; the embattled Duke of Hamilton, who was using it as his headquarters, having died of wounds in this fine mediaeval building, it said to be haunted by his ghost (Wikimedia Commons).

The house in Ely occupied for some years by Oliver Cromwell in the years prior to the outbreak of the Civil War; many visitors have reported a feeling of terror and dread or a sense of an evil presence (author's collection).

Christchurch College, Oxford, one of the many sites claimed to be haunted by Charles I (Wikimedia Commons).

Goodrich Castle, Shropshire; ill-fated lovers, Charles Clifford and Alice Birch, are said to haunt the ramparts (Wikimedia Commons).

Seventeenth-century buildings in Amery Hill, Alton: the site of a fierce action in December 1643, Alton's streets are said to echo to the sound of marching troops (author's collection).

The Great Barn, Basing House: a bastion of the defenders during the two sieges endured by the garrison, the Great Barn boasts the ghost of nomne other than Oliver Cromwell (Wikimedia Commons).

The Red Lion, Avebury: famously the only pub in England situated within a stone circle, the Red Lion is another hostelry associated with the ghost of an unhappy young woman, in this case one Florence (Wikimedia Commons).

Athelhampton Hall, Devon: the two Cavaliers seen duelling in the great hall recall the violent and undisciplined reputation of 'Goring's crew' (Wikimedia Commons).

Llanhydrock Hall, Cornwall; the grounds of this sumptuous mansion, the home of local Parliamentarian commander, Lord Robartes, are haunted by the ghost of a Royalist soldier put to death for pillage (Wikimedia Commons).

in the western wall of his last refuge. With the morale of his men, in a state of collapse, the Royalist commander therefore had to accept that further resistance was futile, and on 6 October he duly laid down his arms.[26]

Needless to say, hardly had Winchester fallen than Cromwell was on his way to Basing House. Appearing before the defences just two days later, he immediately added the five heavy guns he had brought with him to the many artillery pieces already in place in the attackers' siege lines, and on 11 October unleashed a powerful bombardment. By the evening of the next day the walls were breached in a number of places, the morning of 13 October therefore seeing three assault columns hurl themselves upon the 300 defenders. Outnumbered ten to one or more, the defenders fought hard, but they could not prevail, and within a very short space of time all resistance had been overcome. What followed was one of the most unpleasant episodes of the struggle. Infuriated by the losses that they had suffered in the assault, carried away by adrenalin and convinced that not only the Marquis of Winchester but also all his men were Catholics, the victorious Parliamentarians laid about them with great savagery, eventually making an end of as many as three quarters of the garrison, together with an unknown number of civilians, some of them Catholic priests, but others wives and daughters of soldiers of the garrison. To make matters worse, confined in the cellars of the great complex, many of the prisoners perished when fire broke out in the chaos of looting that was the sequel to the collapse of resistance. That nothing of the sort happened anywhere else in England in the whole period from 1642 to 1651 is a comfort - Birmingham, Bolton and Leicester were nothing by comparison - but the fact that the fate of Basing House was exceptional does not make it any the more acceptable or any less terrible.[27]

With the fall of Winchester and Basing House, the south-east's active participation in the war had all but come to an end, all that remained to the king being Donnington Castle and Faringdon, of which the former laid down its arms on 1 April 1646 and the latter following the surrender of Oxford. In the Second Civil War, however, there was a terrible postscript. As in much of the rest of the country, assaults on popular traditions such as, above all, the celebration of Christmas, repeated harvest failures, heavy taxation, the continued need to feed and billet large numbers of troops and the arrogance of many officers and soldiers alike had engendered wholesale popular unrest across the whole region, and in May 1648, in the wake of the outbreak of revolt in Wales, Hampshire, Surrey,

Sussex, Kent and Essex all experienced serious outbreaks of disorder. In the first three instances, order was quickly restored by troops and militia at the cost of a few minor skirmishes, but in the last two the situation was very different. As witness events in Surrey, the disaffection was by no means necessarily Royalist in sympathy: having gathered a large band of Cavalier conspirators around him at Hampton Court, the Earl of Holland set out to attack Reigate Castle, but, for all the outrage at the general situation, failed to win over the inhabitants of the towns and villages round about and was in consequence overwhelmed in a sharp skirmish at Surbiton. However, the Royalist conspirators of Kent and Essex showed much greater awareness and political flexibility, and, placing themselves at the head of the angry crowds, thereby turned riot into insurrection.[28]

What followed was an episode as terrible as anything that had preceded it. Initially, the focus of the revolt was in Kent, a county hitherto almost completely devoid of any military action. Within a matter of days some 10,000 men had rallied to the colours of the local Royalists, but the head of the insurrection, the Earl of Norwich, spread his forces out over a wide area of the north and east of the county, and in consequence opened the way to defeat in detail. Even had he kept his followers together, it is doubtful that they could have made head against even the limited forces – some 6,000 men only – of the New Model Army that were all that was available to deal with the revolt, and all the more so as the Parliamentarian commander was the extremely capable Sir Thomas Fairfax. Thus, while Norwich dithered, Fairfax marched on his headquarters at Maidstone and on 1 June took him completely by surprise, something that undoubtedly helped a great deal here being the fact that it was pouring with rain. Held by only 2,000 men, no more than a handful of them trained soldiers, the town was very vulnerable, and it must therefore have been a matter of some surprise to the Parliamentarian commander to find that his opponents put up a most desperate defence, fighting hard for each and every street, and making a determined last stand in and around the church of Saint Faith before finally laying down their arms.[29]

Defeat at Maidstone did not quite put an end to the insurrection in Kent: aided by firepower from warships of the navy, a large part of which had become so disaffected that it had declared for the king, elements of Norwich's forces had seized Dover Castle and the more modern Henrician artillery forts at Deal, Sandown and Walmer, and the four strongholds had all to be besieged and retaken, a task that was not completed until 5 September. At the same time, after heading an abortive march on London in the course of which most of the men remaining to him deserted, Norwich himself managed to get across the Thames and march into Essex where he joined veteran Royalist Sir Charles Lucas, who had secured Chelmsford at the head of a substantial part of the county's Trained Bands. Together, the two commanders then seized Colchester as the only town in the area that could offer them some protection from the retribution that was now bearing down on them in the shape, once again, of Sir Thomas Fairfax. That said, Lucas and Norwich were not disposed simply to shut themselves up inside its medieval walls. On reaching the environs of Colchester on 13 June, Fairfax therefore found himself confronted by several thousand Royalist troops, and, not only that, but worsted in the fierce battle that followed. When the guns fell silent, the Royalists withdrew into the town, but there was to be no repeat of the assault at Maidstone. On the contrary, the Parliamentarian commander opted to starve the city into surrender. Determined to tie down as many Parliamentarian troops as possible so as to boost the chances of the Scottish invasion on which the hopes of the Royalists were now fastened, Lucas and Norwich hung on for more than two months amid scenes of terrible suffering that saw hundreds of civilians succumb to hunger and disease. When surrender came on 27 August, there was no massacre in the style of Basing House, but, even so, the terms were harsh enough, Lucas and his chief collaborator, Sir George Lisle, both being immediately court-martialled and put to death by firing squad.[30]

With the fall of Colchester, the south-east's direct experience of conflict came to an end. As in other parts of the country, however, the memory of what had passed continued to be engraved on the minds of the populace. We come here, of course, to the ghost-lore of the region, this being something that exists in abundance. One might here begin with the spots where the sounds of fighting, cannon fire or columns of marching troops can be heard – most notably, Alton, Alresford, where the main street supposedly resounds to the tramp of Hopton's retreating army every fourth anniversary of the battle of Cheriton, and Arundel and Donnington Castles[31] – or the list of hauntings on the part of named individuals, known or otherwise. Of these last, there is certainly no lack. Hampton Court, then, is allegedly stalked by the ghosts of Archbishop Laud and Sir Francis Villiers, a younger brother of the Earl of Holland who perished in the Surrey rising of 1648 (executed for his part in the rising, Holland himself was reputed to haunt his long-since demolished London residence, Holland House); the old tithe barn adjoining the ruins of Basing House by that of its conqueror, Oliver Cromwell, the latter also being supposed to frequent the parish church of Saint Nicholas in Chiswick; the White Hart Inn at Andover by that of Charles I, the latter also being associated with Billingham Manor on the Isle of Wight, Hurst Castle and Windsor Castle's Saint George's chapel (respectively a house in which Charles was supposed to have taken refuge during an abortive attempt to escape from Carisbrooke Castle; one of his last places of imprisonment; and the site of his tomb); the Hampshire village of East Wellow by that of Sir William Norton, brother of the Sir Richard Norton who was so prominent in the Parliamentarian cause in the area, a prominent Royalist who brought dishonour on himself by reneging on his allegiance to the king; Red Lion Square in London by those of Oliver Cromwell, Henry Ireton and John Bradshaw, the bodies of all three of whom were laid out in the tavern of that name which the square is called after before their ritual execution at Tyburn in the wake of the Restoration; the Essex town of Manningtree, a place much affected by the 'witch craze' of 1646–47, by the sinister Matthew Hopkins; the Crab and Lobster Inn in the Sussex village of Sidlesham by that of Sir Robert Earnley, a local Royalist mortally wounded in a skirmish outside the building; the parish church of Shipbourne in Kent (in which he is buried) by that of executed regicide Sir Henry Vane the Younger; the Crown Inn at Brading by Louis de la Roche, a French agent supposedly murdered in the building in 1648 while on a secret mission to Charles I, who was then imprisoned at Carisbrooke Castle; and Cassiobury Park in Watford by that of its then owner, Lord Capel, an ardent Royalist who went to the axe in 1649 for his part in the Second Civil War.[32]

In all this, there is but little difference with other regions of the country, while the same is true of the many instances of places for which we have nothing more than vague references to 'a Cavalier' or 'a Roundhead', examples of this category including the site of First Newbury, where the construction of a ring-road across the battlefield in the early 1990s is supposed to have disturbed the spirits of the dead; Towersey in Oxfordshire; Royston, Wigginton Common (a site traditionally supposed to have been the site of a Civil War encampment), Hitchin Priory and Salisbury Hall in Hertfordshire; Hampstead's Flask Inn; Arundel Castle and the sixteenth-century house known as 'The Shelleys' in Lewes, both of them in Sussex; the Bedfordshire village of Pullox Hill's Cross Keys Inn; the

Hampshire sites of Bordean House, Crondall, Hook, and the Tudor Rose Inn at Fordingbridge; Donnington Castle and Henley's Red Lion, both of them in Berkshire; the Essex cases of Colchester, Loughton Hall and Lavenham, together with White's Tyrrels Farm near Chelmsford and Edwin's Hall at South Woodham Ferrers; and finally the Kentish cluster of Dartford Heath, Downe Court House near Orpington, the Museum of Kentish Life at Maidstone, Hollingbourne, and a variety of public houses including Doddington's Chequers Inn, Elham's Abbot's Fireside, Pluckley's Blacksmith's Arms, Maidstone's Fisherman's Arms and Rusthall's Red Lion.[33]

Much though the locations of these hauntings are plausible enough – Arundel Castle, Colchester and Maidstone were all places that had played an important part in the fighting, while obscure Crondall was a key outpost of the garrison of Farnham that saw much action and was eventually burned to the ground by raiders from Basing House – in very few instances do we know anything about the stories that gave rise to them. The exceptions, though, are quite telling in that they all constitute examples of themes with which we are already familiar: thus, in Lavenham, the property concerned – a house in Prentice Street – is said to be the home of a Cavalier who was killed in the siege of Colchester; the ghost at Doddington's Chequers Inn is supposed to be that of a Cavalier murdered in one of its chambers, similar stories being told of the 'in-dwell' at Pullox Hill's Cross Keys and the figure – a headless horseman, no less – that is claimed to appear at Hitchin Priory; at Towersey, the spectre concerned – another headless horseman – is reputed to be the ghost of a Royalist soldier wounded at Chalgrove Field who sought help in the village, but was murdered by the inhabitants and buried in an unmarked grave; and, last but not least, tradition maintains that Hook's ghost – a mounted Cavalier armed with a broken sword – was a courier caught and killed by the Parliamentarians.[34] Once again, then, Cavaliers are remembered as tragic figures, indeed, very often victimised figures, men worthy of a better fate. This, certainly, is the picture painted by the four ghost stories from the region of which we have most detail, namely those concerning Salisbury Hall, the Chequers Inn at Haversham and The Royal Standard of England – a name supposedly granted to the hostelry in question by Charles II in recompense for the loyalty displayed by its owner – at Beaconsfield and finally the Hertfordshire village of Pirton, of which the first is haunted by a Royalist fugitive who killed himself rather than let himself be taken prisoner; the second by a Royalist spy named William who was hung outside the building when he was caught eaves-dropping on a Parliamentarian patrol, the third by a drummer who was among a group of Royalist prisoners put to death in the Turnham Green campaign on the grounds, true or otherwise, that they were Catholics, and the fourth a man (by tradition one Goring, though it may be the case that this was just a famous name plucked out of the air to flesh out the story) who had joined Holland's rising in Surrey and then, like its commander, fled northwards only to be cornered and killed when he sought refuge at a Tudor residence named Highdown House near Pirton, this last being the home of a young woman to whom he was engaged to be married (a detail that is lent added veracity by the fact that at the time of the Civil War the house belonged to the prominent, and deeply Royalist, Dowcra family).[35] And, finally, if Cavaliers were victims, they remained ones who were incorrigibly romantic, the Fordingbridge example being renowned for fondling female patrons of the establishment.[36] Can it be derived from all this, however, that the Royalist hand on the region was somehow lighter than it was elsewhere? Given the fact that much of the material we have to work on in respect of the actions of Royalist commanders and their followers are the allegations of Parliamentarian pamphleteers, it is difficult to hazard an opinion with any certainty, but absolving such figures as the governor of Donnington Castle, Sir John Boys, of the charges that have been made against them is not an easy task, while there are few historians who have not accepted their basic premise.[37]

As elsewhere, then, in the popular recounting of the war, we see a sea-change in the representation of the Cavalier. Something that makes the overwhelming focus on the Royalist cause which characterises the stories we have available to us even more interesting is the fact that, except in parts of Hampshire, throughout the period, it was the Parliamentarian cause that predominated in the region. Yet Parliamentarian spectres are notably scarce and when they do appear, it is usually in an unfavourable light (the one exception is the Crondall ghosts: specifically cited as being 'Cromwellian', these simply flit to and fro in the vicinity of the parish church in neutral fashion). Consider, then, the case of Oliver Cromwell, the places where he is recalled excluding settings that are potentially laudatory – Hampton Court, perhaps, or Westminster Hall – in favour of others where the context is rather negative in the extreme, namely Basing House or Red Lion Square House and Red Lion Square. Equally, the Roundhead soldier whose ghost is heard screaming for mercy before being strung up from the signboard of the Swan Inn in Romsey is seemingly not some heroic spy or courier but rather a villain hanged by his own side on 9 May 1645 for theft and murder.[38] And, finally, if all else fails, there is always Matthew Hopkins, Colchester's ghosts including not just gallant Cavaliers killed fighting bravely in the siege, but also a young girl accused of witchcraft by Hopkins and, however improbably, walled up in a recess and left to die somewhere in the cellars beneath the Fox and Fiddler public house.[39]

Less ravaged by war though much of the south-east was, it therefore offers a wealth of material for the purposes of this study. Some of it is both confused and confusing: the headless Roundhead ghost who is associated with the graveyard of Faringdon parish church is said to be Sir Robert Pye, the commander of the Parliamentarian troops who besieged the Royalist garrison in 1646, but he could just as easily be Pye's son, Hampden, a lieutenant in the Royal Navy who is recorded as having been decapitated by a cannonball in action against the Spaniards.[40] At the same time, those who are inclined to be sceptical will find ample material to satisfy their inclinations once the stories we have retold here have been deconstructed: if the ghost of Sir Henry Vane haunts the parish church of Shipbourne, for example, the fact that his tomb is to be found there provides a fairly obvious reason belief grew in the phenomenon, while questions cannot but be aroused by the fact that the Salisbury Hall we see today was not in fact constructed till 1669, albeit on the site of an earlier Tudor building. Yet at root there is clearly a common core of folk-memory that encompasses not just the dramatic but the mundane: if it is hardly surprising that such events as the storming of Alton or the siege of Arundel Castle should occupy a permanent niche in the popular construct of the past, there is far less reason to expect common recollections of the past to include the idea, say, that, as the legend holds, Hertfordshire's Wigginton Common was once the encampment of a group of Parliamentarian soldiers, nor, for that matter, that men were once hung from the sign-board of Romsey's Swan Inn. As Ian Rodger writes, then, 'It is true that we no longer possess "noble savages" whom we can patronise by occasional tape-recording visits, but what we do possess is an extraordinary community of folk-memory which makes it an everyday event to hear someone tell a story which refers to something in the days of an old man's grandfather.'[41] Since the moment when these words were written, well over half a century has passed, half a century, moreover, in which a dizzying process of social and technological change has heavily eroded, if not destroyed for good, the common perceptions of the past of which Rodger wrote. If this last is the case, though, it does not destroy the basic premise of his remarks, but rather underlines the importance of collecting and analysing such tales of the Pirton horseman, and, where possible, giving them a place, however small, within the historical canon.

Chapter 8

The South-West

The south-west of England, here defined as the five counties of Cornwall, Devon, Somerset, Dorset and Wiltshire, has a unique place in the history of the English Civil War in that, in the first of said counties, it contained England's only substantial Celtic minority, the same region also possessing a number of privileges, customs and traditions that many of its inhabitants were determined to maintain in the face of pressure to bring the county - to them, Kernow - more into line with English norms. Whether this situation predisposed the Cornish to turn to the cause of Royalism is a moot point, but it was in all events to prove an important factor in the four years of fighting that followed the outbreak of hostilities in 1642, not least because in other ways Cornwall and the other counties of the south-west had much in common, whether it was their accentuated Protestantism; the common sea-faring traditions of Devon and its western neighbour; the poverty of much of its inhabitants; and, finally, the tin and lead mining to be found in the Mendips, Dartmoor and the Saint-Just peninsula. Indeed, it is probably not going too far to say that, without the particularism of the Cornish, the five western counties might have had as quiet a war as their counterparts in East Anglia. Tragically, however, this was not the case: bolstered by the army raised by such Cornish gentleman as Bevil Grenville and John Trevanion, the western Royalists were able to make sufficient head for the region to become the scene of protracted fighting that involved both pitched battles such as Stratton, Lansdowne and Langport, and protracted sieges such as those of Bristol, Taunton and Exeter. Devastation, then, was widespread, and it is therefore no surprise to find Civil War ghosts stalking the region from Portland to Penzance.

The ferocity of the manner in which south-west England experienced the Wars of the Three Kingdoms must at first have seemed an unlikely outcome to the political and military situation that developed in the region by the end of 1642. Thus, in general the West Country was not promising ground for King

Charles, not least because recusant families - the group that had played so important a role in Lancashire and other parts of the north of England – were few and far between. From the start it was highly unlikely that the monarch could hope for the support of Plymouth and Exeter, both of which were strongly Puritan, as were many smaller places such as Taunton, Barnstaple, Bideford and Bridgewater, the only major settlement that promised anything different being Bristol, where Puritanism had established less of a hold. Yet even here the Royalists were thwarted: in the event the corporation opted for neutrality, a state that, as was the case everywhere else, lasted just as long as it took armed troops - in this case Parliamentarians - to arrive before the walls.[1] Nor was the countryside of much more help. A considerable number of the gentry in all five counties were Royalist, true, but there were plenty who were not, and in at least some of them - Devon for one, and Wiltshire for another - the propertied classes were solidly Parliamentarian in sympathy: in Wiltshire, indeed, just eight of the county's twenty-nine Members of Parliament declared for the king.[2] To make matters worse, it was not just that Royalists were in a minority among the gentry. Thus, in much of Somerset in particular, Cavalier families such as the Pouletts, the Stawells and the Berkeleys found that it was quite impossible to bring out the local populace in their support: on the contrary, indeed, no sooner had open hostilities broken out in early August than the northern part of the county effectively rose in revolt against the king, thousands of town and countryfolk flocking to a great muster called by the local Parliamentarians at Chewton Mendip armed with whatever weapons came to hand.[3]

What factors underpinned this popular Parliamentarianism? In the long term there is no doubt that there was, first, a long legacy of discontent sparked by economic insecurity. In Somerset in particular, then, the whole county was in the grip of rural overpopulation, while the vital cloth industry had suffered a serious crisis of overproduction following the outbreak of the Thirty Years' War, yet another factor making for social conflict being the onset from 1636 onwards of serious outbreaks of plague.[4] More immediately, there were the effects of Charles' unfailingly disastrous foreign policy *démarches*, whether it was the disorders committed by the soldiers who gathered in Plymouth and other ports preparatory to joining the expeditions to Cádiz and La Rochelle in the first years of the king's reign, not to mention the heavy financial burden that their presence represented, or the widespread use of impressment across the region to produce the men required to fill the ranks.[5] Finally, if Wiltshire was less affected by Charles' efforts to play the Protestant prince, it suffered just as badly from the crisis in the woollen industry, while an issue of particular concern among the poorer classes, and, especially, the cottagers (essentially landless labourers), being de-forestation, a term referring not to the clearing of the area's woodlands but the process whereby the government granted permission to wealthy land-owners to enclose the various royal forests in the area, thereby eradicating such customary rights as grazing livestock and gathering firewood, nuts, mushrooms and wild berries.[6]

What clinched the deal for the Parliamentarians, however, was the spread of Puritanism. Devon has been reckoned as the most Puritan county in the whole of England while Somerset and Wiltshire were not far behind. Why this should be so is not entirely clear. One contributing factor was undoubtedly the conversion of increasing numbers of the gentry to the cause of ecclesiastical reform and the consequent appointment of large numbers of parish clergy who were committed to a preaching ministry, but to cite this phenomenon is but to beg the question of why the leading men of the region were so much at the religious cutting-edge. In any case, it was not just a question of the propertied classes setting the tone. As Wroughton writes, 'Although largely inspired by the Puritan gentry and cloth-makers who controlled the area, [the Puritan revolution] had widespread support from ordinary local people - weavers, artisans, traders, husbandmen and labourers.'[7] Quite so, but this does but lead us back to the question of how Puritanism can have made such strides, and all the more so as detailed research on popular mentalities in such places as Dorchester has suggested that the onward march of Puritanism was bitterly resented by considerable elements of the lower classes at one and the same time bored by the endless sermons, revolted by the perception that godly reformation was a creed of the prosperous, and, above all, perhaps, infuriated by the war waged by the Puritans on drinking, dancing, wassailing, bear-baiting, cock-fighting and virtually every other form of popular entertainment.[8] This is not a question on which the author is equipped to speculate, but one issue that was almost certainly very important was the influence of hatred of the Spaniards. Somerset, Devon and Dorset were all seafaring counties that had contributed dozens of ships and thousands of men to the defeat of the Spanish Armada and the rampages of Sir Francis Drake and his fellow Elizabethan 'sea-dogs' in the Caribbean and elsewhere, and these exploits were looked back upon with enormous pride, a pride, however, that was mixed with nightmare tales of the tortures that had been inflicted on those mariners unfortunate enough to fall into the hands of the enemy. As for the origins of these tortures and, for that matter, that of the Armada, these lay in the fact that Spain was a Catholic country and Catholicism a religion bent on the eradication of English Protestantism. If anything, then, fear of Catholicism blazed even brighter in the south-west than it did in other parts of the country, the result being that the imposition of laudianism – something that was everywhere seen as a move towards Britain's re-catholicisation, even a papist plot – met with ferocious resistance from every level of society. Thus, at Beckington in Somerset, the church-wardens were imprisoned after refusing to reinstate the parish church's 'communion-table' as an altar, while, across the region, 'godly' gentlemen and town councils appointed dozens of preachers whose task it was to deliver daily sermons in the Puritan style.[9]

In the face of this concerted hostility, the king's emissaries could achieve little when the time came to mobilise for war. Other than an abortive attempt that was made to secure Salisbury on the part of one of its two Members of Parliament, Robert Hyde, that ended in the latter's arrest and incarceration, the chief action in the region took place at Wells. Thus, having been appointed by King Charles to take control of the western counties, the Marquis of Hertford headed for Wells, where he gathered around him a considerable number of local gentry and those of their tenants they had managed to mobilise (as will be gathered from what been said, this was far from being an easy task: indeed, passing through the Wiltshire town of Marlborough, around which place he had substantial estates, Hertford had proved unable to gain the support of more than a handful of individuals). Unfortunately for the Royalist cause, the marquis was no general – indeed, he had already given proof of his incapacity by plumping for Wells as his headquarters rather than a Bristol that was ripe for the picking[10] – and he therefore remained largely inactive, thereby giving the Parliamentarians, initially commanded by Sir Alexander Popham, to gather together a far larger force than the few hundred men who were available to the supporters of the king. An attempt to raid the enemy headquarters at Shepton Mallet achieved nothing, while, if successful in itself, an attack on an advance party of Parliamentarians at the hamlet of Marshal's Elm near Street on 4 August did not secure Hertford even so much as a breathing space. Ever more fearful and knowing full well that Wells could not be defended against a serious attack, the marquis therefore evacuated the town and led his little array – no more than a few troops of horse and dragoons and the cadre of an infantry regiment – to Sherborne in the hope that Wiltshire might offer him more recruits than Somerset. This hope, however, proved a delusion, and Hertford fell into a fit of dithering that lasted almost a full month and was only broken when he was beset by a force of some 7,000 men commanded by the Earl of Bedford on 2 September, and left with no option but to take refuge in the castle. The Parliamentarian commander was little more vigorous than Hertford, however, and withdrew after a mere four days, and that despite winning a minor skirmish at Babylon Hill. Badly outnumbered, unable to recruit fresh troops and lacking in experience, the marquis once more fell into a state of inactivity and therefore lost still more time, the only thing that prompted him to action being the arrival on 18 September of the news that Portsmouth had fallen to the enemy. Thus deprived of his one serious hope – in brief, that help might come from outside – in what amounted to a confession of defeat, the Royalist commander therefore fled for Minehead from whence he took ship for South Wales in the hope that he could join King Charles.[11]

With Hertford's departure from the scene, all that the Royalists were left with were a handful of garrisons, including, most notably, Sherborne and Wardour Castles in Wiltshire and Corfe Castle in Dorset, of which the last two happened to be in the charge of the wives of their absent owners, Lord Arundell and the Chief Justice, Sir John Bankes. What changed the situation were the actions of the marquis' cavalry commander, Sir Ralph Hopton, a committed Somerset Puritan and veteran of the Thirty Years' War, who had resolved to put loyalty to the established order ahead of his religion. There having been no shipping available to take his 200 cavalry and dragoons, he therefore opted to head for Cornwall, a county that had shown itself to be predominantly Royalist in sympathy but had nonetheless hitherto remained neutral thanks to an agreement negotiated by leading members of the gentry. Thus far, we have not spoken much of Cornwall, and it is therefore time to do so, and all the more so as the greater favour enjoyed by the Royalist cause there at first appears to be somewhat contradictory: after all, ships had sailed against the Spaniards from Falmouth and Fowey at least as often as they had done from Plymouth, while the Elizabethan naval hero Sir Richard Grenville had hailed from Stowe, a hamlet on the north coast near Bude. Equally, economic conditions were no better in Cornwall than in the rest of the south-west; Cornish Members of Parliament such as Sir John Elliot had taken a prominent role in opposing Charles' policies before 1642; there was a significant Puritan minority among the clergy, albeit one that was concentrated in its eastern parts; and Cornwall had suffered particularly badly from the raids of the swarms of Moorish galleys that had been plying the seas.[12] And, finally, for all that the Duchy of Cornwall was a possession of the Crown, King Charles was no more able to secure the loyalty of his tenants than many other landowners across the region. In the words of Mary Coate:

> So powerful did [the Royalist party] become and so attractive were its leaders ... that later generations forget that ... there existed from the beginning of the war a well-organised opposition. On the Parliamentarian side were Lord Robartes of Llanhydrock, Sir Richard Buller ... John Saint-Aubyn of Clowance, Nicholas Boscawen of Tregothnan, Anthony and Humphrey Nichol, Richard Erisey ... Edmund Prideaux and John Trefusis. If nine Arundells rode for the king, two ... were for the Parliament; Sir Francis Godolphin ... and his son, Sidney the poet were Royalists, but their cousin, Francis Godolphin of Treveneague, was a Parliamentarian.[13]

In practice, then, Cornwall was not a Royalist county *ipso facto*, but rather one that was split down the middle. What changed the situation was simply the arrival of Hopton and his little cavalcade, a number of whom were Cornish gentlemen, at the Grenville mansion at Stowe on 25 September. Like Hopton an opponent of King Charles who had swung behind the latter when Pym and his acolytes had taken the for them unacceptable step of seizing control of the Trained Bands, the current head of the family, the widely liked and respected Sir Bevil Grenville, immediately proffered his support.[14] After this events moved swiftly. Outraged by the threat to Cornwall's neutrality, the Parliamentarian party arraigned Hopton as a disturber of the peace (it so happened that the county assizes were in session) – and called a muster of the Trained Bands, but the court acquitted the Royalist commander, while far fewer men than had been hoped for turned out to resist him, the result being that the initial Parliamentarian leader, Sir Richard Buller, withdrew to Launceston, leaving Hopton to secure the central and western parts of the county for the king. Calling out the Trained Bands in his turn, Hopton had much more success than his opponents and had therefore soon put together a force of 3,500 men with which he proceeded to advance on the Tamar and drive Buller and his followers back into Devon. Also ousted, meanwhile, was a regiment of Scottish foot that the outbreak of war had by sheer happenstance found in Plymouth (destined for employment in Ireland, it had turned up in the port completely unexpectedly when the transports carrying it were blown far out of their way by bad weather) commanded by Colonel William Ruthven, which had crossed the river by boat and seized Saltash. For the time being at least, then, Cornwall was Royalist.[15]

Along with much of Wales, Cornwall enjoys the reputation of being the home of the greatest popular support garnered by King Charles: 'Cornish troops', writes Mark Stoyle, remained the Parliamentarians' most implacable opponents: no English county was so highly praised by the king's propagandists, or so bitterly excoriated by Parliament's, and it seems fair to suggest that no English county did more to assist the Royalist cause.'[16] Almost inevitably, then, there has arisen an abiding myth to the effect that its inhabitants were simple country-folk loyal to their king, their church and their social superiors. Here, for example, is John Baratt:

> Cornish society remained intensely parochial ... [and] also strongly conservative: it had a growing, if relatively small, merchant class, but its towns remained modest in size ... [The] relationship [of many of the Cornish gentry] with their tenants and retainers still had the feudal overtones that were disappearing elsewhere in England ... Most people remained Anglican in belief, though there were a small number of Puritans, mainly in the towns.[17]

This analysis is not entirely without merit: it is, for example, perfectly true to say that Puritanism was much weaker in Cornwall than it was across the Tamar, though such hold as it had was less on the towns as such than on those in the eastern parts of the county; at the same time, it is also the case that there were some members of the gentry who, at least according to legend, were kindly and paternalistic in their dealings with their tenants. Yet, in so far as we have thus far heard them, Barratt's views are insufficient as an explanation for the situation: apart from anything else, Cornwall was not nearly as parochial as his comments imply and had, as we have seen, been fully engaged with the politics of the 1630s. It is, then, but fair to say that Barratt does not just attribute Cornish support for the Royalist cause to devotion to king, parson and squire. Just as important in his eyes was the truculence of a people who had always seen themselves as being set apart from the rest of the country by geography and, in the western parts of the county where Cornish was still clinging on, language.[18] Citing the series of rebellions that affected the region in Tudor times, he therefore claims that 'Cornwall's physical isolation and the ever present reminders of its ancient past had helped to breed a spirit of independence ... among its people'.[19] To independence should probably be added resentment, for, as Mark Stoyle has pointed out, 'Throughout the mediaeval and early-modern periods, the Cornish, like the Welsh, were treated with lofty disdain by their English neighbours, who mocked them as ignorant peasants.'[20] Curiously, this disdain had not been shared by successive English administrations: on the contrary, fear of the Cornish potential for rebellion led to a series of concessions, including, most notably, respect for the 'stannaries' - councils originally set up to regulate the tin trade that had evolved into *de facto* local governments whose presence conveyed a wide range of privileges on the inhabitants - and massive over-representation in Parliament. At the same time, much indulgence was granted in the field of religion, those areas where Cornish remained common being allowed its use in respect of liturgy and sermons alike. However, the problem with this tactic was that, far from keeping the Cornish quiet, it ensured that the moment that English politics turned reformist, as was the case from 1640, there were immediate fears for the survival of Cornish particularism, fears that could not but be reinforced when, in the wake of Hopton's seizure of control, Cornwall found itself completely isolated in political terms and facing the threat of 'foreign' invasion. To recognise this last, though, is to recognise that popular support for the Royalist cause represented something other than devotion to either King Charles or the Anglican Church. Thus, if it is true that the first months of the war saw large crowds of countrymen assemble to fight the enemy, taking the war to said enemy by marching across the Tamar into Devon was another matter altogether, the implication being that what motivated the mass of the people was fear of attack by, or so one assumes, hordes of Devonians: before he could engage in offensive operations, then, Hopton was forced to raise an army of volunteers. Such was the general poverty that these efforts were not wholly unsuccessful[21] - by the turn of the year Hopton had raised five regiments of infantry, two of horse and one of dragoons - but many of the units were badly understrength, while, throughout the war, every attempt to advance into Devon, let alone places further east, was accompanied at the very least by much discontent and desertion and, on occasion, outright mutiny.[22] Nor was the home front entirely quiet: in November, for example, the area round Saint Michael's Mount was disturbed by a serious riot among local fishermen that had to be put down by troops sent from Falmouth.[23]

Secure Cornwall though Hopton and his companions had, their position therefore remained extremely vulnerable, and all the more so as the Parliamentarians in Devon and Somerset had access to greater resources and greater good will. Hearing that they were putting together a field army of their own, in November Hopton in consequence resolved to get his blow in first. Invading Devon (a step he was unable to take without first bribing his troops with a substantial advance in respect of their pay), he duly seized Tavistock and Plympton and made an effort completely unsuccessful to summon the Trained Bands.[24] Attacked and nearly captured at Modbury by a raid led by Ruthven, the Royalist commander first retired on Totnes and then tried to recover the initiative by threatening Exeter. Despite some panic among the population at the approach of the Cornish forces, the city was well garrisoned and strongly fortified, while Ruthven further distinguished himself by mounting as many of his musketeers on requisitioned horses as he could and rushing to the assistance of the defenders. Hopton, meanwhile, was short of food and increasingly threatened by mutiny, while he was further discouraged by a Parliamentarian attack that drove him from an outpost he had recently established at the town of Topsham. Hardly surprisingly, then, all threat to Exeter evaporated, 1 January 1643 seeing the unhappy Royalists evacuate their camps and set off for the Cornish border.[25]

Reach its home territory without further mishap though it did, the Cornish army had scarcely reached safety, for the energetic Ruthven had followed its retreating columns and once more seized Saltash after defeating a small force that had been posted to cover the crossing of the Tamar at Newbridge. Westminster had recently appointed a new commander of the south-western theatre of war in the person of the Earl of Stamford, and Ruthven had been supposed to wait for the latter to gather his forces - all of them new regiments raised in Devon and Somerset - together, before invading Cornwall. Meanwhile, having fallen back across the Tamar, Hopton's troops had recovered their equanimity, while the fortuitous capture of two Parliamentarian ships laden with arms and munitions that were driven into Falmouth by bad weather meant that there was plenty of material with which to make up their wants and, in addition, equip the men of the Trained Bands who answered Hopton's summons to confront the enemy invasion. With Ruthven's isolation worsened still further by the fact that he had decided to march still further into Cornwall, the Royalist commander resolved on a rapid counter-stroke. Gathering together the 5,000 men he had available, on 19 January he therefore launched a surprise attack on Ruthven whose somewhat smaller force had just reached the village of East Taphouse some miles west of Liskeard. Their general having seemingly had second thoughts in respect of his temerity, the Parliamentarians had previously deployed in a reasonable defensive position at Braddock Down, but the blood of the Cornishmen was well and truly up, and a single charge was therefore sufficient to sweep away Ruthven's entire army with the loss of 200 dead, 1,250 prisoners and five cannon, the surviving Parliamentarians fleeing post-haste for Saltash. Attacked in the latter town on 22 January, Ruthven's men put up a fierce fight and held out for the best part of the day, but with the coming of dusk all resistance collapsed, as many as 800 men being killed or taken prisoner in the rout that followed, one of the few who managed to make it back across the Tamar being their now completely discredited commander.[26]

If Braddock Down was the beginning of what became known in the Royalist camp as 'the western wonder', its immediate results were distinctly disappointing. Thus, Hopton decided to follow up his success by invading Devon for a second time and threatening Plymouth, but the Cornish Trained Bands refused point-blank to second this endeavour, and the result was that all Sir Ralph could do was to establish a loose blockade of the town by means of a chain of outposts. Beyond the Royalist positions, however, the local Parliamentarians were astir and they had soon put together a scratch force composed very largely of men from the Devon Trained Bands, the commander being one James Chudleigh, a scion of a local gentry family who had served as a captain in the Bishops' Wars. Though but poorly equipped, on 8 February the militiamen surprised a small Royalist picket at Chagford, among the men who fell in the resultant skirmish being Sidney Godolphin, a noted poet and Member of Parliament who had enlisted as a trooper in the Royalist horse. Not content with this success, having gathered still more men, on 21 February Chudleigh fell on the heavily outnumbered garrison of Modbury, which was eventually driven from the town after a day of fierce fighting. Threatened not just by Chudleigh but also the Earl of Stamford who was marching on his rear from the north, Hopton abandoned his designs on Plymouth and fell back on Tavistock, at which place he succeeded in negotiating a local truce that he hoped to use to recoup his losses (why the Parliamentarians agreed to his request is unclear, but several weeks of winter campaigning had probably left their forces in little better state than their Cornish opponents, and it may be that what they gained - the retreat of the Royalist forces back across the Tamar - therefore seemed preferable to the alternative of a pitched battle).[27]

The truce, however, proved short-lived. Meanwhile, no sooner had it come to an end on 22 April than Chudleigh led the three regiments that were all that Stamford had managed to raise thus far across the border to attack Launceston, only to be repulsed by Hopton at the strong defensive position offered by an eminence just east of the town known as Beacon Hill. Once again, move was followed by counter-move, Hopton promptly striking across the border in his turn in the hope of catching the discomforted Chudleigh at his base at Okehampton. In consequence, the night of 24 April saw the Royalist army trudging eastwards along the highroad that led from Launceston first to that place and then to Exeter. This manoeuvre, however, did not lead to the successful dawn attack for which Hopton had hoped. On the contrary, forewarned of his enemy's approach, Chudleigh rode west at the head of a small force of cavalry and ambushed the Royalist column as it was crossing Sourton Down, a ridge close to the northern fringes of Dartmoor, just as it was struck by the onset of a fortuitous thunder-storm. Already none too pleased at having once more been led across the Tamar and taken completely by surprise - astonishingly enough, no one had troubled to send out any scouts - many of Hopton's troops turned and ran, the only thing that saved their commander from complete destruction being the resistance of a few units who escaped the initial Parliamentarian onslaught. Casualties, true, were not too numerous, but, even so, it was some days before the Royalist commander was in a position to undertake further operations, not least because many of the fugitives had flung away their arms.[28]

By contrast, the Parliamentarians were much heartened, while they were also aware of the need to exploit their victory with the utmost speed, a captured letter having revealed that the Marquis of Hertford was heading for Devon at the head of a substantial body of troops detached from the Royalist forces at Oxford. Gathering all the men he could, Stamford, who had passed the previous few weeks nursing an attack of gout at Exeter, therefore hastened to invade Cornwall in strength, crossing the border near the north coast and taking up a strong defensive position on a steep hill overlooking the town of Stratton, the idea being that Hopton would have no option but to attack him. Like Hopton before him, however, the Parliamentarian commander fell prey to overconfidence and sent off most of his cavalry to forestall any attempt to raise the trained bands. When the Royalists appeared at dawn on the morning of 16 May, Stamford found himself at a considerable disadvantage. That said, he still had a considerable preponderance in terms of numbers, and it is therefore much to the credit of the Cornish infantry that, having previously repulsed a fierce counter-attack headed by Chudleigh, at the end of a long day of fierce fighting, they finally crowned the ridge and put the Parliamentarians to flight. The result was an even greater triumph than Braddock Down: around 1,000 of Stamford's men had been killed, wounded or taken prisoner, while the Royalists had more than made up for the matrial losses thy had suffered at the hands of Chudleigh, their plunder including thirteen cannon, seventy barrels of powder and large quantities of pikes and muskets.[29] Nor did the matter end there: led by James Chudleigh's father, Sir George Chudleigh, the cavalry sent westwards by Stamford had ridden as far as Bodmin and taken the town after a short struggle, but, at the news of Stratton, the townsfolk rose in revolt and soon had them fleeing for Plymouth in great disorder.[30]

With all threat to Cornwall at an end, Hopton was now free to march east to rendezvous with Hertford. More to the point, perhaps, his unruly troops were for the time being prepared to follow his lead, Stratton having filled them with the conviction that their commander was a leader who could be relied upon to win them much plunder.[31] Marching east via Okehampton, he blockaded Plymouth and Exeter and eventually rendezvoused with Hertford and his second-in-command, Prince Rupert's younger brother, Maurice, at Chard. Their combined forces amounting to well over 6,000 men, the Royalist commanders immediately took the offensive, quickly securing Taunton, Bridgewater and Dunster Castle in the face of minimal resistance and dispersing a considerable part of such troops as the Somerset Parliamentarians had at their disposal.[32] However, no sooner had they done so than a new and far more dangerous threat than that posed by Stamford and Chudleigh emerged in the person of the newly appointed Sir William Waller, who, it was learned, was gathering an army at Bath. Driving what remained of the Parliamentarian forces in Somerset before them, the

Royalists therefore marched east and on 12 June occupied Wells, just beyond which their vanguard of cavalry encountered the enemy rearguard drawn up on a local eminence known as Nedge Hill on the fringe of the Mendip hills. The commander on the spot being the notoriously impetuous Prince Maurice, it was not long before the Royalist horse were advancing upon their opponents. These last immediately taking to flight, they were pursued for miles across the moors that crowned the Mendips, but were saved from disaster by the fortuitous appearance at the village of Chewton Mendip of a force of cavalry and dragoons that Waller had sent out from Bath, the result being a confused skirmish fought in a sudden evening mist.[33]

Sharp fight though it was, Chewton Mendip - at one point Prince Maurice was actually captured by the Parliamentarians - ended in a triumph for the Royalists, but they made no attempt to pursue their advantage and instead decided to make use of Hopton's long-standing friendship with Waller in an effort to get the latter to change sides (a goal that did not seem so unlikely: in the wake of the disaster at Stratton, Chudleigh had done just that, while his example had just been followed by the commander of one of Waller's infantry regiments). The result was a justly famous exchange of letters, of which one in particular has been regularly cited as an example of the manner in which decency and humanity continued to survive in Civil War England, but the Parliamentarian commander remained implacable, leaving the Royalists no option but to resume their advance.[34] There followed several days of manoeuvring that essentially saw Hertford's forces envelop Bath from the east and hem Waller, who was badly outnumbered and particularly short of infantry, into a strong defensive position on a lofty ridge known as Lansdown Hill just north of the city. Finally coming face-to-face with their opponent on 5 July, Hertford, Maurice and Hopton rejected the idea of a frontal assault as being likely to be far too costly, and instead started to draw off their troops in the hope of being able to try a further approach elsewhere. Waller, however, had other ideas. Realising that his best chance of success lay in his opponents shredding themselves to pieces on the steep slopes that lay beneath his lines, he sent his horse to harass their retiring columns. A master-stroke, this soon produced the desired effect, the Cornish foot, in particular, becoming vociferous in their demands to be led against the enemy. Unwilling to risk damaging accusations of cowardice, the Royalist commanders gave way, and very soon the whole of their forces were heading back towards Waller, only to discover that discretion would indeed have been the better part of valour. Forced to advance up punishing gradients devoid of cover, the Royalists suffered heavy losses, among them Sir Bevil Grenville, who fell mortally wounded in the middle of a fierce Parliamentarian counter-attack, and succeeded in doing no more than driving their opponents a few hundred yards from the crest of the ridge. During the night, true, Waller evacuated the field rather than face a second day's fighting on ground that was far less favourable to his outnumbered men, but, for all that, the triumphant letters he sent to London claiming victory can be seen to be possessed of considerable justification.[35]

Reeling from losses that ran into many hundreds, the Royalists were now stricken by a fresh disaster in the form of the explosion that almost cost the life of Sir Ralph Hopton (see Chapter 1). With much of their spare ammunition gone in the blast, Hertford and Maurice - temporarily blinded as he was, Hopton was in no state to take part in a council of war - decided to make for Oxford in the hope of getting help, but Waller was soon in hot pursuit. Having routed some laggard Royalist cavalry at Chippenham, on 11 July the Parliamentarian commander caught up with his opponents at the village of Rowde near Devizes, and, after a sharp action, drove them into the town. Realising that to march on regardless would be to risk suffering a major defeat, Hertford resolved to leave the foot to barricade themselves within the place's rather rudimentary defences, while he and Maurice broke out with the cavalry and rode pell-mell for the Royalist capital, still some forty miles away though it was. Desperate as this strategy was, however, it was completely successful. Not only did Hertford and Maurice escape successfully but also they reached Oxford safely and obtained the help of two brigades of horse, whereupon the prince led the 1,800 men to which the relief force amounted straight back to Devizes, the return journey in the end taking no more than eighteen hours. Taken completely by surprise, Waller drew up his entire army to meet the threat on the rolling downland that commanded the town from the north, but, outnumbered almost two to one though he was, Maurice did not hesitate for a moment and rode straight at the Parliamentarians. Completely unnerved, the latter's horse gave way immediately and fled in rout, many of them coming to grief as they plunged down the precipitous slopes to the rear of their positions, the battle concluding by the Royalist infantry marching out of Devizes and taking their beleaguered counterparts in the rear. 'William the Conqueror' no more, Waller got away to Bristol, and with him most of the senior officers, but, for a second time in two months, the 'western wonder' had seen the elimination of an entire Parliamentarian army.[36]

Roundway Down, or, as the jubilant victors called it 'Runaway Down', was but the beginning of the disaster that now afflicted the Parliamentarian cause. No sooner had news of the battle reached Oxford than Charles dispatched Prince Rupert west to join Maurice at the head of the 10,000 men of his main field army who had been left in the city when he headed north to meet with Henrietta Maria and her much-needed convoy of arms and ammunition (see Chapter 5). In the first instance, the objective was Bristol, not only a great city but also the most important port in the kingdom. Having joined forces with the 5,000 men of the western army who had survived the campaign against Waller, on 23 July the prince closed up on the defences, there following two days of preliminary skirmishing. Rightly sensing that the defenders had too few troops to man the many miles of ramparts that ringed the city, the Royalist commanders resolved to avoid a formal siege in favour of an assault, and dawn on 26 July duly saw the united armies advance to the attack from opposite directions, the Oxford troops hitting the high ground that overlooked the city from the north, while the Cornishmen and their allies made for the southern Temple suburb. Nothing daunted, their opponents stood to their arms, and the result was a bloody struggle that cost the attackers several hundred lives and at times looked as if it might result in Parliamentarian victory, but at length Rupert's men broke through and started fighting their way into the heart of the city. Even then, continued resistance might have prevailed, but the governor, Nathaniel Fiennes, was no hero and by the middle of the day was so cast down that he asked for terms.[37]

With Bristol gone, the Royalist offensive continued. Rupert and Maurice, as we have seen, turned north to join the king in attacking Gloucester, leaving a Hopton now recovered from his wounds to hold their conquest with what remained of the Cornish army. To the south, meanwhile, Exeter was already under attack. Blockaded by a strong detachment of the western army commanded by Sir John Berkeley since the beginning of June, the staunchly Parliamentarian city had held out determinedly under the leadership of the Earl of Stamford, but an attempt to storm the key Royalist outpost of Topsham at the head of the estuary of the River Exe was defeated without difficulty, while the defenders were driven from the western suburb of Saint Thomas and most of their other outworks and forced to retire within the medieval walls. With food running short, the outlook was bleak, but on 8 July a stay of execution was obtained when a flotilla of Parliamentarian ships arrived off Exmouth under the Earl of Warwick, the besieging forces having no option but to evacuate many of their positions in case the new arrivals attempted a descent on the coast or tried to make their way up the Exe. In the event, though it took the Parliamentarian admiral ten days to get his forces into position, it was the latter move that was attempted. Warwick had 2,000 troops embarked on his ships, and on 18 July he launched an amphibious assault on Topsham, only for the landing force to be subjected to be such heavy fire that it never reached the shore several of Warwick's ships being sunk or damaged in the process. All Warwick had achieved, then, was a diversion that allowed Stamford to replenish his magazines, though the garrison was sufficiently encouraged to mount a fiercely aggressive defence when their assailants closed in once more, launching a fierce counter-attack that drove the Royalists from all the positions they had occupied in Saint Thomas. At the end of August, however, Prince Maurice arrived before the city at the head of a strong detachment of the Oxford army. With its links with the outside world now completely cut off and all hope of relief gone, Exeter was doomed to succumb to starvation, but the Royalist commanders could not wait for hunger to do its work, and on 3 September they launched a massive attack on the walls that soon had the garrison suing for terms of surrender.[38]

Bad though the fall of Exeter was, it was not the only blow to fall on the western Parliamentarians in the wake of the fall of Bristol. Hearing that troops were gathering in Somerset for the relief of the city, in August Berkeley had dispatched 1,000 troops to Torrington under a Colonel John Digby. Much alarmed at this development, the local Parliamentarians sent the Trained Bands of northern Devon to deal with the interloper, only for the unfortunate militiamen to be ambushed just outside the town and put to flight, a development that led Appledore, Barnstable and Bideford to send word to Prince Maurice that they had resolved to capitulate rather than face the sieges that had become their inevitable lot.[39] With the north of the county secure and Exeter taken, this left Maurice free to turn on the Parliamentarian strongholds still holding out along the southern coast, namely Dartmouth and Plymouth, of which the former was besieged on 20 September and the latter subjected to a loose blockade.[40] At this point, however, the impetus of the Royalist offensive began to slacken, much aided by the onset of heavy autumn rains, the garrison of Dartmouth did not surrender until 5 October, while the troops sent to blockade Plymouth were worsted in sharp skirmishes at Hooe and Knackersknowle. Given that the fall of Dartmouth meant that the men involved were soon reinforced by the whole of Prince Maurice's army, these petty reverses mattered little, but Plymouth nevertheless proved a hard nut to crack. Protected by massive fortifications that had been thrown up in the previous year, possessed of both many guns and powerful naval support, strongly manned and no longer headed by the ineffectual Stamford but rather a professional soldier named James Wardlawe, the defenders stood firm, the only success that the Royalists achieved in the first month of the siege being the capture of the prominent hill on the southern shores of the Catwater known as Mount Stamford that dominated the entrance to the harbour. Not until 3 December was Maurice in a position to launch a major assault, and in the event this was thrown back with heavy losses. Unwilling to concede defeat, the prince set his men to the task of sapping their way to the brink of the ditch that protected the northernmost point of the town's defences, only for the Parliamentarians to launch a sudden sally that cost the soldiers concerned more than 200 casualties. With his men mutinous, hungry and smitten by disease, even Maurice realised that the game was up and on 25 December, he duly evacuated his siege works and fell back on Plympton. For all the Royalists' efforts, then, 1643 ended with the Parliamentarian cause in the west of England bloody but unbowed.[41]

Before pursuing the main thread of the narrative into 1644, we must first turn our attention to experiences of the eastern part of the region in 1643. As we have seen, other than a few isolated strongholds, Wiltshire and Dorset had both been Parliamentarian strongholds from the start. That said, they did not escape the fighting altogether. To begin with Wiltshire, first to suffer in this respect was the town of Marlborough. Somewhere where Puritanism and resentment of Ship Money was strong, the place had quickly been secured for Parliament by a force of volunteers drawn from the Trained Bands and the local inhabitants, whereupon its lack of any defences was remedied by the construction of a line of earthworks blocking the main approaches to the town. That said, its defiance was soon brought to nothing. Thus, on 5 December 1642, a column of 3,000 troops that had been dispatched from Oxford under Henry Wilmot fell upon the defenders and forced their way into the streets. A desperate last stand in the parish church notwithstanding, by the end of the day resistance was at an end, the surviving members of the garrison being marched off into imprisonment and the town both pillaged and in large part fired.[42] Next to experience the horrors of war was Malmesbury. Originally another Parliamentarian stronghold, this had been evacuated by its defenders in the wake of the fall of Cirencester (see Chapter 6), whereupon had become a Royalist garrison. With the arrival of Sir William Waller in the west, however, the days of domination by the king's forces were numbered. Anxious to secure a direct line of communication with London, the Parliamentarian had no sooner reached Bristol than he set off to regain the town with the aid of some infantry gathered from among the local Parliamentarians. Reaching the place at noon on 24 March, he launched a fierce attack on its walls, only twice to be beaten off and finally forced to give up the fight on account (or so he claimed) of lack of ammunition. To his astonishment, however, no sooner had the next day dawned than, seemingly still worse off than their assailants, the defenders sent an emissary to ask for terms.[43]

The success at Malmesbury was soon followed by a much pettier affair. Ever since the start of the war, the 60-year-old Lady Blanche Arundell had been holding the family seat of Wardour Castle some miles east of Shaftesbury for her husband, Lord Arundell, the latter having joined the king at the head of a troop of horse in 1642. Consisting solely of a mere twenty-five armed retainers, the garrison had caused little trouble to the local inhabitants, and the fact that it now became the centre of attention seems to have stemmed from little more than the malice of the commander of the Wiltshire Parliamentarians, Sir Edward Hungerford. Whatever the reason, however, on 2 May the latter approached the castle at the head of as many as 1,300 men and summoned Lady Arundell to surrender. Said summons having been firmly refused, Hungerford promptly placed the castle - in reality little more than a glorified country house - under siege. Attempts to bring down the walls by mining having had little effect, on 8 May resort was had to a storming party that managed to blow in a key gate by means of a petard, the exhausted garrison then capitulating rather than face a full-scale assault it had no means of repelling. Initially taken to Shaftesbury, Lady Arundell was treated decently enough and eventually allowed to seek the protection of the Royalist army, but her home was first thoroughly pillaged and then transformed into a Parliamentarian garrison.[44]

Hitherto almost entirely quiet, Dorset also experienced an outburst of hostilities at this time. Situated in a cleft in the Purbeck Hills midway between

Wareham and Swanage, Corfe Castle was another isolated Royalist outpost held in the absence of its owner, in this case the Lord Chief Justice, Sir John Bankes, by a determined chatelaine. Forty-five years old in 1643, then, Mary, Lady Bankes, quickly showed herself to be someone who was both devoted to King Charles and a person of courage, decision and resource. Like Lady Arundell, she had been left with no more than a handful of retainers to defend her home, and it was therefore just as well that for some considerable time she was left in peace by the local Parliamentarians. At the beginning of May 1643, true, an attempt had been made to secure four small cannon that had been left in the castle, but Lady Bankes had seen off the seemingly rather half-hearted party of sailors who had been sent to remove them, and promptly set about recruiting men from the district. Further reinforced by a handful of troops from Hertford's army, the castle, a place of considerable natural strength that was in excellent repair, was therefore much more ready to face an enemy when the Parliamentarians moved against it for a second time some six weeks later. Led by the less than competent Sir Walter Erle, the latter attempted, first, to breach the walls by bombardment; second, to hack holes in the stonework by parties of men working in the shelter of medieval-style wheeled shelters known as 'sows'; and, finally, to storm the defences by means of an escalade. However, none of these tactics achieved even the most limited success, while at the beginning of August news also arrived that Royalist troops dispatched from Prince Maurice's army under the Earl of Crawford were marching on Dorchester. Much discomforted, Erle therefore abandoned the siege, leaving a triumphant Lady Bankes to be rejoined by her husband in October (sadly, the reunion was short-lived: soon called away to Oxford to resume his duties as Lord Chief Justice, in December Sir John fell sick and died).[45]

The Parliamentarian repulse at Corfe was soon followed by other Royalist successes. Thus, Wareham, Weymouth, Dorchester and Portland Castle were all captured with little or nothing in the way of resistance, the only place that stood fast in the way of this tide of success being the small port of Lyme.[46] Garrisoned by perhaps 1,200 troops together with a number of sailors landed from ships of the Parliamentarian Channel squadron, the tiny settlement was protected by a line of earthern ramparts studded by a series of forts, while the populace were notoriously Puritan in terms of their religious sympathies and the governor, Sir Thomas Sealey, an equally resolute opponent of the king. When

Prince Maurice approached the town on 20 April 1644, then, the fact that he had as many as 6,000 men with him dismayed the defenders not a jot: the very next day, indeed, they beat off an attempt to storm the walls. Following the repulse of a second attack a week later, the Royalist commander then subjected Lyme to many days of bombardment while even at one point attempting to set the town ablaze by the use of which fire-arrows. Yet it was all for naught: firmly supported by the future admiral, Robert Blake, Sealey continued to defy the prince, unleashing several sallies and beating off a third assault on the walls on 8 May. In consequence, with much of its infantry seemingly composed of men pressed in Devon in the autumn of the previous year, the morale of the Royalist army slumped dramatically, and all the more so as numbers of Parliamentarian ships kept appearing in the harbour with fresh supplies of food and ammunition. On 28 May yet another attack was beaten off, and the siege thereafter became a matter of desultory bombardment alone, albeit one not without incident: on 1 June, for example, as many as thirty houses were destroyed in a fire ignited by cannon firing red-hot shot.[47]

The extent to which Lyme was ever really in danger is a moot point. On occasion, true, the Royalists achieved a degree of success, but, for all that their guns, many of which were posted on the undefended headland overlooking the harbour, were able seriously to incommode the vessels that put in with aid for the defenders, Maurice had no chance of victory unless he could find some means of taking on the Parliamentarian fleet, something of, of course, he had no hope. Failure at Lyme, however, was soon to be eclipsed by undreamed-of success. Thus, as we have seen, much taken with the epic nature of the defenders' stand, coupled with the panic-stricken nature of some of the letters describing the siege penned by the Parliamentarian admiral, the Earl of Warwick, the Committee of Safety ordered Waller to abandon the attempt to trap the king at Oxford, and march into the west to effect the town's relief, only for an Essex desperate to shore up his credit in London to insist that he take on the task himself.[48] Needless a piece of politicking as the move was, it nevertheless was quick to achieve its object: hearing that the earl was on his way, on 15 June Maurice abandoned the siege and fell back on Exeter. Even better, the garrisons of Dorchester, Sandersfoote Castle, Melcombe and Weymouth – this last a port crucial to Royalist hopes for support from the Continent – all surrendered without resistance, while Wareham succumbed to a brief siege.[49] What followed, however, was completely unexpected.

Thus, rather than falling back on the Thames Valley as would have been his best move in the circumstances, having first secured the support of the Committee of Both Kingdoms, Essex pushed on for Plymouth (which had remained the subject of a loose blockade), and that despite that the fact that King Charles was marching on his rear with the bulk of what had ever been the main Royalist army.[50]

Having relieved Plymouth by reaching Tavistock and thereby forcing the Royalist troops watching the town under Sir Richard Grenville to flee across the Tamar, 'Old Robin' would have done well to turn and face the king who had long since joined forces with Maurice.[51] However, not least because the army had been stripped of several detachments including 1,000 men left behind to stiffen the Parliamentarian cause in southern Dorset, a column of foot and horse sent to make an attempt on Taunton and, finally, a full brigade dispatched to assist a Parliamentarian uprising that had broken out at Barnstaple, the prospect of a field battle was distinctly unpalatable.[52] In consequence, seemingly persuaded by Cornish exiles such as Lord Robartes that their home county had become so tired of Royalist requisitioning and impressment that it was ripe for the taking, Essex instead marched still further west. As decisions went, scarcely anything could have been more disastrous. Aside from anything else, short of supplies and assailed by the miserable weather typical of the summer of 1644, the Parliamentarian soldiers were becoming ever more undisciplined, and, already bad enough, their pillaging could not but escalate once they crossed into territory that they were convinced was irredeemably hostile. Very soon, then, they were being harassed by bands of angry civilians who frequently put to death the unfortunate stragglers who were falling by the wayside in ever larger numbers on account of the sickness that was winnowing their ranks. With the fact that Cornwall was not going to rise in arms against King Charles now more evident by the day, and no support forthcoming from the east (ordered to do what he could to help, Waller had dispatched a 2,000-strong flying column of cavalry and dragoons to distract the king from his prey, but this had been routed by a small Royalist force it had encountered near Bridgewater), all Essex could do was to head for the port of Fowey in the hope that he and his men could be rescued by the navy.[53]

On this occasion, however, there was to be no Dunkirk. Fowey being commanded by hills on either side of the estuary on which it stood, Essex's plan depended on his army being able to hold off the advancing Royalists, but this did not appear a likely chance. Between them, Charles, Maurice and Grenville could muster nearly 20,000 men, while 'Old Robin' could by now field barely half that number, and many even of them were in no fit state to fight. Starting on 21 August, then, the Royalists steadily reduced the amount of territory held by the Parliamentarians. On this day, then, concentric attacks drove the latter from the ring of hills overlooking Lostwithiel, and the king's men could undoubtedly have gone on to take the town had it not been deemed more important to spend time, first, positioning men and guns on the hills above Fowey so as to obstruct any attempt to rescue Essex by sea, and, second, seizing the countryside round about so as to secure it from enemy foraging parties.[54] Seeing which way events were trending, Essex resolved to save what he could from the impending disaster by ordering his cavalry commander, Sir William Balfour, to break out of the trap and head for Plymouth, this being something that was duly effected without mishap in the small hours of 31 August, some 2,000 men eventually reaching the safety of Saltash after some sharp skirmishes on Coryton Down and at the village of Lee.[55] As for the rest of the army, the same morning it was directed to evacuate Lostwithiel and head for the sea. With the Royalists in hot pursuit, Essex and some of the infantry attempted to make a stand at an Iron Age earthwork halfway to Fowey called Castle Dor. For a time the action was very fierce – some of the Cornish infantry, indeed, were forced to retreat – but, following what appears to have been an attempt at mass desertion on the part of some Devon troops eager to escape to their homes, by the end of the day resistance had completely collapsed. Abandoning the remnants of his army, Essex fled to Fowey where he requisitioned a fishing boat with orders to take him to Plymouth, the next day seeing the commander of the infantry surrender on terms that allowed the officers and men to march away at the cost of all their weapons, the haul amounting to forty cannon, a mortar, muskets and pikes sufficient for 9,000 men and 100 barrels of powder. Marston Moor it was not, but even so sufficient damage had been done to the Parliamentarian cause to tide King Charles over for at least another winter.[56]

Following the defeat of Essex, relative calm once again returned to the south-west, not least because Charles was now intent on nothing more than getting back to Oxford with such men as remained from the troops with which he had marched into the west, the only military episodes of any importance being a brief diversion to relieve Portland Castle, which the relief of Lyme had allowed Sir Walter Erle's Dorset Parliamentarians to besiege, a desultory blockade of Plymouth on the part of the Cornish forces of Sir Richard Grenville, and, last but not least, a determined attempt to reduce staunchly Puritan Taunton.[57] At this last place, however, the fighting was as ferocious as anything experienced in the Civil War. With no defences other than improvised barricades, the town was quickly overrun, but the defenders, who were commanded by the same Sir Robert Blake who had taken a leading role at Plymouth and was quickly establishing himself as a leader of real dynamism, succeeded in withdrawing into the castle from the shelter of whose walls they defied every attempt either to winkle them out or persuade them to surrender. Nor, meanwhile, did their efforts go unrewarded. Thus, as impressed by the courage of the garrison as they had been with that of Lyme, the Committee of Both Kingdoms directed Waller to get a relief force together. With his army in utter disarray, the latter was able to find no more than 500 horse for the endeavour, but the officer he put in command, one Major-General Holborne, managed to gather a number of additional troops from Wiltshire and Dorset and thereby succeeded in relieving Blake and his hard-pressed men.[58]

The relief of Taunton was a useful counterpoint to the defeat of Essex, but the Parliamentarian cause in Somerset and the other western counties remained under great pressure: besieged by Goring, rebellious Barnstaple, for example, was forced to surrender on 17 September.[59] If operations against Blake came to a halt on account of furious quarrels in the local Royalist leadership, at Plymouth 1645 had scarcely dawned when Grenville suddenly closed in on the defences and converted his blockade into a formal siege. Predictably enough, however, he and his men got no further forward than they had the previous year: not only did their cannon have little impact on the ramparts, but two assaults were repelled with heavy losses, the Royalist commander eventually being ordered by the Council of the West - a committee nominally headed by the 14-year-old Prince of Wales that had just been established to settle the many differences that separated the various Royalist grandees and revive the faltering war effort - to abandon active operations there in favour of taking the much more vulnerable (at least, comparatively speaking) target represented by Taunton.[60] If the thinking behind the switch from Plymouth to Taunton was sound enough, in the event Grenville was thwarted once again. Blake had made use of the lull afforded him by the appearance of Holborne's column to erect substantial earthworks around the town, and had also thrown garrisons into a number of country-seats in the vicinity, but this was scarcely the problem: hard-bitten veteran that he was, Grenville was unlikely to be dissuaded from attacking defences that were no stronger than those of conquered Saltash's for very long. However, while reconnoitring the Parliamentarian outpost of Wellington House, Grenville was badly wounded by musket-fire, the task of vanquishing Blake therefore passing to those of Sir George Goring, the latter having in the autumn of 1644 been rewarded for his excellent conduct at Marston Moor with the command of a new western army at the head of which he had since been probing the frontiers of Parliamentarian rule in Hampshire and even Surrey.[61] In some respects, this move was perfectly justified: after all, Goring was a figure of obvious talent of whom it was essential to make good use. Yet, typically enough, the details were not thought through sufficiently, and the result was much confusion. To quote Goring's biographer, Florence Memegalos, 'Was … Goring answerable to the prince's council? Were the other western commanders answerable to Goring? The bitter internecine struggles which emerge over these questions of precedence proved highly detrimental to the king's cause.'[62]

Reassuring though the situation at Taunton at first appeared to be, the Committee of Both Kingdoms had no intention of letting the town succumb to the Royalist attack, and the net result was that, headed by Sir Thomas Fairfax, the brand-new New Model Army was directed to march into Somerset to relieve Blake. That this was the decision taken was just as well: siege operations had begun on 10 April and, within a month, the defenders were in dire straits - indeed, on 8 May the Royalists, who were now headed by the redoubtable Hopton, launched a fierce assault that gained them several footholds in the town. Help, however, was not far away. Fairfax had set off with his army on 30 April, and, having first turned aside to recapture Weymouth, by now was well placed to mount a relief effort. In the event, he was not able to undertake the task himself for Goring, as we have seen, had marched north with his cavalry to rendezvous with the king, it being deemed that the New Model should follow in his wake, but a brigade was detached for the purpose under Surrey Parliamentarian Sir Ralph Weldon, and on 9 May this last force duly appeared before the Royalist lines. Fierce fighting was currently in progress in the very streets, but Hopton appears to have got the impression that he was about to be attacked by Fairfax's entire army rather than a single brigade and therefore ordered a retreat, leaving the way open for Weldon to link up with Blake amid the blazing ruins.[63]

If the inhabitants of Taunton thought that their travails were over, they were sorely mistaken. Having relieved the town, Weldon made to leave the area, only suddenly to be confronted by Goring, the latter having persuaded Charles to permit him to return to the task of subduing the West Country.[64] Had he acted with vigour, Goring could probably have overwhelmed Weldon, who was, after all, caught between two fires, but, worn down by heavy drinking, the Royalist commander was well past his best. Some rather confused skirmishes aside, then, his Parliamentarian opponent managed to get back to Taunton with his forces all but unscathed, the town then being subjected to a further siege, not that this amounted to much more than a loose blockade.[65] Once again, moreover, help was at hand, and this time, not in the form of some scratch force of local troops or a mere brigade, but rather in that of the full weight of the New Model Army. Thus, following the king's defeat at Naseby, Fairfax had been ordered to march west to deal with Grenville, Goring and Hopton. Abandoning his efforts against Taunton, Goring decided to meet the oncoming Parliamentarians head on and to this end took up a strong position behind a stream known the Wagg Rhyne just east of Langport. Ensconced behind high hedges on ground that could only be accessed by a narrow lane leading uphill from a single bridge, the Royalists should have been able to make a good fight of it. That said, Goring had only 7,000 men to Fairfax's 10,000, while months of lack of pay and insufficient rations had reduced his forces to a mutinous rabble. Nor did it help that a substantial part of Goring's cavalry that had been sent to occupy the nearby village of Isle Abbots had only the day before been routed in a surprise attack, When Fairfax attacked on 10 July, then, a single cavalry charge up the lane from the bridge was enough to burst the defenders asunder and have them fleeing in all directions, leaving 300 dead and another 2,000 taken prisoner.[66]

Langport was a body-blow to the Royalist cause in the West Country. A considerable number of troops got away to Bridgewater, where they were joined by a Goring who had been separated from his command in the last moments of the action, but it was clear that another field battle was an impossibility, Bridgewater therefore being given a reinforcement of 1,000 men and what was left of the army put on the road for North Devon. With Goring's remaining troops ever more depleted by desertion and the high command riven by personal disputes, had Fairfax pressed on he might have destroyed the western Royalists there and then, but he was perturbed by the fact there were still enemy garrisons at Sherborne, Bath and Bristol, and therefore turned back to deal with them, albeit not before the defenders of Bridgewater had been overcome in a ferocious action that ended with much of the town in flames.[67] Completely overawed, the garrison of Bath surrendered without a fight on 30 July, but those of Sherborne and Bristol were made of sterner stuff. Thus, headed by Sir Lewis Dyve, the defenders of the former withstood a two-week siege before surrendering on 14 August, while, possessed of no less a person than Prince Rupert as its governor, Bristol threatened to be even harder to overcome. Yet, exactly as Nathaniel Fiennes had discovered in 1643, the fact that the city's fortifications were as imposing as any in England was of little use if there were not enough men to man them. If it was true enough that Rupert had a force of some 4,500 men as opposed to Fiennes' 2,500, the difference was not enough, and, having in late August successfully closed in on the walls despite a series of gallant sorties on the part of the garrison, Fairfax therefore resolved to take the city by storm. In the small hours of 10 September, then, the bulk of the Parliamentarian infantry hurled themselves on the same two sectors of the defences that had been attacked by Rupert just two years earlier. This time, however, the results were very different. While some units put up a fierce fight, others broke and ran, while the foot had no sooner secured the gates than they unbarred them and let a torrent of horse into the city. With the remaining defenders taken in the rear, Rupert was left with no choice but to try to negotiate the best terms he could for his men (a task he achieved quite successfully, the garrison being permitted to march away to join the defenders of Oxford).[68]

The surrender of Bristol completely broke the reputation of Prince Rupert, and, as we have seen, he played little part in the remaining months of the conflict. Though all too many, the travails of the unfortunate prince are not something that need concern us here, what matters being rather the ongoing campaign in the west, this last being resumed with renewed vigour following the diversion occasioned by the siege of Basing House (see Chapter 7). Scattered across Devon and Dorset were a series of scattered garrisons - Portland Castle, Corfe Castle, Dunster Castle, Tiverton, Dartmouth, Barnstaple and Exeter - while Grenville and Goring had between them managed to reconstitute the army beaten at Langport under the command of Hopton, the latter's position as Lord-General of all the Royalist forces in the west having finally been confirmed by the king, and, one-by-one, these all now felt the full weight of Parliament's burgeoning military power.[69] Marching west once more, Fairfax stormed the town of Tiverton on 16 October and took the surrender of its castle three days later.[70] By the beginning of December the Parliamentarians were threatening Exeter, and on 14 December a daring attempt to launch an amphibious attack across the Exe on the Royalist stronghold of Powderham Castle led to a fierce struggle in which the attackers ended up being forced to barricade themselves in the parish church, the next day seeing them retrace their way to the east bank of the estuary. Thanks to the onset of dreadful winter weather, operations than came to a standstill, only for the lull to be broken by an attempt to relieve Exeter on the part of the commander of Hopton's cavalry, Henry Wentworth. However, easily broken by no less a figure than Oliver Cromwell at Bovey Heath on 9 January 1646, all this achieved was a foretaste of the utter calamity that now threatened the Royalist cause. Thus, having chased off Wentworth, the victorious Parliamentarians rounded on Dartmouth, which place was duly stormed after a siege of a mere eight days.[71] Turning north, having stormed the Royalist outpost of Mamhead House, vanquished the troublesome garrison of Powderham Castle and surrounded Exeter, on 17 February Fairfax attacked Hopton, who had concentrated his field army at Torrington, the Royalist forces being driven from the town in rout after a brutal battle that left much of the place in ruins.[72] Further east, meanwhile, if a column of cavalry dispatched from Oxford under Cromwell's cousin, Colonel James Cromwell, had in early February launched a surprise attack on the Parliamentarian soldiers holding Wareham and got a certain amount of food into Corfe Castle, three weeks later the defenders were overcome by a ruse that saw a turncoat officer of the garrison manage to get a strong party of enemy troops inside the walls, the governor and Lady Bankes in consequence having no option but to lay down their arms.[73] Blockaded for the past month or more, on 31 March the governor of Exeter, Sir John Berkeley, was summoned to surrender, a demand to which he acceded on 9 April in exchange for generous terms, while, similarly summoned to surrender, Barnstaple capitulated without a fight four days later.[74] Finally, having been blockaded since the turn of the year, on 6 April Portland Castle surrendered in exchange for terms that were once again very generous, an example that was followed on 30 April by its counterpart at Dunster.[75]

, All that was now left to the Royalists was Cornwall, where Hopton was still at liberty with an army of perhaps 10,000 men, not that this was in any state to fight, the soldiers being uniformly undisciplined and mutinous. Nor was the situation with respect to civil-military relations any better, all sign of such loyalty to the Crown as there had been in the early days of the war having long since succumbed to despair and war-weariness, not to mention fury at Royalist billeting, requisitioning and impressment. As one contemporary observer put it, 'You must take into consideration the large numbers of poor soldiers maimed and hurt and the hard condition they were in …The Cornish looked on themselves as left to sustain all, and the burden of the war lay on them so heavy [that] they were all grown hopeless.'[76] As if this was not enough, Hopton's elevation to the command of the army had angered Sir Richard Grenville and the many Cornish officers associated with him, the former's defiance being so blatant that Hopton had no option but to arrest him and strip him of his commission.[77] Given the circumstances, to expect much from Cornwall was at best a forlorn hope, what followed therefore being a foregone conclusion. No sooner had Fairfax led his army across the Tamar on 24 February, then, than resistance dwindled to nothing other than a few skirmishes, matters being worsened still further for the Royalists by the fact that, unlike Essex, Fairfax kept his forces in check and kept their pillaging to a minimum and in general exercising the utmost restrain. With Hopton all too convinced that the situation was hopeless, there was no fighting, and on 2 March the New Model entered Bodmin, whereupon the Prince of Wales and his council took ship for France, leaving Hopton to obtain such terms as he could, the Royalist army finally surrendering on 9 March at the village of Tresilian near Truro.[78] Setting aside the Scilly Isles, all that was left to the Royalist cause was Pendennis Castle. This Henrician fortress, it was decided, should be clung onto at all costs in the hope that, should the desperate efforts that were currently in train on the part of Henrietta Maria to obtain aid from France come to fruition, it could serve as a *point d'appui*.[79] The governor, 79-year-old Sir John Arundell of Trerice, being a doughty individual and the castle's defences very strong, there followed yet another lengthy siege, but, in the absence of any relief force, this could have but one end, and on 16 August 1646 the famished garrison, the last Royalist force in mainland England, laid down its arms in exchange for generous terms of the sort for which Fairfax had set a precedent at Exeter and Barnstaple.[80]

Thus ended the south-west's experience of the conflicts of 1642-51. For all that the region completely escaped the Second and Third Civil Wars, it was beyond doubt an area of the country that had been very hard hit. As Underdown writes of Somerset, for example, 'It was a ruined and ravaged county. The plague raged alarmingly … poverty was widespread, food prices high and trade hampered by the wartime disruption of already primitive communications.'[81] Places large and small had been besieged, fought over and subjected to much destruction, while the battle of Lansdown, in particular, had been as horrific as any of its fellows elsewhere in the country. And, finally, at the hands of, first, Hopton's Cornish army; second, the soldiers of the Earl of Essex; and, finally, Goring's 'crew', as the remnants of his ever more undisciplined forces were for many years remembered, many areas had been subjected to periods of unremitting pillage. That the period was stamped on the popular memory is therefore anything but a surprise, and, as everywhere else, this has ensured that the region is awash with ghost stories relating to the era. As usual, let us start with the various élite figures said to haunt historic sites around the region, in which respect we can list Queen Henrietta Maria; King Charles II; Royalist officer Sir Sidney Godolphin; archetypal Cavalier Sir Thomas Lunsford; Sir John Saint-John and Sir John Stawell, both of them Wiltshire Royalists who, in the case of the former, lost three sons in the service of the king and, in that of the latter, the whole of his fortune; the defender of Taunton, Robert Blake; and, last but not least, Blanche Arundell, of which the first stalks Barnfield House near Exeter, the country-seat to which she retired for the birth of her last baby; the second Bovey House near Beer, a residence in which he supposedly took refuge during his peregrinations in the wake of the Battle of Worcester; the third the Three Crowns Hotel in Chagford, the building, then a private house, in which he took refuge when he was mortally wounded in a skirmish fought in the village in 1643; the fourth the Bristol alley-way known as Christmas Steps; the fifth, sixth - generally known as 'the Red Cavalier' - and seventh their respective family homes, namely Lydiard House near Swindon, Avebury Manor and a house in the main street of Bridgewater that is now the town's museum; and the eighth the ramparts of Wardour Castle.[82]

Next, of course, comes the list of hauntings that simply feature unknown figures of the period, good examples being the three Cavaliers observed standing in the corner of one of the bars in the Devon village of Buckland Brewer's Coach and Horses Inn; the similar group, albeit this time covered in blood, who haunt the chapel of Gaulden Manor, Somerset; the two Cavaliers who endlessly fight and refight a duel in the great hall of Devon's Athelhampton Hall; the tableau of a similar contest, complete with the death one of the participants, seen by an RNAS pilot near Mullion in 1917; the individual Cavaliers espied at Velly Farm near Clovelly in Devon, at Hound Tor in Dartmoor, at Well's Crown Hotel, at Eggbuckland's long-since demolished Widey Court (for a time in 1644 the headquarters of Prince Maurice), at the sixteenth-century building in Salisbury known as the Wardrobe, at the Highway Inn in Sourton, at the Cridford Inn in Trusham, at the Who'd Have Thought It? inn at Milton Combe, at Longleat House, and at Devizes Castle; the male figure dressed in seventeenth-century clothing who stalks Compton Castle in Devon; the Royalist soldiers reported from Corfe Castle; the Cavalier whistling 'Greensleeves' sometimes spotted on the road leading north from the Wiltshire village of Bulford; the three men in 'Musketeer-style clothing' spotted in Lyme Regis' Volunteer Inn in January 2000; the drummer who walks the grounds of Lydiard House; the man and woman, the former holding a sword and pistol, who lurk in Taunton Castle; the Roundhead, identified, one presumes, by a supposedly so-characteristic lobster-pot helmet, who terrifies walkers in Stapleton Woods near Bristol by walking straight through them; the soldier remembered as one Richard and woman in seventeenth-century clothes (reputedly the mother of the governor, Colonel Wyndham) seen at Dunster Castle; the five Cavaliers, by tradition killed in a skirmish in the town, who are the 'in-dwells' of Weymouth's Boot Inn; and, finally, the rather jollier group consisting of five Cavaliers playing cards forever condemned to haunt Wonson Manor in Devon on account, or so it is said, of fleecing the owner out of his property.[83]

As ever, far more interesting than such cases, the origins of all of which, to reiterate, may well lie in drink, imagination or pure invention, are the various hauntings to which some story can be attached or which suggest themselves as folk-memories of documented events. As ever again, many of the former deal with the sufferings and experience of women. In this respect, the first of them to be highlighted is that of subjugation. If Avebury Manor boasts the ghost of Sir John Stawell, for example, the village's Red Lion Inn is equally the home of a spectre known as Florence, this last by tradition being the ghost of a young woman whose husband murdered her for the crime of taking a lover while he was away at the wars and then threw her body down a well.[84] Moving on to the other extreme of the region, the last refuge of the Royalist cause in the south-west, Pendennis Castle, is reputedly haunted by, first, the governor, Sir John Arundell, and, second, the unhappy spirits of the starving women and children of the garrison, and the grounds of Llanhydrock House, the home of local Parliamentarian notable Lord Robartes, that of a Royalist soldier hung for pillage, while from Poundstock Manor near Bude comes the story of Kate Penfound, this running more-or-less as follows: the daughter of a staunch Royalist, Penfound fell in love with Parliamentarian-favouring John Trebarfoot, and endeavoured to elope with him, only for her father to discover what was afoot and fall on Trebarfoot with his sword; both the woman and her lover being mortally wounded in the subsequent scrimmage, they are seemingly condemned to re-enact the tragic scene for all time.[85] For another unhappy love affair that resulted in a haunting, meanwhile, we can turn to Tiverton Castle. Thus, according to legend, a quarrel broke out between local Royalist Sir Charles Trevor, and one Maurice Fortescue, a young man attached to the garrison, with regard to the favours of the daughter of the governor, Sir Hugh Spencer, a young woman by the name of Alice. Eventually, Trevor challenged Fortescue to a duel, and in the resultant combat, which was fought out on the banks of the River Exe beneath the walls of the castle, the latter was mortally wounded, his contemptuous opponent cementing his victory by throwing his body into the river, which happened to be in spate. Alice, however, had fallen in love with Fortescue, and, having seen what happened, rushed out of the castle in the hope of saving her lover. In this, alas, she was too late, and so, utterly distraught and fearing, too, that her father would force her to marry Trevor, she flung herself into the Exe and was swept away, the story being that she and Fortescue are periodically seen gliding over the water together, united in death.[86]

Sad though the three preceding stories are, there was nothing quintessentially 'Civil War' about them, for adultery had always entailed great risks, while women of the propertied classes could rarely expect to marry who they chose. What changed the situation, of course, was the presence of an added level of danger. This, too, is reflected in ghost stories of the era. Thus, Hanham Court Farm in the Bristol suburb of Hanham Abbots, Shute Barton Manor in Devon and the Wiltshire village of Broad Hinton all have tales that are suggestive of the vulnerability of women to the violence and loss brought by war, the first being haunted by 'Loyal Sally', the ghost of a servant maid killed for refusing to betray the whereabouts of some Royalist fugitives hiding in the area, the second a 'grey lady' reputed to be the ghost of a woman, namely the wife of the then owner, wantonly murdered by marauding Parliamentarian troops at a spot in the grounds known to this day as Lady's Walk, and the graveyard of the third's parish church by the shade of Winifred Glanville, the lady of the local manor and wife of the Speaker of the House of Commons, Sir John Glanville, who reputedly lost her mind in the wake of the death at the siege of Bridgewater of her eldest son, Francis.[87]

Moving on to those stories that suggest themselves as folk-memories of documented events, we come, first, to the claims of ghostly sounds of battle that have been made in respect of the villages of Ashmore in Dorset (a perfectly plausible site for some forgotten skirmish involving, say, Goring's troopers) and Bovey Tracey, Braddock Down, Lansdown, Roundway Down and Lostwithiel, and, in addition, those of the tramp of marching men heard in the streets of Dunster and the stench of burning flesh - the product, one assumes, of wounds being cauterised - that supposedly pervades Portland Castle (for good measure, part of the castle is graced by a much nicer smell, namely that of lavender, this last being associated with a woman, possibly the governor's mistress, said to have perished in the siege).[88] To these, meanwhile, can be joined the stories of apparitions of one sort or another, good examples being the crowds of seventeenth-century soldiers locked in battle that have been claimed suddenly to have sprung up around walkers crossing the site of the battle of Stratton; the shadowy figures of two men and a woman spotted on the battlefield of Lansdown, the fleeing horsemen seen by a couple caught out on Roundway Down by a sudden mist; the figures, seemingly the ghosts of twenty men killed in a skirmish between local clubmen and marauding Parliamentarians at the Devon village of Poyntington on 2 June 1645, glimpsed on a patch of land said to mark their graves; and, last but not least, the soldier, by repute a man killed in the battle of February 1646, that frequents Torrington's Castle Hill.[89] Not all such legacies of the past are quite so grim, however. Thus, situated in the eastern suburb of Bristol known as Saint George, the nature reserve known as Troopers Hill, a logical enough bivouac for troops besieging the city is noted, not for the clash of arms and the screams of wounded and dying men but rather the cheerful laughter of men taking their ease around a campfire.[90]

Across the south-west, then, the Civil War is commemorated via much the same sort of ghost stories that are told of the rest of the country, the overwhelming impression that we have, as usual, being one of violence, suffering and tragedy. That said, there is one notable difference. In many parts of the rest of England, as we have seen, there is a strong tendency to remember the supporters of King Charles in a very positive sense, Cavaliers being presented as veritable icons of courage and nobility reduced in many instances to figures of the utmost pathos dying heroically for a lost cause. In Wiltshire, Dorset, Somerset, Devon and Cornwall, by contrast, there is little of this romanticisation, true though it is that the real villains of some of the stories of Parliamentarian troops murdering defenceless women may in fact be Royalists. Of the much-vaunted Cornish infantry, for example, the only mention that we have is that of a man hung for an act of pillage committed at the family seat of Parliamentarian leader Lord Robartes. Equally, although there are only a few instances in which any characterisation is given to Royalist ghosts, in almost every case in respect to which we have some detail – the duellists of Athelhampton Hall and the card-players of Wonson Manor are the best examples – their image is distinctly negative, from which one can only presume that the depredations of 'Goring's crew' were so bad as to ensure that the folk-memories they left behind were left untarnished by the determination of the Restoration to sanctify the 'good old cause' and canonise its every adherent. Hence, in part at least, the willingness of many parts of the region to rally to the cause of the Duke of Monmouth in 1685 (an event which, unsurprisingly enough, also features very heavily in its ghost stories). As Susan Le Queux has said, 'Understanding the local history of a place can sometimes help to understand and discover what the psychic activity is and possibly why it is there.'[91]

Conclusion: Of Legacy and Memory

A s we have seen, then, there is, indeed, hardly a Civil War site in England that does not boast a spectral Roundhead or Cavalier or some other figure related to the period. Taking the first of our case studies as our baseline, if Rowton Heath is associated with such apparitions, so are Lansdown, Marston Moor and Naseby; if the siege of Chester is commemorated by many ghost stories, so are plenty of others including those of Arundel, Corfe and Hopton Castles, Colchester, Basing House, York and many more; if the noise of battle reputedly echoes in the streets of Chester, so it does in the Hampshire town of Alton and on the battlefield of Edgehill; if Sandbach has a haunted grave, so does Poyntington; if Bolton and Middleton have houses, hostelries or church-yards stalked by the phantoms of murdered Cavaliers, so do Pullox Hill, Fleet and Prestbury and a whole host of others; if Wythenshawe, Duddon and Chester have their share of tragic maidens, so do Goodrich Castle and Shute Barton Manor; if Chester's Blue Bell Inn has a Civil War tale to tell, so does Shrewsbury's Prince Rupert Hotel; and, finally, if Charles I is supposed to haunt the tower of Chester Cathedral and the home of John Bradshaw at Marple, Oliver Cromwell is supposed to do the same with regard to the school he attended at Huntingdon and the house in which he lived at Ely. Nor should any of this come as a surprise. For the generation caught up in it, the Civil War was a shattering experience. Erupting, as it did, from an era of peace and prosperity in which armed conflict had not been known for generations, it spread death and destruction far and wide, imposed heavy demands on the unhappy populace and challenged a whole series of age-old certainties. Even when peace was finally restored, meanwhile, many minds continued to be exercised by what their owners had seen, even to be filled by visions of horror.

From all this, much as had been the case with earlier traumatic episodes such as the Viking invasions and the Norman conquest - though the passage of time, of a full millennium indeed, has ensured that far fewer such tales have survived from them, the contents of many anthologies is such as to suggest that England must once have been awash with them – there emerged the many Civil War ghost stories that we have reviewed and, at least to some extent, attempted to verify. At the simplest of levels, the oral tradition that tales of haunting represented was how a populace with no access to any historical education made sense of its history. That said, it was a tradition that kept reinventing itself. Just as the stories of, for example, King Arthur, that presumably did the rounds of the halls and huts of Anglo-Saxon Britain were supplanted in their turn by stories of Alfred the Great, Harold Godwinson and William the Conqueror, so, six centuries on, the latter were replaced in their turn by stories of the Reformation – a period that could very easily make the subject of a discussion of the sort that has been attempted in this study – and the mid-Stuart crisis. To quote Owen Davies, 'The Civil War [became] the most popular episode in English legendary history, smothering and replacing earlier traditions of Old-English battles and monumental destruction.'[1]

Meanwhile, in the case of the struggles of 1642-51 in particular, ghost stories can be seen to have served another purpose. In those nine years, not only a king but an archbishop of Canterbury had gone to the scaffold; episcopacy had been overthrown and the country's cathedrals appropriated as barracks, prisons or magazines; England's ecclesiastical heritage subjected to a ruthless campaign of iconoclasm; castles and country houses sacked, slighted and burned to the ground; and the whole fabric of society subjected to the most sustained challenge it had faced since the Black Death. As if this was not enough, there had also been widespread breaches of public order as an angry and hard-pressed populace expressed its fury by taking matters into its own hands, most notably through the emergence of the clubmen, spontaneous acts of resistance such as that which reputedly occurred at Poyntington in 1645 and Sandbach in September 1651, and the murder of countless stragglers and fugitives from the ever more undisciplined, and, indeed, ever more defeated, Royalist armies and the isolated garrisons left stranded by their downfall. At the time of the wars all this had had a certain logic: there was, for example, a strong case to be made for the execution of Charles I as the only means of bringing peace to the country, while the fact that the depredations of desperate men acting, in a most literal sense, in cavalier fashion had evoked a violent response was easy to explain away in terms of acts of justifiable revenge and self-defence. However, as time went by, memories faded and the war generations were lost to the grave, so perceptions began to change. No sooner had Charles II been restored to the throne in 1660 than the Restoration régime began, as Erin Peters has put it, to seek to instil society with a sense of collective shame designed, on the one hand, to boost support for the new dispensation, and, on the other, undermine the reputation of the Commonwealth.[2] Here, for example, is an extract from the dedication to a play entitled *The Roundheads* published by the female playwright Avra Behm in 1682, this last being addressed to the Duke of Grafton, then Colonel of the Regiment of Foot-Guards:

> This *play*, for which I humbly beg Your Grace's protection, needs it in a more peculiar manner, it having drawn down legions upon its head for its loyalty – '*What! To name us?*', cries one; '*'Tis most abominable unheard of daring!*', cries another; '*She deserves to be swung!*', cries a third – as if 'twere all a libel, a scandal impossible to be proved, or that their rogueries were of so old a date their reign were past remembrance or history And I am satisfied, that they that will justify the best of these traitors, deserves the fate of the worst, and most manifestly declare to the world by it, [that] they would be at the *old game* their forefathers played with so good success.[3]

Equally scathing, meanwhile, was a broadside ballad published the previous year. Thus:

Now for shame ye zealots be confounded;
Boast no more allegiance,
For a Roundhead is grounded upon the holy sham.
How dare ye talk of loyalty, ye hater of justice, king and law?[4]

Finally, to the chorus of Cavalier and neo-Cavalier voices there was added the trumpet-blasts of repentant Roundheads eager to ingratiate themselves with the Restoration and at the same time, no friends of independency, deeply alienated by the direction that events had taken in the latter part of the war. Here, for example, is Denzil Holles, a Member of Parliament who headed a regiment of infantry in the forces of the Earl of Essex at Edgehill and Brentford and went on to become a champion of the Presbyterian cause, on the New Model Army, a force become, as he put it, 'an excrescence that drew away the whole nourishment of the body, and starved it'. Thus:

> That army was composed for the most part of factious sectaries … [and] grew to be not only an unnecessary grievous burden in respect of charge, but also a let and hindrance to the settling all government, both civil and ecclesiastical, neither submitting themselves to order of Parliament, nor permitting others where they could hinder it, but giving countenance to all disorders, especially in the Church, as breaking open the church doors, doing most unseemly barbarous things, indeed not fit to be related either to modest or Christian ears, and in time of Divine Service interrupting ministers as they were preaching, miscalling [and] reviling them, sometimes pulling them down by violence, beating and abusing them, getting into the pulpits themselves, and venting either ridiculous or scandalous things … countenancing and publishing seditious pamphlets … decrying both King and Parliament and all authority [and] infusing a rebellious spirit into the people, under the pretence of liberty and freedom.[5]

While mud was flung in one direction, of course, white-wash was hurled in the other. 'In the last years of the war, the Cavaliers were hated and feared throughout the length and breadth of the land', writes Ian Roy. 'The defeat of the King's main armies … unleashed numerous straggling, unofficered bands of reformados, intent on pillaging the remaining resources of the countryside … Even close to Oxford, mounted hangers-on … stole horses … and became highwaymen … In north Wales, one of the most rapacious commanders … Sir William Vaughan, [was] nicknamed "the Devil of Shrarawdine".'[6] Yet, even before the Restoration, Royalist poets such as Andrew Marvell were presenting the die-hard Cavaliers of the Second Civil War - men like Sir Charles Lucas and Sir George Lisle, both of them executed at Colchester, and Sir Francis Villiers, slain in the action at Surbiton - as not the robber-barons that, however willy-nilly, they became, but rather peerless exemplars of chivalry, while at the same time straining every nerve to portray the Royalist cause as that of wit and learning.[7] Equally, it is in large measure to the so-called Cavalier poets of the Restoration era that we owe the stereotype of the supporters of King Charles as dashing blades bent on, to purloin the words of one of their poems, 'gathering rosebuds while ye may', and, not just that, but wistful figures, reluctant warriors forced to take arms to satisfy the demands of honour and loyalty.[8]

If historians have been but little interested in the paranormal, at least this transformation is something that has captured their attention. As John Stubbs has written of the supporters of Charles I, '[The] Cavaliers ... were being remade ... Later generations sought to maintain the air of respectability ... The fictitious gentleman of Defoe's *Memoirs of a Cavalier* (1720) actually combines the virtues of a staunch Royalist with those of a godly warrior, fighting for the Protestants in Europe before returning to defend his king.'[9] As if the diatribes of Restoration penitents, *literati* and *sub-literati* were not enough, meanwhile, two centuries on, driven by a mixture of Romanticism and dark fears of the march of progress, a host of Georgian and Victorian writers and artists competed with one another to romanticise the Royalist cause and portray Cromwell and his fellow Parliamentarians as soulless brutes and bullies (one thinks here of such examples as Sir Walter Scott's *Woodstock*, Frederick Marryat's *Children of the New Forest* and William Yeames' painting 'When did you last see your father?'). Thus, King Charles was transformed from being a 'man of blood' into a saintly martyr and his host of fugitive followers from ruthless plunderers who every day committed actions that invited their extermination to lonely champions of a noble cause who were worthy of a better fate. In the process, meanwhile, it would not be surprising to find the demonisation of the Roundhead cause reflected in the retelling of the ghost stories: for example, of Romsey, as we have seen, it is said that the Old Swan Inn resounds to the screams of two Parliamentarian soldiers who were hung outside its doors, but how do we know that, assuming that what we are dealing with here is actually a folk-memory, the two men concerned were not rather Royalist troopers who were either executed by their own side or lynched by townsfolk angered at the depredations of the soldiery? There was, of course, always a radical tradition whose loyalties continued to lie with the Parliamentarians, but, as the triumph of 'Church and King' patriotism in the 1790s suggests, it was not until well into the nineteenth century that it acquired substantial roots in the crowd: it is very noticeable that the number of public houses called 'The Fairfax' or 'The Cromwell', if any such exist at all, is dwarfed by that of those bearing such proud names as 'The King's Head' and 'The Royal Oak'. This being the case, it is at the very least possible to argue that many Civil War ghost stories were in effect expressions of collective guilt in the face of a situation in which the execution of King Charles in Whitehall had on the local level been mirrored by the brutal dispatch of large numbers of men desperate for food and shelter who were rightly or wrongly perceived as a source of danger: if the headless figure of King Charles stalks various sites, of which Chester Cathedral and Christchurch College, Oxford, are but the most exalted, there are literally dozens of tales featuring the murder of isolated Royalist soldiers.

Nor is this the only way the realities of war were distorted in the popular memory. One thing that is quite clear is that, to the extent that the civilian population suffered at the hands of the contending armies, it was the forces of the king that bore the lion's share of the blame. Thus, in the only instances where towns were sacked – Bolton, Birmingham, Liverpool and Leicester – the culprits were Royalist troops, while their superior resources and organisation enabled the Parliamentarians to keep their men fed and supplied much more consistently and thereby to ensure that the soldiery, not all of whom were pious and sober Ironsides by any means, were generally kept within the bounds of military discipline. Yet in almost all the ghost stories that have been found that relate to acts of violence in respect of the populace – the one exception is the case of the Warrington blacksmith Giles Boston – the perpetrators are not Royalists but Roundheads, as witness, for example, the tailor killed at Foulridge in Lancashire; the unfaithful woman murdered by her soldier-husband at Gubberford Bridge; the unfortunate Grace Trygg; the servant-girl slain by Parliamentarian troops in the storm of Wythenshawe Hall; the woman hung at Heskin Hall; and, finally, the Grey Lady of Shute Barton. If Ironsides were as grim as their appearance, then, Cavalier apparitions – good examples are those associated with Speke Hall, the King's Head at Lichfield, the Rake Inn at Littleborough and the Highway Inn at Sourton – were rather often jovial figures clearly fond of a glass whose worst sin was womanising, a characteristic, commemorated, as we have seen, by the presence who is reputed to make a nuisance of himself in Fordingbridge's Tudor Rose pub (that said, one negative characteristic of the Cavaliers that is remembered in the ghost stories is their propensity to duelling, as witness, for example, the stories that we have from Mullion in Cornwall, the Old King's Head in Chester, Athelhampton Hall in Devon and Jesus College in Oxford, though this capacity for violence has but been sanitised as an integral part of their image as 'men of honour').

If the Cavalier became a celebrated figure in the popular mind, even, indeed, an admired figure, it was not just because of a constant barrage of Restoration propaganda. Even before the Civil War, for all the growth of Puritanism, there had been an undercurrent of resistance to its demands, for the insistence that the Sabbath should be kept holy and the condemnation that its more hard-line elements lavished on many aspects of popular culture (most famously music and dancing, but also bowls, gambling, cock-fighting, bear-baiting and such brutal entertainments as shin-kicking contests and bare-knuckle fighting) as threats to public order and morality alike constituted serious infringements of the leisure activities available to the populace. If the 'Olympick Games' organised on a hill near Chipping Campden every year from 1612 onwards by the wealthy and well-connected lawyer Robert Dover became a roaring success, then, it was in part because they represented an act of defiance to Puritan mores, while an important factor in the popular royalism visible in many parts of the country in 1642 was Charles I's promulgation of the so-called 'Book of Sports' in 1633, an action that expressly permitted the populace to engage in at least the less unruly of the pastimes the Puritans in effect sought to ban.[10] Welcomed though it was (and, indeed, because it was) by wide sections of the gentry and people alike, the measure infuriated the 'godly' and the debates of the 'Long Parliament' therefore saw many attacks upon it, the offending document finally being publicly disavowed in 1643. Nor did the offensive stop there: as is widely known, the celebration of Christmas was banned in 1647, while, in many areas at least, the so-called 'rule of the major-generals' was accompanied by further assaults on popular sports and festivities.[11] All this, of course, occasioned much resistance, of which the 'Christmas riot' in Canterbury in December 1647 was but the tip of the iceberg, while it is difficult to imagine the constant diet of sermons on which Puritanism religiosity was centred failing to occasion considerable boredom and resentment among the less biddable elements of the people.[12] We therefore come to a deeper reason for the rehabilitation of the Cavaliers in that they were increasingly seen as being in every respect the antithesis of what the 'rule of the saints' stood for, the personification, indeed, of 'good old days' whose many deficiencies were increasingly forgotten.[13]

Profound though the feelings of remorse suggested by these distortions of the past were, however, even the Civil War was not proof against cultural marginalisation, one of the things that is most clear from the gazetteer that accompanies this work (see appendix) is that, the more urbanised the setting, the less friendly it is to Cavalier and Roundhead ghosts: thus, while conurbations such as Liverpool, Manchester and Birmingham can boast of rich collections of hauntings, the stories that are attached to them mostly date from the nineteenth and twentieth centuries and in consequence reflect an experience of life that was very different. At the same time, the loss of more and more of the built environment of the Stuart period swept away many backdrops that might have assisted in conjuring up visions of Civil War ghosts: the apparition of a woman in seventeenth-century costume reported, as we have seen, from a social club in Farnsworth, Greater Manchester, is very much an exception in this respect (those who specialise in the paranormal make much the same point, but in another way, their belief being that hauntings are necessarily brought to an end by the physical destruction of their setting). Even before the Industrial Revolution began to bite, meanwhile, a new 'ghost of choice' - the highwayman - was beginning to supplant the monks and Cavaliers who had been its predecessors, just as, in the case of Liverpool, the 'May Blitz' of 1941 can be seen to have conjured up a new and more relevant array of ghosts than the victims of Prince Rupert in 1644.[14]

Nor is it just a matter of fresh sets of experiences eclipsing their predecessors. On the contrary, society and technology having moved on apace, the functions that the ghost story once served have long since been rendered redundant: in a de-Christianised society, concepts of Purgatory or the Devil have no meaning. That being the case, one cannot but be extremely sceptical about most of the latter-day apparitions that have been reported: while there are certainly some that are harder to challenge than others, it is impossible not to suspect that many are the fruit of invention, imagination or hallucination, or even, in a few cases, student jokes (to take the instance of Oxford, has Charles I really been seen rushing round the Bodleian Library snatching books from the shelves and has, too, a beheaded Archbishop Laud really been seen kicking his head along the floor football-style in Saint John's College?). If fresh stories of Civil War hauntings continue to crop up from time to time, it is as much as anything because the figure of the Roundhead or Cavalier is extremely well-known, many of the battlefields and other sites of conflict clearly identified and the memory of the conflict further kept alive by the efforts of the gallant re-enactors of the Sealed Knot and the English Civil War Society (one wonders, indeed, whether more than one recent tale of haunting was occasioned by nothing more spectral than a brief glimpse of one of their members).[15] Indeed, with the growth of tourism and, alongside it, the heritage industry, the revival of old ghost stories and the generation of new ones has become endowed with a powerful economic incentive - it is no coincidence that so many stately homes open to the public, so many hotels and so many hostelries boast of spectres of one sort or another, nor, for that matter, that so many of said spectres are Cavaliers (for even those but little versed in history, the followers of King Charles are well enough known to make an obvious choice for those in search of a handy in-dwell). We come here, of course, to the extent to which the Civil War has become embedded in popular culture: if the producers of the popular television series 'Midsomer Murders' had little hesitation in basing an early episode on a haunting involving a ghostly Cavalier, a figure that is also common to the work of many novelists who have made use of the same sort of figure, in each case, the assumption was, of course, that this was a historical theme well within the grasp of the general public.[16] For aristocratic families challenged by the advance of the modern world, meanwhile, a ghost in the house served as a *de facto* badge of exclusivity, an unchallengeable claim, indeed, to status and lineage, while so much the better if the spectral presence to which they laid claim was one that resonated with traditional virtues such as military prowess and loyalty to the throne. Small wonder, then, that Brooks can write, 'The spectral inhabitants of the stately homes of this country are seldom regarded with alarm by their owners. Rather they seem to tolerate them as part of the furnishings, however disturbing their habits, with a kind of off-hand pride.'[17]

To maintain a strong degree of scepticism is therefore eminently sensible. Yet to make these points is not the same as to claim that the ghost story is devoid of historical interest. On the contrary, in the first place, there is the issue of geographical distribution: of the 234 places from which Civil War ghosts have been reported, no fewer than 155 are in the Midlands, the south-east and the south-west, or, in other words, the relatively prosperous and well-found regions in which the bulk of the fighting necessarily took place.[18] In the second, as we have seen in a number of instances, many of the older tales clearly represent genuine folk-memories, some of which - for example, those recorded at Lydiate and Winnington Bridge - capture events that receive scant mention in even the more specialised historiography. And in the third, they give us an insight into the way history is experienced by people who would ordinarily have had no voice. One thinks here, especially, of the women of Stuart Britain. Until very recently denied any coverage in the historiography other than in the case of a few élite figures such as Henrietta Maria and the Countess of Derby, they are now more prominent, there having been much stress on 'she-soldiers' and female preachers and prophetesses. However, if the theme here is the empowerment of women – indeed, the agency of women – the ghost stories tell a very different tale, namely one that centres above all on insecurity and vulnerability, if not violence and death, in which respect one has only to think of the wails of women lamenting husbands and lovers slain in the battle of Edgehill that are said to resound in the Warwickshire village of Lighthorne.

To conclude, then, the hauntings that have been at the heart of this work represent both historic memory and, albeit to a lesser extent, historical narrative. Let them, certainly, be analysed with the most critical of eyes, and let them, too, be set within the context and geography of the actual march of historical events, but let there also be both collection and curation. If the ghosts of Grace Trygg and her many companions cannot tell us very much, they can yet tell us something, while at the same time standing proxy for the many victims of the conflict who have neither grave nor memory. 'Whether you believe in ghosts or not', writes Owen Davies, 'there is no doubt they make ideal guides for exploring the thoughts and emotions of our ancestors.'[19] Keeping that in mind, then, let us close with words written by the leading Puritan divine, Richard Baxter. Thus:

Oh the sad and heart-piercing spectacles that mine eyes have seen in four years' space! Scarce a month, scarce a week, without the sight or noise of blood so that hearing such sad news on one side or the other was our daily work in so much that duly as I was awakened in the morning I expected to hear one come and tell me such a garrison is one or lost or such a defeat received or given. And 'Do you hear the news?' was commonly the first word I heard. So miserable were those bloody days in which he was the most honourable that could kill most of his enemies.[20]

Gazetteer

East Anglia

Cambridge: Oliver Cromwell (Sidney Sussex College).

Ely, Cambridgeshire: Oliver Cromwell (Cromwell's House).

Huntingdon: Oliver Cromwell (Cromwell Museum).

Melford Hall, Suffolk: Lady Rivers, Melford Hall.

Raynham Hall, Norfolk: Cavalier.

Saint Neots, Cambridgeshire: Earl of Holland (New Inn).

Woodcroft Castle, Cambridgeshire: Michael Hudson.

Ireland

Clonegal Castle, Carlow: Royalist soldier accidentally shot dead by a comrade.

Scotland

Balgonie Castle, Fife: seventeenth-century soldier.

Brodick Castle, Arran: servant girl who committed suicide after falling pregnant to a soldier of the garrison.

Edinburgh: drummer (castle); plague victims (Mary King's Close).

Fordell, Fife: apprentice hung by marauding Parliamentarian troops in 1651.

Penkaet Castle, East Lothian: Charles I.

The Midlands

Aston Hall, West Midlands: unknown woman.

Attenborough, Nottinghamshire: troop of Roundheads.

Banbury, Oxfordshire: executed soldier (Reindeer Hotel).

Bolsover Castle, Derbyshire: Marquis of Newcastle.

Bradgate Park, Leicestershire: group of Civil War soldiers.

Bromham, Bedfordshire: Sir Lewis Dyve (parish church).

Bromsgrove, West Midlands: Cavalier (Ye Old Black Crosse).

Broughton Hall, Staffordshire: unknown boy.

Claydon House, Buckinghamshire: Sir Edmund Verney.

Codnor Castle, Derbyshire: soldier of Cromwell's army.

Droitwich, Worcestershire: Cavalier.

East Retford, Nottinghamshire: Cavalier.

Eccleshall Castle, Staffordshire: Cavalier.

Elvaston Castle, Derbyshire: sounds of battle.

Grafton Regis, Northamptonshire: sounds of battle.

Hagley, West Midlands: Cavalier.

Halton, Warwickshire: Cavalier.

Hanborough, Oxfordshire: murdered woman.

Hopton Heath, Staffordshire: scenes of battle.

Kempsey, Worcestershire: Fitzwilliam.

Kineton, Warwickshire: riderless white horse; sounds of battle.

Kings Norton, Warwickshire: maid-servant (Saracen's Head).

Leicester, Leicestershire: screams (Guild Hall).

Lichfield, Staffordshire: Cavalier (King's Head).

Lighthorne, Warwickshire: women bewailing their dead; bloodstains.

Mamble, Worcestershire: Cavalier (Sun and Slipper).

Marston Trussel, Northamptonshire: Royalist fugitives.

Middleton Hall, Northamptonshire: galloping horsemen.

Naseby, Northamptonshire: group of Parliamentarians.

Newark, Nottinghamshire: Prince Rupert (Kirkgate House).

Northampton: Cavalier (Hind Hotel).

Oxford: Charles I (Bodleian Library, Christchurch College); Prudence Bostock (Magpie Lane); Sir Francis Windebank (Merton College); sound of cavalry (New College Lane); Archbishop Laud (Saint John's College); Lord Grandison's rival (Jesus College).

Pavenham, Worcestershire: Royalist fugitive.

Prior's Court, Worcestershire: Royalist fugitive.

Sedgeley, West Midlands: Cavalier (White Lion).

Sinai Park House, Staffordshire: sounds of battle.

Sutton Coldfield, West Midlands: murdered drummer (Three Tuns Hotel); hoof-beats (Yew-Tree Walk).

Swarkestone Bridge, Derbyshire: sound of galloping horses.

Upton-on-Severn, Worcestershire: Cavalier (Tudor House).

Warwick: man put on trial for looting the dead of Edgehill (Anchor Inn).

Wichenford Court, Worcestershire: Elizabeth Washburne.

Worcester: Duke of Hamilton (the Commandery).

Worsham, Oxfordshire: galloping horsemen.

Wordsley, West Midlands: Cavalier (Old Cat Inn).

Youlgreave, Derbyshire: Cavalier and Roundhead engaged in a fierce sword-fight.

The North-West

Appley Bridge, Lancashire: skull (Skull Cottage).

Barton-on-Irwell, Greater Manchester: Cavalier fugitive (Rock Hotel).

Blackburn: William Dutton (Black Bull).

Billinge, Lancashire: murdered Cavalier (Stork Hotel).

Bolton, Greater Manchester: Earl of Derby (Old Man and Scythe); fugitive Cavalier (Hall in the Wood).

Carlisle: Cavalier (city walls).

Carr House, Lancashire: fugitive from the battle of Preston.

Chester: Charles I (cathedral); Earl of Derby (Stanley Palace); sounds of battle (Saint Werburgh's Street, city walls); Henrietta (Blue Bell Inn); Cavaliers, women in seventeenth-century attire (Goblin Tower); male laughter, female moans (Old Boot Inn); severed heads (River Dee); headless man (Tudor House); sentry shot by firing squad for falling asleep at his post (Water Tower); cries of lamentation (Water Tower Gardens); Cavalier (Old King's Head).

Christleton, Cheshire: two seventeenth-century soldiers.

Clitheroe Castle, Lancashire: three Royalist prisoners shot while trying to escape.

Farnsworth, Greater Manchester: seventeenth-century woman (Dixon Green Labour Club).

Foulridge, Lancashire: murdered tailor (Tailor's Cross); victim of the Battle of Preston (New Inn).

Gubberford Bridge, Lancashire: murdered woman.

Heskin Hall, Lancashire: young woman murdered by Roundhead soldiers.

Hockenhall Hall, Cheshire: Grace Trygg.

Hoghton Tower, Lancashire: Roger Starkie.

Littleborough, Greater Manchester: Cavalier (Rake Inn).

Hoole Heath, Cheshire: Cavalier.

Lydiate, Lancashire: sounds of battle.

Marple Hall, Cheshire: Charles I; maidservant.

Middleton, Greater Manchester: two soldiers killed in a skirmish (School Lane); murdered Cavalier fugitive (Ring o'Bells).

Nantwich, Cheshire: Royalist officer (Churche's Mansion); Roundhead officer (Black Lion); sounds of battle (Dead Man's Field).

Newton-le-Willows, Greater Manchester: tramp of marching men.

Rowton Heath, Cheshire: William Lawes, Lord Bernard Stuart, horseman, sounds of battle, ghostly music.

Rivington, Lancashire: rider in seventeenth-century dress.

Rochdale, Greater Manchester: man in seventeenth-century dress (Saint Mary's church).

Sandbach, Cheshire: Scottish piper (Piper's Hollow).

Speke Hall, Merseyside: Cavalier.

Thurnham Hall, Lancashire: Cavalier.

Turton Moor, Lancashire: Cavalier.

Vicar's Cross, Cheshire: Civil War soldiers.

Warrington, Greater Manchester: Giles Boston (Black Horse Inn).

Waverton, Cheshire; Civil War soldiers.

Wincham Hall, Cheshire: Cavalier.

Winnington Bridge, Cheshire: galloping horsemen.

Winwick, Greater Manchester: Scottish soldiers hung by Cromwell.

Wythenshawe Hall, Greater Manchester: Mary Webb.

The North-East

Buckstones, West Yorkshire: mounted Cavaliers.

Cleadon, Tyne and Wear: Cavalier (Britannia Inn).

East Riddlesden Hall, West Yorkshire: woman murdered by her soldier-husband.

Hassop Hall, Derbyshire: Cavalier (Eyre Arms).

Hull: Cavalier (Ye Olde White Hart).

Kirkburton, West Yorkshire: Hester Whitaker (Old Vicarage).

Lincoln: Cavalier (County Assembly Rooms).

Lindisfarne Castle, Northumberland: Cromwellian soldier.

Long Marston Hall, North Yorkshire, Oliver Cromwell.

Marston Moor, North Yorkshire: figures in seventeenth-century costume; headless horseman.

Newcastle: Cavalier (Sally-Port Tower); Charles I (Town Quay, Old George); gunner killed in action (castle keep).

Raby Castle, Northumberland: Henry Vane the Younger.

Sheffield: John Bright (Carbrook Hall); Cavalier (Old Queen's Head).

Watton Priory, Yorkshire: Cavalier; woman murdered by Parliamentarian marauders.

West Boldon, Tyne and Wear; Cavalier (Black Horse).

Wetherby, Yorkshire: soldiers in Civil War dress.

York: cries of wounded men (Old Starre Inn, King's Manor); Cavalier (Stonegate).

The South-East

Andover, Hampshire: Charles I.

Alresford, Hampshire: tramp of marching troops.

Alton, Hampshire: sounds of battle.

Andover, Hampshire: Cavalier (White Hart).

Arundel Castle, West Sussex: cannon fire; Cavalier known as 'the Blue Man'.

Ashdon, Essex: Civil War skirmish.

Basing House, Hampshire: Oliver Cromwell; mounted figure described as a Puritan.

Beaconsfield, Buckinghamshire: drummer (Royal Standard of England).

Billingham Manor, Isle of White: Charles I.

Bordean House, Hampshire: Cavalier.

Brading, Isle of Wight: Louis de la Roche (Crown Inn).

Cassiobury Park, Hertfordshire: Lord Capel.

Chiswick: Oliver Cromwell (parish church).

Colchester, Essex: Cavaliers (castle); girl accused of witchcraft (Fox and Fiddler).

Crondall, Hampshire: Cromwellian soldiers.

Dartford Heath, Kent: mounted Cavalier.

Doddington, Kent: Cavalier (Chequers Inn).

Donnington Castle, Berkshire: sound of battle; sentinel; skirmish.

Downe Court, Kent: Cavalier.

East Wellow, Hampshire: Sir William Norton.

Edwin's Hall, Essex: Cavalier.

Elham, Kent: Cavalier (Abbot's Fireside).

Faringdon House, Oxfordshire: Sir Robert Pye.

Fordingbridge, Hampshire: Cavalier (Tudor Rose Inn).

Haversham, Kent: hanged Royalist spy named William (Chequers Inn).

Henley, Berkshire: Cavalier (Red Lion).

Hampton Court, Middlesex: Archbishop Laud; Sir Francis Villiers.

Haversham, Buckinghamshire: Royalist spy named William (Chequers Inn).

Hitchin Priory, Hertfordshire: headless horseman.

Hook, Hampshire: mounted Cavalier.

Hurst Castle, Hampshire: Charles I.

Lavenham, Essex: Cavalier.

Lewes, West Sussex: Cavalier (The Shelleys).

London: Oliver Cromwell, Henry Ireton and John Bradshaw (Red Lion Square); Cavalier (Flask Inn, Hampstead); Earl of Holland (Holland House, now demolished).

Loughton Hall, Essex: Cavalier.

Maidstone, Kent: Cavalier (Fisherman's Arms).

Manningtree, Essex: Matthew Hopkins.

Newbury, Berkshire: shadowy Civil War figures.

Pirton, Hertfordshire: Cavalier.

Pluckley, Kent: Cavalier (Blacksmith's Arms).

Pullox Hill, Bedfordshire: Cavalier (Cross Keys Inn).

Romsey, Hampshire: hanged Parliamentarians (Old Swan).

Royston, Hertfordshire: Cavalier.

Rusthall, Kent: headless horseman (Hurst Wood); figure dressed in Cromwellian garb (Red Lion).

Salisbury Hall, Hertfordshire: Cavalier.

Sidlesham, West Sussex: five Royalists, among them Sir Edward Earnley (Crab and Lobster Inn).

Shipbourne, Kent: Henry Vane the Younger, Shipbourne (parish church).

Towersey, Oxfordshire: headless horseman.

White's Tyrrel Farm, Essex: Cavalier.

Wigginton Common, Hertfordshire: groups of Roundheads.

Windsor Castle, Berkshire: Charles I.

The South-West

Athelhampton Hall, Devon: duelling Cavaliers.

Avebury, Wiltshire: Florence (the Red Lion); Sir John Stawell (Avebury Manor).

Ashmore, Dorset: sounds of battle.

Aust, Gloucestershire: cries of soldiers lost crossing the Severn.

Barnfield House, Devon: Henrietta Maria.

Bovey House, Devon: Charles II.

Bovey Heathfield Nature Reserve, Devon: sound of battle.

Braddock Down, Cornwall: seventeenth-century soldiers; sound of galloping horses.

Bristol: Sir Thomas Lunsford.

Broadhinton, Wiltshire: Winifred Glanville (parish church).

Buckland Brewer, Devon: group of Cavaliers (Coach and Horses Inn).

Bulford, Wiltshire: whistling Cavalier.

Chagford, Devon: Sydney Godolphin (Three Crowns Hotel).

Chavenage House, Gloucestershire: black carriage driven by a headless horseman.

Cirencester, Gloucestershire: Cavaliers (King's Head Hotel/Fleece Inn).

Clovelly, Devon: Cavalier (Velly Farm).

Compton Castle, Devon: male figure in seventeenth-century clothing.

Corfe Castle, Dorset: Royalist soldiers.

Devizes Castle, Wiltshire: Cavalier.

Dover Hill, Gloucestershire: Roger and Beatrice.

Dunster, Somerset: tramp of marching men.

Dunster Castle, Somerset: soldier; woman in seventeenth-century clothing.

Freezing Hill, Gloucestershire: groups of Civil War soldiers.

Gaulden Manor, Somerset: three bloodstained Cavaliers.

Gloucester: Cavalier (the Dukeries).

Hanham Abbots, Gloucestershire: 'Loyal Sally' (Hanham Court Farm).

Lansdown, Wiltshire: sound of galloping horses; shadowy figures.

Littledean Hall, Gloucestershire: two Royalist colonels named Wigmore and Congreve.

Llanhydrock House, Cornwall: Royalist soldier.

Lostwithiel, Cornwall: sound of horses' hooves.

Lydiard House, Wiltshire: Sir John Saint-John, drummer.

Lyme Regis, Dorset: three men dressed in 'Musketeer-style' clothing (Volunteer Inn).

Milton Coombe, Devon: Cavalier (Who'd Have Thought It? inn).

Mullion, Cornwall: duelling Cavaliers.

Painswick, Gloucestershire: Charles I; men arming for battle.

Pendennis Castle, Cornwall: lamentations of women and children.

Portland Castle, Dorset: smell of burning flesh.

Poundstock Manor, Cornwall: Kate Penfold and John Trebarthen.

Poyntington, Dorset: Royalist soldiers; headless woman.

Prestbury, Gloucestershire: headless horseman.

Roundway Down, Wiltshire: sound of galloping horses.

Salisbury: Cavalier (the Wardrobe).

Shute Barton Manor, Devon: woman murdered by Parliamentarian troops.

Sourton, Devon: Cavalier (Highway Inn).

Stapleton Woods, Somerset: Roundhead.

Stow-on-the-Wold, Gloucestershire: cries of wounded men (King's Arms); Cavalier (Royalist Hotel).

Stratton, Cornwall: sound of battle.

Taunton Castle, Devon: Cavalier; woman in seventeenth-century costume.

Torrington, Devon: seventeenth-century soldier.

Tiverton: Alice Spencer and Maurice Fortescue.

Troopers Hill, Bristol: sound of laughter.

Trusham, Devon: Cavalier (Cridford Inn).

Upton-on-Severn, Gloucestershire: Thomas Bound.

Wardour Castle, Wiltshire: Blanche Arundell.

Wells, Somerset: Cavalier (Crown Hotel).

Weymouth, Dorset: five Cavaliers (Boot Inn).

Widey Court, Devon: Cavalier.

Wonson Manor, Devon: group of Cavaliers playing cards.

Wales and the Marches
Castell Coch, South Glamorgan: Cavalier.

Chatwall, Shropshire: mounted Cavalier.

Goodrich Castle, Shropshire: Charles Clifford and Alice Birch.

Hopton Castle, Shropshire: massacred soldiers.
Llanvihangel, Monmouthshire: Cromwellian soldier (Skirrid Mountain Inn).
Moreton Corbett Castle, Shropshire: Puritan preacher.
Newent, Gwent: Cavalier (Old Courthouse).
Raglan Castle, Monmouthshire: shadowy figure in seventeenth-century clothing.
Saint Fagan's, South Glamorgan: sound of battle.
Shrewsbury, Shropshire: Civil War soldiers (Lion Hotel/Dun Cow Inn).
Wilderhope Manor, Shropshire: Thomas Smallman.

Further Reading

Battles, Campaigns and the Wider War

Abram, A., *More like Lions than Men: Sir William Brereton and the Cheshire Army of Parliament, 1642-1646* (Warwick, 2020)

Adair, J., *By the Sword Divided: Eyewitnesses of the English Civil War* (London, 1983)

Adair, J., *Roundhead General: a Military Biography of Sir William Waller* (London, 1969)

Adair, J., 'The death of Hampden', *History Today*, XXIX, No. 10 (October, 1979), pp. 656-63

Adamson, J., *The Noble Revolt: the Overthrow of Charles I* (London, 2007)

Atkin, M., *Cromwell's Crowning Mercy: the Battle of Worcester, 1651* (Stroud, 1998)

Atkin, M., *The Civil War in Worcestershire* (Stroud, 1995)

Atherton, I., 'Royalist finances in the English Civil War: the case of Lichfield garrison', *Midland History*, XXXIII, No. 1 (Spring 2008), pp. 43-67

Ashley, M., *The English Civil War* (second edition; Stroud, 1990)

Bann, S., *Scenes and Traces of the English Civil War* (London, 2020)

Barratt, J., *'A Rabble of Gentility': the Royalist Northern Horse, 1644-1645* (Solihull, 2017)

Barratt, J., *Cavalier Capital: Oxford in the Civil War, 1642-46* (Solihull, 2015)

Barratt, *Cavalier Generals: King Charles I and his Commanders in the English Civil War, 1642-1646* (Barnsley, 2004)

Barrett, J., *Cavalier Stronghold: Ludlow in the English Civil War* (Little Logaston, 2013)

Barrett, J., *Sieges of the English Civil Wars* (Barnsley, 2009)

Barrett, J., *The Battle of Marston Moor, 1644* (Stroud, 2002)

Barratt, J., *The Civil War in the South-West* (Barnsley, 2005)

Barratt, J., *The First Battle of Newbury* (Stroud, 2005)

Barrett, J., *The Great Siege of Chester* (Stroud, 2011)

Barrett, J., *The Last Army: the Battle of Stow-on-the-Wold and the End of the Civil War in the Welsh Marches, 1646* (Warwick, 2018)

Bayley, A.R., *The Great Civil War in Dorset* (Taunton, 1910)

Beckett, I.F.W., *Wanton Troopers: Buckinghamshire in the Civil Wars, 1640-1660* (Barnsley, 2015)

Bennett, M., *Cromwell at War: the Lord General and his Military Revolution* (London, 2017)

Bennett, M., *The Civil Wars Experienced: Britain and Ireland, 1638-1661* (London, 2000)

Bennett, M., *The English Civil War* (Hereford, 2002)

Binns, J., *Yorkshire in the Civil Wars: Origins, Impact and Outcome* (Pickering, 2004)

Bowen, L., *John Poyer, the Civil Wars in Pembrokeshire and the British Revolutions* (Cardiff, 2020)

Bracher, T., and Emmett, R., *Shropshire in the Civil War* (Shrewsbury, 2000)

Braddick, M., *God's Fury, England's Fire: a New History of the English Civil Wars* (London, 2008)

Brammer, B., *Winceby: the Campaign and the Battle* (Boston, 1994)

Wroughton, J., *An Unhappy Civil War the Experiences of Ordinary People in Gloucestershire, Somerset and Wiltshire, 1642-1646* (Bath, 1999)

Broughton, J., *The Battle of Lansdown, 1643: an Explorer's Guide* (Bath, 2008)

Broxap, E., *The Great Civil War in Lancashire, 1642-1651* (Manchester, 1910)

Bull, S., *"A General Plague of Madness": the Civil Wars in Lancashire, 1640-1660* (Lancaster, 2009)

Bull, S., and Seed, M., *Bloody Preston: the Battle of Preston, 1648* (Lancaster, 1998)

Bull, S., *The Furie of the Ordnance: Artillery in the English Civil Wars* (Woodbridge, 2008)

Carlton, C., *Going to the Wars: the Experience of the British Civil Wars, 1638-1651* (London, 1992)

Carlton, C., *This Seat of Mars: War and the British Isles, 1485-1746* (London, 2011)

Carpenter, S.D.M., *Military Leadership in the British Civil Wars, 1642-1651* (London, 2005)

Casserly, D., *Massacre: the Storming of Bolton* (Stroud, 2011)

Chandler, G., *Liverpool under Charles I* (Liverpool, 1965)

Chapman, G., *The Siege of Lyme Regis* (Lyme Regis, 1982)

Chevis, H., 'Civil War, trade and kinship: the experience of some West-Country clothiers', *Limina: a Journal of Historical and Cultural Studies*, XX, No. 3 (July, 2015), pp. 1-19

Childs, J., 'War, crime waves and the English army in the late seventeenth century', *War and Society*, XV, No. 2 (October 1977), pp. 1-17

Chippendale, N., *The Battle of Brentford, 1642: the Hounslow Area in the Civil War* (Leigh-on-Sea, 1991)

Coate, M., *Cornwall in the Great Civil War and Interregnum, 1642-1660* (Oxford, 1933)

Coates, B., *The Impact of the English Civil War on the Economy of London, 1642-1650* (Abingdon, 2004)

Como, D.R., *Radical Parliamentarians in the English Civil War* (Oxford, 2018)

Cooke, D., *Civil War in Yorkshire: Fairfax versus Newcastle* (Barnsley, 2004)

Cooke, D., *Yorkshire Sieges of the Civil Wars* (Barnsley, 2011)

Cust, R., and Hughes, A. (eds.), *The English Civil War* (London, 1997)

Daniels, R., and Philo, P., *The First Great Civil War in the Tees Valley* (Sunderland, 2018)

Darcy, E., *The Irish Rebellion of 1641 and the Wars of the Three Kingdoms* (Woodbridge, 2013)

Dixon, J., *The Unfortunate Battaille [sic] of Alresford, being an Account of the Campaign and Battle of Cheriton, March 29th 1644* (Nottingham, 2012)

Donagan, B., 'Atrocity, war crime and treason in the English Civil War', *American Historical Review*, XCIX, No. 4 (October, 1999), pp. 1137-66

Donagan, B., 'Family and misfortune in the English Civil War: the sad case of Edward Pitt', *Huntingdon Library Quarterly* LXI, No. 3 (April, 1998), pp. 223-40

Donagan, B., *War in England, 1642-1649* (Oxford, 2008)

Donoghue, J., 'Resisting the 'enslaving design': conscription and the radical politics of the body in England's Atlantic empire, circa 1647–1660', *Labor: Studies in Working-Class History of the Americas*, XIII, No. 3 (July, 2016), pp. 19-36

Dixon, J., *The Business at Acton: the Battle of Nantwich, 1644* (Nottingham, 2012)

Dore, R.N., *The Civil Wars in Cheshire* (Chester, 1966)

Edwards, P., 'Turning ploughshares into swords: the arms and military equipment industries in Staffordshire in the first Civil War, 1642-1646' *Midland History*, XXVII (October, 2002), pp. 52-79

Emberton, W., *Love Loyalty: the Close and Perilous Siege of Basing House, 1643-1645* (Basingstoke, 1972)

Foard, G., *Naseby: the Decisive Campaign* (revised edition, London, 2004)

Gaskill, M., *Witchfinders: a Seventeenth-Century English Tragedy* (London, 2005)

Gaunt, P., *A Nation under Siege: the Civil War in Wales, 1642-48* (London, 1991)

Gaunt, P., *The English Civil War: a Military History* (London, 2014)

Gentles, I., *The New Model Army in England, Scotland and Ireland, 1645-1653* (Oxford, 1993)

Gruber von Arni, E., *Justice to the Maimed Soldier: Nursing, Medical Care and Welfare for Sick and Wounded Soldiers and their Families during the English Civil Wars and Interregnum, 1642-1660* (Aldershot, 2001)

Haythornthwaite, P., *The English Civil War; an Illustrated Military History* (Blandford, 1983)

Haldane, A., *Portraits of the English Civil War* (London, 2017)

Hensman, E.W., 'The Second Civil War in the East Midlands, May to July 1648', *Transactions of the Royal Historical Society*, VI (1923), pp. 126-59

Hibbert, C., *Cavaliers and Roundheads: the English at War, 1642-1649* (London, 1993)

Hill, P.R., and Watkinson, J.M., *'Cromwell hath the honour but ...': Major-General Lambert's Campaigns in the North, 1648* (London, 2012)

Hindle, S., 'Dearth and the English Revolution; the subsistence crisis of 1647-50', *Economic History Review*, LXI, Supplement No. 1 (August 2008), pp. 64-98

Hopper, A.J., '"Fitted for desperation": honour and treachery in Parliament's Yorkshire command, 1642-1643', *History*, LXXXVI, No. 282 (April, 2001), pp. 138-54

Hopper, A.J., 'The clubmen of the West Riding of Yorkshire during the First Civil War: "Bradford club-law"', *Northern History*, XXXVI, No. 1 (March, 2000), pp. 59-72

Hopper, A., '"Tinker" Fox and the politics of garrison warfare in the West Midlands, 1643-50', *Midland History*, XXIV, No. 1 (January, 1999), pp. 98-113

Hudson, R. (ed.), *The Grand Quarrel: Women's Memoirs of the English Civil War* (Stroud, 2000)

Hughes, A., '"The accounts of the Kingdom": memory, community and the English Civil War', *Past and Present*, No. 230 (November, 2016), pp. 311-29

Hunt, T., *The English Civil War at First Hand* (London, 2002)

Hutton, R., *The Royalist War Effort, 1642-1646* (London, 1982)

Jennings, S.B., '"A miserable, stinking, infected town": pestilence, plague and death in a Civil-War garrison - Newark, 1640-1649', *Midland History*, XXVIII, No. 1 (January, 2003), pp. 51-70

Jennings, S.B., 'The anatomy of a Civil-War plague in a rural parish: East Stoke, Nottinghamshire, 1646', *Midland History*, XL, No. 2 (November, 2015), pp. 155-80

Jennings, S.B., 'The third and final siege of Newark (1645-1646) and the impact of the Scottish Army upon Nottinghamshire and adjacent counties', *Midland History*, XXXVII, No.2 (November, 2012), pp. 142-62

Johnson, D., *Adwalton Moor, 1644: the Battle that Changed a War* (Pickering, 2003)

Jones, I, 'A sea of blood? Massacres during the Wars of the Three Kingdoms, 1641-1653', in Dwyer, P., and Ryan, L. (eds.), *Theatres of Violence: Massacre, Mass Killing and Atrocity throughout History* (New York, 2012), pp. 63-78

Jones, P., *The Siege of Colchester, 1648* (Dubai, 2004)

Jones, S. (ed.), *Britain turned Germany: the Thirty Years War and its Impact on the British Isles, 1618-1660* (Warwick, 1918)

Kennedy, D., 'Holy violence and the English Civil War', *Parergon*, XXXII, No. 3 (July, 2015), pp. 17-42

Kenyon J., and Ohlmeyer, J., *The Civil Wars: a Military History of England, Scotland and Ireland, 1638-1600* (London, 1998)

Leask, P., *Valour is the Safest Helm: the Life of Sir Hugh Cholmley and Scarborough during the English Civil War* (Newtown, 1995)

Lynch, J., *For King and Parliament: Bristol and the Civil War* (Stroud, 1999)

Lyndon, B., 'The South and the start of the Second Civil War, 1648', *History*, LXXI, No. 233 (October 1986), pp. 393-407

MacLachlan, T., *The Civil War in Hampshire* (Landford, 1997)

Maggs, S., *The Storming of Canon Frome, 22 July 1645* (n.p., 2018)

Marshall, R.K., *The Intrepid Queen: Henrietta Maria* (London, 1990)

Malcolm, J.L., 'All the King's men: the impact of the Crown's Irish soldiers on the English Civil War', *Irish Historical Studies*, XXII, No. 83 (March, 1979), pp. 239-64

McCall, F., 'Women's experience of violence and suffering as represented in loyalist accounts of the English Civil War', *Women's History Review*, XXVIII, No. 7 (July, 2019), pp. 1136-56

McElligott, J., and Smith, D.L. (eds.), *Royalists and Royalism during the English Civil War* (Cambridge, 2007)

Memegalos, F., *George Goring, 1608-1657* (Aldershot, 2007)

Miles Brown, H., *Battles Royal: Charles I and the Civil War in Cornwall and the West* (Lostwithiel, 1982)

Miller, A.C., *Sir Richard Grenville of the Civil War* (Chichester, 1979)

Morrill, J. (ed.), *The Impact of the English Civil War* (London, 1991)

Newman, P.R., *The Battle of Marston Moor, 1644* (Chichester, 1991)

Newman, P.R., and Roberts, P.R., *Marston Moor, 1644: the Battle of the Five Armies* (Pickering, 2003)

Norman, A., *By Swords Divided: Corfe Castle in the Civil War* (Tiverton, 2003)

Orme, S., '"Bestowing a visit on that little city": Cromwell and the taking of Peterborough, April 1643', *Cromwelliana*, Series III, No. 7 (2018), pp. 85-100

Paddock, J.M., *The Storming of Cirencester in 1643: an Episode in the English Civil War* (Cirencester, 1995)

Parker, G., *Global Crisis: War, Climate Change and Catastrophe in the Seventeenth Century* (London, 2013)

Plowden, A., *Women All on Fire: the Women of the English Civil War* (Stroud, 1997)

Porter, S., *The Blast of War: Destruction in the English Civil Wars* (Stroud, 1994)

Porter, S., and Marsh, S., *The Battle for London* (Stroud, 2012)

Pringle, P., *Stand and Deliver: the Story of the Highwayman* (San Francisco, 2016)

Ray, M.E., 'John Taylor and the ghost of Long Meg of Westminster: authorship and poetic authority in *The Women's Sharpe Revenge*', *Studies in Philology*, CXIII, No. 4 (September, 2016), pp. 919–46

Richardson, R.C. (ed.), *The English Civil Wars: Local Aspects* (Stroud, 1997)

Ross, D., *Royalist but ... Herefordshire in the English Civil War, 1640-1651* (Little Logaston, 2012)

Royle, T., *Civil War: the Wars of the Three Kingdoms, 1638-1660* (London, 2004)

Scott, C., and Turton, A., *'Hey for Old Robin!' The Campaigns and Armies of the Earl of Essex during the Civil Wars, 1642-44* (Solihull, 2017)

Serdivill, R., and Sadler, J., *The Great Siege of Newcastle, 1644* (Stroud, 2011)

Scott, C.L., *Edgehill: the Battle Reinterpreted* (London, 2005)

Sherwood, R.E., *Civil Strife in the Midlands, 1642-1651* (Chichester, 1974)

Spence, R.T., *Skipton Castle in the Great Civil War, 1642-1645* (Skipton, 1991)

Stoyle, M.J., *From Deliverance to Destruction: Rebellion and Civil War in an English City* (Exeter, 1996)

Stoyle, M.J., *Loyalty and Locality: Popular Allegiance in Devon during the English Civil War* (Exeter, 1994)

Stoyle, M.J., 'Pagans or paragons? Images of the Cornish during the English Civil War', *English Historical Review*, CXI, No. 441 (April, 1996), pp. 299-323

Stoyle, M.J., *Plymouth in the Civil War* (Exeter, 1998)

Stoyle, M.J., *Soldiers and Strangers: an Ethnic History of the English Civil War* (London, 2005)

Stoyle, M.J., *The Black Legend of Rupert's Dog: Witchcraft and Propaganda during the English Civil War* (Liverpool, 2014)

Stubbs, J., *Reprobates: the Cavaliers of the English Civil War* (London, 2011)

Stuckley, J., *Sir Bevil Grenville and His Times, 1596-1643* (Chichester, 1983)

Thomas, W.S.K., *Stuart Wales* (Llandyssul, 1988)

Thomas-Stanford, C., *Sussex in the Great Civil War, 1642-1660* (London, 1910)

Toynbee, M., and Young, P., *Cropredy Bridge, 1644: the Campaign and the Battle* (Kineton, 1970)

Trease, G., *Portrait of a Cavalier: William Cavendish, First Duke of Newcastle* (London, 1979)

Tucker, N., *North Wales and Chester in the Civil War* (second edition, Ashbourne, 2003)

Turnbull, E., 'Anti-popery in early-modern England: war and print, 1617-1635', University of Oxford Ph.D. thesis, 2016

Underdown, D., *Fire from Heaven: Life in an English Country Town in the Seventeenth Century* (London, 1993)

Underdown, D., *Somerset in the Civil War and Interregnum* (Newton Abbott, 1973)

Underdown, D., 'The chalk and the cheese: contrasts among the English clubmen', *Past and Present*, No. 85 (November, 1979), pp. 25-48

Venning, T., *An Alternative History of Britain: the English Civil War* (Barnsley, 2015)

Wanklyn, M., *Decisive Battles of the English Civil War* (Barnsley, 2006)

Wanklyn, M., *Supreme Command and Politics during the British Wars, 1649-1651* (Barnsley, 2019)

Wanklyn, M., and Jones, F., *A Military History of the English Civil War: Strategy and Tactics* (London, 2005)

Wardman, *The Forgotten Battle: Torrington, 1646* (Torrington, 1996)

Wedgwood, C.V., *The King's War, 1641-1647* (London, 1958)

Wenham, P., *The Great and Close Siege of York* (Kineton, 1970)

Willis-Bund, J.W., *The Civil War in Worcestershire, 1642-6, and the Scotch Invasion of 1651* (Worcester, 1905)

Wood, A., *The Politics of Social Conflict: the Peak Country, 1560-1720* (Cambridge, 2009)

Woolrych, A., *Battles of the English Civil War* (London, 1961)

Worden, B., *The English Civil Wars, 1640-1660* (London, 2009)

Worton, J., *To Settle the Crown: Waging the Civil War in Shropshire, 1642-48* (Solihull, 2016)

Wright, S., *With Guns and Drums: Civil War in Birmingham* (Birmingham, 1997)

Wroughton, J., *The Battle of Lansdown, 1643: an Explorer's Guide* (Bath, 2008)

Yaxley, S., *The Siege of King's Lynn, 1643* (Dereham, 1993)

Young, P., *Edgehill, 1642: the Campaign and the Battle* (Kineton, 1976)

Young, P., *The Cavalier Army: its Organization and Daily Life* (London, 1974)

Young, P., and Emberton, W., *Sieges of the Great Civil War* (London, 1978)

The Theory and History of Ghost Stories

Ackroyd, P., *The English Ghost: Spectres through Time* (London, 2010)

Chesters, T., *Ghost Stories in Late-Renaissance France: Walking by Night* (Oxford, 2011)

Davies, O., *The Haunted: a Social History of Ghosts* (Basingstoke, 2007)

Davidson, H.R.E. (ed.), *The Folklore of Ghosts* (Cambridge, 1980)

Enright, D.J. (ed.), *The Oxford Book of the Supernatural* (Oxford, 1994)

Finucane, R.C., *Ghosts: Appearances of the Dead and Cultural Transformation* (New York, 1996)

Marshall, P., *Beliefs and the Dead in Reformation England* (Oxford, 2002)

Martin, A., *Ghoul Britannia: Notes from a Haunted Isle* (London, 2009)

Oldridge, D., 'Land of the walking dead', *BBC History,* January 2006, pp. 20-1

Oldridge, D., *The Supernatural in Tudor and Stuart England* (London, 2016)

O'Lynn, A., 'Ghosts of war and spirits of place: spectral belief in early-modern England and Protestant Germany', University of Bristol Ph.D. thesis, 2019

Pollmann, J., *Memory in Early-Modern Europe, 1500-1800* (Oxford, 2017)

Rodger, I., 'The headless horseman: an amateur inquiry', *Journal of the Folklorz Institute,* II, No. 3 (December, 1965), pp. 266-71

Sangha, L., 'The social, political and spiritual dynamics of ghost stories in early-modern England', *Historical Journal,* LXIII, No. 2 (March 2020), pp. 339-59

Thomas, K., *Religion and the Decline of Magic: Studies in Popular Beliefs in Sixteenth and Seventeenth Century England* (London, 1971)

Wilson, I., *In Search of Ghosts* (London, 1995)

Haunted Houses and Other Sites of Memory

Acorah, D., *Derek Acorah's Ghost Towns* (London, 2006)

Acorah, D., *Haunted Britain: over 100 of the UK's Scariest Places to Visit* (London, 2006)

Andrews, R., *The Paranormal Tourist Guide to Gloucestershire* (privately published, 2013)

Anon., *Cheshire Ghost Stories* (Sheffield, n.d.)

Arnold, N., *Haunted Maidstone* (Stroud, 2011)

Bellanger, J., *Ghosts of War: Restless Spirits of Soldiers, Spies and Saboteurs* (Franklin Lakes, New Jersey, 2006)

Bennett, W.S. and Steer, L., *Birmingham Ghosts* (Birmingham, n.d.)

Bradford, A., and Roberts, B., *Midland Ghosts and Hauntings* (Birmingham, 1994)

Brandon, D., *Haunted Chester* (Stroud, 2008)

Brooks, J.A., *Britain's Haunted Heritage* (Norwich, 1990)

Codd, D., *Paranormal Devon* (Stroud, 2009)

Codd, D., *Paranormal Lancashire* (Stroud, 2011)

Drake, P.M., *The Spooky South: an A-Z of Haunted Locations of Hampshire and the Isle of White* (privately published, 2015)

Eyre, K., *Lancashire Ghosts* (Clapham, 1986)

Florek, B., *Totally Haunted UK; Cornwall* (n.p., 2014)

Fry, E., and Harvey, R., *Haunted Gloucester* (Stroud, 2004)

Gater, P., *Ghosts at War: an Anecdotes Book* (Buxton, 2009)

Gray, R., *Scottish Ghosts* (Broxburn, 2013)

Guthrie, R., *The Haunted Locations of Lancashire: a Look at Ghostly Lancashire Hotspots* (n.p., n.d.)

Haughton, B., *Haunted Spaces, Sacred Spaces; a Field Guide to Stone Circles, Crop Circles, Ancient Tombs and Supernatural Landscapes* (Franklin Lakes, New Jersey, 2008)

Holland, J., *Wiltshire Ghost Stories* (Sheffield, n.d.)

Holland, J., *Somerset and Bristol Ghost Stories* (Sheffield, n.d.)

Holland, R., *Shropshire Ghost Stories* (Sheffield, 2015)

Holland, R., *Lancashire Ghost Stories* (Sheffield, 2014)

Hynes, K., *Haunted Plymouth* (Stroud, 2010)

Ingram, J., *The Haunted Homes and Family Traditions of Great Britain: Second Series* (London, 1884)

King, W.H., *Haunted Bedford* (n.p., n.d.)

Le Queux, S., *Haunted Bristol* (Stroud, 2004)

Love, D., *Scottish Ghosts: Ghouls, Ghosts and Beasties* (London, 1995)

Mackay, C., *Memoirs of Extraordinary Popular Delusions* (London, 1841)

Marsden, S., *This Sceptred Isle: a Journey through Haunted England* (Swindon, 2005)

Matthews, R., *Haunted Chester* (Andover, 1992)

Matthews, R., *Haunted Places of Wiltshire* (Newbury, 2004)

Matthews, R., *Haunted York* (Stroud, 2009)

McKenzie, R., *They Still Serve: a Complete Guide to the Military Ghosts of Britain* (self-published, 2008)

McLachlan, S., *The Ghosts of Wales: a Collection of Ghost Stories from Across the Welsh Nation* (n.p., n.d.)

Pearson, J., *Haunted Places of Cheshire: on the Trail of the Paranormal* (Newbury, 2006)

Poulton-Smith, A., *Haunted Worcestershire* (Stroud, 2009)

Price, M., *Folktales and Legends of Gloucestershire* (self-published, 2013)

Robinson, J., *Oxfordshire Ghosts* (Barnsley, 2000)

Slemen, T., *Haunted Cheshire* (Liverpool, 2013)

Slemen, T., *Haunted Liverpool*, 31 volumes (Liverpool, 1996-2018)

Sly, N., *A Ghostly Almanac of Devon and Cornwall* (Stroud, 2009)

Solomon, P., *Haunted Staffordshire* (n.p., n.d.)

Stevens Bassett, R.A., *Ghostly Tales and Hauntings of Northamptonshire* (Chichester, 2014)

Toner, A., *The Ghosts of Wales* (self-published, 2018)

Tyler, N., *Haunted Yorkshire* (Cheltenham, 2019)

Underwood, P., *A Gazetteer of British Ghosts: an Illustrated Guide to 236 Haunted Sites* (self-published, n.d.)

Underwood, P., *Ghosts of Hampshire and the Isle of Wight* (self-published, 1982)

Underwood, P., *Where the Ghosts Walk: the Gazetteer of Haunted Britain* (London, 2013)

Walters, R., *Haunted Oxford* (Stroud, 2007)

Whitaker, T.W., *Lancashire Ghosts and Legends* (London, 1980)

White, D., *Haunted Cotswolds* (Stroud, 2010)

Whittington-Egan, R., *Liverpool Ghosts and Ghouls* (Neston, 1986)

Wood, A.C., *Military Ghosts: Naval, Military and Military Ghosts and Legends – a Gazetteer Guide for Ghost Researchers and Others* (Stroud, 2013)

Woods, F., *Cheshire Ghosts and Legends* (Newbury, 1990)

Notes

Preface

1. For the story of the Moddey Doo, see S. Morrison (ed.), *Manx Fairy Tales* (Ramsey, 2013), pp. 68-9. However encouraging the fate of the soldier concerned may have been, the inhabitants of the island did not have to trust to supernatural protection to save them from the horrors of war. On the contrary, when the Parliamentarian authorities sent an expedition to take control of the island in 1651, led by Derby's Receiver General, William Christian, the trained bands mutinied and overpowered the garrison's few regular troops in a bloodless coup before the New Model Army had even set foot on the island, an act which led to Christian's execution by a vengeful Charles II ten years later. Known by his nickname of Illiam Dhone, or Brown Willie, Christian is to this day revered as the island's greatest national hero. For these events, see W. Harrison, *Illiam Dhone and the Manx Rebellion, 1651* (Douglas, 1877).

2. M. O'Leary, *Hampshire and Isle-of-Wight Ghost Tales* (Stroud, n.d.), pp. 49-56. There is a sequel to this story in that, a century later, the elm began to emit, or so it was claimed, the most piercing groans and for a while became a veritable tourist attraction! One presumes, then, that the story was invented to lend the hoax (for so it was, of course) a certain verisimilitude, but it yet remains a very interesting example of how the Civil War was viewed among the common people.

3. Not that many historians have. With regard to the English Civil War, the one contribution that I know of is a solitary paragraph from Charles Carlton. Thus: 'Battles were the epitome of what was invariably described as "these *unnatural* civil wars". In consequence, it is not surprising that, after them, supernatural events were frequently reported. Even before fighting started, people reported seeing fully equipped musketeers and horsemen fighting in the skies above the Cotswolds and angels clashing above the college roof-tops in Cambridge ... Such apparitions continued throughout the war: for hundreds of years tales were told of heavenly hosts contesting above Naseby ... At Newmarket three men were seen duelling in the heavens; at Thetford a sword and pike appeared to hover in the sky; at Brandon a whole fleet, flags flying, was espied sailing across the skies ... "What all this doth

portend, God only knoweth", wrote one pamphleteer, "but doubtless it is a sign of His wrath." C. Carlton, *Going to the Wars: the Experience of the English Civil Wars, 1638-1651* (London, 1992), pp. 148-9. What all this did portend, indeed? Perceptive though Carlton's remarks are, they offer but the sketchiest of introductions to the topic: hence, in part, the need for the current book.

4. For example, excellent a work in many respects though it is, the most recent work on the historical memory of the conflicts of 1642-1651, Stephen Banns' *Scenes and Traces of the English Civil War* (London, 2020) mentions the subject not at all, even though the presence of the monuments to various combatants that he discusses at some length were prime candidates for the generation of tales of haunting.

5. The sites that crop up in such places include Basing House, Littlecote House, Broughton Castle and Scarborough Castle, the figure seen in the last instance - a man smoking a pipe who appeared to fall from a wall as if shot - corresponding to that of a spectre which is seemingly spotted quite regularly.

Chapter 1

1. The visions seen at Mons are discussed at length by D. Clarke, *The Angel, Phantom Soldiers and Ghostly Guardians of Mons* (Chichester, 2004). For some good examples of First World War ghost stories current among the front-line troops, see T. Cook, 'Grave beliefs: stories of the supernatural and the uncanny among Canada's Great-War trench soldiers', *Journal of Military History*, LXXVII, No. 2 (April, 2013), pp. 521-42. Meanwhile, the battlefields of that conflict are replete with latter-day tales of ghostly visions of all sorts, in which respect, see, for example, M. da Silva and A. Hind, *Ghost Stories of the First World War* (Vancouver, 2014).

2. See, for example, D. Asfar and E. Thay, *Ghost Stories of the Civil War* (Vancouver, 2003), and M. Nesbit, *Ghosts of Gettysburg: Spirits, Apparitions and Haunted Places of the Battlefield* (Gettysburg, Pennsylvania, 1996).

3. For the 'Wild Hunt', see A. O'Lynn, 'Ghosts of war and spirits of place: spectral belief in early-modern England and Protestant Germany', University of Bristol Ph.D. thesis, 2019, pp. 194-6.

4. H. Kwon, *Ghosts of War in Vietnam* (Cambridge, 2008).

5. See < haunted battlefields and the ghosts of soldiers, from the paranormal database >, accessed 16 March 2021.

6. For an account of this event, see C.J. Esdaile, *Fighting Napoleon: Guerrillas, Bandits and Adventurers in Spain, 1808-1814* (London, 2004), p. 63. A natural explanation of the incident might be the appearance in the sky of a 'false sun' or 'sun dog', a reflection of the sun that can appear at some distance to one side or the other

as a result of the refraction of sunlight by ice crystals in the atmosphere: judging from the author's own experience of such phenomena, it would not be impossible to imagine that what was on show was a palm tree.

7. R. Hargreaves, *Hitler's Final Fortress: Breslau, 1945* (Barnsley, 2011), p. 32.

8. Carlton, *Going to the Wars*, p. 202. The issue of men who disappeared without trace was a particular problem for the wives they left behind. In this respect, see I. Peck, 'The great unknown: the negotiation and narration of death by English war-widows, 1647-1660', *Northern History*, LIII, No. 2 (July, 2016), pp. 220-35.

9. C. Carlton, *This Seat of Mars: War and the British Isles, 1485-1746* (London, 2011), p. 147.

10. S.B. Jennings, '"A miserable, stinking, infected town": pestilence, plague and death in a Civil-War garrison - Newark, 1640-1649', *Midland History*, XXVIII, No. 1 (January, 2003), pp. 51-70.

11. S.B. Jennings, 'The anatomy of a Civil-War plague in a rural parish: East Stoke, Nottinghamshire, 1646', *Midland History*, XL, No. 2 (November, 2015), pp. 155-80.

12. J.A. Dils, 'Epidemics, mortality and the Civil War in Berkshire, 1642-6', in R.C. Richardson (ed.), *The English Civil Wars: Local Aspects* (Stroud, 1997), pp. 145-55; J. Binns, *Yorkshire in the Civil Wars: Origins, Impact and Outcome* (Pickering, 2004), p. 159; Carlton, *Going to the Wars*, p. 157.

13. *Cit.* M.J. Stoyle, *Loyalty and Locality: Popular Allegiance in Devon during the English Civil War* (Exeter, 1994), p. 30.

14. For the material losses inflicted by the Civil Wars, see S. Porter, *The Blast of War: Destruction in the English Civil Wars* (Stroud, 1994). The extent of the destruction can be suggested by a comparison with the major fires that were a constant scourge in seventeenth-century England. Thus, 'There were eighteen fires that destroyed more than 100 houses in provincial towns in the seventeenth century excluding the years of civil war, but, during the six years of conflict in the 1640's at least twenty-three, and possibly as many as thirty, towns lost property on that scale.' *Ibid.*, p. 88. Among the places that suffered accidental conflagrations - a category from which the effects of siege, battle or bombardment are exempted - were Beaminster, Diss, Leighton Buzzard, Lowestoft, Oxford and Wrexham. See Carlton, *Going to the Wars*, p. 158; J. Barrett, *Cavalier Capital: Oxford in the Civil War, 1642-46* (Solihull, 2015), pp. 144-5. With regard to the deliberate destruction of stately homes and manor houses, the Naseby campaign alone saw the loss of Bagworth House, Burley House, Barton House, Hawkesley House, Cofton Hall and Campden House. See R.E. Sherwood, *Civil Strife in the Midlands* (Chichester, 1974), pp. 186-9, 195.

15. *Cit.* J. Lynch, *For King and Parliament: Bristol and the Civil War* (Stroud, 1999), p. 163.

16. P. Tennant, 'Parish and people: South Warwickshire in the Civil War', in Richardson, *English Civil Wars*, pp. 176-81; for a general discussion of the impact of garrisons in their neighbourhoods, see Carlton, *Going to the Wars*, pp. 151-3.

17. For an unpleasant episode in which a young woman was preyed upon by a Scottish officer billeted on her family in Yorkshire in 1644, see R. Hudson, *The Grand Quarrel: Women's Memoirs of the English Civil War* (Stroud, 2000), pp. 132-5. Meanwhile, for two liaisons with soldiers that resulted in illegitimate births in Exeter, see M.J. Stoyle, *From Deliverance to Destruction: Rebellion and Civil War in an English City* (Exeter, 1996), pp. 138-9.

18. *Cit.* Carlton, *This Seat of Mars*, p. xviii.

19. F. McCall, 'Women's experience of violence and suffering as represented in loyalist accounts of the English Civil War', *Women's History Review*, XXVIII, No. 7 (July, 2019), p. 1143.

20. Barrett, *Cavalier Capital*, pp. 72-3.

21. *Cit.* C. Hibbert, *Cavaliers and Roundheads: the English at War, 1642-1649* (London, 1993), p. 70.

22. Tennant, 'Parish and people', p. 163.

23. I.F.W. Beckett, *Wanton Troopers: Buckinghamshire in the Civil Wars, 1640-1660* (Barnsley, 2015), p. 129; R. Hutton, *The Royalist War Effort* (Harlow, 1982), p. 98.

24. *Cit. ibid.*, p. 62; for a discussion of the cost of Parliamentarian requisitioning in particular, see A. Hughes, '"The accounts of the Kingdom": memory, community and the English Civil War', *Past and Present*, No. 230 (November, 2016), pp. 311-29.

25. *Cit.* Beckett, *Wanton Troopers*, p. 66. On occasion, the behaviour of the Parliamentarian troops was worsened by particular circumstances. For example, when the army of the Earl of Essex invaded Cornwall in the summer of 1644, such was the lather that the Parliamentarian news-sheets had worked up against the Cornish in response to their loyalty to the king - they were invariably portrayed as being brutal, ignorant, backward and cruel, not to mention traitors to the good people of England as a whole - that they fell upon the countryside with the utmost licence, stripping it of all it contained and causing the populace to flee in panic. See M.J. Stoyle, 'Pagans or paragons? Images of the Cornish during the English Civil War', *English Historical Review*, CXI, No. 441 (April, 1996), p. 308.

26. *Cit.* C.V. Wedgwood, *The King's War, 1641-1647* (London, 1958), p. 222.

27. See, for example, S.B. Jennings, 'The third and final siege of Newark (1645-1646) and the impact of the Scottish Army upon Nottinghamshire and adjacent counties', *Midland History*, XXXVII, No.2 (April, 2012), pp. 142-62.

28. One place where this last occurred was Nottingham, of which Lucy Hutchinson wrote, 'The wives, children and servants of such as were in the enemy's garrisons and armies [Mr Hutchinson] thought it not safe to suffer ... to be in the town, and therefore commanded them all to depart, not sparing some of his own relations.' *Cit.* Hudson, *The Grand Quarrel*, p. 165.

29. *Cit. ibid.*, p. 74.

30. M.J. Stoyle, '"Whole streets converted to ashes": property destruction in Exeter during the English Civil War', in Richardson, *English Civil Wars*, p. 140. The terrible sufferings endured by the poor are shown all too well by the case of Reading: three times greater than normal in the town as a whole in the spring and summer of 1643, in its poorest district - the parish of Saint Giles - it peaked at a level twice as much again. Dils, 'Epidemics, mortality and the Civil War in Berkshire', p. 150.

31. Wedgwood, *King's War*, pp. 188-95.

32. Sherwood, *Civil Strife in the Midlands*, p. 116.

33. I. Atherton, 'Royalist finances in the English Civil War: the case of Lichfield garrison', *Midland History*, XXXIII, No. 1 (Spring, 2008), pp. 43-67. In the summer of 1643, albeit on a local level only and then in a completely different area, this prophecy came to dramatic fruition when solidly Parliamentarian East Anglia was stunned by an armed revolt on the part of the population of King's Lynn in protest at the spiralling level of taxation. See Wedgwood, *King's War*, p. 248.

34. Sherwood, *Civil Strife in the Midlands*, p. 106.

35. *Cit.* Beckett, *Wanton Troopers*, pp. 124-5.

36. *Cit.* B. Coates, *The Impact of the English Civil War on the Economy of London, 1642-1650* (Abingdon, 2004), p. 220.

37. *Cit. ibid.*, p. 219.

38. For the experiences of the Wiltshire cloth industry, see H. Chevis, 'Civil War, trade and kinship: the experience of some West-Country clothiers', *Limina: a Journal of Historical and Cultural Studies*, XX, No. 3 (July, 2015), pp. 1-19.

39. To quote one authority on Civil War Newcastle, 'The effect on the coal trade was immediate and economically damaging ... Unemployment undoubtedly gave a boost to [Royalist] recruiting.' R. Serdiville and J. Sadler, *The Great Siege of Newcastle, 1644* (Stroud, 2011), pp. 48-9. Just as badly hit, meanwhile, were the lead mines of the Peak District, though in this case the problem was less the general disruption consequent on the war as the decision of the Earl of Newcastle on the one hand and the Earl of Manchester on the other to place embargos on the region for fear that they would be unable to stop their opponents from deriving too great a share of the metal dug up from the pits. See A. Wood, *The Politics of Social Conflict: the Peak Country, 1560-1720* (Cambridge, 2009), p. 274

40. Hibbert, *Cavaliers and Roundheads*, pp. 81-3. For a discussion of the impact of the Little Ice Age, see G. Parker, *Global Crisis: War, Climate Change and Catastrophe in the Seventeenth Century* (London, 2013) while the near famine of the latter half of the 1640s is discussed in S. Hindle, 'Dearth and the English Revolution; the subsistence crisis of 1647-50', *Economic History Review*, LXI, Supplement No. 1 (August, 2008), pp. 64-98.

41. *Cit.* T. Hunt, *The English Civil War at First Hand* (London, 2002), p. 98.

42. *Cit.* B. Donagan, 'Family and misfortune in the English Civil War: the sad case of Edward Pitt', *Huntingdon Library Quarterly* LXI, No. 3 (April, 1998), p. 230. The Pitt family had a tragic war, indeed: seen, despite Pitt's efforts to remain neutral, as Royalist sympathisers, they saw their properties in Westminster and the Hampshire village of Stratfield Saye pillaged, while Pitt himself spent many months in close confinement in Windsor Castle, suffered the loss of his wife from fever, and finally died of the effects of his imprisonment just days after his release. As for the Verneys, aside from Sir Edmund, they lost both a son and a son-in-law, while Lady Verney also lost a brother-in-law. Beckett, *Wanton Troopers*, p. 74.

43. *Cit.* Wedgwood, *King's War*, p. 163.

44. Hibbert, *Cavaliers and Roundheads*, pp. 38-42 *passim*.

45. The extent to which the bonds that held society together were actually threatened is a moot point. Thus, even in the New Model Army most officers tended to come from the gentry: that a significant number of those who originated in the forces of the Eastern Association came from relatively humble backgrounds is true enough, but no less a figure than Oliver Cromwell, the man most responsible for this development, at the very least implied that such men were raised *faut de mieux* and, further, that he would have preferred that they were gentlemen as well as honest 'men of spirit'. See M. Bennett, *Cromwell at War: the Lord General and his Military Revolution* (London, 2017), pp. 47-50. In general, meanwhile, local structures of status and authority survived more-or-less intact and were frequently able to continue to pursue the same projects - the draining of the fens and the enclosure of the forests, for example - that had occupied them before 1642: to take just one example, in Warwickshire no family appears to have fallen from the ranks of the gentry and only two or three individuals appear to have joined them. See A. Hughes, *Politics, Society and Civil War in Warwickshire, 1620-60* (Cambridge, 1987), pp. 263-70. Nevertheless, among the propertied classes there was a strong sense of moral panic that continued to exert a powerful effect long after the Restoration had ensured that, not just the king, but also the self-same propertied classes had finally,

to paraphrase the words of the greatest Royalist anthem of the war, come to enjoy their own again. For a discussion of all this, see J. Morrill and J. Walter, 'Order and disorder in the English Revolution' in R. Cust and A. Hughes (eds.), *The English Civil War* (London, 1997), pp. 310-39. See also J. Walter, 'The impact on society: a world turned upside-down', in J. Morrill (ed.), *The Impact of the English Civil War* (London, 1991), pp. 104-22.

46.   In the words of Fiona McCall, 'Although historians debate the relative significance of change over continuity in changing women's lives, few would contest that the 1640's and 1650's witnessed striking challenges to patriarchy ... Women's volubility was apparent, but also seen as requiring control and correction by men.' McCall, 'Women's experience of violence and suffering', p. 1139. For an interesting discussion that on the one hand emphasises just how limited the occurrence of cross-dressing was, while on the other detailing the moral panic to which it gave rise, see M.J. Stoyle, '"Give me a souldier's coat": female cross-dressing during the English Civil War', *History*, CIII, No. 354 (January, 2018), pp. 7-26.

47.   Donagan, 'Family and misfortune in the English Civil War', p. 225. See 'The World Turned Upside Down', < https://en.wikipedia.org/wiki/The_World_Turned_Upside_D it own#Lyrics >, accessed 18 October 2020.

48.   *Cit.* Hibbert, *Cavaliers and Roundheads*, p. 145.

49.   *Cit.* J. Adair, *By the Sword Divided: Eyewitnesses of the English Civil War* (London, 1983), p. 104. There is clearly an interesting backstory to this letter and, indeed, the one that precedes it. As members of the Trained Bands, Rodway and Owen alike were volunteers and were therefore men who had made a conscious decision to become soldiers, this being a decision of which their wives most definitely disapproved. Implicit in both letters, meanwhile, is the suggestion that they should follow the example currently being set by many of their comrades - they were written in the middle of the Newbury campaign of 1643 - and desert their colours for the comforts of home. Desertion being something that was obviously all too easy to get away with, we are therefore left with a snapshot of the way the war could be manipulated for the purposes of the day-to-day struggle that was family life: far from being unhappy conscripts, then, Rodway and Owen were likely examples of the many men who regard war as an adventure, not to mention release from the daily grind.

50.   J. Donoghue, 'Resisting the 'enslaving design': conscription and the radical politics of the body in England's Atlantic empire, circa 1647-1660', *Labor: Studies in Working-Class History of the Americas*, XIII, No. 3 (July, 2016), p. 21.

51.   For these reports, see S. Murdoch, *'Nicrina ad heroas anglos*: an overview of the British and the Thirty Years War', in S. Jones (ed.), *Britain Turned Germany: the*

Thirty Years War and its Impact on the British Isles, 1618-1660 (Warwick, 2019), p. 21. Something of the pain involved in these departures is captured in the entirely different British and Scottish folk songs with the common title of 'High Germany'. See C.J. Esdaile, '"Bullets, baggages and ballads" revisited: forgotten sources for the experience of British women in the Revolutionary and Napoleonic Wars revised and expanded', *British Journal of Military History*, I, No. 3 (June, 2015), pp. 80-95.

52. For an excellent study of conscription and its impact in one particular region, see J. Broughton, *An Unhappy Civil War the Experiences of Ordinary People in Gloucestershire, Somerset and Wiltshire, 1642-1646* (Bath, 1999), pp. 42-50.

53. Hibbert, *Cavaliers and Roundheads*, p. 266. For the views of the Levellers, meanwhile, see Donoghue, 'Resisting the "enslaving design"', pp. 21-3.

54. Stoyle, 'Pagans or paragons?', pp. 319-23; Wedgwood, *Kings War*, p. 108.

55. Anon., *The Art of Martiall Discipline*, (n.p., n.d.), pp. 61-4.

56. In fairness, the wounds inflicted even by edged weapons were grim enough. As one eyewitness wrote of the aftermath of the skirmish at Powicke Bridge on 23 September 1642, for example, 'Many ... Cavaliers, being fled into Worcester ... were seen in the streets most woefully cut and mangled, some having their ears cut off, some the flesh of their heads sliced off, some with their very skulls hanging down and they ready to fall down dead.' *Cit.* E. Gruber von Arni, *Justice to the Maimed Soldier: Nursing, Medical Care and Welfare for Sick and Wounded Soldiers and their Families during the English Civil Wars and Interregnum, 1642-1660* (Aldershot, 2001), p. 43.

57. *Cit.* S. Bull, *The Furie of the Ordnance: Artillery in the English Civil Wars* (Woodbridge, 2008), p. 31.

58. *Cit.* Hibbert, *Cavaliers and Roundheads*, pp. 118-9.

59. T. Ellison Gibson (ed.), *A Cavalier's Note-Book being Notes, Anecdotes and Observations of William Blundell of Crosby, Lancashire, England, Captain of Dragoons under Major-Gen. Sir Thomas Tyldesley, Knt., in the Royalist Army of 1642* (London, 1880), pp. 25-6; Gruber von Arni, *Justice to the Maimed Soldier*, p. 49.

60. For the examples of Marston Trussel and Stow-on-the-Wold, see D. White, *Haunted Cotswolds* (Stroud, 2010), p. 57, and R.A. Stevens Bassett, *Ghostly Tales and Hauntings of Northamptonshire* (Chichester, 2014), p. 67. For Harston, meanwhile, see < Harston & English Civil War | New contributions, Wartime | Harston History >, accessed 18 March 2021.

61. *Cit.* Adair, *By the Sword Divided*, p. 108.

62. For a detailed study of the response of the inhabitants of much of Somerset to the coming of war in 1642, see D. Underdown, *Somerset in the Civil War and Interregnum* (Newton Abbott, 1973), pp. 37-9.

63. Such popular underpinning of the Parliamentarian cause is something of a theme in the manner in which the rebel war-effort is envisaged, and it is possible to trace this back to the pamphlet literature of the era. By contrast, there are few, if any, examples of the genre from the Royalist camp, the fact being that the majority of townsfolk tended to have little sympathy for the king. In consequence, accounts of the siege of such Royalist strongholds as Newark and Worcester are bereft of plausible mentions of participation on the part of the crowd.

64. Stoyle, *Loyalty and Locality*, pp. 118-31.

65. Hutton, *Royalist War Effort*, pp. 159-64; C. Thomas-Stanford, *Sussex in the Great Civil War, 1642-1660* (London, 1910), pp. 169-71; D. Underdown, 'The chalk and the cheese: contrasts among the English clubmen', *Past and Present*, No. 85 (November, 1979), pp. 25-48. In this latter article, Underdown attempts to show that the clubmen of the West Country were for or against the rival sides in accordance with the ecology of their places of origin - in brief, support for the king was associated with arable areas and support for Parliament with arable ones - but this analysis has been challenged by more recent research, and it seems probable that the clubmen were rather neutralist and ready to take arms against whichever side whose hand happened to be the heaviest in the desperate straits to which the districts from which they came were reduced by the summer of 1645.

66. Stoyle, *Loyalty and Locality*, pp. 63-4; Thomas-Stanford, *Sussex in the Great Civil War*, p. 166; Sherwood, *Civil Strife in the Midlands*, pp. 201, 235.

67. For the proponents of the idea that the English Civil War has been overly idealised, see B. Donagan, 'Atrocity, war crime and treason in the English Civil War', *American Historical Review*, XCIX, No. 4 (October, 1999), p. 1137-66; I. Jones, 'A sea of blood? Massacres during the Wars of the Three Kingdoms, 1641-1653', in P. Dwyer and L. Ryan (eds.), *Theatres of Violence: Massacre, Mass Killing and Atrocity throughout History* (New York, 2012), pp. 63-78. As will become clear, however, many of the examples that such pieces cite were either tales that grew wildly in the counting or actions that would have been seen as being within the laws of war as they were then understood.

68. C. Gerrard *et al*, *Lost Lives, New Voices: Unlocking the Stories of the Scottish Soldiers at the Battle of Dunbar, 1650* (Durham, 2018). Few, if any, English Civil War ghost stories have been discovered in respect of County Durham, but cynics might well suggest that, given the publicity afforded the discoveries at Palace Green, it will not be long before such a sighting comes to light.

69. P. Gater, *Ghosts at War: an Anecdotes Book* (Buxton, 2009), p. 46. Lest it be thought either that the treatment meted out to the Scottish prisoners held at Durham and Chapel-en-le-Frith was occasioned by the fact that they were perceived in terms

of a demonised 'other', it is worth remembering that the phrase 'sent to Coventry' is a reference to the notoriously miserable conditions of Royalists held captive in that town. Nor was it only Parliamentarians who were guilty of such behaviour, as witness the manner in which the prisoners taken by the Royalist troops who stormed Cirencester in March 1643 were sent off to Oxford stripped of much of their clothing and roped together two-by-two. Hibbert, *Cavaliers and Roundheads*, p. 106. Of one individual – a soldier named Peter who was wounded and taken prisoner by a party of Shropshire Royalists in a skirmish near Ludlow – in particular, we know a great deal, Brilliana Harley sending a veritable hymn of complaint in his respect to her son, Ned. Thus, 'Turks could have used him no worse: a Lieutenant-Colonel Morrow would come every day and kick him up and down, and they laid him in a dungeon on foul straw.' *Cit.* Hudson, *The Grand Quarrel*, p. 69.

70. For an introduction to this topic, see D. Kennedy, 'Holy violence and the English Civil War', *Parergon*, XXXII, No. 3 (July, 2015), pp. 17–42. There is, of course, no desire to demonise the cause of Parliament here: had the Royalists acquired the upper hand as the conflict dragged on, there is little doubt that their forces would have evinced a desire for revenge that was just as bloodthirsty. To return to the Parliamentarians, however, the move towards greater levels of ferocity was fuelled by the fact that, in the latter part of the First Civil War and most of the Second and Third, the New Model Army and its auxiliaries were either operating in the Celtic fringe – Cornwall, Wales and Scotland – or Lancashire and Westmorland, these being areas that were perceived as being backward, un-English and papistical, or fighting troops drawn from those same regions; for all this, see M. Stoyle, *Soldiers and Strangers: an Ethnic History of the English Civil War* (London, 2005). Finally, the presence of the radical undercurrents in Parliamentarian politics from the very beginning of the fighting is discussed in D.R. Como, *Radical Parliamentarians in the English Civil War* (Oxford, 2018), pp. 138-55.

71. For a discussion of the impact of the Thirty Years' War on England, see E. Turnbull, 'Anti-popery in early-modern England: war and print, 1617-1635', University of Oxford Ph.D. thesis, 2016.

72. M. Braddick, *God's Fury: England's Fire: a New History of the English Civil Wars* (London, 2008), p. 171; for a detailed assessment of the manner in which the Irish revolt was manipulated by the English press, see E. Darcy, *The Irish Rebellion of 1641 and the Wars of the Three Kingdoms* (Woodbridge, 2013). Once retribution fell upon the Irish from 1649 onwards, of course, Catholics had their own stories to tell. One such was Lancashire Royalist William Blundell. Thus: 'Major Monce hanged a gentlewoman only because she looked (as he was pleased to phrase it) like

an Irish lady ... A gentlewoman, big with child, was hanged on the arch of a bridge ... Mr Comain, who never bore arms, was roasted ... alive by Captain Gines ... Mrs Eustace ... of eighty years of age ... was murdered ... with another old gentlewoman and a girl of eight ... Mr Cauley of West Meath, showing his protection [i.e. safe conduct] was killed with a shot, the protection being laid on his breast to try if it were proof.' Ellison Gibson, *Cavalier's Note-Book*, pp. 231-2.

73. *Cit.* Hunt, *English Civil War*, p. 62.

74. *Cit.* Hudson, *The Grand Quarrel*, p. 66.

75. J. Adamson, *The Noble Revolt: the Overthrow of Charles I* (London, 2007), pp. 306-7.

76. P. Pringle, *Stand and Deliver: the Story of the Highwayman* (San Francisco, 2016), pp. 41-64.

77. J. Childs, 'War, crime waves and the English army in the late seventeenth century', *War and Society*, XV, No. 2 (October 1977), p. 12.

78. As Mark Stoyle has shown, there is also a more political slant to the witch hunts in that they emerged from the ever stronger notion in the Parliamentarian camp that, given that its cause was so evidently Godly, the only explanation for Royalist battlefield successes was resort to witchcraft. At the heart of this development was the treatment afforded to Prince Rupert's pet poodle, Boy, a constant companion of the Royalist general until the unfortunate animal's' death on the field of Marston Moor. In the eyes of all and sundry among the Parliamentarians, said creature was a clear instance of a 'familiar' (in this respect it doubtless did not help that poodles – a German breed – were all but unknown in England), this being something that was quite enough to ensure that the prince's talents as a commander were attributed to the Devil. Hence, then, the manner in which Matthew Hopkins, the so-called 'Witchfinder-General', was able to whip up so much mass hysteria. Curiously, however, despite the prevalence of demonic dogs in British folklore, there is no account of the ghost of Boy having been seen at Marston Moor or anywhere else. For all this, see M. Stoyle, *The Black Legend of Rupert's Dog: Witchcraft and Propaganda during the English Civil War* (Liverpool, 2014). On the witch-hunts in general, see M. Gaskill, *Witchfinders: a Seventeenth-Century English Tragedy* (London, 2005).

79. *Cit.* R. Askew, *Muskets and Altars: Jeremy Taylor and the Last of the Anglicans* (London, 1997), pp. 151-2.

80. *Cit.* Thomas-Stanford, *Sussex in the Great Civil War*, p. 103.

81. *Cit.* B. Worden, *The English Civil Wars, 1640-1660* (London, 2009), p. 165. In this respect, it is interesting that William Blundell's famous notebook (see fn. 33) does not contain a single reference to his experiences in the service of the Royalist cause in Lancashire, and precious little even on the wars as a whole.

82. *Ibid.,* p. 72. In fairness, it should be noted that 'history painting' of the sort exemplified by 'The Surrender of Breda' was still very much in its infancy at the time of the Civil War. As Bann has pointed out, there was no substantial *corpus* of canvasses depicting scenes from the conflicts of 1642-51 until the middle of the nineteenth century, while most of the work involved was redolent with a sense of remorse at the fate of Charles I and his cause and might not have appeared at all had the travails of the Royalist cause not been taken up as a suitable subject by the French Romantic painter Paul Delaroche. Bann, *Scenes and Traces of the English Civil War,* pp. 157-208.

Chapter 2

1. Wedgwood, *The King's War,* p. 575.
2. I. Peck, '"A chronology of some memorable accidents": the representation of the recent past in English almanacs, 1648-1660', *Historical Research,* XCII, No. 255 (February, 2019), pp. 97-117.
3. For the emergence of ghost stories as an aid in medieval catechetics, see C.S. Watkins, 'Sin, penance and purgatory in the Anglo-Norman realm: the evidence of visions and ghost stories', *Past and Present,* No. 175 (May, 2002), pp. 3-33, and A. Joynes (ed.), *Mediaeval Ghost Stories: an Anthology of Miracles, Marvels and Prodigies* (Woodbridge, 2003). As has also been pointed, they also figure in the very first work of English literature, namely Chaucer's *Canterbury Tales,* in which respect see A. Martin, *Ghoul Britannia: Notes from a Haunted Isle* (London, 2009), pp. 38-9. In fairness, it has to be admitted that the Reformation did not put paid to ghost stories. Denounced though the concept was by Protestant divines as a survival of papist superstition, visions and visitations remained common currency with the result that ghosts were co-opted as either messengers from Heaven - in effect, angels – come to exhort, comfort or counsel, or demons bent on either temptation or possession. For a discussion of this issue, see P. Marshall, *Beliefs and the Dead in Reformation England* (Oxford, 2002), pp. 233-64.
4. For a discussion of the impact of the Wars of Religion on French tales of the supernatural, see T. Chesters, *Ghost Stories in Late-Renaissance France: Walking by Night* (Oxford, 2011).
5. O'Lynn, 'Ghosts of war', pp. 183-5.
6. P. Young, *Edgehill, 1642: the Campaign and the Battle* (Kineton, 1976), pp. 162-4.
7. D. Purkiss, 'Dismembering and remembering: the English Civil War and male identity', in C.L. Summers and T.L. Pebworth, (eds.), *The English Civil Wars in the Literary Imagination* (Columbia, Missouri, 1999), p. 221.

8. For all this, see D. Oldridge, 'Land of the walking dead', *BBC History*, January 2006, pp. 20-1.

9. D. Oldridge, *The Supernatural in Tudor and Stuart England* (London, 2016), p. 155. In fairness to Thomas, while he is firm in his conviction that, from the Reformation onwards, there was a general move in the direction of rationalism - a move, indeed, that ensured that from time to time particular ghost stories were in some quarters greeted with ridicule - he accepts that until the late seventeenth century not just the bulk of the population, but even convinced Protestants - ministers of religion included - continued to believe in the phenomenon without question. K. Thomas, *Religion and the Decline of Magic: Studies in Popular Beliefs in Sixteenth and Seventeenth Century England* (London, 1971), pp. 701-24. That said, it has been claimed that there was a change in what people saw. To quote R. C. Finucane, 'Summing up seventeenth-century English apparitions, their freedom from purgatorial punishment clearly distinguishes them from their mediaeval counter-parts.' R.C. Finucane, *Ghosts: Appearances of the Dead and Cultural Transformation* (New York, 1996), p. 149.

10. For the full text of this work, see < https://quod.lib.umich.edu/e/eebo/ A26888.0001.001?view=toc >, accessed 20 October 2020. Meanwhile, the context of such works is discussed in L. Sangha, 'The social, political and spiritual dynamics of ghost stories in early-modern England', *Historical Journal*, LXIII, No. 2 (March 2020), pp. 339-59.

11. Oldridge, *Supernatural in Tudor and Stuart England*, p. 155.

12. *Ibid.*

13. K. Lindley and D. Scott (eds.), *The Journal of Thomas Juxon, 1644-47* (Cambridge, 1999), p. 47.

14. For all this, see J. Mullan, 'Ghosts in Shakespeare', < https://www.bl.uk/ shakespeare/articles/ghosts-in-shakespeare >, accessed 1 November 2020.

15. M.E. Ray, 'John Taylor and the ghost of Long Meg of Westminster: authorship and poetic authority in *The Women's Sharpe Revenge*', *Studies in Philology*, CXIII, No. 4 (September, 2016), pp. 919-46; Anon., *Tom Nash his Ghost to the Three Scurvy Fellows of the Upstart Family of the Snufflers, Rufflers and Shufflers, the Thrice Treble-Troublesome Scufflers in the Church and State, the only Lay Ecclesiass* [sic] *I call Generallissimos, being like Job's Three Comforters, or the Church's Three Anti-Disciples, the Clergy's Three Persecuters, the State's Three Horse-Leeches, the Devil's Three Chaplains, namely the Anabaptist, the Libertine, and the Brownist. Written by Thomas Nash his Ghost, with Pap* [sic] *with a Hatchet, a Little Revived since the Thirtieth Year of the Late Queen Elizabeth's Reign when Martin Mar-Prelate was as Mad as any of his Tub-Men are Now* (York, 1642).

16. Anon., *The Earl of Strafford's Ghost complaining of the Cruelties of his Country-Men in killing One Another. and persuading all Great Men to live honestly that desire to die honourably.* Herein also are his Bad Practises manifested, and the Sad Condition of England and Ireland, expressed and commiserated (London, 1644).

17. *Cit.* Anon., 'Enter Ghost: Elizabethan ghost-lore', *cit.* < http://elsinore.ucsc.edu/Ghost/ghostLore.html >, accessed 1 November 2020. Though it dates from a century or more later, also worth giving here is the testimony of the essayist Joseph Addison (1672-1719). Thus: 'My friend, Sir Roger, has often told me, with a great deal of mirth that, at his first coming to his estate, he found three parts of his house altogether useless; that the best room in it had the reputation of being haunted and by that means was locked up; that the door of one of his chambers was nailed up because there went a story in the family that a butler had formally hanged himself in it; and that his mother, who lived to a great age had shut up half the rooms in the house, in which either a husband, a son or a daughter had died … I should not have been thus particular on these ridiculous horrors did I not find them so very much prevail in all parts of the country.' *Cit.* D.J. Enright (ed.), *The Oxford Book of the Supernatural* (Oxford, 1994), p. 510.

18. Carlton, *This Seat of Mars*, p. xv.

19. See < https://unbound.com/boundless/2020/01/02/whatever-happened-to-the-headless-horseman/ >, accessed 31 October 2020.

20. O'Lynn, *Ghosts of War*, pp. 150-1.

21. For a good example of this process, see Hunt, *English Civil War*, pp. 74-5.

22. P. Ackroyd, *The English Ghost: Spectres through Time* (London, 2010), p. 7.

23. Martin, *Ghoul Britannia*, p. 99. As the same author continues, belief in ghosts was accentuated by the fact that street-lighting ranged from the limited to the entirely non-existent, and illumination in the home dependent entirely on hearths, candles or rush-lights. Thus, 'Walk down a country road on a moonless night without a torch … and you will see a ghost, I guarantee … The Enlightenment, which brought the banishment of ghosts from everyday life, must in part have been a literal enlightening: the proper lighting of domestic and public spaces was not far behind after all.' *Ibid.*, pp. 99-100.

24. It is also possible, of course, that the shepherds simply invented the story as a good tale for their local tavern, only to find that their invention took flight and completely escaped their control: we simply do not know. Meanwhile, it is possibly worthy of note that the spectral re-enactment was first spotted by representatives of a rather lowly element in society. As Jacqueline Pearson has pointed out, claims to have seen ghosts were extremely common among such marginalised groups as serving girls, this suggesting

that coming forward with such accounts provided the powerless with a means of voicing fears, frustrations and complaints that would otherwise have found no safe means of expression. J. Pearson, "'Then she asked it, what were its sisters names?'": reading between the lines in seventeenth-century pamphlets of the supernatural', *Seventeenth Century*, XXVIII, No. 1 (March, 2013), pp. 64-5. Nor is it surprising to find that servant girls who died as a result of being mistreated or cast out by their masters are a common theme in ghost stories of the era, two examples from Chester alone being the tales attached to the Falcon Inn and the Old Bear and Billet, both of which are in Lower Bridge Street. D. Brandon, *Haunted Chester* (Stroud, 2008), pp. 42-3, 48-9.

25. For the ergot theory, see P. Underwood, *Where the Ghosts Walk: the Gazetteer of Haunted Britain* (London, 2013), p. 86.

26. For the political exploitation of the supernatural, see < https://www.culture24.org.uk/history-and-heritage/military-history/pre-20th-century-conflict/art533303-strange-news-north-ghost-sightings-used-political-gain-17th-century-yorkshire >, accessed 23 February 2019.

27. Underwood, *Where the Ghosts Walk*, p. 221.

28. M. Price, *Folktales and Legends of Gloucestershire* (privately published, 2013), pp. 45-7. Like the headless horseman, the phantom coach also featured in ghost stories dating from before the Civil War: at Burford, for example, after the death of a particularly greedy local gentleman named Lawrence Tanfield, his coach-and-four was repeatedly seen flying over the town. Martin, *Ghoul Britannia*, p. 156.

29. E.g. *Bradshaw's Ghost: being a Dialogue between the Said Ghost and an Apparition of the Late King Charles, wherein are laid down Several Transactions that did occur in the Many Passages of his Life, never known before* (London, 1659); Anon., *A New Meeting of Ghosts at Tyburn: being a discourse of Oliver Cromwell, John Bradshaw, Henry Ireton, Thomas Pride, Thomas Scot, Secretary to the Rump, [Thomas] Harrison and Hugh Peters, the Devil's Chaplain* (London, 1660).

30. Anon., *Colonel Rainsborough's Ghost or a True Relation of the Manner of his Death, murdered in his Bed-Chamber at Doncaster by Three of Pontefract's Soldiers who pretended that They had Letters from Lieutenant-General Cromwell to deliver unto him* (London, 1648). 'Slee' is an archaic form of 'slyness' or 'deceit'.

31. C. Mackay, *Memoirs of Extraordinary Popular Delusions* (London, 1841), pp. 598-601. Curiously, Thomas ascribes this incident to a poltergeist, a phenomenon that is widely recognised as being the fruit of psychic disturbances unleashed by the presence of a troubled mind or personality, something that is rendered more credible by the fact that it is difficult to see how some of the incidents featured could have been precipitated by human hands without the perpetrator being seen in the act. If

so, then Collins must have seized on what had occurred as a means of ingratiating himself with the Restoration. Thomas, *Religion and the Decline of Magic*, p. 708. That said, the phenomenon was well enough known in the seventeenth century for it to be entirely possible for Collins to have heard of it and decided to make use of it for his own purposes. See Martin, *Ghoul Britannia*, pp. 148-50. For another such case, see Stoyle, *Loyalty and Locality*, pp. 66-7. In this latter instance, according to a long-standing Tavistock tradition, a troop of Parliamentarian horse who were pillaging the town were put to flight by a local woman who came up with the bright idea of faking an apparition.

32. E. Murphy, "'I remain an airy phantom": Lucy Hutchinson's Civil-War ghost-writing', *ELH: a Journal of English Literary History*, LXXXII, No. 1 (Spring, 1982), pp. 87-113. Even among the staunchest Protestants, however, old ideas died hard. As an example we can cite the Earl of Middleton, a Scottish Presbyterian who was captured at the battle of Worcester and imprisoned in the Tower. Seemingly concerned about the reality of the after-life, he had some years earlier made a pact with an old friend whereby the two of them agreed that whoever died first would come back to tell the other what he had seen. Lying in the Tower, then, Middleton was suddenly confronted by said friend who not only reassured him as to the nature of what came after death but also promised that he would escape in three days, something that duly came to pass, the earl managing to get out by disguising himself in his wife's clothes when the latter was allowed in to visit him. Finucane, *Ghosts*, pp. 143-4.

33. This story was first recounted by Daniel Defoe, but it is generally believed to have emanated from an account penned by John Ruddle. See < https://www.thepost.uk.com/article.cfm?id=110190&headline=Tales+of+death%2C+ghosts+and+consequence+in%3FSouth+Petherwin&sectionIs=news&searchyear=2018 >, accessed 23 October 2020.

34. See O'Lynn, *Ghosts of War*, pp. 175-81 *passim*.

35. D. Love, *Scottish Ghosts* (London, 1995), p. 87. For almost the past 150 years, meanwhile, Edinburgh had also been the source of tales of a phantom herald who had appeared early one morning at the Mercat Cross to a merchant named Richard Lawson a few days before the Battle of Flodden, and not only proclaimed the news of the terrible Scottish defeat that this produced but also gave an accurate list of all the persons of quality who perished, starting with King James IV. *Ibid.*, pp. 85-6.

36. For the story of Strafford's supposed intervention in the campaign of Naseby, see J. Ingram, *The Haunted Homes and Family Traditions of Great Britain: Second Series* (London, 1884), pp. 59-61.

37. J.A. Brooks, *Britain's Haunted Heritage* (Norwich, 1990), pp. 151-2. There is no evidence whatsoever that Newcastle, an individual who was renowned for his decency and sense of chivalry, gave any such orders. That said, it is clear that the populace were convinced that they would indeed be slaughtered should his men take the town, not least because the murder of the Royalist officer was all too real, the fatal blow having been struck by one Ralph Atkinson to the accompaniment of jeers that the unfortunate man would receive 'Bradford quarter'. See < https://e-voice. org.uk/claytonhistorygroup/bradford-in-the-civil-war >, accessed 7 January 2021.

38. Oldridge, *Supernatural in Tudor and Stuart England*, p. 59.

39. There are certainly cases from the period in which stories of haunting were contrived for private purposes, one such concerning a certain Mistress Leakey. A resident of Minehead in Somerset, Leakey died in 1634, only for her son and daughter-in-law supposedly to be plagued for months by constant visitations on the part of the old woman's ghost. What happened next is too long and complex a story to recount in any detail, but it seems that the whole tale was concocted as a means of blackmailing an Anglican cleric named John Atherton who was currently Bishop of Waterford, but had previously been a member of the local clergy and, not just that, but the husband of one of her two daughters (in brief, Leakey's daughter-in-law insisted that the ghost had told her that she would only leave her and her husband in peace if she would travel to Waterford and advise him to repent, this being a task that was far from impossible to carry out given the fact that her husband was a merchant who carried on a regular trade with Ireland). So far so good, but, when the case reached the ears of the religious authorities, it was investigated and pronounced completely bogus. The fact that the object was blackmail did not come out, but Atherton had been a noted philanderer during his ministry in Somerset, and, still worse, fathered a child by his sister-in-law, namely Leakey's other daughter, and it is probable that the family therefore decided to profit from his indiscretions, indiscretions that had meanwhile been piling up at such a rate that Atherton ended up being executed for sodomy in 1640. T. Brown, 'The ghost of old Mrs Leakey', in H.R.E. Davidson (ed.), *The Folklore of Ghosts* (Cambridge, 1980), pp. 141-54.

40. For a general discussion, see E. Peters, 'Trauma narratives of the English Civil War', *Journal for Early Modern Cultural History*, XVI, No. 1 (Winter, 2016), pp. 78-94.

41. For all this, see Carlton, *This Seat of Mars*, p. xix.

42. While it is difficult to know how representative they are, Carlton cites a number of cases of men who failed to write about their experiences when, as members of the propertied classes, they might easily have done so, and rightly enough stresses

how few personal recollections of the fighting we have. See Carlton, *Going to the Wars*, pp. 343-4. Particularly interesting in this respect is a comment written by the diarist John Evelyn. Thus: 'I will not go too far in repeating the sorrowes which are vanish't, or uncover the buried memory of the evils past.' *Cit.* Peters, 'Trauma narratives', p. 83. More explicit still, meanwhile, are the memories of Kaspar Preis, a peasant from the Fulda area, of the Thirty Years' War. As he wrote many years later, 'To tell of all the miseries and misfortune is not within my power, not even what I know and have seen myself ... and if I did report everything which I have seen and so painfully experienced no-one living in a better age would believe it.' *Cit.* J. Pollmann, *Memory in Early-Modern Europe, 1500-1800* (Oxford, 2017), p. 163.

43. O'Lynn, 'Ghosts of war and spirits of place', p. 198.

44. *Ibid.*, p. 199.

45. *Cit.* Peters, 'Trauma narratives', pp. 82-3.

46. M. Stoyle, 'Memories of the maimed': the testimony of Charles I's former soldiers, 1660–1730', *History*, LXXXVIII, No. 2 (April, 2003), p. 214.

47. *Cit.* Hudson, *The Grand Quarrel*, p. 167.

48. *Cit. ibid.*, p. 92.

49. *Cit. ibid.*, p. 119.

50. *Cit.* R. Baxter, *The Certainty of the Worlds of Spirits and, consequently, of the Immortality of Souls, of the Malice and Misery of the Devils and the Damned, and of the Blessedness of the Justified, fully evinced by the Unquestionable Histories of Apparitions, Operations, Witchcrafts, Voices, etc., written as an Addition to many other Treatises for the Conviction of Sadducees and Infidels* (London, 1691), pp. 24-5.

51. Baxter was not the only man of learning to attempt this task. On the contrary, seven years before the professor of mathematics at the University of Glasgow, one George Sinclair wrote a pamphlet in which he recounted the story of a corpse that suddenly came to life in the middle of its funeral and was thrust into the grave kicking and struggling (that the unfortunate person concerned had not been dead at all seemed never to occur to Sinclair). See Oldfield, 'Land of the walking dead', p. 20.

52. For a fascinating discussion of popular perceptions of the combatants of the Civil War, see Anon. 'Ghosts of the English Civil War', < https://mysterioustimes. wordpress.com/2014/02/24/ghosts-of-the-english-civil-war/ >, accessed 30 March 2019. In brief, what is described in the pieces concerned is an experiment in which some 500 people were shown models of a pikeman, a musketeer and a cavalryman, of whom the last was cunningly dressed neither in a hat nor a helmet but a montero (a species of seventeenth-century balaclava helmet) and asked various questions of their identity. Not surprisingly, it was only the cavalryman who was widely

associated with the Civil War, and, even then, only a small minority of the people surveyed spotted that he could equally well have been serving on either side. From this, there follow two conclusions, namely, first, that claims as to the identity of Civil War ghosts cannot be trusted, and, second, at least potentially, that many such spectres have gone completely unrecognised.

53. The best guide to the clothing and equipment of Civil War armies is beyond doubt P. Haythornthwaite, *The English Civil Wars: an Illustrated Military History* (London, 1983).

54. For a wonderful collection of such portraits, see A. Haldane, *Portraits of the English Civil War* (London, 2017).

55. The Civil War is not the only period of history that could be so treated. As one county study observes, 'Ghostly 'ladies' floating about the halls of old Lancashire are often an indication of illicit Roman-Catholic activities in centuries gone by ... With only a few exceptions, this county's old halls and houses which claim a feminine apparition can trace a story back to Catholicism in those days of horror and tension.' K. Ayre, *Lancashire Ghosts* (Clapham, 1976), pp. 18-19.

56. *Cit.* J. Bellanger, *Ghosts of War: Restless Spirits of Soldiers, Spies and Saboteurs* (Franklin Lakes, New Jersey, 2006), p. 52. From this it follows that ghost stories can be a valuable weapon for struggling educators. As Priestly continues, 'A lot of children ... find the Civil War a very dry subject, but, if you add a headless ghost into it, then it helps them remember it.' *Ibid.*

57. Davidson, *Folklore of Ghosts*, p. vii.

58. Brooks, *Britain's Haunted Heritage*, p. 34.

59. For a discussion of this issue, see K.M. Briggs, 'Tradition and invention in ghost stories' in Davidson, *ibid.*, pp. 3-12.

60. For the story of the Brodick Castle ghost, see Love, *Scottish Ghosts*, p. 121.

61. D. Acorah, *Derek Acorah's Ghost Towns* (London, 2006), pp. 211-12.

62. Underwood, *Where the Ghosts Walk*, p. 95.

63. *Cit. ibid.*, p. 107. For the Shrewsbury investigation, see Bellanger, *Ghosts of War*, pp. 48-9.

64. Eyre, *Lancashire Ghosts*, p. 7.

65. Bellanger, *Ghosts of War*, p. 48. Accounts of such sightings litter the internet. One such that is particularly pertinent to this pamphlet concerns a ghostly image that was spotted on a photograph that was taken of what used to be the graveyard of Saint James' church in a ghost-tour of Liverpool, said image supposedly being that of a Civil War soldier. See < https://mysteriousuniverse.org/2018/03/saint-james-cemetery-liverpool-ghost-photograph/ > and < https://www.dailymail.co.uk/news/

article-5545973/Ghost-17th-century-soldier-spotted-Liverpool-cemetery.html >, accessed 28 February 2019. For two more, this time from the sites of the battle of Naseby and Saint Fagan's, see < https://www.telegraph.co.uk/news/uknews/2401393/ English-Civil-War-ghost-captured-on-film-by-paranormal-enthusiasts.html > and < https://www.unexplained-mysteries.com/forum/topic/300495-english-civil-war-ghosts-spying-on-child/ >, accessed 30 March 2019. For a ruthless demolition of such photographs, see I. Wilson, *In Search of Ghosts* (London, 1995), pp. 27-41.

Chapter 3

1. See M. Ashley, *The English Civil War* (second edition; Stroud, 1990), pp. 93, 99.
2. H.C.B. Rogers, *Battles and Generals of the Civil Wars, 1642-1651* (London, 1968), p. 62.
3. For a particularly good example of a work that attempts to meld the Civil War in the localities with major campaigns such as Edgehill, Marston Moor and Naseby, see P. Gaunt, *The English Civil War: a Military History* (London, 2014).
4. S. Bull, *"A General Plague of Madness: the Civil Wars in Lancashire, 1640-1660* (Lancaster, 2009), pp. 73-8.
5. R.N. Dore, *The Civil Wars in Cheshire* (Chester, 1966), pp. 9-22.
6. In fairness to Derby, despite having been one of King Charles' first adherents, he received little support or encouragement from his royal master, the latter having seemingly been persuaded that, coming as he did from a family with a long record of being 'over-mighty' subjects, he was a figure cast in the same mould as such rebel grandees as the Earls of Warwick, Essex and Northumberland. See J. Kewley Draskau, *Lady Derby: the Great Whore of Babylon* (Douglas, 2020), pp. 147-9.
7. For all this, see E. Broxap, *The Great Civil War in Lancashire, 1642-1651* (Manchester, 1910), pp. 41-65; Bull, *General Plague of Madness*, pp. 92-127.
8. Broxap, *Great Civil War,* pp. 66-81; Bull, *General Plague of Madness*, pp. 127-50.
9. Broxap., *Great Civil War,* pp. 82-8; Bull, *General Plague of Madness*, pp. 151-62. Though French, De La Trémoille was a staunch Protestant and for that reason had earned the enmity of Henrietta Maria and been denied favour at court. That said, when war came she from the start proved a vigorous adherent to the Royalist cause, and seems to have been the chief influence in persuading her husband - initially an opponent of hostilities who was desperate for compromise – into declaring for King Charles. See Kewley Draskau, *Lady Derby*, pp. 143-4.
10. That quiet reigned at Lathom House was in large part the work of some clever politicking on the part of Lady Derby, the latter having in effect negotiated a truce with the Lancashire Parliamentarians whereby she promised to live quietly within the immediate bounds of her home and, in particular, abstain from raiding the countryside

round about for supplies, in exchange for being left in peace and allowed to maintain a garrison for her personal protection. Kewley Draskau, *Lady Derby*, p. 170.

11. Bull, *General Plague of Madness*, pp. 164-70.

12. Dore, *Civil Wars in Cheshire*, p. 15.

13. *Ibid.*, pp. 25-8; A. Abram, *More like Lions than Men: Sir William Brereton and the Cheshire Army of Parliament, 1642-1646* (Warwick, 2020), pp. 31-3. For the battle of Middlewich, in particular, see P. Gaunt, 'Wedged up in the church like billets in a woodpile': new light on the battle of Middlewich, 13 March, 1643', in I. Pells (ed.), *New Approaches to the Military History of the English Civil War*, pp. 27-56.

14. Hutton, *Royalist War Effort*, pp. 59-67; J. Worton, *To Settle the Crown: Waging the Civil War in Shropshire, 1642-48* (Solihull, 2016), pp. 205-7.

15. For the Parliamentarian invasion of North Wales in 1643, see P. Gaunt. *A Nation under Siege: the Civil War in Wales, 1642-48* (London, 1991), pp. 36-7; Abram, *More like Lions than Men*, pp. 45-9.

16. For details of the fall of Beeston, see J. Barrett, *Sieges of the English Civil Wars* (Barnsley, 2009), pp. 45-9.

17. Abram, *More like Lions than Men*, pp. 50-3. The incident at Barthomley has often been represented as a massacre of innocent civilians. However, the most recent research suggests that this interpretation is based on little more than Parliamentarian pamphlets of the time, and that the victims were rather soldiers who were certainly dealt with harshly but were yet put to death in accordance with what were then commonly accepted as the laws of war. G. Hudson, 'Northern Civil-War atrocity story at Barthomley church revisited', *Northern History*, XLVI, No. 2 (September, 2009), pp. 329-32.

18. Given the events of 1641, the arrival of the troops from Ireland, the first contingent of some 25,000 men who were dispatched from various Irish ports in the period November 1643-May 1644, was a seminal moment, and all the more so as, despite Royalist insistence that all the men concerned were Protestant Englishmen recruited before the outbreak of the Civil War, between two fifths and one half of the whole can be shown to have been native Irish who had been driven by poverty to enlist in the forces of the Crown. If the new arrivals temporarily turned the war in Cheshire and North Wales - without them it seems likely that Chester would have fallen very shortly - in the north-west and elsewhere alike, the fact that the king had acted as he had caused consternation among neutral opinion and imbued the conflict with a savagery that it had hitherto mostly been lacking: if hardened veterans of the Irish war were responsible for killing prisoners in cold blood at Barthomley, the Parliamentarians were responsible for a particularly unpleasant incident that took

place in May 1644 when a Royalist ship was captured in the Irish Sea and all the men on board judged to be Irish by birth roped together and thrown overboard. For all this, see J.L. Malcolm, 'All the King's men: the impact of the Crown's Irish soldiers on the English Civil War', *Irish Historical Studies*, XXII, No. 83 (March, 1979), pp. 239-64.

19. For a full account of the Nantwich campaign, see J. Dixon, *The Business at Acton: the Battle of Nantwich, 25th January 1644, and the Civil War in Cheshire, 1642-1646* (Nottingham, 2012). See also J. Lowe, 'The campaign of the Irish Royalist army in Cheshire, November 1643-January 1644', *Transactions of the Historical Society of Lancashire and Cheshire*, III (1959), pp. 47-76. Desperate, perhaps, to save themselves from being labelled as papists and but little inclined to face months or even years of incarceration in the most miserable of conditions, as many as half the 1,500 prisoners quickly proceeded to 'turn their coats' and enlist in the forces of Parliament. A. Hopper, *Turncoats and Renegadoes: Changing Sides during the English Civil Wars* (Oxford, 2012), p. 89.

20. Abram, *More like Lions then Men*, pp. 59-60.

21. For the strategic background to Rupert's campaign in the north-west and subsequent march on York, see M. Wanklyn and F. Jones, *A Military History of the English Civil War* (Harlow, 2005), pp. 173-5. As for the collapse of the truce that had protected Lathom House since the battle of Whalley (see fn. 10), it appears that the Parliamentarian leaders had, quite rightly, if somewhat belatedly, woken up to the fact Lady Derby had been quietly playing them for fools and doing all she could to prepare her domains for a siege. Kewley Draskau, *Lady Derby*, pp. 171-2.

22. For the attack on Lathom House, see Barrett, *Sieges of the English Civil War*, pp. 83-92. Of the defences we know little, for almost nothing has survived of the seventeenth-century site, but there was clearly a massive earthern rampart, while the garrison appear to have been well provided with cannon. Bull, *General Plague of Madness*, pp. 185-211.

23. D. Casserly, *Massacre: the Storming of Bolton* (Stroud, 2011), pp. 111-23; Broxap, *Great Civil War*, pp. 120-4; Bull, *General Plague of Madness*, pp. 219-24.

24. For all this, see G. Chandler, *Liverpool under Charles I* (Liverpool, 1965), pp. 21-2. According to tradition, Rupert established his headquarters in the humble home of some tenant farmer on Everton heights. The building, alas, has long since disappeared, but in 1851 it was still marked on the local Ordnance Survey map while its memory is perpetuated by the modern street-name 'Rupert Drive'. Not far away, meanwhile, stands Prince Rupert's Tower, a name erroneously appended to a round parish lock-up that was erected nearby in 1787.

25. Bull, *General Plague of Madness*, pp. 262-5.

26. *Ibid.*, pp. 267-80; Barrett, *Sieges of the English Civil Wars*, pp. 92-4.

27. Abram, *More like Lions than Men*, p. 71.

28. J. Barratt, '*A Rabble of Gentility*': *the Royalist Northern Horse, 1644-1645* (Solihull, 2017), pp. 33-5.

29. Gaunt, *Nation under Siege*, pp. 48-9.

30. Abram, *More like Lions than Men*, pp. 70-3.

31. J. Barrett, *The Great Siege of Chester* (Stroud, 2011), pp. 64-83.

32. *Ibid.*, pp. 84-6.

33. *Ibid.*, pp. 90-1.

34. For the battle of Rowton Heath, as the clash of 24 September became known, see *ibid.*, pp. 93-106; Barratt, *Rabble of Gentility*, pp. 71-8. Meanwhile, according to legend, not to mention the plaque that today marks the spot, King Charles watched the battle from the Phoenix Tower rather than the cathedral. However, given the position of said Phoenix Tower at the north-easternmost point of the city walls, this story is most implausible, although it may be that the king spent some time there watching the troops who were supposed to attack the besiegers from the rear file round from the North Gate, the more obvious route through the East Gate having been firmly barricaded in the wake of the attack of 19 September. While on the tower of the cathedral, meanwhile, Charles was almost killed when a ball from a wall-piece – essentially a giant musket – that the Parliamentarians had carried up to the roof of the tower of Saint John's Priory struck down an officer who was standing beside him.

35. Barrett, *Great Siege of Chester*, pp. 118-22.

36. *Ibid.*, pp. 123-65.

37. For the fall of Beeston, see Barrett, *Sieges of the English Civil Wars*, pp. 55-9.

38. For the early stages of the campaign of 1648, see P.R. Hill and J.M. Watkinson, '*Cromwell hath the honour but ...*': *Major-General Lambert's Campaigns in the North, 1648* (London, 2012), pp. 49-94.

39. The most up-to-date account of the battle is constituted by S. Bull and M. Seed, *Bloody Preston: the Battle of Preston, 1648* (Lancaster, 1998), pp. 63-74. Also very useful is M. Wanklyn, *Decisive Battles of the English Civil War: Myth and Reality* (Barnsley, 2006), pp. 184-99. For two discussions of Cromwell's generalship in the campaign, see M. Bennett, *Cromwell at War: the Lord General and his Military Revolution* (London, 2017), pp. 252-8., and F. Kitson, *Old Ironsides: the Military Biography of Oliver Cromwell* (London, 2004), pp. 151-9.

40. There is no detailed print source for the battle of Winwick, though Bull and Seed provide enough information to follow the story. See *ibid.*, pp. 79-84. However, for

an excellent website, see < https://historicengland.org.uk/listing/the-list/list-entry/1412878 >.

41. For the battle of Wigan Lane, see Bull, *General Plague of Madness*, pp. 375-80.

42. Rebuilt in its current form though it was in 1636, the Old Man and Scythe dates from the thirteenth century and is supposed to be the fourth-oldest hostelry in the entire country. Among its prize possessions is a chair said to have been sat in by Derby while he was waiting for his execution although this is beyond doubt a fake.

43. R. Matthews, *Haunted Chester* (Andover, 1992), p. 13; D. Acorah, *Haunted Britain: Over 100 of the UK's Places to Visit* (London, 2006), p. 86. There is a bizarre post-script to the Bolton part of Derby's various hauntings. Thus, some time after closing time one night in 2014, the owner of the Old Man and Scythe suddenly heard a glass shatter in the bar. Rushing downstairs, he found the remains of the glass on the floor and looked up to see a shadowy figure standing whom he recognised as none other than the Earl of Derby, it later being discovered that the apparition had been picked up by the pub's CCTV system. See < https://www.dailymail.co.uk/news/article-2561419/Is-proof-ghost-Ye-Olde-Man-Scythe-Or-spirits.html >, accessed 19 March 2019. However, matters did not end there. On the contrary, the resultant video having been released to the press, a Chinese artist named Lu Pingyuan saw it and travelled to England to capture Derby's shade so that he could incorporate it into an art exhibit. To achieve this purpose, he came equipped with a steel flask and managed to entice the ghost into this by casting a spell. Success having been achieved in this fashion, he then travelled back to China with said flask (complete with said ghost!) and duly put it on show, much to the fury of the despoiled licensee who, having discovered the theft via the internet, promptly got in touch with the local paper and demanded Derby's return forthwith! See < https://mysteriousuniverse.org/2016/09/haunted-pubs-owner-wants-stolen-ghost-returned/ >, accessed 19 March 2019.

44. < http://affetside.org.uk/pub_history.htm >, accessed 24 March 2014. Details of how the skull manifests its displeasure are unknown, but there are one or two stories of people who had stolen it for a joke or borrowed it for a lecture returning it in great haste in a state of some alarm.

45. D. Brandon, *Haunted Chester* (Stroud, 2008), p. 75; F. Woods, *Cheshire Ghosts and Legends* (Newbury, 1990), p. 54.

46. Brandon, *Haunted Chester*, pp. 19-20.

47. *Ibid.*, p. 83. Anon., *Cheshire Ghost Stories* (Sheffield, n.d.), p. 44. For good measure, on the anniversary of the battle, its site is supposedly roamed by a ghostly horseman in the person of Charles I's cousin, Lord Bernard Stuart, who was slain in a cavalry

charge, while the ghostly music said to have been heard in the area is associated with another victim of the fighting in the person of William Lawes, a court musician who was serving in the King's Lifeguard of Horse. See < https://www.hauntedrooms. co.uk/rowton-moor-chester >, accessed 30 March 2019.

48. J. Pearson, *Haunted Places of Cheshire: On the Trail of the Paranormal* (Newbury, 2006), p. 55. Given that Nantwich was almost permanently in the hands of the Parliamentarians, it is hard not to wonder how it came to be that this ghost was a Royalist. Speculation, of course, is useless, but it is not impossible that prisoners of rank were at some point housed in the building. For the story in respect of the Black Lion, meanwhile, see < http://billpearson.co.uk/ghosts-in-nantwich-public-houses/ >, accessed 27 March, 2019. It should perhaps be noted, however, that the current building only dates from 1664.

49. *Cheshire Ghost Stories*, p. 59. Assuming, as is usually said, that the men concerned were fugitives from some Royalist defeat, it may be that they were survivors of the troops defeated by Brereton at Middlewich in March 1643. However, a much more likely candidate for the action concerned is the brief skirmish that took place near the bridge on 19 August 1659 in the uprising of Colonel George Booth, this being an abortive Royalist attempt to overthrow the Commonwealth and bring back Charles II from exile. If it is indeed the case that it is this affair that is remembered via the story of the two horsemen, then, as in the case of the battle of Ormskirk (see below), what we have is the case of an obscure historical detail being preserved in the form of a folk-memory.

50. For the ghost of Speke Hall, see < https://signaturesliverpool.co.uk/the-spookiest-stories-in-liverpool/ >, accessed 24 March 2019.

51. Whitaker, *Lancashire Ghosts and Legends*, p. 49; *Haunted Locations of Lancashire*, p. 19. The 'laughing Cavalier' is not Littleborough's only association with the Civil War. On the contrary, nearby stood an old cottage in which Cromwell is reputed to have stayed, a spot now commemorated by a street named 'Oliver Close'.

52. *Ibid.*, p. 63. There are several Lancashire ghost stories that relate to priest hunting, but tying these to the period of the Civil War is somewhat problematic. Certainly, the hunt for Catholic clergy had but little abated, no fewer than thirty-one such men dying in prison or being put to death between 1640 and 1660, but much confusions caused by the leading role played in England's Protestant Reformation by Thomas Cromwell, the result, of course, being that tales of priests being hunted and killed by 'Cromwell's men' are as likely to refer to the sixteenth century as they are to the seventeenth. Meanwhile, for details of the English martyrs, see < https://en.wikipedia.org/wiki/List_of_Catholic_martyrs_of_the_English_Reformation#1606%E2%80%931680 >, accessed 31 March 2019.

53. D. Codd, *Paranormal Lancashire* (Stroud, 2011), < https://books.google.co.uk/ books?id=RoKoAwAAQBAJ&printsec=frontcover&dq=paranormal+lancashire& hl=en&sa=X&ved=0ahUKEwiAqda5sqzhAhVzpHEKHalgD14QuwUILTAA#v= onepage&q=paranormal%20lancashire&f=false >, accessed 31 March 2019. This story does not ring true when applied to the New Model Army, it being much more likely that the tailor was rather the victim of the increasingly desperate troops of the Duke of Hamilton.

54. T.W. Whitaker, *Lancashire Ghosts and Legends* (London, 1980), p. 47.

55. O. Davies, *The Haunted: a Social History of Ghosts* (Basingstoke, 2007), p. 40. One oddity of Lancashire's list of Civil War hauntings is the absence of anything from Liverpool. Given the brutality of the then town's experiences, it would be surprising if the latter had not been remembered by its inhabitants in the form of ghost stories. Yet, despite the many books written on 'haunted Liverpool' by Tom Slemen and others, nothing relevant has been located other than the rather dubious photograph of a ghostly figure in Saint James' cemetery noted in Chapter 1. Evidently, the complete absence of the seventeenth-century townscape and the city's cosmopolitan nature have between them obliterated the city's older cultural traditions and replaced them with a new set of myths.

56. Whitaker, *Lancashire Ghosts and Legends*, p. 97.

57. For the story of the Nantwich battlefield, see < http://mythsandlegendsofcheshire. blogspot.com/2011/02/battle-of-nantwich-1644.html >, accessed 27 March 2019. Meanwhile, for the Chester case, see Brandon, *Haunted Chester*, pp. 72, 75. With regard to the fighting in Saint Werbugh's Street, for which mute evidence may be found in the form of a number of bullet marks in the wall of the cathedral, this incident is often placed in the context of the aftermath of the battle of Rowton Heath, but this is erroneous: at the time of the battle the East Gate was firmly blocked up, the result being that the combat can only have taken place during the assault of 22 September.

58. R. Holland, *Lancashire Ghost Stories* (Sheffield, 2014), p. 25.

59. Eyre, *Lancashire Ghosts*, p. 65.

60. Whitaker, *Lancashire Ghosts and Legends*, p. 96; < https://www.paranormaldatabase. com/calendar/Pages/aug.php >, accessed 2 November 2020. Further north, meanwhile, it is presumably the campaign of 1648 that in some way accounted for a vision of a large army that was seen advancing across the fells on a number of occasions near Penrith in the period 1735-40. See S. Marsden, *This Sceptred Isle: a Journey through Haunted England* (Swindon, 2005), p. 153. For good measure, Hermitage Green Lane is also reported as playing host to the sound of running feet and loud drumming.

61. Ayre. *Lancashire Ghosts*, p. 9. Whitaker, *Lancashire Ghosts and Legends*, p. 63.

62. Whitaker, *Lancashire Ghosts and Legends*, p. 137; R. Guthrie, *The Haunted Locations of Lancashire: a Look at Ghostly Lancashire Hotspots* (n.p., n.d.) , pp. 11, 23.

63. R. McKenzie, *They Still Serve: a Complete Guide to the Military Ghosts of Britain* (self-published, 2008), p. 62; Davies, *The Haunted*, p. 37. The stories that have come down to us in respect of Middleton are rather muddled and it is not at all clear whether the hauntings reported to have occurred in School Lane are connected with the Ring o'Bells' Edward, while matters are further confused by claims that said hostelry was the haunt of a group of Royalist conspirators who went down fighting after they were surprised by Parliamentarian troops. Sadly, however, the only connection that has been established between Middleton and the Civil Wars is the fact that some of the prisoners from the battle of Wigan Lane were housed in the parish church, though it is also claimed that a number of bodies that were identified as being of seventeenth-century provenance were at some point unearthed in the cellar. Guthrie, *Haunted Locations of Lancashire*, p. 22.

64. McKenzie, *They Still Serve*, p. 62.

65. *Ibid.*, p. 61.

66. The story of the fight at Sandbach and the subsequent hauntings is retold in a Facebook site entitled 'Sandbach Ghost Stories', accessed 3 November 2020. The fact that the haunting centres on a piper instantly renders it slightly suspect: classic symbol of Scotland though they are, pipers were not a feature of the Lowland regiments that fought in the Worcester campaign. That said, it is clear that the civilian population had good cause for their anger: Warrington's Black Horse Inn, for example, is haunted by the ghost of one Giles Boston, a blacksmith supposedly shot to death by Royalist troops. See < 7 of Warrington's spookiest ghost stories on Halloween | Warrington Guardian >, accessed 12 November 2021.

67. This point is impossible to prove in any tangible sense, but it is by no means to be scorned. To quote Barbara Donaghan, 'The internalised honour that derived from uncompromised personal integrity ... played a crucial part in shaping the conduct enemies to each other and in justifying conduct against critics of one's own side ... At Chester in 1645, the opposing commanders, Lord Byron and Sir William Brereton, invoked the reciprocity of "civil and soldierly proceedings" ... Failure to adhere to standards of courage and good faith damaged an officer's standing in the eyes of others ... and his ideal sense of himself. He was motivated by "feare of shame" as well as "a certaine desire of excellencie".' B. Donagan, *War in England, 1642-1642* (Oxford, 2008), pp. 228-9.

68. Brandon, *Haunted Chester*, pp. 20, 72. For good measure, the Water Tower is haunted by the ghost of a soldier put to death for falling asleep on sentryduty.

69. *Ibid.*, p. 71.

70. Holland, *Lancashire Ghost Stories*, pp. 32-3. According to report, the house does not just have an 'in-dwell' but also from time to time is visited by the sound of gunfire.

71. *Cheshire Ghosts*, pp. 71-2. Whereas Mary Webb was at least cut down in the heat of battle, Grace Trygg fell victim to gratuitous violence. While the general opinion among scholars is that women were usually spared such treatment, the north-west boasts at least two other ghost stories that suggest that there were exceptions. First, then, we have the case of Heskin Hall's 'white lady', according to legend a daughter of the household who was killed in a raid on the house by troops looking for a Catholic priest who was known to be hiding in the building. Whitaker, *Lancashire Ghosts and Legends*, p. 129. And, second, there is that of the ghost associated with Gubberford Bridge near Garstang, the figure reported as having been seen in this vicinity supposedly being the wife of a man named Peter Broughton, who was one of the Parliamentarian troops currently besieging Garstang Castle. Mistress Broughton, it seems, was a somewhat wayward woman, and, discovering that she had been having an affair, not just with another man, but with a Royalist sympathiser, her husband murdered her on the bridge before burying her body on the riverbank. Codd, *Paranormal Lancashire*.

72. Brandon, *Haunted Chester*, pp. 32-3. Another ghost who the literature recalls as having lost her love is associated with Marple Hall in Cheshire, the story being that the spectre in question is that of a young maidservant who fell in love with a Royalist officer, only to see him murdered by the then owner, Henry Bradshaw (in some versions of the story, the murder victim is rather the girl, and, not just that, but Bradshaw's own daughter). See < Marple Hall – Mysterious Britain & Ireland >, accessed 12 November 2021.

73. *Ibid.*, p. 50. Given the distance of the Tudor House from the north wall, it may be justifiably asked whether such a hit could have been achieved, but a ball from a heavy cannon such as a culverin could easily have spanned the distance, while the building is tall enough for the top floor to be easily attainable. On top of this, that the area suffered from the bombardment cannot be doubted: as we have seen, the nearby building that occupied the site of the Old Bear and Billet was heavily damaged, if not totally destroyed.

74. Virtually the only Civil War ghost story that we have from Carlisle consists of a vague report to the effect that Cavaliers have been sighted on the surviving stretches of the city walls. See < Cumbria Guide | Haunted Carlisle - Tales from the Crypt | Cumbria Guide >, accessed 12 November 2021.

Chapter 4

1. Some eyebrows may be raised by the inclusion in the region of the Nottinghamshire town of Newark, but this can be justified by reference to the facts, first, that it was throughout the period 1643-44 a dependency of the Marquis of Newcastle, and, second, that events that took place there had much influence on the situation in Yorkshire and Lincolnshire.

2. Hibbert, *Cavaliers and Roundheads*, p. 41.

3. Wedgwood, *King's War*, pp. 80-1. This was not the first attempt on the part of Charles to secure the city. Thus, hardly had the king departed from Hampton Court than he ordered the Marquis of Newcastle, a prominent courtier who had until his enforced dismissal the year before at the hands of Pym and his allies been the tutor of the future Charles II to do just that. Then resident at his Nottinghamshire estate at Welbeck, the duke had ridden post-haste to the city the moment he received the king's missive, but, while he talked his way in easily enough, he had brought no men with him other than two or three servants and in consequence lacked the force to take over, eventually having no option but to submit to demands from Parliament that he should travel to London to explain himself forthwith, a demand with which Charles, his bluff firmly called, directed him to comply. G. Trease, *Portrait of a Cavalier: William Cavendish, First Duke of Newcastle* (London, 1979), pp. 90-1.

4. P. Young and W. Emberton, *Sieges of the Great Civil War* (London, 1978), pp. 47-8.

5. The split in the Yorkshire gentry was at least three to two in favour of the king, one factor that particularly benefited the Royalists being the relatively large number of families - according to one estimate some 157 - who had remained faithful to Catholicism. See Binns, *Yorkshire in the Civil Wars*, pp. 42-5. Meanwhile, strategically situated Skipton was a particularly valuable acquisition: not only was its castle a particularly impressive fortification but it also happened to house no fewer than seven artillery pieces, of which one was a demi-culverin, three culverins and one a demi-cannon. See R.T. Spence, *Skipton Castle in the Great Civil War, 1642-1645* (Skipton, 1991), p. 3.

6. Trease, *Portrait of a Cavalier*, pp. 92-4.

7. Binns, *Yorkshire in the Great Civil War*, p. 55. Throughout the campaigns in Yorkshire, Sir Thomas Fairfax was but Lieutenant-General of the Horse in his father's army, but it is nonetheless quite clear that he was the leading light in the latter's operations. For a recent study, see A. Hopper, *Black Tom: Sir Thomas Fairfax and the English Revolution* (Manchester, 2007).

8. Binns, *Yorkshire in the Civil Wars*, p. 55.

9. In view of the fact that the Yorkshire gentry was so heavily split in favour of the king, this judgement may seem a little adventurous, and all the more so as the Parliamentarians were bedevilled by personal rivalries in that the Hothams had been far more energetic in their opposition to the king than Lord Fairfax, while yet having little interest in the latter's religious radicalism, and were therefore deeply resentful of the latter's appointment to the command. See A.J. Hopper, '"Fitted for desperation": honour and treachery in Parliament's Yorkshire command, 1642-1643', *History*, LXXXVI, No. 282 (April, 2001), p. 139. However, Cumberland was so flaccid a figure and so short of resources that it is difficult to see how he could possibly have triumphed unaided. Meanwhile, for a collection of useful thumbnail sketches of the leading personalities in the region, see 'Portrait Gallery of Important Characters from Civil-War Yorkshire', < https://www.yas.org.uk/Resources/Civil-War-Characters >, accessed 17 January 2021.

10. For the battle of Piercebridge, see R. Daniels and P. Philo, *The First Great Civil War in the Tees Valley* (Sunderland, 2018).

11. The action at Tadcaster was fiercely contested, and the Fairfaxes were, in fact, still in control of the town at the end of the day, but gave it up during the night on account of lack of ammunition. D. Cooke, *Civil War in Yorkshire: Fairfax versus Newcastle* (Barnsley, 2004), pp. 21-8.

12. For the attack on Bradford, see Binns, *Yorkshire in the Civil Wars*, pp. 58-60; < https://e-voice.org.uk/claytonhistorygroup/bradford-in-the-civil-war > accessed 7 January 2021. The rising of the local populace in defence marked the beginning of a major phenomenon in the area in the formaumnted HeritageHaunted |Heritage (Nortwich, 1990), pp. 151-2 in the form of a major anti-Royalist insurgency. Badly hit in economic terms by the damaging impact of the outbreak of war on the clothing trade, the people were strongly Puritan in their sympathies and were therefore easily won over to the standard of Lord Fairfax, who had for some time been showing himself to be an ardent opponent of laudianism. As we shall see very shortly, however, the emergence of popular Parliamentarianism did some damage to the Parliamentarian cause in Yorkshire in political terms, while its military value was at best limited. See A.J. Hopper, 'The clubmen of the West Riding of Yorkshire during the First Civil War: "Bradford club-law"', *Northern History*, XXXVI, No. 1 (March, 2000), pp. 59-72.

13. Cooke, *Civil War in Yorkshire*, pp. 39-44.

14. For the campaign of Guisborough and Yarm, see P. Leask, *Valour is the Safest Helm: the Life of Sir Hugh Cholmley and Scarborough during the English Civil War* (Newtown, 1995), pp. 8-9.

15. R.K. Marshall, *The Intrepid Queen: Henrietta Maria* (London, 1990), pp. 104-6. Baulked of their target, Parliamentarian ships opened fire on the queen and her party as they reached the shore, only to be forced to desist by the Dutch warships that had escorted them across the North Sea.

16. For the Battle of Seacroft Moor, see < http://www.barwickinelmethistoricalsociety. com/8513.html >, accessed 18 January 2020. Meanwhile, the treatment of the hundreds of prisoners captured by Goring gave rise to a bitter controversy. In brief, possibly to distract attention from the disaster, not to mention to maintain the fervour of his popular following, Fairfax accused Newcastle of behaving towards the men concerned in the most barbaric fashion and neglecting even to treat their wounds, the response of the marquis being to issue a furious public denial of anything of the sort. Exactly what happened is, of course, impossible to establish, but it seems likely that, given Newcastle's chivalrous character, the Royalists were simply overwhelmed by the number of troops who had fallen into their hands, the result being that many of them went hungry and were left languishing in the most fetid and uncomfortable of conditions. See < https://www.civilwarpetitions.ac.uk/blog/the-story-after-the-battle-before-the-wounded-prisoners-of-seacroft-moor/ >, accessed 18 January 2021.

17. Leask, *Valour is the Safest Helm*, pp. 10-11. Cholmley is an interesting case. A fierce opponent of the king in the crisis of 1641-42, he was yet a firm adherent of the established church and hated Puritanism and, possibly driven on by concern at the growing social agitation gripping the West Riding clothing towns in support of the Fairfaxes, was soon urging peace negotiations. Hopper, "'Fitted for desperation'", pp. 139-41.

18. Young and Emberton, *Sieges of the Great Civil War*, pp. 129-30; Spence, *Skipton Castle*, pp. 38-41.

19. Cooke, *Civil War in Yorkshire*, pp. 53-60.

20. For Newcastle's offensive of the early summer of 1643, see D. Johnson, *Adwalton Moor, 1644: the Battle that Changed a War* (Pickering, 2003).

21. S.D.M. Carpenter, *Military Leadership in the British Civil Wars, 1642-1651* (London, 2005), p. 72.

22. See < https://e-voice.org.uk/claytonhistorygroup/bradford-in-the-civil-war >, accessed 7 January 2021.

23. Formed of the counties of Hertfordshire, Essex, Norfolk, Suffolk, Cambridgeshire, Huntingdonshire and Lincolnshire, the Eastern Association was one of a number of *de facto* military and administrative districts set up in the winter of 1642-43 to run the Parliamentarian war effort at the regional level (there were also Northern, Midland, Southern and Western Associations).

24. For the Grantham campaign, see < http://bcw-project.org/military/english-civil-war/midlands-and-east/lincolnshire-1643 >, accessed 7 January 2021; Bennett, *Cromwell at War*, pp. 63-4.

25. The most recent biography of Oliver Cromwell goes much further than this, alleging not only that the then colonel went out of his way to magnify the importance of what was in reality little more than a petty skirmish but also that his famous charge only routed half the Royalist forces and, still worse, that his regiment got out of control and proceeded to chase their defeated opponents for a considerable distance, leaving the other half of the Parliamentarian command to fight it out alone. R. Hutton, *The Making of Oliver Cromwell* (London, 2021), pp. 108–11.

26. For the Gainsborough campaign, see M. Bennett, *Cromwell at War: the Lord General and his Military Revolution* (London, 2017), pp. 67-72.

27. For the fall of the Hothams, see Hopper, '"Fitted for desperation"', pp. 140-44.

28. Young and Emberton, *Sieges of the Great Civil War*, pp. 48-50.

29. For the Winceby campaign, see B. Brammer, *Winceby and the Battle* (Boston, 1994).

30. Young and Emberton, *Sieges of the Great Civil War*, pp. 130-1.

31. For the relief of Newark, see Reid, *All the King's Armies*, pp. 148-51.

32. *Ibid.*, p. 163.

33. *Ibid.*, pp. 166-7.

34. Cooke, *Civil War in Yorkshire*, pp. 98-9.

35. Carpenter, *Military Leadership in the British Civil Wars*, pp. 85-6. 'In this series of small-scale engagements', writes Carpenter, 'Lambert proved exceptionally talented as an independent commander detached from the main body of the army, striking swiftly and decisively.'

36. Cooke, *Civil War in Yorkshire*, pp. 101-6.

37. The most detailed source on the siege of York is P. Wenham, *The Great and Close Siege of York* (Kineton, 1970).

38. For Marston Moor, see P.R. Newman, *The Battle of Marston Moor, 1644* (Chichester, 1991); P.R. Newman and P.R. Roberts, *Marston Moor, 1644: the Battle of the Five Armies* (Pickering, 2003); and J. Barrett, *The Battle of Marston Moor, 1644* (Stroud, 2002).

39. For the siege of Newcastle, see R. Serdivill and J. Sadler, *The Great Siege of Newcastle, 1644* (Stroud, 2011); as for events in Yorkshire, see Binns, *Yorkshire in the Civil Wars*, pp. 114-16.

40. Spence, *Skipton Castle*, pp. 67-70.

41. Leaske, *Valour is the Safest Helm*, pp. 26-35; Binns, *Yorkshire in the Civil Wars*, pp. 17-19.

42. Barratt, *Rabble of Gentility*, pp. 47-62; Spence, *Skipton Castle*, p. 78.

43. Spence, *Skipton Castle*, p. 75.

44. Space does not allow more than a brief reference to Montrose. However, in brief, in 1644 the marquis had risen against the ruling Covenanters at the head of a mixed force of highlanders and regular troops brought over from Ireland and won a series of dazzling victories.

45. Barratt, *Rabble of Gentility*, pp. 79-87; Binns, *Yorkshire in the Civil Wars*, pp. 119-24. For the siege of Skipton Castle in particular, see Spence, *Skipton Castle*, pp. 93-100.

46. The details of this quarrel need not concern us here, but, in brief, given free passage to join the king following his surrender of Bristol (see Chapter 8), Rupert made for Newark, only to find himself accused of having given up the fight for treasonous motives. Thoroughly outraged, Rupert managed to persuade Charles that the claims - the work of the increasing enmity that he had been facing among certain elements of the court - were unfounded, but a further row broke out when Charles decided to replace the governor, Sir Richard Willys, with the Royalist commander who had been defeated at Selby, Lord Belasyse, the prince taking it into his head that this was intended as a personal slight. Wedgwood, *King's War*, pp. 469-73.

47. For the storm of Shelford House, see < https://www.bbc.co.uk/news/uk-england-nottinghamshire-54973017 >.

48. Wood, *Nottinghamshire in the Civil War*, pp. 102-6.

49. Young and Emberton, *Sieges of the Great Civil War*, pp. 132-5.

50. For the events of 1649, see Binns, *Yorkshire in the Civil Wars*, pp. 135-41.

51. For the Lindisfarne, Buckstones, Knaresborough, Lincoln, Cleadon, West Bolden, Watton Priory, Hassop, Sheffield, Newcastle and Wetherby apparitions, see Underwood, *Where the Ghosts Walk*, p. 327, < https://www.tapatalk.com/groups/supernaturalearth/a640-near-nont-sarah-pub-buckstones-t56.html >; https://www.paranormaldatabase.com/yorkshire/Pages/yorkdata.php?pageNum_paradata=12&totalRows_paradata=525 >; < https://www.pridemagazines.co.uk/lincolnshire/highlights/top-10-most-haunted-places-in-lincolnshire/11-2018 >; < https://www.mysteriousbritain.co.uk/hauntings/the-toby-carvery-cleadon/ >; < 13 of the most haunted pubs in South Shields, Jarrow, Whitburn, Cleadon and Boldon - and the ghosts said to walk them | Shields Gazette >, < https://www.haunted-yorkshire.co.uk/driffieldsightings.htm >; < Spooky Stories of the Peak District | Peak District Online >; < https://www.chroniclelive.co.uk/whats-on/whats-on-news/10-best-places-see-ghost-1372946 >; < https://www.wetherbycivicsociety.org.uk/ghost-stories/ >; < https://www.higgypop.com/hauntings/sallyport-tower/ >; all accessed 16 January 2021.

52. In fairness, setting aside the tale of the headless horseman who supposedly regularly gallops across the battlefield from one side to the other, the apparitions at Marston Moor - generally groups of weary figures trudging dejectedly along the road from Long Marston to Tockwith who are observable for a few minutes before suddenly vanishing - have in many instances taken place in daylight, while the stories are not of the 'it is said' or 'according to legend' varieties, but are often rather associated with particular witnesses and particular dates. See < https://www.tapatalk.com/groups/supernaturalearth/marston-moor-hauntings-t574.html >, accessed 16 January 2021. All the cases referred to in this post were reported by people from other parts of the country who happened to be driving across the moor, but many stories are also current among the inhabitants of the district, many of whom profess to being frightened of walking its lanes and fields even in daylight. For a collection of local eyewitness accounts collected for an episode of the television show *Ghosthunters*, see < http://forteanfindings.blogspot.com/2017/08/ghost-hunters-spirits-of-civil-war.html >, accessed 16 January 2021.

53. For these examples, see < https://www.tapatalk.com/groups/supernaturalearth/marston-moor-hauntings-t574.html >, < https://www.chroniclelive.co.uk/news/north-east-news/story-old-george-haunted-ghost-14475121 >, < https://www.paranormaldatabase.com/yorkshire/Pages/yorkdata.php?pageNum_paradata=20&totalRows_paradata=525 >, all accessed 16 January 2021. The fact that Bright, hardly a well-known figure, appears alongside Cromwell and Charles I is interesting, suggesting, as it does, a long-standing oral tradition founded in deep-seated local knowledge. With regard to Newark, meanwhile, another building that is reputed to be haunted is the sixteenth-century house in Kirkgate where Henrietta-Maria stayed when she passed through the city in 1643, though such evidence as there is consists solely of spectral noises - ghostly footsteps and the clashes of pots and pans - and there are no specific claims to the effect that the 'in-dwell' is the queen. R. Robb, *Ghosts and Legends of Newark* (Newark, 1987), pp. 33-4.

54. See < https://www.chroniclelive.co.uk/whats-on/whats-on-news/10-best-places-see-ghost-1372946 >, accessed 16 January 2021.

55. See < https://www.mirror.co.uk/news/weird-news/soldiers-ghost-snapped-haunted-pub-6197280 >, accessed 17 January 2021.

56. M. Wray, *The Ghosts and Ghouls of the East Riding* (n.p., n.d; Kindle edition), n.p.

57. Ingram, *Haunted Homes and Family Traditions*, II, pp. 273-8.

58. See < https://www.paranormaldatabase.com/yorkshire/Pages/yorkdata.php?pageNum_paradata=12&totalRows_paradata=525 >, accessed 16 January 2021.

59. See < https://www.chroniclelive.co.uk/whats-on/whats-on-news/10-best-places-see-ghost-1372946 >, accessed 16 January 2021.

60. R. Matthews, *Haunted York* (Stroud, 2009), pp. 30-1, 60-2.
61. Wray, *Ghosts and Ghouls of the East Riding*, n.p.
62. Robb, *Ghosts and Legends of Newark*, pp. 10-11.
63. The absence of any memory of the Scots is doubly odd: not only where they are an identifiably foreign 'other', but, whereas all English troops looked much alike whichever side they fought for and, the New Model Army aside, were dressed in a wide range of hues, their Scottish counterparts wore what amounted to a national uniform consisting of hodden grey suits and blue bonnets and fought under colours bearing the saltire.

Chapter 5

1. 'The Midlands' is, of course, a debatable concept. For the purposes of this work, the region will be defined as comprising the West Midlands, Staffordshire, Warwickshire, Leicestershire, Rutland, Bedfordshire, Huntingdonshire, Cambridgeshire, the southern parts of Derbyshire and Nottinghamshire, the eastern parts of Worcestershire and Shropshire and the northern parts of Oxfordshire and Buckinghamshire. It is accepted that the inclusion of Huntingdonshire and Cambridgeshire may raise some eyebrows, but the fact is that the material on East Anglia is too thin to merit a chapter of its own. Thus, just one ghost story apiece have been found in respect of Norfolk and Suffolk, while the grand total for the four counties that make up the region as a whole just fourteen. Nor is this surprising, East Anglia being an area of the country that military action hardly touched.
2. The classic account of Edgehill remains Young's *Edgehill*. However, this should be supplemented by C.L. Scott, *Edgehill: the Battle Reinterpreted* (London, 2005).
3. For the aftermath of Edgehill, see Wanklyn and Jones, *Military History of the English Civil War*, pp. 56-7. Whether an immediate march on London would really have won the war for Charles is a matter of debate, for, commanded by the able and popular Sir Phillip Skippon, London's Trained Bands were capable of putting up a good fight, while, so energised was public opinion in the capital, that they would undoubtedly have been backed by substantial numbers of civilian volunteers. Accessible as a consolation prize, true, was the royal seat of Hampton Court, but, with Essex on the loose to the north, it is difficult to see how the Royalists could have maintained such a position for very long. On balance, then, Charles was probably correct in heading for Oxford despite the implications of such a course. For all this, see T. Venning, *An Alternative History of Britain: the English Civil War* (Barnsley, 2015), pp. 79-81.
4. Control of the Black Country was possibly the most important factor in allowing Charles to keep the field for as long as he did, for, without it, he would have been dependent on captures from the Parliamentarians or the receipt of arms from abroad, neither of which could be depended on overmuch. See P. Edwards,

'Turning ploughshares into swords: the arms and military equipment industries in Staffordshire in the first Civil War, 1642-1646' *Midland History*, XXVII (October, 2002), pp. 52-79.

5. For the Stafford campaign, see P. Young, 'The Battle of Hopton Heath, 19 March 1643', *Journal of the Society of Army Historical Research*, XXXIII, No. 133 (Spring, 1955), pp. 35-9.

6. E.g. Hibbert, *Cavaliers and Roundheads*, pp. 107-9.

7. For the experiences of Birmingham, see S. Wright, *With Guns and Drums: Civil War in Birmingham* (Birmingham, 1997).

8. Sherwood, *Civil Strife in the Midlands*, p. 67.

9. S. Orme, '"Bestowing a visit on that little city": Cromwell and the taking of Peterborough, April 1643', *Cromwelliana*, Series III, No. 7 (2018), pp. 85-100; < The Siege of Crowland - South Holland Life Heritage and Crafts including Chain Bridge Forge (heritagesouthholland.co.uk) >, accessed 19 March 2021. Though much acclaimed by admirers of Cromwell, the Crowland Abbey affair was not much of a triumph, the defenders fleeing by boat through the wetlands by which it was largely surrounded as soon as the Parliamentarians put in an appearance. See Hutton, *Making of Oliver Cromwell* (London, 2021), p. 103.

10. *Ibid.*, p. 66. M. Atkin, *The Civil War in Worcestershire* (Stroud, 1995), pp. 50-1.

11. Burton had been having a particularly difficult war. Initially Royalist, it was, as we have seen, taken by the Parliamentarians in December 1642. The latter, however, had not remained in control for very long, being driven out after barely one month by Lord Loughborough. Yet Loughborough was to prove no luckier than the opponent he had ousted, for the town was recaptured in April. By the time Henrietta Maria headed south towards Oxford, then, the place had changed hands four times in eight months.

12. The best account of Henrietta Maria's march from York to Stratford is offered by S. Reid, *All the King's Armies: a Military History of the English Civil War, 1642-1651* (Stroud, 2007), pp. 84-6.

13. For the siege of Burghley House, see < History Article Around Stamford | Stamford and the Civil War 1642-45 (visitoruk.com) >, accessed 19 March 2021.

14. For the siege of King's Lynn, see S. Yaxley, *The Siege of King's Lynn, 1643* (Dereham, 1993).

15. Sherwood, *Civil Strife in the Midlands*, pp. 93-5. Meanwhile, for the capture of Bagworth House in particular, see < Battle at Bagworth - Lord Thomas Grey's Regiment of Foote (weebly.com) >, accessed 17 March 2021. These minor affairs could yet be substantial military operations: although the midwinter siege of Grafton

House lasted but three days, for example, it yet involved an attacking force of 3,500 men. See Beckett, *Wanton Troopers*, p. 72.

16. A.C. Wood, *Nottinghamshire in the Civil War* (Oxford, 1937), pp. 59-63.

17. *Ibid.*, pp. 63-5.

18. For all this, see A. Hopper, '"Tinker" Fox and the politics of garrison warfare in the West Midlands, 1643-50', *Midland History*, XXIV, No. 1 (January, 1999), pp. 98-113.

19. Sherwood, *Civil Strife in the Midlands*, pp. 127-8.

20. For the operations against Biddulph House and Hillesden House, see *ibid.*, pp. 123-4, and Beckett, *Wanton Troopers*, pp. 75-6.

21. For the action at Market Drayton, see Reid, *All the King's Armies*, p. 146.

22. The best account of the decision to divide the Royalist armies can be found in M. Wanklyn, *Supreme Command and Politics during the British Wars, 1649-1651* (Barnsley 2019), pp. 42-3. Why Essex and Waller decided to switch roles is unclear, but Wedgwood suggests that the decisive factor was the key part being played in the defence of Lyme Regis by a naval squadron commanded by the Parliamentarian's chief admiral, the Earl of Warwick, the result being that Essex, who was, after all, a cousin of the former, was the obvious candidate to relieve Lyme. See Wedgwood, *The King's War*, p. 304. As for the issue of responsibilities, while the initiative came from the Committee of Both Kingdoms, the two generals cannot be resolved of all guilt in that they were evidently so consumed by their personal dislike for one another that they jumped at the chance of splitting their forces rather than trying to hold out for the obvious strategic priority.

23. There remains little explanation for the Committee of Both Kingdoms' decision other than a desire to satisfy public opinion. What is more interesting is why it chose Waller for the march on Lyme rather than Essex: in so far as this is concerned, the answer is, first, the desire of some members to advance the star of the former at the expense of that of the latter, and, second and more generally, a perception that Waller, a commander who had, as we shall see, acquired a considerable reputation for rapid manoeuvre, was a more appropriate choice.

24. For a detailed analysis of the Cropredy campaign, see Wanklyn and Jones, *Military History of the English Civil War*, pp. 164-9. See also M. Toynbee and P. Young, *Cropredy Bridge, 1644: the Campaign and the Battle* (Kineton, 1970).

25. Sherwood, *Civil Strife in the Midlands*, pp. 141-4.

26. Hutton, *Making of Oliver Cromwell*, pp. 246-7.

27. Wedgwood, *The King's War*, pp. 414-16.

28. Wanklyn and Jones, *Military History of the English Civil War*, pp. 233-6; Sherwood, *Civil Strife in the Midlands*, pp. 190-2.

29. *Cit.* Sherwood, *Civil Strife in the Midlands*, p. 242.

30. The best work on the Naseby campaign by far is G. Foard, *Naseby: the Decisive Campaign* (revised edition, London, 2004).

31. Atkin, *Civil War in Worcestershire*, pp. 97–8.

32. Sherwood, *Civil Strife in the Midlands*, p. 209.

33. For the collapse of the Royalist cause in the Midlands, see Sherwood, *War and Civil Strife in the Midlands*, pp. 210-18 *passim,* while the sieges of Oxford and Worcester in particular are discussed in Barrett, *Cavalier Capital,* pp. 196-205 and Barrett, *Sieges of the English Civil Wars*, pp. 99-104. There is no space here to go into the ever more polarised politics of the Parliamentarian cause in any detail, but a succinct introduction may be found in Wedgwood, *The King's War*, pp. 324-8.

34. See Reid, *All the King's Armies*, p. 321; Adair, *Cavaliers and Roundheads*, pp. 68-9; E.W. Hensman, 'The Second Civil War in the East Midlands, May to July 1648', *Transactions of the Royal Historical Society*, VI (1923), pp. 126-159.

35. For the battle of Worcester, see M. Atkin, *Cromwell's Crowning Mercy: the Battle of Worcester, 1651* (Stroud, 1998).

36. For the ghosts of Charles I, Archbishop Laud and Francis Windebank, see < Ghost Fest is here! How haunted is Oxford? - Oxford Castle & Prison (oxfordcastleandprison. co.uk) > and < Could this floating orb be Oliver Cromwell's ghost? - Cambridgeshire Live (cambridge-news.co.uk) >, accessed 16 March 2021, while the Windebank case is discussed in more detail in R. Walters, *Haunted Oxford* (Stroud, 2007), pp. 76-80. For the Wichenford Court, Bromham and Bolsover apparitions, see A. Poulton-Smith, *Haunted Worcestershire* (Stroud, 2009), p. 111; W.H. King, *Haunted Bedford* (n.p., n.d.), pp. 37-8; < Haunted House (real-british-ghosts.com) >, accessed 17 March 2021, and < Bolsover Castle Rated English Heritage's Spookiest Site by Staff | English Heritage (english-heritage.org.uk) >, accessed 16 March 2021. Finally, for Dudley Castle, see Hutton, *Royalist War Effort*, p. 199. With regard to Oxford, in particular, it has to be said that the stories emanating from the Bodleian Library and Merton College sound very much as if they had their origins in undergraduate jokes, the idea of Charles I rushing round the Bodleian seizing books from the shelves or Archbishop Laud rolling his head along the floor of the Great Hall being very hard to take seriously (all the more is the case with regard to the archbishop as Laud never had any connection with Merton College).

37. See < Guildhall Leicester - Most Haunted : A Tribute : A Fan Site (tributemosthaunted.co.uk) >, accessed 18 March 2021; < Haunted places to visit in Northamptonshire | Northampton Chronicle and Echo >, accessed 16 March 2021; P. Solomon, *Haunted Staffordshire* (n.p., n.d.), pp. 64, 78; A. Bradford and B. Roberts,

Midland Ghosts and Hauntings (Birmingham, 1994), p. 19; Poulton-Smith, *Haunted Worcestershire,* pp. 76, 107; J. Robinson, *Oxfordshire Ghosts* (Barnsley, 2000), pp. 86-7; < english haunted houses and ghost stories, from the paranormal database >, accessed 18 March 2021; < haunted battlefields and the ghosts of soldiers, from the paranormal database >, accessed 10 April 2021.

38. The Hopton Heath and Grafton Regis incidents are discussed at < A Mysterious Battle: Ghosts or Time Traveling? | Mysterious Universe >, and < The Phantom Army of Grafton Regis | Supernatural England – Countryside Books >, accessed 16 March 2021.

39. See < The History of Lichfield, Staffordshire (historic-uk.com) >, accessed 18 March 2021; King, *Haunted Bedford,* pp. 62, 67; Solomon, *Haunted Staffordshire,* p. 67; < haunted battlefields and the ghosts of soldiers, from the paranormal database >, accessed 10 April 2021.

40. Bradford and Roberts, *Midland Ghosts and Hauntings,* pp. 125-6.

41. See < Ghost Fest is here! How haunted is Oxford? - Oxford Castle & Prison (oxfordcastleandprison.co.uk) >, accessed 16 March 2021. W.S. Bennett and L. Steer, *Birmingham Ghosts* (Birmingham, n.d.), pp. 16-17. The site of the bivouac set up by the troops accompanying Henrietta Maria is supposedly commemorated by the name of nearby Camp Road.

42. Robinson, *Oxfordshire Ghosts,* pp. 73-4.

43. Bradford and Roberts, *Midlands Ghosts and Hauntings,* p. 8. Given that drummers are commonly imagined as young boys, this particular story is worth an additional note. In reality, the key here is not age, but rather status. Far from being mere children, drummers were grown men - something that was, not least, required by the very large dimensions of the instruments they were required to manipulate - and, what is more, grown men who could be relied on for missions requiring tact and diplomacy, one of the tasks entrusted to them being the conveyance of such documents as terms of surrender. More importantly in this context, meanwhile, they were regarded as non-combatants, what the story commemorates therefore being something rather different from the murder of a child.

44. See < The New Inn, St Neots – Mysterious Britain & Ireland > and < Woodcroft Castle | Ghosts | Fandom >, accessed 18 March 2021.

45. In another version of the Banbury story, the ghost is simply a Cavalier. See < BOO! Haunted Banbury | The Banburian >, accessed 18 March 2021.

46. For the Lichfield Cavalier, see Solomon, *Haunted Staffordshire,* p. 64; < Ghosts | Pub Lore (wordpress.com) >, accessed 18 March 2021.

47. Poulton-Smith, *Haunted Worcestershire,* pp. 66-8.

48. Walters, *Haunted Oxford,* pp. 80-6. Grandison was indeed grievously wounded at Bristol, and is recorded of dying of his wounds on 29 September 1643. His tomb can be seen in Christchurch Cathedral, but it was erected by his daughter, Lady Barbara Villiers, and so it is entirely possible that he was originally interred elsewhere, the latter being just 2 years old at the time of his death.

49. For the stories concerning Ye Old Black Cross, Prior's Court and Droitwich, see *ibid.*, pp. 36-7, 46. Meanwhile, the Marston Trussel and Pavenham ghosts are catalogued in Stevens Bassett, *Ghostly Tales and Hauntings of Northamptonshire*, p. 67 and King, *Haunted Bedford*, p. 71.

50. Whatever the truth of these individual stories, the ruthless violence of which they are redolent is by no means wholly an invention: in the closing stages of the Battle of Worcester, for example, a large mass of Scottish fugitives fleeing from the fighting on the hills that overlooked the city from the east who tried to reach the safety of its streets via the Sidbury gate met a terrible fate. In the words of one chronicler of the battle, 'Here the great slaughter took place. The Scots ... could not get inside as the gate was so narrow that only a few could pass at a time ... Riding down on the fugitives were Cromwell's horsemen, pressing in, stern, relentless, smiting hip and thigh, showing no mercy to the children of Amalek ... They did not want to be guilty of the sin of Saul ... and they were not. The victors ... were full of zeal for the Lord ... [and] showed their gratitude by free use of their swords.' J.W. Willis-Bund, *The Civil War in Worcestershire, 1642-6, and the Scotch Invasion of 1651* (Worcester, 1905), pp. 245-8.

51. Poulton-Smith, *Haunted Worcestershire*, pp. 104-5.

52. Bradford and Roberts, *Midland Ghosts and Hauntings*, p. 8.

Chapter 6

1. It having proved impossible to trace more than one or two Welsh Civil War ghosts, no attempt will be made to retell the experiences of the region in the conflicts of 1642-51. However, readers wishing to enquire into the matter are referred to Gaunt, *Nation Under Siege*; W.S.K. Thomas, *Stuart Wales* (Llandyssul, 1988), pp. 17-56; and L. Bowen, *John Poyer, the Civil Wars in Pembrokeshire and the British Revolutions* (Cardiff, 2020).

2. T. Bracher and R. Emmett, *Shropshire in the Civil War* (Shrewsbury, 2000), pp. 8-23 *passim*; Worton, *To Settle the Crown*, pp. 37-42.

3. Broughton, *Unhappy Civil War*, pp. 18-20.

4. Atkin, *Civil War in Worcestershire*, p. 40; D. Ross, *Royalist but ... Herefordshire in the English Civil War, 1640-1651* (Little Logaston, 2012), pp. 35-46.

5. J. Barrett, *Cavalier Stronghold: Ludlow in the English Civil War* (Little Logaston, 2013), p. 27.

6. Ross, *Herefordshire in the English Civil War*, pp. 50-1.

7. For the attack on Cirencester, see J.M. Paddock, *The Storming of Cirencester in 1643: an episode in the English Civil War* (Cirencester, 1995).

8. J. Adair, *Roundhead General: a Military Biography of Sir William Waller* (London, 1969), p. 55.

9. *Ibid.*, p. 62.

10. *Ibid.*, pp. 62-9. Ross, *Herefordshire in the English Civil War*, pp. 62-4. As we have seen, Hereford was nominally Royalist, but neither against Stamford nor Waller.

11. Ross, *Herefordshire in the English Civil War*, p. 68.

12. Abram, *More like Lions than Men*, pp. 37-8.

13. A. Plowden, *Women All on Fire: the Women of the English Civil War* (Stroud, 1997), pp. 52-8.

14. For the siege of Gloucester, see Broughton, *Unhappy Civil War*, pp. 173-92.

15. For the events at Hopton Castle, see Cross, *Herefordshire in the English Civil War*, pp. 78-9.

16. *Ibid.*, pp. 79-84.

17. Worton, *To Settle the Crown*, pp. 203-9.

18. Ross, *Herefordshire in the English Civil War*, p. 85.

19. *Ibid.*, pp. 91-5. For the lesser disturbances in Shropshire and western Worcestershire, see Atkin, *Civil War in Worcestershire*, pp. 95-7; Bracher and Emmett, *Shropshire in the Civil War*, pp. 37-9.

20. Bracher and Emmett, *Shropshire in the Civil War*, p. 36.

21. *Ibid.*, pp. 39-40; Worton, *To Settle the Crown*, pp. 209-13.

22. Ross, Herefordshire in the English Civil War, pp. 101-9; S. Maggs, The Storming of Canon Frome, 22 July 1645 (n.p., 2018).

23. For the Stow-on-the-Wold campaign, see J. Barrett, *The Last Army: the Battle of Stow-on-the-Wold and the End of the Civil War in the Welsh Marches, 1646* (Warwick, 2018).

24. Barrett, *Cavalier Stronghold*, pp. 83-90; Atkin, *Civil War in Worcestershire*, pp. 100-105; Ross, *Herefordshire in the English Civil War*, pp. 137-8.

25. Atkin, *Civil War in Worcestershire*, p. 150.

26. Bracher and Emmett, *Shropshire in the Civil War*, p. 61.

27. R. Holland, *Shropshire Ghost Stories* (Sheffield, 2015), p. 51; White, *Haunted Cotswolds*, p. 57; R. Andrews, *The Paranormal Tourist Guide to Gloucestershire* (privately published, 2013), I, n.p.

28. < Nine of Gloucestershire spookiest ghost stories and haunted sites – Gloucestershire Live >, accessed 7 July 2021. In addition to the galloping horseman, Prestbury also boasts a Cavalier who is said to wander the streets. See < Most haunted: 25 of Gloucestershire's spookiest spots – Gloucestershire Live Jul 2021.>, accessed

29. White, *Haunted Cotswolds*, pp. 23, 54, 61 (for good measure, Painswick boasts an additional sighting in the form of ghostly lights suggestive of flaming torches). Andrews, *Paranormal Tourist Guide to Gloucestershire*, I, n.p; E. Fry and R. Harvey, *Haunted Gloucester* (Stroud, 2004), p. 41.

30. Holland, *Shropshire Ghost Stories*, p. 45.

31. This story is more than somewhat spoilt by the fact that the eldest of Birch's three daughters was not born until 1645. That said, there is no reason to suppose that the legend is wholly without foundation.

32. Andrews, *Paranormal Tourist Guide to Gloucestershire*, I, n.p.

33. *Ibid.*

34. Poulton-Smith, *Haunted Worcestershire*, pp. 104-5.

35. Holland, *Shropshire Ghost Stories*, pp. 55-6.

36. Andrews, *Paranormal Tourist Guide to Gloucestershire*, I, n.p. The impact of the Civil War on sexual mores awaits its historian, but there is some reason to believe that they were at the very least undermined. Of Chepstow, for example, Martyn Bennett claims that there was only one illegitimate child baptised in the town in 1642 as opposed to three in 1644 and four in 1645. See M. Bennet, *The Civil Wars Experienced: Britain and Ireland, 1648-1651* (London, 2000), p. 97.

Chapter 7

1. *Cit.* Thomas-Stanford, *Sussex in the Great Civil War*, p. 157.

2. T. MacLachlan, *The Civil War in Hampshire* (Landford, 1997), p. 400.

3. *Cit. ibid.*, p. 394.

4. *Cit.* Adair, *By the Sword Divided*, p. 228.

5. MacLachlan, *Civil War in Hampshire*, pp. 26-7; Thomas-Stanford, *Sussex in the Great Civil War*, p. 54. For a study of Sussex that stresses the overwhelmingly strong hold that Puritanism had on Sussex and, by extension, the strength of its support for Parliament, see A. Fletcher, *A County Community in Peace and War: Sussex, 1600-1660* (London, 1975).

6. See < Kentish Petition, March 1642 (luminarium.org) >, accessed 1 April 2021.

7. For the attack on Brentford, see N. Chippendale, *The Battle of Brentford, 1642: the Hounslow Area in the Civil War* (Leigh on Sea, 1991).

8. For Turnham Green, see S. Porter and S. Marsh, *The Battle for London* (Stroud, 2012).

9. Young and Emberton, *Sieges of the Great Civil War,* pp. 9-14. Awarded generous terms, Goring was allowed to sail into exile, only, as we have seen, to return a few months later to command the cavalry of the Marquis of Newcastle.

10. Adair, *Roundhead General,* pp. 50-1; MacLachlan, *Civil War in Hampshire,* pp. 77-9. In the same fashion as its counterpart in Chichester, in the days that followed the cathedral was subjected to much vandalism.

11. Adair, *Roundhead General,* pp. 51-3. Thomas-Stanford, *Sussex in the Great Civil War,* pp. 42-55.

12. Young and Embleton, *Sieges of the Great Civil War,* pp. 19-23.

13. For the action at Chalgrove Field, see J. Adair, 'The death of Hampden', *History Today,* XXIX, No. 10 (October, 1979), pp. 656-63.

14. The most detailed account of Newbury that is available is contained in Day, *Gloucester and Newbury,* pp. 146-205. It is Day's contention that, though certainly short of ammunition, the Royalist army had sufficient to hold its ground for long enough to force the exhausted Parliamentarians to lay down their arms, the real reason for its abandonment of the field rather being loss of the nerve on the part of the king and, in particular, his distress at the loss of several peers of the realm, including his secretary of state, Lord Falkland. This, however, looks like mere speculation: it is, for example, supported by neither Wanklyn nor Reid. See also J. Barratt, *The First Battle of Newbury* (Stroud, 2005).

15. MacLachlan, *Civil War in Hampshire,* pp. 108-12, 114-15, 131.

16. W. Emberton, *Love Loyalty: the Close and Perilous Siege of Basing House, 1643-1645* (Basingstoke, 1972), pp. 38-46.

17. Reid, *All the King's Armies,* pp. 230-2. Why Hopton acted as he did is unclear. According to his own version of events, he spread his men out to ease the problem of keeping them supplied with food and forage, but this could have been achieved just as easily elsewhere and, what is more, in an area far less vulnerable to attack. In all probability, encouraged by Waller's defeat at Roundway Down (see Chapter 8), Hopton regarded Waller as something of a spent force, while, in so far as the advance on Arundel was concerned, he may have been pushed into taking action by pressure from the leader of Sussex Royalism, Sir Edward Ford.

18. For the attack on Alton, see Adair, *Roundhead General,* pp. 124-9.

19. Thomas-Stanford, *Sussex in the Great Civil War,* pp. 86-94.

20. MacLachlan, *Civil War in Hampshire,* pp. 201-39. Meanwhile, the most recent account of Cheriton is constituted by J. Dixon, *The Unfortunate Battaille* [sic] *of Alresford, being an Account of the Campaign and Battle of Cheriton, March 29th 1644* (Nottingham, 2012).

21. Even Winchester had almost been lost: attacked by Waller on 8 April, the garrison had managed to escape disaster by withdrawing into the castle, and the town would have been lost altogether had not Waller withdrawn for lack of the means to mount a major siege.

22. Emberton, *Love Loyalty*, pp. 65-75.

23. Young and Emberton, *Sieges of the Great Civil War*, pp. 121-2.

24. The most recent account of the Newbury campaign is constituted by J. Barrett, *The Second Battle of Newbury* (Stroud, 2020). However, see also M. Wanklyn, *Decisive Battles of the English Civil War* (Barnsley, 2006), pp. 145-58. As Wanklyn admits, the contemporary accounts of the battle are so fragmentary that it is impossible to prove any argument one way or the other, but what is clear enough is that, for whatever reason, Cromwell's cavalry showed little of its usual prowess.

25. MacLachlan, *Civil War in Hampshire*, pp. 314-25. A commanding height to the south of the city from which Cromwell is reputed to have conducted the siege is to this day called Oliver's Battery.

26. *Ibid.*, pp. 358-68; Young and Emberton, *Sieges of the Great Civil War*, pp. 83-6.

27. Emberton, *Love Loyalty*, pp. 82-90.

28. For all this, see B. Lyndon, 'The South and the start of the Second Civil War, 1648', *History*, LXXI, No. 233 (October, 1986), pp. 393-407. At the time that he published this article, the author, Brian Lyndon, was a part-time Ph.D. student at the University of Southampton. Tragically, however, he was killed in a road accident shortly after its appearance, it being no exaggeration to say that the historical profession was thereby deprived of a great talent and the world of a most decent human being. Rest in peace.

29. Reid, *All the King's Armies*, pp. 310-11.

30. For the Colchester campaign, see P. Jones, *The Siege of Colchester, 1648* (Dubai, 2004).

31. See < haunted battlefields and the ghosts of soldiers, from the paranormal database >, < Arundel Castle – The Haunted Place In Sussex, England - I-Newz | DailyHunt > and < Donnington Castle. Berkshire - Haunted Island >, accessed 10 April 2021.

32. P. Underwood, *A Gazetteer of British Ghosts: an Illustrated Guide to 236 Haunted Sites* (n.p., n.d.), p. 164; P. Underwood, *Ghosts of Hampshire and the Isle of Wight* (n.p., 1982), pp. 21, 48-9, 69, 86; J. Ingram, *The Haunted Homes and Family Traditions of Great Britain: Second Series* (London, 1884), pp. 127-8; < Red Lion Square (historic-uk.com) >, < Basing House - The Ghost of Oliver Cromwell (haunted-britain.com) >, < https://www.hauntedplaces.org/item/st-nicholas-chiswick/ >;

< Haunted Watford | Ghosts of Watford | Watford Ghosts | Watford Hauntings | Cassiobury Park Ghosts (greatbritishghosttour.co.uk) >, < Manningtree, Mistley and the Ghost of the Witchfinder General (timetravel-britain.com) >, accessed 10 April 2021; < haunted pubs in the united kingdom and ireland (paranormaldatabase. com) >, < Page:Notes and Queries - Series 10 - Volume 7.djvu/504 - Wikisource, the free online library >, all accessed 8 April 2021. The story of the haunting at Billingham Manor is particularly grisly. In brief, one night in 1928 the entire household was woken by the noise of heavy footsteps and clanking swords. Coming, as it was, from the hidden compartment in which the king was supposed to have hidden, this was hastily opened to reveal a vision of the latter's severed head. Meanwhile, with respect to Chiswick parish church, this houses the private vault of the Cromwell family, the story being that, after his disinterment and symbolic execution, two of Cromwell's daughters managed to secure the body and give it a decent burial in said vault.

33. P. Underwood, *Where the Ghosts Walk: the Gazetteer of Haunted Britain*, pp. 142-3, 293; N. Arnold, *Haunted Maidstone* (Stroud, 2011), pp. 55, 70, 78; Brooks, *Britain's Haunted Heritage*, p. 104; < Some Notes on the History of Pirton Village - Pirton Local History Group (pirtonhistory.org.uk) >, < Wigginton Common – Mysterious Britain & Ireland >, < Salisbury Hall, I Was A Child Obsessed With Ghosts! | Spooky Isles >, < Tales of hauntings in the New Forest | Bournemouth Echo > and < haunted battlefields and the ghosts of soldiers, from the paranormal database >, all accessed 10 April 2021.

34. See < Hauntings in Lavenham – De Vere House >, < Home | Chequers Inn, (chequersinndoddington.co.uk) >, < haunted pubs in the united kingdom and ireland (paranormaldatabase.com) >, < Towersey Morris - Our Emblem (towerseymorrismen.org.uk) > and < haunted battlefields and the ghosts of soldiers, from the paranormal database >, all accessed 10 April 2021; Underwood, *Gazetteer of British Ghosts*, p. 483.

35. See < Salisbury Hall, I Was A Child Obsessed With Ghosts! | Spooky Isles >, < November 2015 – Mysterious Britain & Ireland >, < The Royal Standard of England, Beaconsfield – Mysterious Britain & Ireland > and < Microsoft Word - WEB 6 - The Headless Horseman of High Down.doc (icknieldwaypath.co.uk), all accessed 10 April 2021. Again, there is reason to believe that such stories have a basis in reality: in the fevered atmosphere of 1642, it is wholly possible that there were instances in which Catholic prisoners were lynched, while several cases are known of Royalist spies or couriers being subjected to summary justice. E.g. Thomas-Stanford, *Sussex in the Great Civil War*, p. 88. That said, muddle and confusion abound: thus, in some

versions of the Pirton story, the chief protagonist merely haunts Highdown House, while in others, sometimes headless and sometimes not, he is rather seen galloping along the road from Pirton to Hitchin on 15 June, the supposed anniversary of his death; equally, once asked to come up with something interesting about their village, quite a number of Pirton children duly recounted the tale, but did not always have Goring as a Cavalier, the most favoured option being rather that he was a highwayman. Finally, one point to note is that, if the man concerned was indeed called Goring, he could not have been the commander of that name as the latter played no part in the Second Civil War. See I. Rodger, 'The headless horseman: an amateur inquiry', *Journal of the Folklore Institute*, II, No. 3 (December, 1965), pp. 266-71.

36. It is, of course, accepted that the image of the jovial Cavalier much addicted to 'wenching' cloaks a much darker reality, namely, that of the soldier as sexual predator, that it is, indeed, utterly repulsive to modern eyes. However, it was not this second side of the coin that stuck in the popular imagination.

37. E.g. MacLachlan, *Civil War in Hampshire*, p. 339.

38. Drake, *Spooky South*), n.p. For the incident on which this haunting is probably based, see MacLachlan, *Civil War in Hampshire*, p. 347.

39. See < BBC - Essex - History - A Colchester Ghost Walk>, accessed 10 April 2021.

40. See < Berkshire History: The Ghost of Hampden Pye (Faringdon), Part 1 >, accessed 10 April 2021.

41. Rodger, 'Headless horseman', p. 271.

Chapter 8

1. For events in Bristol, see J. Lynch, *For King and Parliament: Bristol and the Civil War* (Stroud, 1999), pp. 20-4.

2. Broughton, *Unhappy Civil War*, p. 16. The strongly Parliamentarian tendencies of the gentry of the south-west were driven by many of the same concerns as those visible elsewhere, but there were also causes particular to the region, including, not least, what was perceived as the failure of the régime to protect the coasts of Somerset, Cornwall, Devon and Dorset from the raids of the so-called 'Barbary Corsairs'. Andriette, *Devon and Exeter in the Civil War*, pp. 31-3.

3. Underdown, *Somerset in the Civil War and Interregnum*, pp. 36-8.

4. *Ibid.*, pp. 15-18. Plague was also a factor in Devon, no fewer than 2,300 of the inhabitants succumbing to the dreaded disease in Exeter alone in the winter of 1625-6, while the county's cloth industry was hit by much the same set of issues as that of Somerset. Andriette, *Devon and Exeter in the Civil War*, p. 25; Stoyle, *Loyalty and Locality*, pp. 15-16.

5.   Andriette, *Devon and Exeter in the Civil War*, pp. 25-8, 40-1.

6.   Broughton, *Unhappy Civil War*, p. 5.

7.   *Ibid.*, *Unhappy Civil War*, p. 9.

8.   For this anti-Puritan undercurrent, see D. Underdown, *Fire from Heaven: Life in an English Country Town in the Seventeenth Century* (London, 1993), pp. 160-6.

9.   Broughton, *Unhappy Civil War*, p. 7; Underdown, *Somerset in the Civil War and Interregnum*, p. 23. To a certain extent, the spread of Puritanism depended on personalities: thus, although the city was very much the sort of place where the reform party tended to flourish, Bristol remained solidly Anglican, the reason in part being that it had no equivalent to Ignatius Jurdain, a fiery alderman and sometime Member of Parliament who championed the Puritan cause in Exeter. For Jurdain, see Stoyle, *From Deliverance to Destruction*, pp. 19-37.

10. Why Hertford opted for Wells as his headquarters is a mystery, the town's only advantage being its central position: perhaps he assumed that so mercantile a city as Bristol would automatically fall into the Parliamentarian camp.

11. J. Barratt, *The Civil War in the South-West* (Barnsley, 2005), pp. 13-14; Reid, *All the King's Armies*, pp. 68-70; Underdown, *Somerset in the Civil War and Interregnum*, pp. 31-8.

12. H. Miles Brown, *Battles Royal: Charles I and the Civil War in Cornwall and the West* (Lostwithiel, 1982), pp. 8-12.

13. M. Coate, *Cornwall in the Great Civil War and Interregnum, 1642-1660* (Oxford, 1933), p. 32.

14. For a useful biography of Grenville, see J. Stuckley, *Sir Bevil Grenville and His Times, 1596-1643* (Chichester, 1983).

15. Reid, *All the King's Armies*, p. 70; Miles Brown, *Battles Royal*, pp. 18-19.

16. M. Stoyle, *Soldiers and Strangers: an Ethnic History of the English Civil War* (London, 2005), p. 33.

17. Barratt, *Civil War in the South-West*, pp. 8-9.

18. The issue of language has possibly been made too much of. Thus, Cornish was only spoken in the area west of Truro, the rest of the county being strongly Anglophone, while the senior officers of the Royalist forces without exception came from backgrounds that were very much English in cultural terms.

19. Barratt, *Civil War in the South-West*, p. 8.

20. M.J. Stoyle, 'English nationalism, Celtic particularism and the English Civil War', *Historical Journal*, XLIII, No. 4 (December, 2000), p. 1121.

21. It is but fair to say here that there are some hints in contemporary accounts to the effect that at least some of the recruits were brought in thanks to heavy pressure on

the part of the gentry whose fields they tilled or mines they excavated. See Barratt, *Civil War in the South-West*, p. 18.

22. Miles Brown, *Battles Royal*, p. 17.
23. Coates, *Cornwall in the Great Civil War*, p. 40.
24. Although Hopton proved unsuccessful on this occasion, in the two years that followed, the Royalists were able to obtain at least some recruits from Devon. As the bulk of these came from the tin-mining districts which spread across Dartmoor and its environs, districts were covered by the stannary laws just as much as their Cornish counterparts, it may be assumed that the deciding factor here was the same fear of reform. See Stoyle, *Loyalty and Locality*, pp. 55-74.
25. Reid, *All the King's Armies*, pp. 71-2; Stoyle, *From Deliverance to Destruction*, pp. 69-71.
26. Miles Brown, *Battles Royal*, pp. 21-4; Barratt, *Civil War in the South-west*, pp. 22-5.
27. Barratt, *Civil War in the South-West*, pp. 26-7.
28. *Ibid.*, pp. 28-31.
29. *Ibid.*, pp. 34-7.
30. Miles Brown, *Battle Royal*, p. 30.
31. In the weeks that followed, as chief theatre of the campaign, Somerset suffered greatly from pillage at the hands of the Royalist forces, and there can be no doubt that the Cornishmen played a full part in the havoc. See Underdown, *Somerset in the Civil War and Interregnum*, pp. 54-5.
32. *Ibid.*, pp. 50-1. In view of the fervour in favour of the Parliamentarian cause displayed by the populace the previous year, the absence of popular resistance is somewhat surprising. However, the Royalist forces were infinitely more imposing than they had been in 1642, the probable result being a widespread feeling that discretion was the better part of valour.
33. Barratt, *Civil War in the South-West*, pp. 41-4.
34. For the idea that the exchange of letters between Hopton and Waller was an attempt to get the latter to change sides, see Underdown, *Somerset in the Civil War and Interregnum*, pp. 55-6. Whether Underdown is correct in his interpretation is, of course, impossible to say, but the principle that a plot was afoot was certainly taken on board by Waller's only biographer. See Adair, *Roundhead General*, p. 75.
35. For the battle of Lansdowne, see J. Wroughton, *The Battle of Lansdown, 1643: an Explorer's Guide* (Bath, 2008).
36. *Ibid.*, pp. 89-95.
37. Lynch, *For King and Parliament*, pp. 74-87.
38. Stoyle, *From Deliverance to Destruction*, pp. 78-83.

39. Andriette, *Devon and Exeter in the Civil War*, pp. 92-3.

40. *Ibid.*, pp. 95-7.

41. M. Stoyle, *Plymouth in the Civil War* (Exeter, 1998), pp. 23-30.

42. For the sack of Marlborough, see < https://towerandtown.org.uk/pdfs/168153436020190719907463462.pdf >, accessed 26 October 2021. Silent witness is borne to the ferocity of fighting by the numerous impacts of musket balls that pockmark the walls of the parish church.

43. Adair, *Roundhead General*, pp. 60-2.

44. A. Plowden, *'Women all on Fire': the Women of the English Civil War* (Stroud, 1998), pp. 35-7.

45. A. Norman, *By Swords Divided: Corfe Castle in the Civil War* (Tiverton, 2003), pp. 31-52.

46. For the fall of Dorchester, see Underdown, *Fire from Heaven*, pp. 203-4. Much given though they had been to grandiloquent declarations of support for the Parliamentarian cause, the leaders of the Puritan faction in the town had no sooner heard that Royalist troops were approaching the town than they took to flight with as much of their property as they could manage.

47. For the siege of Lyme, see, G. Chapman, *The Siege of Lyme Regis* (Lyme Regis, 1982).

48. In the wake of Roundway Down, it might be thought that Waller's reputation would have been damaged beyond repair. However, the radical element in Westminster politics were increasingly suspicious of Essex, whom they deemed, at the very least, lacking in pugnacity and, at the worst, inclined to favour a compromise peace, whereas in their eyes Waller was a commander who could be relied upon to fight the king to the utmost and oppose peace negotiations, as well as one who had a much more convincing war record. Far from being dismissed, then, when Waller got to London, he was greeted as a hero and the Committee of Safety, as it then was, overawed into offering him the command of the new army that was currently being raised to cover the southern approaches to London. Adair, *Roundhead General*, pp. 98-101. Badly tarnished in the summer of 1643 by his perceived inaction, Essex's credit had been temporarily restored by the relief of Gloucester, but many months had gone by since then without Essex seeing any further action whereas Waller had triumphed at Cheriton. If the earl wanted command of the Lyme expedition, it was therefore wholly understandable.

49. Norman, *By Swords Divided*, p. 60; C. Scott and A. Turton, *'Hey for Old Robin!' The Campaigns and Armies of the Earl of Essex during the Civil Wars, 1642-44* (Solihull, 2017), pp. 134-5.

50. The decision to march into Devon may have been sanctioned by the Committee of Both Kingdoms, but it is abundantly clear that the impetus came not from

Westminster but rather Essex and his kinsman, the Earl of Warwick. As to the reasons the two commanders were so desirous of continuing with the western offensive, on one level they were purely military and political: not only was Maurice seemingly on the run, but to march Essex's army back to the Midlands or the Thames Valley would effectively take it out of the fight for the whole of what remained of the campaign season; not to be scorned, meanwhile, was the hope of capturing the queen, Henrietta Maria having been sent to the safety of Exeter for the duration of her last confinement. Also present, however, was vanity and personal ambition: not only had the hero of Edgehill, Gloucester and Newbury been out of the eye of the pamphleteers for almost a full year but also he feared that Waller's many friends in London would enveigle the Committee of Both Kingdoms into ordering him to take charge in the west instead of Essex. Scott and Turton, 'Hey for Old Robin!', pp. 135-8.

51. Younger brother to the more famous Sir Bevill Grenville, Grenville has been the subject of bitter controversy. As his biographer, Amos Miller, writes, 'Among the military leaders of the English Civil War, few ... aroused more violent feeling than ... Sir Richard Grenville. The Roundheads hated him as ... an enemy who hanged prisoners of war and relentlessly harassed Parliamentarian supporters in the civilian population. Many Royalists, on the other hand, regarded Grenville with almost equal aversion. In his famous *History of the Rebellion*, [for example,] Edward Hyde, Earl of Clarendon, describes the mocking cruelty with which he used his military authority to pay off private grudges and for personal enrichment ... [and argues that] Grenville's constant quarrels with other officers and outright insubordination towards those in authority over him contributed to the defeat of the Royalist cause.' A.C. Miller, *Sir Richard Grenville of the Civil War* (Chichester, 1979), p. 1. According to Miller, the case thus made against Grenville is overblown, but it is no task of the current author to discuss such matters. Suffice to say that Grenville was a tough professional soldier who had learned his trade in the Thirty Years' War, the Bishops' Wars and the Irish rebellion, in which last he had acquired a reputation for extreme ruthlessness.

52. In fairness to Essex, these subsidiary operations were uniformly successful, the defenders of Taunton - a mere eighty men who had taken refuge in the castle - surrendering after a brief siege, and Barnstaple being transformed into a Parliamentarian garrison. Scott and Turton, 'Hey for Old Robin', p. 136; Underdown, *Somerset in the Civil War and Interregnum*, p. 74.

53. The best account of Essex's decision to invade Cornwall may be found in Scott and Turton, 'Hey for Old Robin!', pp. 138-40; however, see also Andriette, *Devon and Exeter in the Civil War*, p. 111.

54. Barratt, *Civil War in the South-West*, pp. 89-93; Miles Brown, *Battles Royal*, p. 52.

55. Reid, *All the King's Armies*, p. 254.

56. Barratt, *Civil War in the South-West*, pp. 97-108; Miles Brown, *Battles Royal*, pp. 57-62.

57. For Grenville's attack on Plymouth, see Miller, *Sir Richard Grenville*, pp. 91-102. So ineffective was the cannonade with which he began his operations that the inhabitants nicknamed the eminence on which he planted his guns 'Vapouring Hill'. That said, on 7 October Grenville did succeed in storming Saltash, slaying 500 of his opponents and taking 300 more prisoners, a considerable number of these being hung on the grounds that the garrison had refused to surrender despite the fact that a practicable breach had been opened in their defences.

58. Underdown, *Somerset in the Civil War and Interregnum*, pp. 80-1.

59. Andriett, *Devon and Exeter in the Civil War*, p. 128.

60. Stoyle, *Plymouth in the Civil War*, pp. 32-4.

61. Underdown, *Somerset in the Civil War and Interregnum*, pp. 93-4; J. Barratt, *Cavalier Generals: King Charles I and his Commanders in the English Civil War, 1642-1646* (Barnsley, 2004), pp. 110-12.

62. F. Memegalos, *George Goring, 1608-1657* (Aldershot, 2007), p. 215.

63. Underdown, *Somerset in the Civil War and Interregnum*, pp. 93-5.

64. The decision to allow Goring to return to the campaign in the west was perhaps the greatest strategic error committed by the Royalists in the entire war for, had the 10,000 troops that he could muster been present at Naseby, it is entirely possible that the Royalists could have overcome the New Model Army. Why it was taken, however, remains unclear. Clarendon suggests that a Rupert already burdened with too many enemies in Charles' court had no desire for the presence of a man who was at the very least an ambitious rival, if not an outright enemy, but there were other pressures at work, namely the determination of Sir John Digby to limit the prince's authority by any means available. In the end, however, the final responsibility lay with Charles, who, unable to make his mind up between the rival merits of campaigning in the west or in the north typically enough ended up compromising by trying to do both at once. Memegalos, *George Goring*, pp. 250-1.

65. Underdown, *Somerset in the Civil War and Interregnum*, pp. 96-7.

66. Barratt, *Civil War in the South-West*, pp. 118-27; Memegalos, *George Goring*, pp. 279-90; I. Gentles, *The New Model Army in England, Scotland and Ireland, 1645-1653* (Oxford, 1993), pp. 67-9.

67. Gentles, *New Model Army*, pp. 69-70.

68. For the fall of Bristol in particular, see Barratt, *Sieges of the English Civil Wars*, pp. 39-44; Lynch, *For King and Parliament*, pp. 145-61. Meanwhile, for the fall of Sherborne, see Gentles, *New Model Army*, pp. 71-2.

69. The decision to make Hopton supreme commander in the west greatly angered Goring, who responded by sailing into exile in disgust. Memegalos, *George Goring*, p. 317.

70. Gentles, *New Model Army*, p. 78.

71. *Ibid.*, pp. 80-1.

72. For the battle of Torrington, see J. Wardman, *The Forgotten Battle: Torrington, 1646* (Torrington, 1996).

73. Norman, *By Swords Divided*, pp. 63-5; A.R. Bayley, *The Great Civil War in Dorset, 1642-1660* (Taunton, 1910), p. 299.

74. Andriette, *Devon and Exeter in the Civil War*, pp. 165-9. For the siege of Exeter in particular, see Stoyle, *From Deliverance to Destruction*, pp. 109-35.

75. Bayley, *Great Civil War in Dorset*, p. 309; Underdown, *Somerset in the Civil War and Interregnum*, p. 115. According to tradition, the siege of Dunster Castle featured an unpleasant episode in which, having captured the mother of the governor, Sir Francis Wyndham, the Parliamentarian commander (Robert Blake) threatened to have the woman shot unless the garrison surrendered forthwith, to which she allegedly responded by shouting to her son that he should do his duty come what may. Eventually released in recognition of her bravery, she is nevertheless reputed to haunt the grounds of the castle. Anon., *Somerset and Bristol Ghost Stories* (Sheffield, n.d., p. 35).

76. *Cit.* Coates, *Cornwall in the Great Civil War*, p. 191.

77. *Ibid.*, p. 199.

78. *Ibid.*, pp. 208-10.

79. In the face of the threat to her person implicit in Essex's invasion of the west, in July 1644 the queen had taken ship for her homeland where she threw herself into the task of trying to get help for her husband's cause.

80. Barrett, *Sieges of the English Civil War*, pp. 106-11.

81. Underdown, *Somerset in the Civil War and Interregnum*, pp. 122-3.

82. For the examples of Henrietta Maria, Charles II and Godolphin, see D. Codd, *Paranormal Devon* (Stroud, 2009), n.p. Meanwhile, for Stawell, see J. Holland, *Wiltshire Ghost Stories* (Sheffield, n.d.), p. 56; for Lady Arundell and Sir John St John, R. Matthews, *Haunted Places of Wiltshire* (Newbury, 2004), pp. 44-5, 80-1; for Lunsford, < https://www.bristol247.com/news-and-features/features/things-you-didnt-know-oct-2018/ >, accessed 27 October 2021; and, for Robert Blake, J. Holland, *Somerset and Bristol Ghost Stories* (Sheffield, n.d.), p. 16. With respect to Bovey House, there is unfortunately no record of Charles having stayed there, though he may have called in his excursion to the Dorset coast in the hope of obtaining passage for France at Charmouth.

83. Codd, *Paranormal Devon*, n.p; Holland, *Wiltshire Ghost Stories*, pp. 19, 27; Matthews, *Haunted Places of Wiltshire*, p. 59; Holland, *Somerset and Bristol Ghost Stories*, pp. 35, 66, 71; Wood, *Military Ghosts*, n.p; N. Sly, *A Ghostly Almanac of Devon and Cornwall* (Stroud, 2009), pp. 149-50; McKenzie, *They Still Serve*, pp. 56, 57, 63, 65, 68; < https://www.somersetlive.co.uk/news/somerset-news/most-haunted-somerset-bath-places-3457039 >, accessed 27 October 2021; < https://news.dorsetcouncil.gov.uk/dorset-history-centre-blog/2020/10/30/a-dorset-house-and-its-ghosts/ >, accessed 27 October 2021.

84. Holland, *Wiltshire Ghost Stories*, p. 57.

85. B. Florek, *Totally Haunted UK; Cornwall* (n.p., 2014), pp. 64-5; Sly, *Ghostly Almanac of Devon and Cornwall* (Stroud, 2009), pp. 60, 63-6.

86. Codd, *Paranormal Devon*, n.p.

87. S. Le Queux, *Haunted Bristol* (Stroud, 2004), p. 94; < https://www.spookyisles.com/shute-barton-manor/ >, accessed 28 October 2021; < https://www.paranormaldatabase.com/reports/battlefields.php >, accessed 27 October 2021; < http://hauntedwiltshire.blogspot.com/2009/12/st-peters-church-broad-hinton.html >, accessed 21 October 2021; Matthews, *Haunted Places of Wiltshire*, pp. 72-4. There are several more-or-less incredible legends associated with Lady Glanville, of which one has her burning down the manor house rather than see it fall into the hands of the Parliamentarians and another burying a cache of treasure in the village, which has remained undiscovered to this day. Be all this as it may, what is true is that Saint Peter's parish church boasts the tomb of Francis Glanville.

88. For all this, see Matthews, *Haunted Places of Wiltshire*, p. 31; Sly, *Ghostly Almanac of Devon and Cornwall*, pp. 12-13; R. Jeffers, < The Haunting of Portland Castle | Every Woman Dreams… (reginajeffers.blog) >, accessed 23 October 2021.

89. See Matthews, *Haunted Places of Wiltshire*, p. 32; < https://www.yalhs.org.uk/1997-apr-pg31_he-dyed-kings-service/ >, accessed 21 October 2021. The origins of the Poyntington story are shrouded in mystery, the only fact known for a certainty being that the dead included one Baldwin Malet, the son of the Royalist-supporting lord of the manor, Sir Thomas Malet (he is commemorated as having been killed in the action by a memorial tablet in the church). However, given the wider context, the traditional version of events - namely, that the arrival of the Parliamentarian party saw Malet rush to the aid of the beleaguered villagers and take charge of their attempt to defend their homes - is open to question: it is, then, far from impossible that the marauders were actually Royalists and Malet not the champion of the villagers but rather their victim.

90. Le Queux, *Haunted Bristol*, p. 94.

91. *Ibid.*, p. 11.

Conclusion

1. Davies, *The Haunted*, p. 41.
2. For an introduction to the work of the Restoration in this respect, see E. Peters, '"The greatest and most shameful laughing-stock in the world": narrating national shame in 1660', *Dix-Septième Siècle*, CCLXXV, No. 2 (April, 2017), pp. 269-84.
3. A. Behm, *The Roundhead's or the Good Old Cause: a Comedy* (London, 1682), n.p; < https://search-proquest-com.liverpool.idm.oclc.org/docview/2240918255/11956572#? >, accessed 7 November 2020. For a detailed discussion of this work, see M. Mowry, 'Irreconcilable Differences: Royalism, personal politics and history', in Aphra Behn's *The Roundhead, Women's Writing*, XXIII, No. 3, pp. 286-97.
4. Anon., *Riddle of the Roundhead: an Excellent New Ballad* (London, 1681), < https://search-proquest-com.liverpool.idm.oclc.org/docview/2264207705/fulltextPDF/3CF289FFF10E44D1PQ/1?accountid=12117 >, accessed 7 November 2020.
5. D. Holles, *Memoirs of Denzil, Lord Holles, Baron of Ifield in the County of Sussex from the Year 1641 to 1648*, pp. 70-1, < Memoirs of Denzil Lord Holles, Baron of Ifield in Sussex, from the year 1641 to 1648 - ProQuest (oclc.org) >, accessed 22 April 2021.
6. I. Roy, 'Royalist reputations: the Cavalier ideal and the reality', in J. McElligott and D.L. Smith (eds.), *Royalists and Royalism during the English Civil Wars* (Cambridge, 2007), pp. 109-10.
7. B. Worden, 'The poetry of Andrew Marvell', *ibid.*, pp. 214-38.
8. For an introduction to the political poetry of the Interregnum, see R. Skelton, 'The Cavalier Poets', in I. Scott-Kilvert (ed.), *Poets American and British* (New York, 1998), I, pp. 298-313.
9. Stubbs, *Reprobates*, p. 469.
10. See < https://www.olimpickgames.co.uk/history >, accessed 16 November 2021; A. Dougall, *The Devil's Book: Charles I, the Book of Sports and Puritanism in Tudor and Early Stuart England* (Exeter, 2011).
11. For the latter topic, see C. Durston, *Cromwell's Major-Generals: Godly Government During the English Revolution* (Manchester, 2001).
12. For some examples from Exeter, see Stoyle, *From Deliverance to Destruction*, pp. 25-7.
13. Underlying this paragraph is an issue that is far too complex to be dealt with here. In brief, while it is widely maintained that many towns and cities, and, not just that, but wide areas of the country, were strongly Puritan in 1642, it is yet clear that there

was a fundamental clash between godly ideals and popular culture, and, further that, even in districts that gave strong support to the Parliamentarian cause, there was a great reluctance to embrace its mores in so far as they touched upon cherished pastimes, sports and community festivities (such, at least, is one of the matters revealed by Durston). In short, with Puritanism by no means all-embracing in its dominance, it could be argued that it could provide little defence against revisionism of a spectral nature.

14. In one sense, highwaymen were quite literally ghosts of the Civil War: not only were the first recruits to the phenomenon Royalist officers and cavalry troopers thrown on the roads by misfortune but also their strenuous assertion that they were gentlemen via exaggerated displays of courage, courtesy and chivalry helped perpetuate the myth of the Cavalier. See E. Mackie, *Rakes, Highwaymen and Pirates: the Making of the Modern Gentleman in the Eighteenth Century* (Baltimore, 2009).

15. One interesting point to note in respect of the re-enactment world is that experience suggests that there have always been far more would-be Cavaliers than would-be Roundheads.

16. Instances of such books are easy to find: see, for example, M. Lindsay, *The Last Cavalier: the Secret of Hardwood House* (self-published, 2018); A.D. Hawkins, *The Time Princess* (self-published, 2012); P. Thomson, *A Ghost-Light in the Attic* (London, 1997).

17. Brooks, *Britain's Haunted Heritage*, p. 6.

18. If broken down still further, these statistics can be seen to correspond with the geographical distribution of the fighting even more closely. Thus, all but untouched by violence, the whole of East Anglia has only yielded seven sites of haunting and the county of Surrey none at all, whereas fiercely contested Worcestershire, Hampshire and Oxfordshire have eight, eleven and seven, respectively. Equally, in the north, Cumbria and Northumberland (Newcastle included), which both saw little action, have turned up just four such places, whereas Yorkshire can boast of ten.

19. Brooks, *Britain's Haunted Heritage,* p. 9.

20. *Cit.* J. Adair, *By the Sword Divided: Eyewitnesses of the English Civil War* (London, 1983), p. 163.

Index